The Academy Classics

PALGRAVE'S
GOLDEN TREASURY

SELECTED FROM THE BEST SONGS AND
LYRICAL POEMS IN THE ENGLISH LAN-
GUAGE AND ARRANGED WITH NOTES

*EDITED WITH NOTES, QUESTIONS
AND BIOGRAPHIES*

BY

A. B. DE MILLE

SIMMONS COLLEGE, BOSTON

1948

ALLYN AND BACON

BOSTON   NEW YORK   CHICAGO
ATLANTA   SAN FRANCISCO   DALLAS

COPYRIGHT, 1926 AND 1930

BY ALLYN AND BACON

IER

Norwood Press
J. S. Cushing Co. — Berwick & Smith Co.
Norwood, Mass., U.S.A.

FOREWORD

THE aim of the present edition of *The Golden Treasury* is to guide the modern high school student towards an appreciation of the best lyric poetry. To appreciate, however, he must first understand; and hence such practical aids have been provided as experience shows to be definitely useful. Literary criticism is reduced to a minimum, the comment is as simple and straightforward as possible, and the book is treated as a collection to be read and enjoyed, not as a problem in historical literature.

The Appendix contains many helps for the pupil. The section on the study of poetry, with special reference to the lyric, forms an introduction to the field covered by the anthology. The suggestions for oral work and the discussion of methods of approach will help both teacher and pupil to plan wisely. A feature of unusual interest is the list of musical settings, which will add materially to the pleasure of class presentation.

The notes are informative rather than critical. Grouped according to books, they include suggestive questions and topics for discussion, as well as biographical sketches of the authors. Further questions, taken from papers of the College Entrance Examination Board, are placed at the end of the volume, and

Foreword

will serve as a valuable test of general knowledge. A full index forms a means of ready reference.

The illustrations are reproduced chiefly from paintings in the National Portrait Gallery, London. Other pictures have been added to interpret the spirit of various poems.

A. B. DE MILLE

SIMMONS COLLEGE, BOSTON

CONTENTS

	PAGE
LIST OF ILLUSTRATIONS	vii
PALGRAVE'S DEDICATION	ix
PALGRAVE'S PREFACE	xi
BOOK FIRST	1
BOOK SECOND	69
BOOK THIRD	169
BOOK FOURTH	253
APPENDIX	
The Study of Poetry	449
Lyric Poetry	452
Rhythm and Metre	455
How to Study Palgrave	465
Suggestions for Oral Work	474
Musical Settings to the Poems	477
EXPLANATORY NOTES	
Book First	485
Questions and Topics for Discussion	503
Biographical Sketches	504
Book Second	510
Questions and Topics for Discussion	540
Biographical Sketches	540
Book Third	545
Questions and Topics for Discussion	562
Biographical Sketches	563
Book Fourth	567
Questions and Topics for Discussion	598
Biographical Sketches	599
General Questions on the Four Books	604
Examination Questions	605

Contents

INDEX INCLUDING AUTHORS, TITLES, AND FIRST LINES	609
GROUP-INDEX OF POEMS BY AUTHORS	630
WORD-LISTS	643
LIST OF PROPER NAMES	646

ILLUSTRATIONS

Poets' Corner, Westminster Abbey	*Frontispiece*
	FACING PAGE
William Shakespeare	2
Stratford-on-Avon	9
Durham Cathedral *. . . an ever-fixéd mark That looks on tempests, and is never shaken*	24
Glastonbury Abbey *Bare ruin'd choirs*	28
John Milton	70
Westminster Abbey *Here's a world of pomp and state Buried in dust, once dead by fate*	93
Milton Dictating "Paradise Lost" to His Daughters	96
Ben Jonson	116
Windsor Castle *Towers and battlements it sees Bosom'd high in tufted trees*	148
Canterbury Cathedral *. . . the high-embowéd roof, With antique pillars massy-proof*	156
John Dryden	164
Thomas Gray	180
Robert Burns	200
Church, Stoke Poges *. . . from yonder ivy-mantled tower The moping owl does to the moon complain*	220

viii   Illustrations

                                                    FACING PAGE

Eton College, from the Thames
Ye distant spires, ye antique towers
That crown the watery glade 237

John Keats 254

Samuel Taylor Coleridge 258

Percy Bysshe Shelley 264

William Wordsworth 274

Sir Walter Scott 286

In Mid-Ocean
A wet sheet and a flowing sea,
A wind that follows fast 301

Lord Byron 324

Roslin Chapel 344

Derwentwater
The sun upon the lake is low 393

King's College Chapel, Cambridge
. . . that branching roof
Self-poised 428

Grasmere
I hear the echoes through the mountains throng,
The winds come to me from the fields of sleep . . . 442

Shakespeare's Birthplace, Stratford-on-Avon . . . 508

To
ALFRED TENNYSON
POET LAUREATE

This book in its progress has recalled often to my memory a man with whose friendship we were once honoured, to whom no region of English Literature was unfamiliar, and who, whilst rich in all the noble gifts of Nature, was most eminently distinguished by the noblest and the rarest, — just judgment and high-hearted patriotism. It would have been hence a peculiar pleasure and pride to dedicate what I have endeavoured to make a true national Anthology of three centuries to Henry Hallam. But he is beyond the reach of any human tokens of love and reverence; and I desire therefore to place before it a name united with his by associations which, while Poetry retains her hold on the minds of Englishmen, are not likely to be forgotten.

Your encouragement, given while traversing the wild scenery of Treryn Dinas, led me to begin the work; and it has been completed under your advice and assistance. For the favour now asked I have thus a second reason: and to this I may add, the homage which is your right as Poet, and the gratitude due to a Friend, whose regard I rate at no common value.

Permit me then to inscribe to yourself a book which, I hope, may be found by many a lifelong fountain of innocent and exalted pleasure; a source of animation to friends when they meet; and able to sweeten solitude itself with best society, — with the companionship of the wise and the good, with the beauty which the eye cannot see, and the music only heard in silence. If this Collection proves a storehouse of delight to Labour and to Poverty, — if it teaches those indifferent to the Poets to love them, and those who love them to love them more, the aim and the desire entertained in framing it will be fully accomplished.

F. T. P.

MAY, 1861

PREFACE

This little Collection differs, it is believed, from others in the attempt made to include in it all the best original Lyrical pieces and Songs in our language (save a very few regretfully omitted on account of length), by writers not living, — and none beside the best. Many familiar verses will hence be met with; many also which should be familiar: — the Editor will regard as his fittest readers those who love Poetry so well, that he can offer them nothing not already known and valued.

The Editor is acquainted with no strict and exhaustive definition of Lyrical Poetry; but he has found the task of practical decision increase in clearness and in facility as he advanced with the work, whilst keeping in view a few simple principles. Lyrical has been here held essentially to imply that each Poem shall turn on some single thought, feeling, or situation. In accordance with this, narrative, descriptive, and didactic poems, — unless accompanied by rapidity of movement, brevity, and the colouring of human passion, — have been excluded. Humourous poetry, except in the very unfrequent instances where a truly poetical tone pervades the whole, with what is strictly personal, occasional, and religious, has been considered foreign to the idea of the book. Blank verse and the ten-syllable couplet, with all pieces markedly dramatic, have been rejected as alien from what is commonly understood by Song, and rarely conforming to Lyrical conditions in treatment. But it is not anticipated, nor is it possible, that all readers shall think the line accurately drawn. Some poems, as Gray's Elegy, the Allegro and Penseroso, Wordsworth's Ruth or Campbell's Lord Ullin, might be claimed with perhaps equal justice for a narrative or descriptive selection: whilst with reference especially to Ballads and Sonnets, the Editor can only state that he has taken his utmost pains to decide without caprice or partiality.

This also is all he can plead in regard to a point even more liable to question; — what degree of merit should give rank among the Best. That a poem shall be worthy of the writer's genius, — that it shall reach a perfection commensurate with its aim, — that we should require finish in proportion to brevity, — that passion, colour, and originality cannot atone for serious imperfections in clearness, unity or truth, — that a few good lines do not make a good poem, that popular estimate is serviceable as a guidepost more than as a compass, — above all, that excellence should be looked for rather in the whole than in the parts, — such and other such canons have been always steadily regarded. He may however add that the pieces chosen, and a far larger number rejected, have been carefully and repeatedly considered; and that he has been aided throughout by two friends of independent and exercised judgment, besides the distinguished person addressed in the Dedication. It is hoped that

Preface

by this procedure the volume has been freed from that one-sidedness which must beset individual decisions: — but for the final choice the Editor is alone responsible.

Chalmers' vast collection, with the whole works of all accessible poets not contained in it, and the best Anthologies of different periods, have been twice systematically read through: and it is hence improbable that any omissions which may be regretted are due to oversight. The poems are printed entire, except in a very few instances where a stanza or passage has been omitted. These omissions have been risked only when the piece could be thus brought to a closer lyrical unity: and, as essentially opposed to this unity, extracts, obviously such, are excluded. In regard to the text, the purpose of the book has appeared to justify the choice of the most poetical version, wherever more than one exists; and much labour has been given to present each poem, in disposition, spelling, and punctuation, to the greatest advantage.

In the arrangement, the most poetically-effective order has been attempted. The English mind has passed through phases of thought and cultivation so various and so opposed during these three centuries of Poetry, that a rapid passage between old and new, like rapid alteration of the eye's focus in looking at the landscape, will always be wearisome and hurtful to the sense of Beauty. The poems have been therefore distributed into Books corresponding, I to the ninety years closing about 1616, II thence to 1700, III to 1800, IV to the half century just ended. Or, looking at the Poets who more or less give each portion its distinctive character, they might be called the Books of Shakespeare, Milton, Gray, and Wordsworth. The volume, in this respect, so far as the limitations of its range allow, accurately reflects the natural growth and evolution of our Poetry. A rigidly chronological sequence, however, rather fits a collection aiming at instruction than at pleasure, and the wisdom which comes through pleasure: — within each book the pieces have therefore been arranged in gradations of feeling or subject. And it is hoped that the contents of this Anthology will thus be found to present a certain unity, 'as episodes,' in the noble language of Shelley, 'to that great Poem which all poets, like the co-operating thoughts of one great mind, have built up since the beginning of the world.'

As he closes his long survey, the Editor trusts he may add without egotism, that he has found the vague general verdict of popular Fame more just than those have thought, who, with too severe a criticism, would confine judgments on Poetry to 'the selected few of many generations.' Not many appear to have gained reputation without some gift or performance that, in due degree, deserved it: and if no verses by certain writers who show less strength than sweetness, or more thought than mastery of expression, are printed in this volume, it should not be imagined that they have been excluded without much hesitation and regret, — far less that they have been slighted. Throughout this vast and pathetic array of Singers now silent, few have been honoured with the name Poet, and have not possessed a skill in words, a sympathy with beauty,

Preface

a tenderness of feeling, or seriousness in reflection, which render their works, although never perhaps attaining that loftier and finer excellence here required, — better worth reading than much of what fills the scanty hours that most men spare for self-improvement, or for pleasure in any of its more elevated and permanent forms. — And if this be true of even mediocre poetry, for how much more are we indebted to the best! Like the fabled fountain of the Azores, but with a more various power, the magic of this Art can confer on each period of life its appropriate blessing: on early years Experience, on maturity Calm, on age, Youthfulness. Poetry gives treasures 'more golden than gold,' leading us in higher and healthier ways than those of the world, and interpreting to us the lessons of Nature. But she speaks best for herself. Her true accents, if the plan has been executed with success, may be heard throughout the following pages: — wherever the poets of England are honoured, wherever the dominant language of the world is spoken, it is hoped that they will find fit audience.

1861

Some poems, especially in Book I, have been added: — either on better acquaintance; — in deference to critical suggestions; — or unknown to the Editor when first gathering his harvest. For aid in these aftergleanings he is specially indebted to the excellent reprints of rare early verse given us by Dr. Hannah, Dr. Grosart, Mr. Arber, Mr. Bullen, and others, — and (in regard to the additions of 1883) to the advice of that distinguished Friend, by whom the final choice has been so largely guided. The text has also been carefully revised from authoritative sources. It has still seemed best, for many reasons, to retain the original limit by which the selection was confined to those then no longer living. But the editor hopes that, so far as in him lies, a complete and definitive collection of our best Lyrics, to the central year of this fast-closing century, is now offered.

1883–1890–1891

FRANCIS T. PALGRAVE

*Εἰς τὸν λειμῶνα καθίσας,
ἔδρεπεν ἕτερον ἐφ' ἑτέρῳ
αἰρόμενος ἄγρευμ' ἀνθέων
ἁδομένᾳ ψυχᾷ*———

"Sitting in the meadow he gathered spoil of flowers, plucking them one by one with a joyful heart."

Euripides.

THE GOLDEN TREASURY

BOOK FIRST

I

SPRING

Spring, the sweet Spring, is the year's pleasant king;
Then blooms each thing, then maids dance in a ring,
Cold doth not sting, the pretty birds do sing,
   Cuckoo, jug-jug, pu-we, to-witta-woo!

The palm and may make country houses gay,
Lambs frisk and play, the shepherds pipe all day,
And we hear aye birds tune this merry lay,
   Cuckoo, jug-jug, pu-we, to-witta-woo!

The fields breathe sweet, the daisies kiss our feet,
Young lovers meet, old wives a-sunning sit,
In every street these tunes our ears do greet,
   Cuckoo, jug-jug, pu-we, to-witta-woo!
     Spring! the sweet Spring!

T. Nash

2

THE FAIRY LIFE

i

Where the bee sucks, there suck I:
In a cowslip's bell I lie;
There I couch, when owls do cry:
On the bat's back I do fly
After summer merrily.
    Merrily, merrily, shall I live now,
    Under the blossom that hangs on the bough!

3

ii

Come unto these yellow sands,
    And then take hands:
Courtsied when you have, and kiss'd
    The wild waves whist,
Foot it featly here and there;
And, sweet Sprites, the burthen bear.
    Hark, hark!
        Bow-wow.
    The watch-dogs bark:
        Bow-wow.
    Hark, hark! I hear
The strain of strutting chanticleer
    Cry, Cock-a-diddle-dow!

W. Shakespeare

WILLIAM SHAKESPEARE

Book First

4

SUMMONS TO LOVE

Phoebus, arise!
And paint the sable skies
With azure, white, and red:
Rouse Memnon's mother from her Tithon's bed
That she may thy career with roses spread: 5
The nightingales thy coming each-where sing:
Make an eternal Spring!
Give life to this dark world which lieth dead;
Spread forth thy golden hair
In larger locks than thou wast wont before,   10
And emperor-like decore
With diadem of pearl thy temples fair:
Chase hence the ugly night
Which serves but to make dear thy glorious light.

— This is that happy morn,   15
That day, long-wishéd day
Of all my life so dark,
(If cruel stars have not my ruin sworn
And fates my hopes betray),
Which, purely white, deserves   20
An everlasting diamond should it mark.
This is the morn should bring unto this grove
My Love, to hear and recompense my love.
Fair King, who all preserves,
But show thy blushing beams,   25
And thou two sweeter eyes
Shalt see than those which by Penéus' streams

Did once thy heart surprize.
Now, Flora, deck thyself in fairest guise:
If that ye winds would hear
A voice surpassing far Amphion's lyre,
Your furious chiding stay;
Let Zephyr only breathe,
And with her tresses play.
— The winds all silent are,
And Phoebus in his chair
Ensaffroning sea and air
Makes vanish every star:
Night like a drunkard reels
Beyond the hills, to shun his flaming wheels:
The field with flowers are deck'd in every hue,
The clouds with orient gold spangle their blue;
Here is the pleasant place —
And nothing wanting is, save She, alas!

W. Drummond of Hawthornden

5

TIME AND LOVE

i

When I have seen by Time's fell hand defaced
The rich proud cost of out-worn buried age;
When sometime lofty towers I see down-razed,
And brass eternal slave to mortal rage;

When I have seen the hungry ocean gain
Advantage on the kingdom of the shore,

And the firm soil win of the watery main,
Increasing store with loss, and loss with store;

When I have seen such interchange of state,
Or state itself confounded to decay, 10
Ruin hath taught me thus to ruminate —
That Time will come and take my Love away:

— This thought is as a death, which cannot choose
But weep to have that which it fears to lose.
W. Shakespeare

6

ii

Since brass, nor stone, nor earth, nor boundless sea,
But sad mortality o'ersways their power,
How with this rage shall beauty hold a plea,
Whose action is no stronger than a flower?

O how shall summer's honey breath hold out 5
Against the wreckful siege of battering days,
When rocks impregnable are not so stout
Nor gates of steel so strong, but time decays?

O fearful meditation! where, alack!
Shall Time's best jewel from Time's chest lie hid? 10
Or what strong hand can hold his swift foot back,
Or who his spoil of beauty can forbid?

O! none, unless this miracle have might,
That in black ink my love may still shine bright.
W. Shakespeare

7

THE PASSIONATE SHEPHERD TO HIS LOVE

Come live with me and be my Love,
And we will all the pleasures prove
That hills and valleys, dale and field,
And all the craggy mountains yield.

There will we sit upon the rocks
And see the shepherds feed their flocks,
By shallow rivers, to whose falls
Melodious birds sing madrigals.

There will I make thee beds of roses
And a thousand fragrant posies,
A cap of flowers, and a kirtle
Embroider'd all with leaves of myrtle.

A gown made of the finest wool,
Which from our pretty lambs we pull,
Fair linéd slippers for the cold,
With buckles of the purest gold.

A belt of straw and ivy buds
With coral clasps and amber studs:
And if these pleasures may thee move,
Come live with me and be my Love.

Thy silver dishes for thy meat
As precious as the gods do eat,
Shall on an ivory table be
Prepared each day for thee and me.

The shepherd swains shall dance and sing 25
For thy delight each May-morning:
If these delights thy mind may move,
Then live with me and be my Love.

C. Marlowe

8

OMNIA VINCIT

Fain would I change that note
To which fond Love hath charm'd me
Long long to sing by rote,
Fancying that that harm'd me:
Yet when this thought doth come 5
'Love is the perfect sum
　　Of all delight,'
I have no other choice
Either for pen or voice
　　To sing or write. 10

O Love! they wrong thee much
That say thy sweet is bitter,
When thy rich fruit is such
As nothing can be sweeter.
Fair house of joy and bliss, 15
Where truest pleasure is,
　　I do adore thee:
I know thee what thou art,
I serve thee with my heart,
　　And fall before thee! 20

Anon.

9

A MADRIGAL

Crabbed Age and Youth
Cannot live together:
Youth is full of pleasance,
Age is full of care;
Youth like summer morn,
Age like winter weather,
Youth like summer brave,
Age like winter bare:

Youth is full of sport,
Age's breath is short,
Youth is nimble, Age is lame:
Youth is hot and bold,
Age is weak and cold,
Youth is wild, and Age is tame! —
Age, I do abhor thee,
Youth, I do adore thee;
O! my Love is young!
Age, I do defy thee —
O sweet shepherd, hie thee,
For methinks thou stay'st too long.

W. Shakespeare

10

Under the greenwood tree
Who loves to lie with me,
And turn his merry note
Unto the sweet bird's throat —

STRATFORD-ON-AVON

Come hither, come hither, come hither!
    Here shall he see
    No enemy
But winter and rough weather.

  Who doth ambition shun
  And loves to live i' the sun,
  Seeking the food he eats
  And pleased with what he gets —
Come hither, come hither, come hither
    Here shall he see
    No enemy
But winter and rough weather.

W. Shakespeare

11

It was a lover and his lass
  With a hey and a ho, and a hey nonino!
That o'er the green corn-field did pass
In the spring time, the only pretty ring time,
When birds do sing hey ding a ding:
  Sweet lovers love the Spring.

Between the acres of the rye
These pretty country folks would lie:
This carol they began that hour,
How that life was but a flower:

And therefore take the present time
  With a hey and a ho and a hey nonino!
For love is crownéd with the prime
In spring time, the only pretty ring time,
When birds do sing hey ding a ding:
  Sweet lovers love the Spring.

W. Shakespeare

12

PRESENT IN ABSENCE

Absence, hear thou this protestation
    Against thy strength,
    Distance, and length;
Do what thou canst for alteration:
    For hearts of truest mettle
Absence doth join, and Time doth settle.

Who loves a mistress of such quality,
    His mind hath found
    Affection's ground
Beyond time, place, and mortality.
    To hearts that cannot vary
Absence is present, Time doth tarry.

By absence this good means I gain,
    That I can catch her,
    Where none can match her,
In some close corner of my brain:
    There I embrace and kiss her;
And so I both enjoy and miss her.

J. Donne

13

VIA AMORIS

High-way, since you my chief Parnassus be,
And that my Muse, to some ears not unsweet,
Tempers her words to trampling horses' feet
More oft than to a chamber melody, —

Now, blesséd you bear onward blesséd me
To her, where I my heart, safe-left, shall meet;
My Muse and I must you of duty greet
With thanks and wishes, wishing thankfully;

Be you still fair, honour'd by public heed;
By no encroachment wrong'd, nor time forgot;
Nor blamed for blood, nor shamed for sinful deed;
And that you know I envy you no lot

Of highest wish, I wish you so much bliss, —
Hundreds of years you Stella's feet may kiss!

Sir P. Sidney

14

ABSENCE

Being your slave, what should I do but tend
Upon the hours and times of your desire?
I have no precious time at all to spend
Nor services to do, till you require:

Nor dare I chide the world-without-end-hour
Whilst I, my sovereign, watch the clock for you,
Nor think the bitterness of absence sour
When you have bid your servant once adieu:

Nor dare I question with my jealous thought
Where you may be, or your affairs suppose,
But like a sad slave, stay and think of nought
Save, where you are, how happy you make those; —

So true a fool is love, that in your will
Though you do anything, he thinks no ill.

W. Shakespeare

15

How like a winter hath my absence been
From Thee, the pleasure of the fleeting year!
What freezings have I felt, what dark days seen,
What old December's bareness everywhere!

And yet this time removed was summer's time:
The teeming autumn, big with rich increase,
Bearing the wanton burden of the prime
Like widow'd wombs after their lords' decease:

Yet this abundant issue seem'd to me
But hope of orphans, and unfather'd fruit;
For summer and his pleasures wait on thee,
And, thou away, the very birds are mute;

Or if they sing, 'tis with so dull a cheer,
That leaves look pale, dreading the winter's near.
W. Shakespeare

16

A CONSOLATION

When in disgrace with fortune and men's eyes
I all alone beweep my outcast state,
And trouble deaf heaven with my bootless cries,
And look upon myself, and curse my fate;

Wishing me like to one more rich in hope,
Featured like him, like him with friends possest,
Desiring this man's art, and that man's scope,
With what I most enjoy contented least;

Yet in these thoughts myself almost despising,
Haply I think on Thee — and then my state,
Like to the lark at break of day arising
From sullen earth, sings hymns at heaven's gate;

For thy sweet love remember'd, such wealth brings
That then I scorn to change my state with kings.
W. Shakespeare

17

THE UNCHANGEABLE

O never say that I was false of heart,
Though absence seem'd my flame to qualify:
As easy might I from myself depart
As from my soul, which in thy breast doth lie;

That is my home of love; if I have rangéd,
Like him that travels, I return again,
Just to the time, not with the time exchangéd,
So that myself bring water for my stain.

Never believe, though in my nature reign'd
All frailties that besiege all kinds of blood,
That it could so preposterously be stain'd
To leave for nothing all thy sum of good:

For nothing this wide universe I call,
Save thou, my rose: in it thou art my all.
W. Shakespeare

18

To me, fair Friend, you never can be old,
For as you were when first your eye I eyed
Such seems your beauty still. Three winters' cold
Have from the forests shook three summers' pride;

Three beauteous springs to yellow autumn turn'd
In process of the seasons have I seen,
Three April perfumes in three hot Junes burn'd,
Since first I saw you fresh, which yet are green.

Ah! yet doth beauty, like a dial-hand,
Steal from his figure, and no pace perceived;
So your sweet hue, which methinks still doth stand,
Hath motion, and mine eye may be deceived:

For fear of which, hear this, thou age unbred, —
Ere you were born, was beauty's summer dead.

W. Shakespeare

19

ROSALINE

Like to the clear in highest sphere
Where all imperial glory shines,
Of selfsame colour is her hair
Whether unfolded, or in twines:
    Heigh ho, fair Rosaline!
Her eyes are sapphires set in snow,
Resembling heaven by every wink;
The Gods do fear whenas thy glow,
And I do tremble when I think:
    Heigh ho, would she were mine!

Book First

Her cheeks are like the blushing cloud
That beautifies Aurora's face,
Or like the silver crimson shroud
That Phoebus' smiling looks doth grace;
   Heigh ho, fair Rosaline!   15
Her lips are like two budded roses
Whom ranks of lilies neighbour nigh,
Within which bounds she balm encloses
Apt to entice a deity:
   Heigh ho, would she were mine!   20

Her neck is like a stately tower
Where Love himself imprison'd lies,
To watch for glances every hour
From her divine and sacred eyes:
   Heigh ho, for Rosaline!   25
Her paps are centres of delight,
Her breasts are orbs of heavenly frame,
Where Nature moulds the dew of light
To feed perfection with the same:
   Heigh ho, would she were mine!   30

With orient pearl, with ruby red,
With marble white, with sapphire blue
Her body every way is fed,
Yet soft in touch and sweet in view:
   Heigh ho, fair Rosaline!   35
Nature herself her shape admires;
The Gods are wounded in her sight;
And Love forsakes his heavenly fires
And at her eyes his brand doth light:
   Heigh ho, would she were mine!   40

Then muse not, Nymphs, though I bemoan
The absence of fair Rosaline,
Since for a fair there's fairer none,
Nor for her virtues so divine:
    Heigh ho, fair Rosaline;
Heigh ho, my heart! would God that she were mine!

T. Lodge

20

COLIN

Beauty sat bathing by a spring
  Where fairest shades did hide her;
The winds blew calm, the birds did sing,
  The cool streams ran beside her.
My wanton thoughts enticed mine eye
  To see what was forbidden:
But better memory said, fie!
  So vain desire was chidden:—
    Hey nonny nonny O!
    Hey nonny nonny!

Into a slumber then I fell,
  When fond imagination
Seeméd to see, but could not tell
  Her feature or her fashion.
But ev'n as babes in dreams do smile,
  And sometimes fall a-weeping,
So I awaked, as wise this while
  As when I fell a-sleeping:—
    Hey nonny nonny O!
    Hey nonny nonny!

(A. Munday) The Shepherd Tonie

21

A PICTURE

Sweet Love, if thou wilt gain a monarch's glory,
Subdue her heart, who makes me glad and sorry:
    Out of thy golden quiver
    Take thou thy strongest arrow
    That will through bone and marrow,
And me and thee of grief and fear deliver: —
But come behind, for if she look upon thee,
Alas! poor Love! then thou art woe-begone thee!
Anon.

22

A SONG FOR MUSIC

Weep you no more, sad fountains: —
    What need you flow so fast?
Look how the snowy mountains
    Heaven's sun doth gently waste!
      But my Sun's heavenly eyes
        View not your weeping,
        That now lies sleeping
    Softly, now softly lies,
            Sleeping.

Sleep is a reconciling,
    A rest that peace begets: —
Doth not the sun rise smiling,
    When fair at even he sets?

—Rest you, then, rest, sad eyes!
  Melt not in weeping!
  While She lies sleeping
Softly, now softly lies,
  Sleeping!

Anon.

23
TO HIS LOVE

Shall I compare thee to a summer's day?
Thou art more lovely and more temperate:
Rough winds do shake the darling buds of May,
And summer's lease hath all too short a date:

Sometime too hot the eye of heaven shines,
And often is his gold complexion dimm'd:
And every fair from fair sometime declines,
By chance, or nature's changing course, untrimm'd.

But thy eternal summer shall not fade
Nor lose possession of that fair thou owest;
Nor shall Death brag thou wanderest in his shade,
When in eternal lines to time thou growest: —

So long as men can breathe, or eyes can see,
So long lives this, and this gives life to thee.

W. Shakespeare

24
TO HIS LOVE

When in the chronicle of wasted time
I see descriptions of the fairest wights,
And beauty making beautiful old rhyme
In praise of ladies dead, and lovely knights;

Then in the blazon of sweet beauty's best
Of hand, of foot, of lip, of eye, of brow,
I see their antique pen would have exprest
Ev'n such a beauty as you master now.

So all their praises are but prophecies
Of this our time, all, you prefiguring;
And for they look'd but with divining eyes,
They had not skill enough your worth to sing:

For we, which now behold these present days,
Have eyes to wonder, but lack tongues to praise.
W. Shakespeare

25

BASIA

   Turn back, you wanton flyer
   And answer my desire
      With mutual greeting.
   Yet bend a little nearer, —
   True beauty still shines clearer
      In closer meeting!
   Hearts with hearts delighted
   Should strive to be united,
Each other's arms with arms enchaining, —
      Hearts with a thought,
Rosy lips with a kiss still entertaining.

   What harvest half so sweet is
   As still to reap the kisses
      Grown ripe in sowing?

15 And straight to be receiver
      Of that which thou art giver,
          Rich in bestowing?
      There is no strict observing
      Of times' or seasons' swerving,
20   There is ever one fresh spring abiding;
      Then what we sow with our lips
      Let us reap, love's gains dividing.

                                    T. Campion

26

ADVICE TO A GIRL

Never love unless you can
Bear with all the faults of man!
Men sometimes will jealous be
Though but little cause they see,
5 And hang the head as discontent,
And speak what straight they will repent.

Men, that but one Saint adore,
Make a show of love to more;
Beauty must be scorn'd in none,
10 Though but truly served in one:
For what is courtship but disguise?
True hearts may have dissembling eyes.

Men, when their affairs require,
Must awhile themselves retire;
15 Sometimes hunt, and sometimes hawk,
And not ever sit and talk: —
If these and such-like you can bear,
Then like, and love, and never fear!

                                    T. Campion

27

LOVE'S PERJURIES

On a day, alack the day!
Love, whose month is ever May,
Spied a blossom passing fair
Playing in the wanton air:
Through the velvet leaves the wind,   5
All unseen, 'gan passage find:
That the lover, sick to death,
Wish'd himself the heaven's breath.
Air, quoth he, thy cheeks may blow;
Air, would I might triumph so!   10
But, alack, my hand is sworn
Ne'er to pluck thee from thy thorn:
Vow, alack, for youth unmeet;
Youth so apt to pluck a sweet.
Do not call it sin in me   15
That I am forsworn for thee:
Thou for whom Jove would swear
Juno but an Ethiope were,
And deny himself for Jove,
Turning mortal for thy love.   20

W. Shakespeare

28

A SUPPLICATION

Forget not yet the tried intent
Of such a truth as I have meant;
My great travail so gladly spent,
  Forget not yet!

Forget not yet when first began
The weary life ye know, since whan
The suit, the service none tell can;
    Forget not yet!

Forget not yet the great assays,
The cruel wrong, the scornful ways,
The painful patience in delays,
    Forget not yet!

Forget not! O forget not this,
How long ago hath been, and is
The mind that never meant amiss —
    Forget not yet!

Forget not then thine own approved
The which so long hath thee so loved,
Whose steadfast faith yet never moved —
    Forget not this!

Sir T. Wyatt

TO AURORA

O if thou knew'st how thou thyself dost harm,
And dost prejudge thy bliss, and spoil my rest;
Then thou would'st melt the ice out of thy breast
And thy relenting heart would kindly warm.

O if thy pride did not our joys controul,
What world of loving wonders should'st thou see
For if I saw thee once transform'd in me,
Then in thy bosom I would pour my soul:

Then all my thoughts should in thy visage shine,
And if that aught mischanced thou should'st not moan
Nor bear the burthen of thy griefs alone;
No, I would have my share in what were thine:

And whilst we thus should make our sorrows one,
This happy harmony would make them none.
W. Alexander, Earl of Sterline

30

IN LACRIMAS

    I saw my Lady weep,
And Sorrow proud to be advancéd so
In those fair eyes where all perfections keep.
    Her face was full of woe,
But such a woe (believe me) as wins more hearts
Than Mirth can do with her enticing parts.

    Sorrow was there made fair,
And Passion, wise; Tears, a delightful thing;
Silence, beyond all speech, a wisdom rare:
    She made her sighs to sing,
And all things with so sweet a sadness move
As made my heart at once both grieve and love.

    O fairer than aught else
The world can show, leave off in time to grieve!
Enough, enough: your joyful look excels:
    Tears kill the heart, believe.
O strive not to be excellent in woe,
Which only breeds your beauty's overthrow.
Anon.

31

TRUE LOVE

Let me not to the marriage of true minds
Admit impediments. Love is not love
Which alters when it alteration finds,
Or bends with the remover to remove:—

O no! it is an ever-fixéd mark
That looks on tempests, and is never shaken;
It is the star to every wandering bark,
Whose worth's unknown, although his height be taken.

Love's not Time's fool, though rosy lips and cheeks
Within his bending sickle's compass come;
Love alters not with his brief hours and weeks,
But bears it out ev'n to the edge of doom:—

If this be error, and upon me proved,
I never writ, nor no man ever loved.

W. Shakespeare

32

A DITTY

My true-love hath my heart, and I have his,
By just exchange one for another given:
I hold his dear, and mine he cannot miss,
There never was a better bargain driven:
    My true-love hath my heart, and I have his.

His heart in me keeps him and me in one,
My heart in him his thoughts and senses guides:

. . . *an ever-fixéd mark*
That looks on tempests, and is never shaken.

He loves my heart, for once it was his own,
I cherish his because in me it bides:
> My true-love hath my heart, and I have his.
>> *Sir P. Sidney*

33

LOVE'S INSIGHT

Though others may Her brow adore
Yet more must I, that therein see far more
Than any other's eyes have power to see:
> She is to me
More than to any others she can be!
I can discern more secret notes
That in the margin of her cheeks Love quotes,
Than any else besides have art to read:
> No looks proceed
From those fair eyes but to me wonder breed.
>> *Anon.*

34

LOVE'S OMNIPRESENCE

Were I as base as is the lowly plain,
And you, my Love, as high as heaven above,
Yet should the thoughts of me your humble swain
Ascend to heaven, in honour of my Love.

Were I as high as heaven above the plain,
And you, my Love, as humble and as low
As are the deepest bottoms of the main,
Whereso'er you were, with you my love should go.

Were you the earth, dear Love, and I the skies,
My love should shine on you like to the sun,
And look upon you with ten thousand eyes
Till heaven wax'd blind, and till the world were done.

Whereso'er I am, below, or else above you,
Whereso'er you are, my heart shall truly love you.

J. Sylvester

35
CARPE DIEM

O Mistress mine, where are you roaming?
O stay and hear! your true-love's coming
   That can sing both high and low.
Trip no further, pretty sweeting,
Journeys end in lovers meeting —
   Every wise man's son doth know.

What is love? 'tis not hereafter;
Present mirth hath present laughter;
   What's to come is still unsure:
In delay there lies no plenty, —
Then come kiss me, Sweet-and-twenty,
   Youth's a stuff will not endure.

W. Shakespeare

36
AN HONEST AUTOLYCUS

Fine knacks for ladies, cheap, choice, brave, and new;
Good penny-worths, — but money cannot move:
I keep a fair but for the Fair to view;
   A beggar may be liberal of love.
Though all my wares be trash, the heart is true —
          The heart is true.

Great gifts are guiles and look for gifts again;
   My trifles come as treasures from my mind;
It is a precious jewel to be plain;
   Sometimes in shell the orient'st pearls we find: — 10
Of others take a sheaf, of me a grain!
                Of me a grain!

Anon.

37

WINTER

When icicles hang by the wall
   And Dick the shepherd blows his nail.
And Tom bears logs into the hall,
And milk comes frozen home in pail;
When blood is nipt, and ways be foul,   5
Then nightly sings the staring owl
           Tu-whit!
To-who!   A merry note!
While greasy Joan doth keel the pot.

When all about the wind doth blow   10
   And coughing drowns the parson's saw,
And birds sit brooding in the snow,
   And Marian's nose looks red and raw;
When roasted crabs hiss in the bowl —
Then nightly sings the staring owl   15
           Tu-whit!
To-who!   A merry note!
While greasy Joan doth keel the pot.

W. Shakespeare

38

That time of year thou may'st in me behold
When yellow leaves, or none, or few, do hang
Upon those boughs which shake against the cold,
Bare ruin'd choirs, where late the sweet birds sang:

5 In me thou see'st the twilight of such day
As after sunset fadeth in the west,
Which by and by black night doth take away,
Death's second self, that seals up all in rest:

In me thou see'st the glowing of such fire,
10 That on the ashes of his youth doth lie
As the death-bed whereon it must expire,
Consumed with that which it was nourish'd by:

— This thou perceiv'st, which makes thy love more strong,
To love that well which thou must leave ere long.

W. Shakespeare

39

MEMORY

When to the sessions of sweet silent thought
I summon up remembrance of things past,
I sigh the lack of many a thing I sought,
And with old woes new wail my dear time's waste;

5 Then can I drown an eye, unused to flow,
For precious friends hid in death's dateless night,
And weep afresh love's long-since-cancell'd woe,
And moan the expense of many a vanish'd sight.

Bare ruin'd choirs . . . .

Then can I grieve at grievances foregone,
And heavily from woe to woe tell o'er
The sad account of fore-bemoanéd moan,
Which I new pay as if not paid before:

— But if the while I think on thee, dear Friend,
All losses are restored, and sorrows end.
W. Shakespeare

40

SLEEP

Come, Sleep: O Sleep! the certain knot of peace,
The baiting-place of wit, the balm of woe,
The poor man's wealth, the prisoner's release,
Th' indifferent judge between the high and low;

With shield of proof shield me from out the prease
Of those fierce darts Despair at me doth throw:
O make in me those civil wars to cease;
I will good tribute pay, if thou do so.

Take thou of me smooth pillows, sweetest bed,
A chamber deaf of noise and blind of light,
A rosy garland and a weary head:
And if these things, as being thine in right,

Move not thy heavy grace, thou shalt in me,
Livelier than elsewhere, Stella's image see.
Sir P. Sidney

41

REVOLUTIONS

Like as the waves make towards the pebbled shore
So do our minutes hasten to their end;
Each changing place with that which goes before,
In sequent toil all forwards do contend.

Nativity, once in the main of light,
Crawls to maturity, wherewith being crown'd,
Crooked eclipses 'gainst his glory fight,
And Time that gave, doth now his gift confound.

Time doth transfix the flourish set on youth,
And delves the parallels in beauty's brow;
Feeds on the rarities of nature's truth,
And nothing stands but for his scythe to mow:—

And yet, to times in hope, my verse shall stand
Praising Thy worth, despite his cruel hand.

W. Shakespeare

42

Farewell! thou art too dear for my possessing,
And like enough thou know'st thy estimate:
The charter of thy worth gives thee releasing;
My bonds in thee are all determinate.

For how do I hold thee but by thy granting?
And for that riches where is my deserving?
The cause of this fair gift in me is wanting,
And so my patent back again is swerving.

Thyself thou gav'st, thy own worth then not knowing,
Or me, to whom thou gav'st it, else mistaking; 10
So thy great gift, upon misprision growing,
Comes home again, on better judgment making.

Thus have I had thee as a dream doth flatter;
In sleep, a king; but waking, no such matter.
W. Shakespeare

43

THE LIFE WITHOUT PASSION

They that have power to hurt, and will do none.
That do not do the thing they most do show,
Who, moving others, are themselves as stone,
Unmovéd, cold, and to temptation slow, —

They rightly do inherit heaven's graces, 5
And husband nature's riches from expense;
They are the lords and owners of their faces,
Others, but stewards of their excellence.

The summer's flower is to the summer sweet,
Though to itself it only live and die; 10
But if that flower with base infection meet,
The basest weed outbraves his dignity:

For sweetest things turn sourest by their deeds;
Lilies that fester smell far worse than weeds.
W. Shakespeare

44

THE LOVER'S APPEAL

And wilt thou leave me thus?
Say nay! say nay! for shame,
To save thee from the blame
Of all my grief and grame.
And wilt thou leave me thus?
Say nay! say nay!

And wilt thou leave me thus,
That hath loved thee so long
In wealth and woe among:
And is thy heart so strong
As for to leave me thus?
Say nay! say nay!

And wilt thou leave me thus,
That hath given thee my heart
Never for to depart
Neither for pain nor smart:
And wilt thou leave me thus?
Say nay! say nay!

And wilt thou leave me thus,
And have no more pity
Of him that loveth thee?
Alas! thy cruelty!
And wilt thou leave me thus?
Say nay! say nay!

Sir T. Wyatt

45

THE NIGHTINGALE

As it fell upon a day
In the merry month of May,
Sitting in a pleasant shade
Which a grove of myrtles made,
Beasts did leap and birds did sing,
Trees did grow and plants did spring;
Every thing did banish moan
Save the Nightingale alone.
She, poor bird, as all forlorn,
Lean'd her breast up-till a thorn,
And there sung the dolefull'st ditty
That to hear it was great pity.
Fie, fie, fie, now would she cry;
Teru, teru, by and by:
That to hear her so complain
Scarce I could from tears refrain:
For her griefs so lively shown
Made me think upon mine own.
— Ah, thought I, thou mourn'st in vain,
None takes pity on thy pain:
Senseless trees, they cannot hear thee,
Ruthless beasts, they will not cheer thee:
King Pandion, he is dead,
All thy friends are lapp'd in lead:
All thy fellow birds do sing
Careless of thy sorrowing:
Even so, poor bird, like thee
None alive will pity me.   *R. Barnefield*

46

Care-charmer Sleep, son of the sable Night,
Brother to Death, in silent darkness born,
Relieve my languish, and restore the light;
With dark forgetting of my care return.

And let the day be time enough to mourn
The shipwreck of my ill-adventured youth:
Let waking eyes suffice to wail their scorn,
Without the torment of the night's untruth.

Cease, dreams, the images of day-desires,
To model forth the passions of the morrow;
Never let rising Sun approve you liars,
To add more grief to aggravate my sorrow:

Still let me sleep, embracing clouds in vain,
And never wake to feel the day's disdain.

S. Daniel

47

The nightingale, as soon as April bringeth
  Unto her rested sense a perfect waking,
While late-bare earth, proud of new clothing, springeth,
  Sings out her woes, a thorn her song-book making
    And mournfully bewailing,
    Her throat in tunes expresseth
    What grief her breast oppresseth
For Tereus' force on her chaste will prevailing.

O Philomela fair, O take some gladness,
That here is juster cause of plaintful sadness:
    Thine earth now springs, mine fadeth;
Thy thorn without, my thorn my heart invadeth.

Alas, she hath no other cause of anguish
  But Tereus' love, on her by strong hand wroken,
Wherein she suffering, all her spirits languish,
  Full womanlike complains her will was broken.
    But I, who, daily craving,
      Cannot have to content me,
      Have more cause to lament me,
Since wanting is more woe than too much having.

O Philomela fair, O take some gladness
That here is juster cause of plaintful sadness:
    Thine earth now springs, mine fadeth;
Thy thorn without, my thorn my heart invadeth.
                       Sir P. Sidney

48

FRUSTRA

  Take, O take those lips away
  That so sweetly were forsworn,
  And those eyes, the break of day,
  Lights that do mislead the morn:
  But my kisses bring again,
      Bring again —
  Seals of love, but seal'd in vain,
      Seal'd in vain!
                       W. Shakespeare

49

LOVE'S FAREWELL

Since there's no help, come let us kiss and part, —
Nay I have done, you get no more of me;
And I am glad, yea, glad with all my heart,
That thus so cleanly I myself can free;
Shake hands for ever, cancel all our vows,
And when we meet at any time again,
Be it not seen in either of our brows
That we one jot of former love retain.

Now at the last gasp of love's latest breath,
When his pulse failing, passion speechless lies,
When faith is kneeling by his bed of death,
And innocence is closing up his eyes,

—Now if thou would'st, when all have given him over
From death to life thou might'st him yet recover!

M. Drayton

50

IN IMAGINE PERTRANSIT HOMO

Follow thy fair sun, unhappy shadow!
  Though thou be black as night
  And she made all of light,
Yet follow thy fair sun, unhappy shadow!

Follow her, whose light thy light depriveth!
  Though here thou liv'st disgraced,
  And she in heaven is placed,
Yet follow her whose light the world reviveth!

Follow those pure beams, whose beauty burneth,
   That so have scorchéd thee
   As thou still black must be
Till her kind beams thy black to brightness turneth.

Follow her, while yet her glory shineth!
   There comes a luckless night
   That will dim all her light;
— And this the black unhappy shade divineth.

Follow still, since so thy fates ordainéd!
   The sun must have his shade,
   Till both at once do fade, —
The sun still proved, the shadow still disdainéd.
T. Campion

51

BLIND LOVE

O me! what eyes hath Love put in my head
Which have no correspondence with true sight:
Or if they have, where is my judgment fled
That censures falsely what they see aright?

If that be fair whereon my false eyes dote,
What means the world to say it is not so?
If it be not, then love doth well denote
Love's eye is not so true as all men's: No.

How can it? O how can love's eye be true,
That is so vex'd with watching and with tears?
No marvel then though I mistake my view:
The sun itself sees not till heaven clears.

O cunning Love! with tears thou keep'st me blind,
Lest eyes well-seeing thy foul faults should find!

W. Shakespeare

52

Sleep, angry beauty, sleep and fear not me!
   For who a sleeping lion dares provoke?
It shall suffice me here to sit and see
   Those lips shut up that never kindly spoke:
What sight can more content a lover's mind
Than beauty seeming harmless, if not kind?

My words have charm'd her, for secure she sleeps,
   Though guilty much of wrong done to my love;
And in her slumber, see! she close-eyed weeps:
   Dreams often more than waking passions move.
Plead, Sleep, my cause, and make her soft like thee
That she in peace may wake and pity me.

T. Campion

53

THE UNFAITHFUL SHEPHERDESS

While that the sun with his beams hot
Scorchéd the fruits in vale and mountain,
Philon the shepherd, late forgot,
Sitting beside a crystal fountain,
   In shadow of a green oak tree
   Upon his pipe this song play'd he:
Adieu, Love, adieu, Love, untrue Love,
Untrue Love, untrue Love, adieu, Love;
Your mind is light, soon lost for new love.

So long as I was in your sight
I was your heart, your soul, and treasure;
And evermore you sobb'd and sigh'd
Burning in flames beyond all measure:
— Three days endured your love to me,
  And it was lost in other three!
Adieu, Love, adieu, Love, untrue Love,
Untrue Love, untrue Love, adieu, Love;
Your mind is light, soon lost for new love.

Another Shepherd you did see
To whom your heart was soon enchainéd;
Full soon your love was leapt from me,
Full soon my place he had obtainéd.
  Soon came a third, your love to win,
  And we were out and he was in.
Adieu, Love, adieu, Love, untrue Love,
Untrue Love, untrue Love, adieu, Love;
Your mind is light, soon lost for new love.

Sure you have made me passing glad
That you your mind so soon removéd,
Before that I the leisure had
To choose you for my best belovéd:
  For all your love was past and done
  Two days before it was begun: —
Adieu, Love, adieu, Love, untrue Love,
Untrue Love, untrue Love, adieu, Love;
Your mind is light, soon lost for new love.

Anon.

54

ADVICE TO A LOVER

The sea hath many thousand sands,
The sun hath motes as many;
The sky is full of stars, and Love
As full of woes as any:
Believe me, that do know the elf,
And make no trial by thyself!

It is in truth a pretty toy
For babes to play withal: —
But O! the honeys of our youth
Are oft our age's gall!
Self-proof in time will make thee know
He was a prophet told thee so;

A prophet that, Cassandra-like,
Tells truth without belief;
For headstrong Youth will run his race,
Although his goal be grief: —
Love's Martyr, when his heat is past,
Proves Care's Confessor at the last.

Anon.

55

A RENUNCIATION

Thou art not fair, for all thy red and white,
  For all those rosy ornaments in thee, —
Thou art not sweet, though made of mere delight,

Nor fair, nor sweet — unless thou pity me!
I will not soothe thy fancies; thou shalt prove
That beauty is no beauty without love.

— Yet love not me, nor seek not to allure
  My thoughts with beauty, were it more divine:
Thy smiles and kisses I cannot endure,
  I'll not be wrapp'd up in those arms of thine:
— Now show it, if thou be a woman right —
Embrace and kiss and love me in despite!

T. Campion

56

Blow, blow, thou winter wind,
Thou art not so unkind
  As man's ingratitude;
Thy tooth is not so keen
Because thou art not seen,
  Although thy breath be rude.
Heigh ho! sing heigh ho! unto the green holly:
Most friendship is feigning, most loving mere folly:
  Then, heigh ho! the holly!
  This life is most jolly.

Freeze, freeze, thou bitter sky,
Thou dost not bite so nigh
  As benefits forgot:
Though thou the waters warp,
Thy sting is not so sharp
  As friend remember'd not.

Heigh ho! sing heigh ho! unto the green holly:
Most friendship is feigning, most loving mere folly:
    Then, heigh ho! the holly!
    This life is most jolly.

W. Shakespeare

57

A SWEET LULLABY

Come little babe, come silly soul,
Thy father's shame, thy mother's grief,
Born as I doubt to all our dole,
And to thyself unhappy chief:
    Sing Lullaby and lap it warm,
    Poor soul that thinks no creature harm.

Thou little think'st and less dost know,
The cause of this thy mother's moan,
Thou want'st the wit to wail her woe,
And I myself am all alone:
    Why dost thou weep? why dost thou wail?
    And knowest not yet what thou dost ail.

Come little wretch, ah silly heart,
Mine only joy, what can I more?
If there be any wrong thy smart
That may the destinies implore:
    'Twas I, I say, against my will,
    I wail the time, but be thou still.

And dost thou smile, oh thy sweet face!
Would God Himself He might thee see,
No doubt thou would'st soon purchase grace,

I know right well, for thee and me:
  But come to mother, babe, and play,
  For father false is fled away.

Sweet boy, if it by fortune chance, 25
Thy father home again to send,
If death do strike me with his lance,
Yet mayst thou me to him commend:
  If any ask thy mother's name,
  Tell how by love she purchased blame. 30

Then will his gentle heart soon yield,
I know him of a noble mind,
Although a Lion in the field.
A Lamb in town thou shalt him find:
  Ask blessing, babe, be not afraid, 35
  His sugar'd words hath me betray'd.

Then mayst thou joy and be right glad,
Although in woe I seem to moan,
Thy father is no rascal lad,
A noble youth of blood and bone: 40
  His glancing looks, if he once smile,
  Right honest women may beguile.

Come, little boy, and rock asleep,
Sing lullaby and be thou still,
I that can do nought else but weep; 45
Will sit by thee and wail my fill:
God bless my babe, and lullaby
  From this thy father's quality!

Anon.

58

With how sad steps, O Moon, thou climb'st the skies!
How silently, and with how wan a face!
What, may it be that e'en in heavenly place
That busy archer his sharp arrows tries!

5 Sure, if that long-with-love-acquainted eyes
Can judge of love, thou feel'st a lover's case,
I read it in thy looks; thy languish'd grace,
To me, that feel the like, thy state descries.

Then, e'en of fellowship, O Moon, tell me,
10 Is constant love deem'd there but want of wit?
Are beauties there as proud as here they be?
Do they above love to be loved, and yet

Those lovers scorn whom that love doth possess?
Do they call virtue, there, ungratefulness?

Sir P. Sidney

59

O CRUDELIS AMOR

When thou must home to shades of underground,
And there arrived, a new admired guest,
The beauteous spirits do engirt thee round,
White Iopé, blithe Helen, and the rest,
5 To hear the stories of thy finish'd love
From that smooth tongue whose music hell can move;

Then wilt thou speak of banqueting delights,
Of masques and revels which sweet youth did make,
Of tourneys and great challenges of Knights,
And all these triumphs for thy beauty's sake:
When thou hast told these honours done to thee,
Then tell, O tell, how thou didst murder me!

T. Campion

60

SEPHESTIA'S SONG TO HER CHILD

Weep not, my wanton, smile upon my knee;
When thou art old there's grief enough for thee.
    Mother's wag, pretty boy,
    Father's sorrow, father's joy;
    When thy father first did see
    Such a boy by him and me,
    He was glad, I was woe,
    Fortune changéd made him so,
    When he left his pretty boy,
    Last his sorrow, first his joy.

Weep not, my wanton, smile upon my knee,
When thou art old there's grief enough for thee.
    Streaming tears that never stint,
    Like pearl drops from a flint,
    Fell by course from his eyes,
    That one another's place supplies;
    Thus he grieved in every part,
    Tears of blood fell from his heart,

When he left his pretty boy,
20   Father's sorrow, father's joy.

Weep not, my wanton, smile upon my knee,
When thou art old, there's grief enough for thee.
   The wanton smiled, father wept,
   Mother cried, baby leapt;
25   More he crow'd, more we cried,
   Nature could not sorrow hide:
   He must go, he must kiss
   Child and mother, baby bless,
   For he left his pretty boy,
30   Father's sorrow, father's joy.
Weep not, my wanton, smile upon my knee,
When thou art old, there's grief enough for thee.

R. Greene

61

A LAMENT

My thoughts hold mortal strife;
I do detest my life,
And with lamenting cries
Peace to my soul to bring
5 Oft call that prince which here doth monarchize:
But he, grim grinning King,
Who caitiffs scorns, and doth the blest surprize,
Late having deck'd with beauty's rose his tomb,
Disdains to crop a weed, and will not come.

W. Drummond

Book First

62

DIRGE OF LOVE

Come away, come away, Death,
And in sad cypres let me be laid;
 Fly away, fly away, breath;
I am slain by a fair cruel maid.
My shroud of white, stuck all with yew,
 O prepare it!
My part of death, no one so true
 Did share it.

Not a flower, not a flower sweet
On my black coffin let there be strown;
 Not a friend, not a friend greet
My poor corpse, where my bones shall be thrown:
A thousand thousand sighs to save,
 Lay me, O where
Sad true lover never find my grave,
 To weep there.

W. Shakespeare

63

TO HIS LUTE

My lute, be as thou wert when thou didst grow
With thy green mother in some shady grove,
When immelodious winds but made thee move,
And birds their ramage did on thee bestow.

Since that dear Voice which did thy sounds approve,
Which wont in such harmonious strains to flow,
Is reft from Earth to tune those spheres above,
What art thou but a harbinger of woe?

Thy pleasing notes be pleasing notes no more,
But orphans' wailings to the fainting ear;
Each stroke a sigh, each sound draws forth a tear;
For which be silent as in woods before:

Or if that any hand to touch thee deign,
Like widow'd turtle, still her loss complain.

W. Drummond

64

FIDELE

Fear no more the heat o' the sun
    Nor the furious winter's rages;
Thou thy worldly task has done,
    Home art gone and ta'en thy wages.
Golden lads and girls all must,
As chimney-sweepers, come to dust.

Fear no more the frown o' the great,
    Thou art past the tyrant's stroke;
Care no more to clothe and eat;
    To thee the reed is as the oak:
The sceptre, learning, physic, must
All follow this, and come to dust.

Fear no more the lightning-flash
    Nor the all-dreaded thunder-stone;
Fear not slander, censure rash;
    Thou has finish'd joy and moan:
All lovers young, all lovers must
Consign to thee, and come to dust.

W. Shakespeare

65

A SEA DIRGE

Full fathom five thy father lies:
    Of his bones are coral made;
Those are pearls that were his eyes:
    Nothing of him that doth fade,
But doth suffer a sea-change
Into something rich and strange.
Sea-nymphs hourly ring his knell:
    Hark! now I hear them,—
        Ding, dong, bell.

W. Shakespeare

66

A LAND DIRGE

Call for the robin-redbreast and the wren
Since o'er shady groves they hover
And with leaves and flowers do cover
The friendless bodies of unburied men.
Call unto his funeral dole
The ant, the field-mouse, and the mole
To rear him hillocks that shall keep him warm
And (when gay tombs are robb'd) sustain no harm;
But keep the wolf far thence, that's foe to men,
For with his nails he'll dig them up again.

J. Webster

67

POST MORTEM

If Thou survive my well-contented day
When that churl Death my bones with dust shall cover,
And shalt by fortune once more re-survey
These poor rude lines of thy deceaséd lover;

5 Compare them with the bettering of the time,
And though they be outstripp'd by every pen,
Reserve them for my love, not for their rhyme
Exceeded by the height of happier men.

O then vouchsafe me but this loving thought—
10 'Had my friend's Muse grown with this growing age,
A dearer birth than this his love had brought,
To march in ranks of better equipage:

But since he died, and poets better prove,
Theirs for their style I'll read, his for his love.'

W. Shakespeare

68

THE TRIUMPH OF DEATH

No longer mourn for me when I am dead
Than you shall hear the surly sullen bell
Give warning to the world, that I am fled
From this vile world, with vilest worms to dwell;

5 Nay, if you read this line, remember not
The hand that writ it; for I love you so,

That I in your sweet thoughts would be forgot
If thinking on me then should make you woe.

O if, I say, you look upon this verse
When I perhaps compounded am with clay,
Do not so much as my poor name rehearse,
But let your love even with my life decay;

Lest the wise world should look into your moan,
And mock you with me after I am gone.
W. Shakespeare

69

YOUNG LOVE

    Tell me where is Fancy bred,
      Or in the heart, or in the head?
      How begot, how nourishéd?
        Reply, reply.

    It is engender'd in the eyes;
      With gazing fed; and Fancy dies
      In the cradle where it lies:
    Let us all ring Fancy's knell;
    I'll begin it,—Ding, dong, bell.
      —Ding, dong, bell.
W. Shakespeare

70

A DILEMMA

Lady, when I behold the roses sprouting
    Which clad in damask mantles deck the arbours,
    And then behold your lips where sweet love harbours,

My eyes present me with a double doubting:
For viewing both alike, hardly my mind supposes
Whether the roses be your lips, or your lips the roses.

Anon.

71

ROSALYND'S MADRIGAL

Love in my bosom, like a bee,
    Doth suck his sweet;
Now with his wings he plays with me,
    Now with his feet.
    Within mine eyes he makes his nest,
    His bed amidst my tender breast;
    My kisses are his daily feast,
    And yet he robs me of my rest:
    Ah! wanton, will ye?

And if I sleep, then percheth he
    With pretty flight,
And makes his pillow of my knee
    The livelong night.
    Strike I my lute, he tunes the string;
    He music plays if so I sing;
    He lends me every lovely thing,
    Yet cruel he my heart doth sting:
    Whist, wanton, will ye?

Else I with roses every day
    Will whip you hence,
And bind you, when you long to play,
    For your offence;

I'll shut my eyes to keep you in;
I'll make you fast it for your sin;
I'll count your power not worth a pin;
—Alas! what hereby shall I win,
    If he gainsay me?

What if I beat the wanton boy
    With many a rod?
He will repay me with annoy,
    Because a god.
Then sit thou safely on my knee,
And let thy bower my bosom be;
Lurk in mine eyes, I like of thee,
O Cupid! so thou pity me,
    Spare not, but play thee!

T. Lodge

72

CUPID AND CAMPASPE

Cupid and my Campaspé play'd
At cards for kisses; Cupid paid:
He stakes his quiver, bow, and arrows,
His mother's doves, and team of sparrows;
Loses them too; then down he throws
The coral of his lip, the rose
Growing on's cheek (but none knows how);
With these, the crystal of his brow,
And then the dimple on his chin;
All these did my Campaspé win:

And last he set her both his eyes—
She won, and Cupid blind did rise.
   O Love! has she done this to thee?
   What shall, alas! become of me?

J. Lylye

73

Pack, clouds, away, and welcome day,
   With night we banish sorrow;
Sweet air blow soft, mount larks aloft
   To give my Love good-morrow!
Wings from the wind to please her mind
   Notes from the lark I'll borrow;
Bird, prune thy wing, nightingale sing,
   To give my Love good-morrow;
      To give my Love good-morrow
      Notes from them both I'll borrow.

Wake from thy nest, Robin-red-breast,
   Sing, birds, in every furrow;
And from each hill, let music shrill
   Give my fair Love good-morrow!
Blackbird and thrush in every bush,
   Stare, linnet, and cock-sparrow
You pretty elves, amongst yourselves
   Sing my fair Love good-morrow;
      To give my Love good-morrow
      Sing, birds, in every furrow!

T. Heywood

74
PROTHALAMION

Calm was the day, and through the trembling air
Sweet-breathing Zephyrus did softly play—
A gentle spirit, that lightly did delay
Hot Titan's beams, which then did glister fair;
When I, (whom sullen care,   5
Through discontent of my long fruitless stay
In princes' court, and expectation vain
Of idle hopes, which still do fly away
Like empty shadows, did afflict my brain)
Walk'd forth to ease my pain   10
Along the shore of silver-streaming Thames;
Whose rutty bank, the which his river hems,
Was painted all with variable flowers,
And all the meads adorn'd with dainty gems
Fit to deck maiden's bowers,   15
And crown their paramours
Against the bridal day, which is not long:
    Sweet Thames! run softly, till I end my song.

There in a meadow by the river's side
A flock of nymphs I chancéd to espy,   20
All lovely daughters of the flood thereby,
With goodly greenish locks all loose untied
As each had been a bride;
And each one had a little wicker basket
Made of fine twigs, entrailéd curiously,   25
In which they gather'd flowers to fill their flasket,
And with fine fingers cropt full feateously
The tender stalks on high.

Of every sort which in that meadow grew
30 They gather'd some; the violet, pallid blue
The little daisy that at evening closes,
The virgin lily and the primrose true.
With store of vermeil roses,
To deck their bridegrooms' posies
35 Against the bridal day, which was not long:
    Sweet Thames: run softly, till I end my song.

With that I saw two Swans of goodly hue
Come softly swimming down along the lee;
Two fairer birds I yet did never see;
40 The snow which doth the top of Pindus strow
Did never whiter show,
Nor Jove himself, when he a swan would be
For love of Leda, whiter did appear;
Yet Leda was (they say) as white as he,
45 Yet not so white as these, nor nothing near;
So purely white they were
That even the gentle stream, the which them bare,
Seem'd foul to them, and bade his billows spare
To wet their silken feathers, lest they might
50 Soil their fair plumes with water not so fair,
And mar their beauties bright
That shone as Heaven's light
Against their bridal day, which was not long:
    Sweet Thames! run softly, till I end my song.

55 Eftsoons the nymphs, which now had flowers their fill,
Ran all in haste to see that silver brood
As they came floating on the crystal flood;

Book First

Whom when they saw, they stood amazéd still
Their wondering eyes to fill;
Them seem'd they never saw a sight so fair 60
Of fowls, so lovely, that they sure did deem
Them heavenly born, or to be that same pair
Which through the sky draw Venus' silver team;
For sure they did not seem
To be begot of any earthly seed, 65
But rather Angels, or of Angels' breed;
Yet were they bred of summer's heat, they say,
In sweetest season, when each flower and weed
The earth did fresh array;
So fresh they seem'd as day, 70
Ev'n as their bridal day, which was not long:
  Sweet Thames! run softly, till I end my song.

Then forth they all out of their baskets drew
Great store of flowers, the honour of the field,
That to the sense did fragrant odours yield, 75
All which upon those goodly birds they threw
And all the waves did strew,
That like old Peneus' waters they did seem
When down along by pleasant Tempe's shore
Scatter'd with flowers, through Thessaly they stream, 80
That they appear, through lilies' plenteous store,
Like a bride's chamber-floor.
Two of those nymphs meanwhile two garlands bound
Of freshest flowers which in that mead they found,
The which presenting all in trim array, 85
Their snowy foreheads therewithal they crown'd;

Whilst one did sing this lay
Prepared against that day,
Against the bridal day, which was not long:
    Sweet Thames! run softly, till I end my song.

' Ye gentle birds! the world's fair ornament,
And Heaven's glory, whom this happy hour
Doth lead unto your lovers' blissful bower,
Joy may you have, and gentle heart's content
Of your love's couplement;
And let fair Venus, that is queen of love,
With her heart-quelling son upon you smile,
Whose smile, they say, hath virtue to remove
All love's dislike, and friendship's faulty guile
For ever to assoil.
Let endless peace your steadfast hearts accord,
And blessèd plenty wait upon your board;
And let your bed with pleasures chaste abound,
That fruitful issue may to you afford
Which may your foes confound,
And make your joys redound
Upon your bridal day, which is not long:
    Sweet Thames! run softly, till I end my song.'

So ended she; and all the rest around
To her redoubled that her undersong,
Which said their bridal day should not be long:
And gentle Echo from the neighbour ground
Their accents did resound.
So forth those joyous birds did pass along
Adown the lee that to them murmur'd low,
As he would speak but that he lack'd a tongue;

Book First

Yet did by signs his glad affection show,
Making his stream run slow.
And all the fowl which in his flood did dwell
'Gan flock about these twain, that did excel
The rest, so far as Cynthia doth shend
The lesser stars. So they, enrangéd well,
Did on those two attend,
And their best service lend
Against their wedding day, which was not long:
   Sweet Thames! run softly, till I end my song.

At length they all to merry London came,
To merry London, my most kindly nurse,
That to me gave this life's first native source,
Though from another place I take my name,
An house of ancient fame:
There when they came whereas those bricky towers
The which on Thames' broad agéd back do ride,
Where now the studious lawyers have their bowers,
There whilome wont the Templar-knights to bide,
Till they decay'd through pride;
Next whereunto there stands a stately place,
Where oft I gainéd gifts and goodly grace
Of that great lord, which therein wont to dwell,
Whose want too well now feels my friendless case;
But ah! here fits not well
Old woes, but joys to tell
Against the bridal day, which is not long:
   Sweet Thames! run softly, till I end my song.

Yet therein now doth lodge a noble peer,
Great England's glory and the world's wide wonder,

Whose dreadful name late through all Spain did thunder,
And Hercules' two pillars standing near
Did make to quake and fear:
150 Fair branch of honour, flower of chivalry!
That fillest England with thy triumphs' fame
Joy have thou of thy noble victory,
And endless happiness of thine own name
That promiseth the same;
155 That through thy prowess and victorious arms
Thy country may be freed from foreign harms,
And great Elisa's glorious name may ring
Through all the world, fill'd with thy wide alarms,
Which some brave Muse may sing
160 To ages following:
Upon the bridal day, which is not long:
  Sweet Thames! run softly, till I end my song.

From those high towers this noble lord issúing
Like radiant Hesper, when his golden hair
165 In th' ocean billows hath bathéd fair,
Descended to the river's open viewing
With a great train ensuing.
Above the rest were goodly to be seen
Two gentle knights of lovely face and feature.
170 Beseeming well the bower of any queen,
With gifts of wit and ornaments of nature,
Fit for so goodly stature,
That like the twins of Jove they seem'd in sight
Which deck the baldric of the Heavens bright;
175 They two, forth pacing to the river's side,
Received those two fair brides, their love's delight;

Which, at th' appointed tide,
Each one did make his bride
Against their bridal day, which is not long:
    Sweet Thames! run softly, till I end my song.
E. Spenser

75

THE HAPPY HEART

Art thou poor, yet hast thou golden slumbers?
    O sweet content!
Art thou rich, yet is thy mind perplex'd?
    O punishment!
Dost thou laugh to see how fools are vex'd
To add to golden numbers, golden numbers?
O sweet content! O sweet, O sweet content!
  Work apace, apace, apace, apace;
  Honest labour bears a lovely face;
Then hey nonny nonny, hey nonny nonny!

Canst drink the waters of the crispéd spring?
    O sweet content!
Swimm'st thou in wealth, yet sink'st in thine own tears?
    O punishment!
Then he that patiently want's burden bears
No burden bears, but is a king, a king!
O sweet content! O sweet, O sweet content!
  Work apace, apace, apace, apace;
  Honest labour bears a lovely face;
Then hey nonny nonny, hey nonny nonny!
T. Dekker

76

SIC TRANSIT

Come, cheerful day, part of my life to me;
  For while thou view'st me with thy fading light
Part of my life doth still depart with thee,
  And I still onward haste to my last night:
Time's fatal wings do ever forward fly—
So every day we live a day we die.

But O ye nights, ordain'd for barren rest,
  How are my days deprived of life in you
When heavy sleep my soul hath dispossest,
  By feignéd death life sweetly to renew!
Part of my life, in that, you life deny:
So every day we live, a day we die.

T. Campion

77

This Life, which seems so fair,
Is like a bubble blown up in the air
By sporting children's breath,
Who chase it everywhere
And strive who can most motion it bequeath.
And though it sometimes seem of its own might
Like to an eye of gold to be fix'd there,
And firm to hover in that empty height,
That only is because it is so light.
—But in that pomp it doth not long appear;
For when 'tis most admired, in a thought,
Because it erst was nought, it turns to nought.

W. Drummond

78

SOUL AND BODY

Poor Soul, the centre of my sinful earth,
[Foil'd by] those rebel powers that thee array,
Why doth thou pine within, and suffer dearth,
Painting thy outward walls so costly gay?

Why so large cost, having so short a lease,
Dost thou upon thy fading mansion spend?
Shall worms, inheritors of this excess,
Eat up thy charge? is this thy body's end?

Then, Soul, live thou upon thy servant's loss,
And let that pine to aggravate thy store;
Buy terms divine in selling hours of dross;
Within be fed, without be rich no more:—

So shalt thou feed on death, that feeds on men,
And death once dead, there's no more dying then.
W. Shakespeare

79

The man of life upright,
    Whose guiltless heart is free
From all dishonest deeds,
    Or thought of vanity;

The man whose silent days
    In harmless joys are spent,
Whom hopes cannot delude
    Nor sorrow discontent:

    That man needs neither towers
        Nor armour for defence,
    Nor secret vaults to fly
        From thunder's violence:

    He only can behold
        With unaffrighted eyes
    The horrors of the deep
        And terrors of the skies.

    Thus scorning all the cares
        That fate or fortune brings,
    He makes the heaven his book,
        His wisdom heavenly things;

    Good thoughts his only friends,
        His wealth a well-spent age,
    The earth his sober inn
        And quiet pilgrimage.

T. Campion

80

THE LESSONS OF NATURE

Of this fair volume which we World do name
If we the sheets and leaves could turn with care,
Of Him who it corrects, and did it frame,
We clear might read the art and wisdom rare:

Find out His power which wildest powers doth tame
His providence extending everywhere,

His justice which proud rebels doth not spare,
In every page, no period of the same.

But silly we, like foolish children, rest
Well pleased with colour'd vellum, leaves of gold,
Fair dangling ribbands, leaving what is best,
On the great Writer's sense ne'er taking hold;

Or if by chance we stay our minds on aught,
It is some picture on the margin wrought.
W. Drummond

81

Doth then the world go thus, doth all thus move?
Is this the justice which on earth we find?
Is this that firm decree which all doth bind?
Are these your influences, Powers above?

Those souls which vice's moody mists most blind,
Blind Fortune, blindly, most their friend doth prove;
And they who thee, poor idol Virtue! love,
Ply like a feather toss'd by storm and wind.

Ah! if a Providence doth sway this all
Why should best minds groan under most distress?
Or why should pride humility make thrall,
And injuries the innocent oppress?

Heavens! hinder, stop this fate; or grant a time
When good may have, as well as bad, their prime!
W. Drummond

82

THE WORLD'S WAY

Tired with all these, for restful death I cry—
As, to behold desert a beggar born,
And needy nothing trimm'd in jollity,
And purest faith unhappily forsworn,

And gilded honour shamefully misplaced,
And maiden virtue rudely strumpeted,
And right perfection wrongfully disgraced,
And strength by limping sway disabled,

And art made tongue-tied by authority,
And folly, doctor-like, controlling skill,
And simple truth miscall'd simplicity,
And captive Good attending captain Ill :—

—Tired with all these, from these would I be gone,
Save that, to die, I leave my Love alone.

W. Shakespeare

83

A WISH

Happy were he could finish forth his fate
In some unhaunted desert, where, obscure
From all society, from love and hate
Of worldly folk, there should he sleep secure ;

Then wake again, and yield God ever praise ;
Content with hip, with haws, and brambleberry ;

In contemplation passing still his days,
And change of holy thoughts to make him merry:

Who, when he dies, his tomb might be the bush
Where harmless robin resteth with the thrush:
—Happy were he!
R. Devereux, Earl of Essex

84

SAINT JOHN BAPTIST

The last and greatest Herald of Heaven's King
Girt with rough skins, hies to the deserts wild,
Among that savage brood the woods forth bring,
Which he more harmless found than man, and mild.

His food was locusts, and what there doth spring,
With honey that from virgin hives distill'd;
Parch'd body, hollow eyes, some uncouth thing
Made him appear, long since from earth exiled.

There burst he forth: All ye whose hopes rely
On God, with me amidst these deserts mourn,
Repent, repent, and from old errors turn!
—Who listen'd to his voice, obey'd his cry?

Only the echoes, which he made relent,
Rung from their flinty caves, Repent! Repent!
W. Drummond

BOOK SECOND

85

ODE ON THE MORNING OF CHRIST'S NATIVITY

This is the month, and this the happy morn
Wherein the Son of Heaven's Eternal King
Of wedded maid and virgin mother born,
Our great redemption from above did bring;
For so the holy sages once did sing 5
That He our deadly forfeit should release,
And with His Father work us a perpetual peace.

That glorious Form, that Light unsufferable,
And that far-beaming blaze of Majesty
Wherewith He wont at Heaven's high council-table 10
To sit the midst of Trinal Unity,
He laid aside; and, here with us to be,
Forsook the courts of everlasting day,
And chose with us a darksome house of mortal clay.

Say, heavenly Muse, shall not thy sacred vein 15
Afford a present to the Infant God?
Hast thou no verse, no hymn, or solemn strain
To welcome Him to this His new abode,
Now while the heaven, by the sun's team untrod,

20 Hath took no print of the approaching light,
And all the spangled host keep watch in squadrons bright?

See how from far, upon the eastern road,
The star-led wizards haste with odours sweet:
O run, prevent them with thy humble ode
25 And lay it lowly at His blessed feet;
Have thou the honour first thy Lord to greet,
And join thy voice unto the Angel quire
From out His secret altar touch'd with hallow'd fire.

THE HYMN

It was the winter wild
30 While the heaven-born Child
All meanly wrapt in the rude manger lies;
Nature in awe to Him
Had doff'd her gaudy trim,
With her great Master so to sympathize:
35 It was no season then for her
To wanton with the sun, her lusty paramour.

Only with speeches fair
She woos the gentle air
To hide her guilty front with innocent snow;
40 And on her naked shame,
Pollute with sinful blame,
The saintly veil of maiden white to throw;
Confounded, that her Maker's eyes
Should look so near upon her foul deformities.

JOHN MILTON

Book Second

But He, her fears to cease,   45
Sent down the meek-eyed Peace;
She, crown'd with olive green, came softly sliding
Down through the turning sphere,
His ready harbinger,
With turtle wing the amorous clouds dividing;   50
And waving wide her myrtle wand,
She strikes a universal peace through sea and land.

No war, or battle's sound
Was heard the world around:
The idle spear and shield were high uphung;   55
The hookéd chariot stood
Unstain'd with hostile blood;
The trumpet spake not to the arméd throng,
And kings sat still with awful eye,
As if they surely knew their sovran Lord was by.   60

But peaceful was the night
Wherein the Prince of Light
His reign of peace upon the earth began:
The winds, with wonder whist,
Smoothly the waters kist   65
Whispering new joys to the mild ocean—
Who now hath quite forgot to rave,
While birds of calm sit brooding on the charméd wave.

The stars, with deep amaze,
Stand fix'd in steadfast gaze,   70
Bending one way what their precious influence;
And will not take their flight
For all the morning light,

Or Lucifer that often warn'd them thence;
75 But in their glimmering orbs did glow
Until their Lord Himself bespake, and bid them go.

And though the shady gloom
Had given day her room,
The sun himself withheld his wonted speed,
80 And hid his head for shame,
As his inferior flame
The new-enlighten'd world no more should need;
He saw a greater Sun appear
Than his bright throne, or burning axletree could bear.

85 The shepherds on the lawn
Or ere the point of dawn
Sate simply chatting in a rustic row;
Full little thought they than
That the mighty Pan
90 Was kindly come to live with them below:
Perhaps their loves, or else their sheep
Was all that did their silly thoughts so busy keep:—

When such music sweet
Their hearts and ears did greet
95 As never was by mortal finger strook—
Divinely-warbled voice
Answering the stringéd noise,
As all their souls in blissful rapture took:
The air, such pleasure loth to lose,
100 With thousand echoes still prolongs each heavenly close.

Book Second

Nature, that heard such sound
Beneath the hollow round
Of Cynthia's seat the airy region thrilling,
Now was almost won
To think her part was done,　　　　　　　　105
And that her reign had here its last fulfilling;
She knew such harmony alone
Could hold all Heaven and Earth in happier union.

At last surrounds their sight
A globe of circular light　　　　　　　　110
That with long beams the shamefaced night array'd;
The helmèd Cherubim
And sworded Seraphim
Are seen in glittering ranks with wings display'd,
Harping in loud and solemn quire　　　　　　　　115
With unexpressive notes, to Heaven's new-born Heir.

Such music (as 'tis said)
Before was never made
But when of old the Sons of Morning sung,
While the Creator great　　　　　　　　120
His constellations set
And the well-balanced world on hinges hung;
And cast the dark foundations deep,
And bid the weltering waves their oozy channel keep.

Ring out, ye crystal spheres!　　　　　　　　125
Once bless our human ears,
If ye have power to touch our senses so;
And let your silver chime
Move in melodious time;

130 And let the bass of heaven's deep organ blow;
And with your ninefold harmony
Make up full consort to the angelic symphony.

For if such holy song
Enwrap our fancy long,
135 Time will run back, and fetch the age of gold;
And speckled Vanity
Will sicken soon and die,
And leprous Sin will melt from earthly mould;
And Hell itself will pass away,
140 And leave her dolorous mansions to the peering day.

Yea, Truth and Justice then
Will down return to men,
Orb'd in a rainbow; and, like glories wearing,
Mercy will sit between
145 Throned in celestial sheen,
With radiant feet the tissued clouds down steering;
And Heaven, as at some festival,
Will open wide the gates of her high palace-hall.

But wisest Fate says No;
150 This must not yet be so;
The Babe yet lies in smiling infancy
That on the bitter cross
Must redeem our loss
So both Himself and us to glorify:
155 Yet first, to those ychain'd in sleep
The wakeful trump of doom must thunder through the deep;

With such a horrid clang
As on Mount Sinai rang
While the red fire and smouldering clouds outbrake:
The aged Earth aghast 160
With terror of that blast
Shall from the surface to the centre shake,
When, at the world's last sessión,
The dreadful Judge in middle air shall spread His throne.

And then at last our bliss 165
Full and perfect is,
But now begins; for from this happy day
The old Dragon under ground,
In straiter limits bound,
Not half so far casts his usurpéd sway; 170
And, wroth to see his kingdom fail,
Swinges the scaly horror of his folded tail.

The Oracles are dumb;
No voice or hideous hum
Runs through the archéd roof in words deceiving. 175
Apollo from his shrine
Can no more divine,
With hollow shriek the steep of Delphos leaving:
No nightly trance or breathéd spell
Inspires the pale-eyed priest from the prophetic cell. 180

The lonely mountains o'er
And the resounding shore
A voice of weeping heard, and loud lament;
From haunted spring and dale
Edged with poplar pale 185

The parting Genius is with sighing sent;
With flower-inwoven tresses torn
The Nymphs in twilight shade of tangled thickets mourn.

In consecrated earth
And on the holy hearth
The Lars and Lemures moan with midnight plaint;
In urns, and altars round
A drear and dying sound
Affrights the Flamens at their service quaint;
And the chill marble seems to sweat,
While each peculiar Power foregoes his wonted seat.

Peor and Baalim
Forsake their temples dim,
With that twice-batter'd god of Palestine;
And moonéd Ashtaroth
Heaven's queen and mother both,
Now sits not girt with tapers' holy shine;
The Lybic Hammon shrinks his horn:
In vain the Tyrian maids their wounded Thammuz mourn.

And sullen Moloch, fled,
Hath left in shadows dread
His burning idol all of blackest hue;
In vain with cymbals' ring
They call the grisly king,
In dismal dance about the furnace blue;
The brutish gods of Nile as fast,
Isis, and Orus, and the dog Anubis, haste.

Nor is Osiris seen
In Memphian grove, or green,
Trampling the unshower'd grass with lowings loud: 215
Nor can he be at rest
Within his sacred chest;
Nought but profoundest Hell can be his shroud;
In vain with timbrell'd anthems dark
The sable-stoléd sorcerers bear his worshipt ark. 220

He feels from Juda's land
The dreaded Infant's hand;
The rays of Bethlehem blind his dusky eyn;
Nor all the gods beside
Longer dare abide, 225
Not Typhon huge ending in snaky twine:
Our Babe, to show His Godhead true,
Can in His swaddling bands control the damnéd crew.

So, when the sun in bed
Curtain'd with cloudy red 230
Pillows his chin upon an orient wave,
The flocking shadows pale
Troop to the infernal jail,
Each fetter'd ghost slips to his several grave;
And the yellow-skirted fays 235
Fly after the night-steeds, leaving their moon-loved maze.

But see! the Virgin blest
Hath laid her Babe to rest;
Time is, our tedious song should here have ending:

240 Heaven's youngest-teeméd star
　　Hath fix'd her polish'd car,
　Her sleeping Lord with hand-maid lamp attending:
　　And all about the courtly stable
　Bright-harness'd Angels sit in order serviceable.

J. Milton

86

SONG FOR ST. CECILIA'S DAY, 1687

From Harmony, from heavenly Harmony
　　This universal frame began:
　　When Nature underneath a heap
　　　Of jarring atoms lay
5　　And could not heave her head,
The tuneful voice was heard from high,
　　Arise, ye more than dead!
Then cold and hot and moist and dry
In order to their stations leap,
10　　And Music's power obey.
From harmony, from heavenly harmony
　　This universal frame began:
　　From harmony to harmony
Through all the compass of the notes it ran,
15　The diapason closing full in Man.

What passion cannot Music raise and quell?
　　When Jubal struck the chorded shell
　　His listening brethren stood around,
　　And, wondering, on their faces fell
20　　To worship that celestial sound.

Less than a god they thought there could not dwell
    Within the hollow of that shell
    That spoke so sweetly and so well.
What passion cannot Music raise and quell?

    The trumpet's loud clangor   25
        Excites us to arms,
    With shrill notes of anger
        And mortal alarms.
    The double double double beat
        Of the thundering drum   30
        Cries 'Hark! the foes come;
Charge, charge, 'tis too late to retreat!'

    The soft complaining flute
        In dying notes discovers
        The woes of hopeless lovers,   35
Whose dirge is whisper'd by the warbling lute.

      Sharp violins proclaim
    Their jealous pangs and desperation,
    Fury, frantic indignation,
    Depth of pains, and height of passion   40
        For the fair disdainful dame.

    But oh! what art can teach,
    What human voice can reach
        The sacred organ's praise?
    Notes inspiring holy love,   45
    Notes that wing their heavenly ways
        To mend the choirs above.

Orpheus could lead the savage race,
And trees unrooted left their place
    Sequacious of the lyre:
But bright Cecilia raised the wonder higher:
When to her Organ vocal breath was given
An Angel heard, and straight appear'd—
    Mistaking Earth for Heaven.

Grand Chorus

As from the power of sacred lays
    The spheres began to move,
And sung the great Creator's praise
    To all the blest above;
So when the last and dreadful hour
This crumbling pageant shall devour,
The trumpet shall be heard on high,
The dead shall live, the living die,
And Music shall untune the sky.

J. Dryden

87

ON THE LATE MASSACRE IN PIEDMONT

Avenge, O Lord! Thy slaughter'd saints, whose bones
Lie scatter'd on the Alpine mountains cold;
Even them who kept Thy truth so pure of old
When all our fathers worship stocks and stones,

Forget not: In Thy book record their groans
Who were Thy sheep, and in their ancient fold
Slain by the bloody Piemontese, that roll'd
Mother with infant down the rocks. Their moans

The vales redoubled to the hills, and they
To Heaven.   Their martyr'd blood and ashes sow
O'er all the Italian fields, where still doth sway

The triple Tyrant: that from these may grow
A hundred-fold, who, having learnt Thy way,
Early may fly the Babylonian woe.

J. Milton

88

HORATIAN ODE UPON CROMWELL'S RETURN FROM IRELAND

The forward youth that would appear,
Must now forsake his Muses dear,
    Nor in the shadows sing
    His numbers languishing.

'Tis time to leave the books in dust,
And oil the unuséd armour's rust,
    Removing from the wall
    The corslet of the hall.

So restless Cromwell could not cease
In the inglorious arts of peace,
    But through adventurous war
    Urgéd his active star:

And like the three-fork'd lightning, first
Breaking the clouds where it was nurst,
    Did thorough his own Side
    His fiery way divide:

For 'tis all one to courage high,
The emulous, or enemy;
 And with such, to enclose
 Is more than to oppose;

Then burning through the air he went
And palaces and temples rent:
 And Caesar's head at last
 Did through his laurels blast.

'Tis madness to resist or blame
The face of angry heaven's flame;
 And if we would speak true,
 Much to the Man is due

Who, from his private gardens, where
He lived reservéd and austere,
 (As if his highest plot
 To plant the bergamot,)

Could by industrious valour climb
To ruin the great work of time,
 And cast the Kingdoms old
 Into another mould;

Though Justice against Fate complain,
And plead the ancient Rights in vain—
 But those do hold or break
 As men are strong or weak;

Nature, that hateth emptiness,
Allows of penetration less,
 And therefore must make room
 Where greater spirits come.

What field of all the civil war 45
Where his were not the deepest scar?
    And Hampton shows what part
    He had of wiser art,

Where, twining subtle fears with hope,
He wove a net of such a scope 50
    That Charles himself might chase
    To Carisbrook's narrow case,

That thence the Royal actor borne
The tragic scaffold might adorn:
    While round the arméd bands 55
    Did clap their bloody hands.

He nothing common did or mean
Upon that memorable scene,
    But with his keener eye
    The axe's edge did try; 60

Nor call'd the Gods, with vulgar spite,
To vindicate his helpless right;
    But bow'd his comely head
    Down, as upon a bed.

—This was that memorable hour 65
Which first assured the forcéd power:
    So when they did design
    The Capitol's first line,

A Bleeding Head, where they begun,
Did fright the architects to run; 70
    And yet in that the State
    Foresaw its happy fate!

And now the Irish are ashamed
To see themselves in one year tamed:
    So much one man can do
    That does both act and know.

They can affirm his praises best,
And have, though overcome, confest
    How good he is, how just
    And fit for highest trust.

Nor yet grown stiffer with command,
But still in the Republic's hand—
    How fit he is to sway
    That can so well obey!

He to the Commons' feet presents
A Kingdom for his first year's rents,
    And (what he may) forbears
    His fame, to make it theirs:

And has his sword and spoils ungirt
To lay them at the Public's skirt.
    So when the falcon high
    Falls heavy from the sky,

She, having kill'd, no more doth search
But on the next green bough to perch,
    Where, when he first does lure,
    The falconer has her sure.

Book Second

—What may not then our Isle presume
While victory his crest does plume?
    What may not others fear
    If thus he crowns each year?

As Caesar he, ere long, to Gaul,
To Italy an Hannibal,
    And to all States not free
    Shall climacteric be.

The Pict no shelter now shall find
Within his parti-colour'd mind,
    But from this valor sad
    Shrink underneath the plaid—

Happy, if in the tufted brake
The English hunter him mistake,
    Nor lay his hounds in near
    The Caledonian deer.

But Thou, the War's and Fortune's son,
March indefatigably on;
    And for the last effect
    Still keep the sword erect:

Besides the force it has to fright
The spirits of the shady night,
    The same arts that did gain
    A power, must it maintain.

A. Marvell

89

LYCIDAS

Elegy on a Friend drowned in the Irish Channel
1637

    Yet once more, O ye laurels, and once more
Ye myrtles brown, with ivy never sere,
I come to pluck your berries harsh and crude,
And with forced fingers rude
Shatter your leaves before the mellowing year.
Bitter constraint and sad occasion dear
Compels to me to disturb your season due:
For Lycidas is dead, dead ere his prime,
Young Lycidas, and hath not left his peer.
Who would not sing for Lycidas? he knew
Himself to sing, and build the lofty rhyme.
He must not float upon his watery bier
Unwept, and welter to the parching wind,
Without the meed of some melodious tear.

    Begin then, Sisters of the sacred well
That from beneath the seat of Jove doth spring;
Begin, and somewhat loudly sweep the string.
Hence with denial vain and coy excuse:
So may some gentle Muse
With lucky words favour my destined urn;
And as he passes, turn
And bid fair peace be to my sable shroud.

    For we were nursed upon the self-same hill,
Fed the same flock by fountain, shade, and rill:

Book Second

Together both, ere the high lawns appear'd 25
Under the opening eyelids of the Morn,
We drove a-field, and both together heard
What time the gray-fly winds her sultry horn,
Battening our flocks with the fresh dews of night,
Oft till the star that rose at evening bright 30
Toward heaven's descent had sloped his westering wheel.
Meanwhile the rural ditties were not mute,
Temper'd to the oaten flute,
Rough Satyrs danced, and Fauns with cloven heel
From the glad sound would not be absent long; 35
And old Damoetas loved to hear our song.

But, oh! the heavy change, now thou art gone,
Now thou art gone, and never must return!
Thee, Shepherd, thee the woods and desert caves
With wild thyme and the gadding vine o'ergrown, 40
And all their echoes, mourn:
The willows and the hazel copses green
Shall now no more be seen
Fanning their joyous leaves to thy soft lays:—
As killing as the canker to the rose, 45
Or taint-worm to the weanling herds that graze,
Or frost to flowers, that their gay wardrobe wear
When first the white-thorn blows;
Such, Lycidas, thy loss to shepherd's ear.

Where were ye, Nymphs, when the remorseless deep 50
Closed o'er the head of your loved Lycidas?
For neither were ye playing on the steep

Where your old bards, the famous Druids, lie,
Nor on the shaggy top of Mona high,
55 Nor yet where Deva spreads her wizard stream:
    Ay me! I fondly dream—
    Had ye been there. . . For what could that have done?
What could the Muse herself that Orpheus bore,
The Muse herself, for her enchanting son,
60 Whom universal nature did lament,
When by the rout that made the hideous roar
His gory visage down the stream was sent,
Down the swift Hebrus to the Lesbian shore?

    Alas! what boots it with uncessant care
65 To tend the homely, slighted, shepherd's trade
And strictly meditate the thankless Muse?
Were it not better done, as others use,
To sport with Amaryllis in the shade,
Or with the tangles of Neaera's hair?
70 Fame is the spur that the clear spirit doth raise
(That last infirmity of noble mind)
To scorn delights, and live laborious days;
But the fair guerdon when we hope to find,
And think to burst out into sudden blaze,
75 Comes the blind Fury with the abhorréd shears
And slits the thin-spun life. 'But not the praise'
Phoebus replied, and touch'd my trembling ears;
'Fame is no plant that grows on mortal soil,
Not in the glistering foil
80 Set off to the world, nor in broad rumour lies:
But lives and spreads aloft by those pure eyes

And perfect witness of all-judging Jove;
As he pronounces lastly on each deed,
Of so much fame in heaven expect thy meed.'

O fountain Arethuse, and thou honour'd flood 85
Smooth-sliding Mincius, crown'd with vocal reeds,
That strain I heard was of a higher mood.
But now my oat proceeds,
And listens to the herald of the sea
That came in Neptune's plea; 90
He ask'd the waves, and ask'd the felon winds,
What hard mishap hath doom'd this gentle swain?
And question'd every gust of rugged wings
That blows from off each beakéd promontory:
They knew not of his story; 95
And sage Hippotadés their answer brings,
That not a blast was from his dungeon stray'd;
The air was calm, and on the level brine
Sleek Panopé with all her sisters play'd.
It was that fatal and perfidious bark 100
Built in the eclipse, and rigg'd with curses dark,
That sunk so low that sacred head of thine.

Next Camus, reverend sire, went footing slow,
His mantle hairy, and his bonnet sedge
Inwrought with figures dim, and on the edge 105
Like to that sanguine flower inscribed with woe:
'Ah! who hath reft,' quoth he, 'my dearest pledge!'
Last came, and last did go
The Pilot of the Galilean lake;
Two massy keys he bore of metals twain 110
(The golden opes, the iron shuts amain);

He shook his mitred locks, and stern bespake:
'How well could I have spared for thee, young swain,
Enow of such, as for their bellies' sake
Creep and intrude and climb into the fold!
Of other care they little reckoning make
Than how to scramble at the shearer's feast,
And shove away the worthy bidden guest.
Blind mouths! that scarce themselves know how to hold
A sheep-hook, or have learn'd aught else the least
That to the faithful herdman's art belongs!
What recks it them? What need they? They are sped;
And when they list, their lean and flashy songs
Grate on their scrannel pipes of wretched straw;
The hungry sheep look up, and are not fed,
But swoln with wind and the rank mist they draw
Rot inwardly, and foul contagion spread:
Besides what the grim wolf with privy paw
Daily devours apace, and nothing said:
—But that two-handed engine at the door
Stands ready to smite once, and smite no more.'

Return, Alphéus; the dread voice is past
That shrunk thy streams; return, Sicilian Muse,
And call the vales, and bid them hither cast
Their bells and flowerets of a thousand hues.
Ye valleys low, where the mild whispers use
Of shades, and wanton winds, and gushing brooks
On whose fresh lap the swart star sparely looks;
Throw hither all your quaint enamell'd eyes

That on the green turf suck the honey'd showers 140
And purple all the ground with vernal flowers.
Bring the rathe primrose that forsaken dies,
The tufted crow-toe, and pale jessamine,
The white pink, and the pansy freak'd with jet,
The glowing violet, 145
The musk-rose, and the well-attired woodbine,
With cowslips wan that hang the pensive head,
And every flower that sad embroidery wears:
Bid amarantus all his beauty shed,
And daffadillies fill their cups with tears 150
To strew the laureat hearse where Lycid lies.
For, so to interpose a little ease,
Let our frail thoughts dally with false surmise:—
Ay me! whilst thee the shores and sounding seas
Wash far away,—where'er thy bones are hurl'd 155
Whether beyond the stormy Hebrides
Where thou perhaps, under the whelming tide,
Visitest the bottom of the monstrous world;
Or whether thou, to our moist vows denied,
Sleep'st by the fable of Bellerus old, 160
Where the great Vision of the guarded mount
Looks toward Namancos and Bayona's hold,
—Look homeward, Angel, now, and melt with ruth:
—And, O ye dolphins, waft the hapless youth!

Weep no more, woeful shepherds, weep no more, 165
For Lycidas, your sorrow, is not dead,
Sunk though he be beneath the watery floor:
So sinks the day-star in the ocean-bed,
And yet anon repairs his drooping head

170 And tricks his beams, and with new-spangled ore
Flames in the forehead of the morning sky:
So Lycidas sunk low, but mounted high
Through the dear might of Him that walk'd the waves;
Where, other groves and other streams along,
175 With nectar pure his oozy locks he laves,
And hears the unexpressive nuptial song
In the blest kingdoms meek of joy and love.
There entertain him all the Saints above
In solemn troops, and sweet societies,
180 That sing, and singing, in their glory move,
And wipe the tears for ever from his eyes.
Now, Lycidas, the shepherds weep no more;
Henceforth thou art the Genius of the shore
In thy large recompense, and shalt be good
185 To all that wander in that perilous flood.

    Thus sang the uncouth swain to the oaks and rills,
While the still morn went out with sandals gray;
He touch'd the tender stops of various quills,
With eager thought warbling his Doric lay:
190 And now the sun had stretch'd out all the hills,
And now was dropt into the western bay:
At last he rose, and twitch'd his mantle blue:
To-morrow to fresh woods, and pastures new.

J. Milton

90

ON THE TOMBS IN WESTMINSTER ABBEY

Mortality, behold and fear
What a change of flesh is here!

*Here's a world of pomp and state
Buried in dust, once dead by fate.*

Think how many royal bones
Sleep within these heaps of stones;
Here they lie, had realms and lands,
Who now want strength to stir their hands,
Where from their pulpits seal'd with dust
They preach, 'In greatness is no trust.'
Here's an acre sown indeed
With the richest royallest seed
That the earth did e'er suck in
Since the first man died for sin:
Here the bones of birth have cried
'Though gods they were, as men they died.'
Here are sands, ignoble things,
Dropt from the ruin'd sides of kings:
Here's a world of pomp and state
Buried in dust, once dead by fate.

F. Beaumont

91

THE LAST CONQUEROR

Victorious men of earth, no more
  Proclaim how wide your empires are;
Though you bind-in every shore
  And your triumphs reach as far
    As night or day,
  Yet you, proud monarchs, must obey
And mingle with forgotten ashes, when
Death calls ye to the crowd of common men.

Devouring Famine, Plague, and War
  Each able to undo mankind,

Death's servile emissaries are;
   Nor to these alone confined,
      He hath at will
   More quaint and subtle ways to kill;
A smile or kiss, as he will use the art,
Shall have the cunning skill to break a heart.

J. Shirley

92

DEATH THE LEVELLER

The glories of our blood and state
   Are shadows, not substantial things;
There is no armour against fate;
   Death lays his icy hand on kings:
      Sceptre and Crown
      Must tumble down,
And in the dust be equal made
With the poor crooked scythe and spade.

Some men with swords may reap the field,
   And plant fresh laurels where they kill:
But their strong nerves at last must yield;
   They tame but one another still:
      Early or late
      They stoop to fate,
And must give up their murmuring breath
When they, pale captives, creep to death.

The garlands wither on your brow;
   Then boast no more your mighty deeds;
Upon Death's purple altar now
   See where the victor-victim bleeds:

Your heads must come
To the cold tomb;
Only the actions of the just
Smell sweet, and blossom in their dust.

J. Shirley

93

WHEN THE ASSAULT WAS INTENDED TO THE CITY

Captain, or Colonel, or Knight in Arms,
Whose chance on these defenceless doors may seize,
If deed of honour did thee ever please,
Guard them, and him within protect from harms.

He can requite thee; for he knows the charms
That call fame on such gentle acts as these,
And he can spread thy name o'er lands and seas,
Whatever clime the sun's bright circle warms.

Lift not thy spear against the Muses' bower:
The great Emathian conqueror bid spare
The house of Pindarus, when temple and tower

Went to the ground: and the repeated air
Of sad Electra's poet had the power
To save the Athenian walls from ruin bare.

J. Milton

94

ON HIS BLINDNESS

When I consider how my light is spent
Ere half my days, in this dark world and wide,

And that one talent which is death to hide
Lodged with me useless, though my soul more bent

To serve therewith my Maker, and present
My true account, lest He returning chide,—
Doth God exact day-labour, light denied?
I fondly ask:—But Patience, to prevent

That murmur, soon replies; God doth not need
Either man's work, or His own gifts: who best
Bear His mild yoke, they serve Him best: His state

Is kingly; thousands at His bidding speed
And post o'er land and ocean without rest:—
They also serve who only stand and wait.

J. Milton

95

CHARACTER OF A HAPPY LIFE

How happy is he born and taught
That serveth not another's will;
Whose armour is his honest thought
And simple truth his utmost skill!

Whose passions not his masters are,
Whose soul is still prepared for death,
Untied unto the world by care
Of public fame, or private breath;

Who envies none that chance doth raise
Nor vice; Who never understood
How deepest wounds are given by praise;
Nor rules of state, but rules of good:

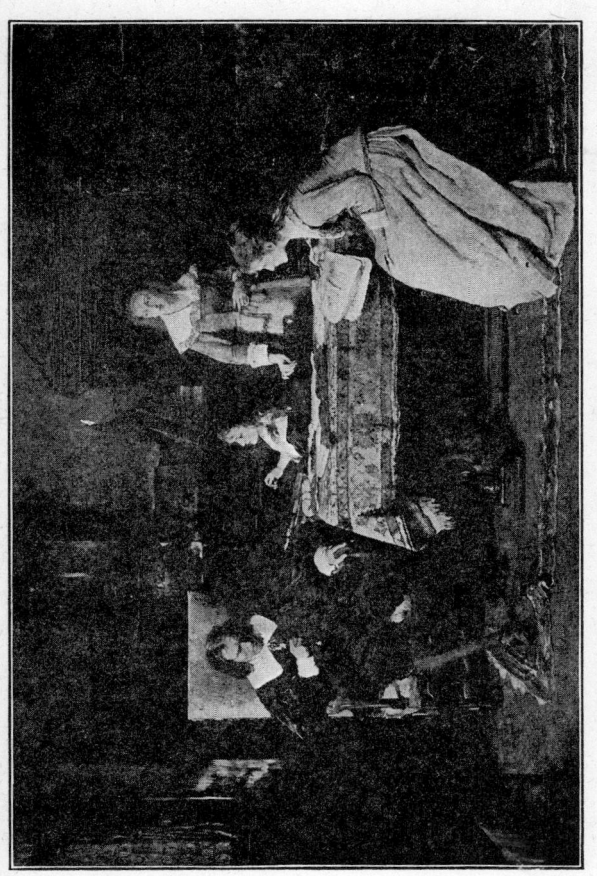

Milton Dictating "Paradise Lost" to His Daughters

Who hath his life from rumours freed,
Whose conscience is his strong retreat;
Whose state can neither flatterers feed,   15
Nor ruin make oppressors great;

Who God doth late and early pray
More of His grace than gifts to lend;
And entertains the harmless day
With a religious book or friend;   20

—This man is freed from servile bands
Of hope to rise, or fear to fall;
Lord of himself, though not of lands;
And having nothing, yet hath all.
Sir H. Wotton

96

THE NOBLE NATURE

It is not growing like a tree
  In bulk, doth make Man better be;
Or standing long an oak, three hundred year,
To fall a log at last, dry, bald, and sere:
     A lily of a day   5
      Is fairer far in May,
   Although it fall and die that night —
  It was the plant and flower of Light.
In small proportions we just beauties see;
And in short measures life may perfect be.   10
B. Jonson

97

THE GIFTS OF GOD

When God at first made Man,
Having a glass of blessings standing by;
Let us (said He) pour on him all we can:
Let the world's riches, which disperséd lie,
    Contract into a span.

So strength first made a way;
Then beauty flow'd, then wisdom, honour, pleasure:
When almost all was out, God made a stay,
Perceiving that alone, of all His treasure,
    Rest in the bottom lay.

For if I should (said He)
Bestow this jewel also on My creature,
He would adore My gifts instead of Me,
And rest in Nature, not the God of Nature,
    So both should losers be.

Yet let him keep the rest,
But keep them with repining restlessness:
Let him be rich and weary, that at least,
If goodness lead him not, yet weariness
    May toss him to My breast.

G. Herbert

THE RETREAT

Happy those early days, when I
Shined in my Angel-infancy!
Before I understood this place
Appointed for my second race,
Or taught my soul to fancy aught   5
But a white, celestial thought;
When yet I had not walk'd above
A mile or two from my first Love,
And looking back, at that short space
Could see a glimpse of His bright face;   10
When on some gilded cloud or flower
My gazing soul would dwell an hour,
And in those weaker glories spy
Some shadows of eternity;
Before I taught my tongue to wound   15
My conscience with a sinful sound,
Or had the black art to dispense
A several sin to every sense,
But felt through all this fleshly dress
Bright shoots of everlastingness.   20

O how I long to travel back,
And tread again that ancient track!
That I might once more reach that plain
Where first I left my glorious train;
From whence th' enlighten'd spirit sees   25
That shady City of palm trees!

But ah! my soul with too much stay
Is drunk, and staggers in the way: —
Some men a forward motion love,
But I by backward steps would move;
But when this dust falls to the urn,
In that state I came, return.

H. Vaughan

99

TO MR. LAWRENCE

Lawrence, of virtuous father virtuous son,
Now that the fields are dank and ways are mire,
Where shall we sometimes meet, and by the fire
Help waste a sullen day, what may be won

From the hard season gaining? Time will run
On smoother, till Favonius re-inspire
The frozen earth, and clothe in fresh attire
The lily and rose, that neither sow'd nor spun.

What neat repast shall feast us, light and choice,
Of Attic taste, with wine, whence we may rise
To hear the lute well touch'd, or artful voice

Warble immortal notes and Tuscan air?
He who of those delights can judge, and spare
To interpose them oft, is not unwise.

J. Milton

100

TO CYRIACK SKINNER

Cyriack, whose grandsire, on the royal bench
Of British Themis, with no mean applause
Pronounced, and in his volumes taught, our laws,
Which others at their bar so often wrench;

To-day deep thoughts resolve with me to drench 5
In mirth, that after no repenting draws;
Let Euclid rest, and Archimedes pause,
And what the Swede intend, and what the French.

To measure life learn thou betimes, and know
Toward solid good what leads the nearest way; 10
For other things mild Heaven a time ordains,

And disapproves that care, though wise in show,
That with superfluous burden loads the day,
And, when God sends a cheerful hour, refrains.
J. Milton

101

A HYMN IN PRAISE OF NEPTUNE

Of Neptune's empire let us sing,
At whose command the waves obey;
To whom the rivers tribute pay,
Down the high mountains sliding;
To whom the scaly nation yields 5
Homage for the crystal fields
    Wherein they dwell;

    And every sea-god pays a gem
      Yearly out of his watery cell,
    To deck great Neptune's diadem.

    The Tritons dancing in a ring,
    Before his palace gates do make
    The water with their echoes quake,
    Like the great thunder sounding:
    The sea-nymphs chaunt their accents shrill,
    And the Syrens taught to kill
      With their sweet voice,
    Make every echoing rock reply,
    Unto their gentle murmuring noise,
    The praise of Neptune's empery.

T. Campion

HYMN TO DIANA

    Queen and Huntress, chaste and fair,
      Now the sun is laid to sleep,
    Seated in thy silver chair
      State in wonted manner keep:
        Hesperus entreats thy light,
        Goddess excellently bright.

    Earth, let not thy envious shade
      Dare itself to interpose;
    Cynthia's shining orb was made
      Heaven to clear when day did close:
        Bless us then with wishéd sight,
        Goddess excellently bright.

Lay thy bow of pearl apart
    And thy crystal-shining quiver;
Give unto the flying hart
    Space to breathe, how short soever:
        Thou that mak'st a day of night,
        Goddess excellently bright!

                      B. Jonson

WISHES FOR THE SUPPOSED MISTRESS

Whoe'er she be,
That not impossible She
That shall command my heart and me;

Where'er she lie,
Lock'd up from mortal eye
In shady leaves of destiny:

Till that ripe birth
Of studied Fate stand forth,
And teach her fair steps tread our earth;

Till that divine
Idea take a shrine
Of crystal flesh, through which to shine:

— Meet you her, my Wishes,
Bespeak her to my blisses,
And be ye call'd, my absent kisses.

I wish her beauty
That owes not all its duty
To gaudy tire, or glist'ring shoe-tie:

      Something more than
20   Taffata or tissue can,
      Or rampant feather, or rich fan.

      A face that's best
      By its own beauty drest,
      And can alone commend the rest:

25   A face made up
      Out of no other shop
      Than what Nature's white hand sets ope.

      Sidneian showers
      Of sweet discourse, whose powers
30   Can crown old Winter's head with flowers.

      Whate'er delight
      Can make day's forehead bright
      Or give down to the wings of night.

      Soft silken hours,
35   Open suns, shady bowers;
      'Bove all, nothing within that lowers.

      Days, that need borrow
      No part of their good morrow
      From a fore-spent night of sorrow:

40   Days, that in spite
      Of darkness, by the light
      Of a clear mind are day all night.

      Life, that dares send
      A challenge to his end,
45   And when it comes, say, 'Welcome, friend.'

I wish her store
Of worth may leave her poor
Of wishes; and I wish —— no more.

Now, if Time knows
That Her, whose radiant brows   50
Weave them a garland of my vows;

Her that dares be
What these lines wish to see:
I seek no further, it is She.

'Tis She, and here   55
Lo! I unclothe and clear
My wishes' cloudy character.

Such worth as this is
Shall fix my flying wishes,
And determine them to kisses.   60

Let her full glory,
My fancies, fly before ye;
Be ye my fictions: — but her story.

R. Crashaw

104

THE GREAT ADVENTURER

Over the mountains
And over the waves,
Under the fountains
And under the graves;

Under floods that are deepest,
    Which Neptune obey;
Over rocks that are steepest
    Love will find out the way.

Where there is no place
    For the glow-worm to lie;
Where there is no space
    For receipt of a fly;
Where the midge dares not venture
    Lest herself fast she lay;
If love come, he will enter
    And soon find out his way.

You may esteem him
    A child for his might;
Or you may deem him
    A coward from his flight;
But if she whom love doth honour
    Be conceal'd from the day,
Set a thousand guards upon her,
    Love will find out the way.

Some think to lose him
    By having him confined;
And some do suppose him,
    Poor thing, to be blind;
But if ne'er so close ye wall him,
    Do the best that you may,
Blind love, if so ye call him,
    Will find out his way.

You may train the eagle
To stoop to your fist;
Or you may inveigle　　　　　　　　　　35
The phoenix of the east;
The lioness, ye may move her
To give o'er her prey;
But you'll ne'er stop a lover:
He will find out his way.　　　　　　　　40
　　　　　　　　Anon.

105

THE PICTURE OF LITTLE T.C. IN A PROSPECT OF FLOWERS

See with what simplicity
This nymph begins her golden days!
In the green grass she loves to lie,
And there with her fair aspect tames
The wilder flowers, and gives them names;　　5
But only with the roses plays,
　　　　　　And them does tell
What colours best become them, and what smell.

Who can foretell for what high cause
This darling of the Gods was born?　　　　10
Yet this is she whose chaster laws
The wanton Love shall one day fear,
And, under her command severe,
See his bow broke, and ensigns torn.
　　　　　　Happy who can　　　　　　15
Appease this virtuous enemy of man!

O then let me in time compound
And parley with those conquering eyes,
Ere they have tried their force to wound;
Ere with their glancing wheels they drive
In triumph over hearts that strive,
And them that yield but more despise:
           Let me be laid,
Where I may see the glories from some shade.

Meantime, whilst every verdant thing
Itself does at thy beauty charm,
Reform the errors of the Spring;
Make that the tulips may have share
Of sweetness, seeing they are fair,
And roses of their thorns disarm,
           But most procure
That violets may a longer age endure.

But O young beauty of the woods,
Whom Nature courts with fruits and flowers,
Gather the flowers, but spare the buds;
Lest FLORA, angry at thy crime
To kill her infants in their prime,
Should quickly make th' example yours;
           And ere we see —
Nip in the blossom — all our hopes and thee.

A. Marvell

106

CHILD AND MAIDEN

Ah, Chloris! could I now but sit
    As unconcern'd as when
Your infant beauty could beget
    No happiness or pain!
When I the dawn used to admire,   5
    And praised the coming day,
I little thought the rising fire
    Would take my rest away.

Your charms in harmless childhood lay
    Like metals in a mine;   10
Age from no face takes more away
    Than youth conceal'd in thine.
But as your charms insensibly
    To their perfection prest,
So love as unperceived did fly,   15
    And center'd in my breast.

My passion with your beauty grew,
    While Cupid at my heart,
Still as his mother favour'd you,
    Threw a new flaming dart: 20
Each gloried in their wanton part;
    To make a lover, he
Employ'd the utmost of his art —
    To make a beauty, she.

Sir C. Sedley

107

CONSTANCY

I cannot change, as others do,
    Though you unjustly scorn,
Since that poor swain that sighs for you,
    For you alone was born;
No, Phyllis, no, your heart to move
    A surer way I'll try, —
And to revenge my slighted love,
    Will still love on, and die.

When, kill'd with grief, Amintas lies,
    And you to mind shall call
The sighs that now unpitied rise,
    The tears that vainly fall,
That welcome hour that ends his smart
    Will then begin your pain,
For such a faithful tender heart
    Can never break in vain.

J. Wilmot, Earl of Rochester

108

COUNSEL TO GIRLS

Gather ye rose-buds while ye may,
    Old Time is still a-flying:
And this same flower that smiles to-day,
    To-morrow will be dying.

The glorious Lamp of Heaven, the Sun,
    The higher he's a-getting

The sooner will his race be run,
   And nearer he's to setting.

That age is best which is the first,
   When youth and blood are warmer;
But being spent, the worse, and worst
   Times, still succeed the former.

Then be not coy, but use your time;
   And while ye may, go marry:
For having lost but once your prime,
   You may for ever tarry.
R. Herrick

109

TO LUCASTA, ON GOING TO THE WARS

Tell me not, Sweet, I am unkind
   That from the nunnery
Of thy chaste breast and quiet mind,
   To war and arms I fly.

True, a new mistress now I chase,
   The first foe in the field;
And with a stronger faith embrace
   A sword, a horse, a shield.

Yet this inconstancy is such
   As you too shall adore;
I could not love thee, Dear, so much,
   Loved I not Honour more.
Colonel Lovelace

110

ELIZABETH OF BOHEMIA

You meaner beauties of the night,
    That poorly satisfy our eyes
More by your number than your light,
    You common people of the skies,
5   What are you, when the Moon shall rise?

You curious chanters of the wood
    That warble forth dame Nature's lays,
Thinking your passions understood
    By your weak accents; what's your praise
10   When Philomel her voice doth raise?

You violets that first appear,
    By your pure purple mantles known
Like the proud virgins of the year,
    As if the spring were all your own,—
15   What are you, when the Rose is blown?

So when my Mistress shall be seen
    In form and beauty of her mind,
By virtue first, then choice, a Queen,
    Tell me, if she were not design'd
20   Th' eclipse and glory of her kind?

                              Sir H. Wotton

III

TO THE LADY MARGARET LEY

Daughter to that good Earl, once President
Of England's Council and her Treasury,
Who lived in both, unstain'd with gold or fee,
And left them both, more in himself content,

Till the sad breaking of that Parliament
Broke him, as that dishonest victory
At Chaeroneia, fatal to liberty,
Kill'd with report that old man eloquent; —

Though later born than to have known the days
Wherein your father flourish'd, yet by you,
Madam, methinks I see him living yet;

So well your words his noble virtues praise,
That all both judge you to relate them true,
And to possess them, honour'd Margaret.

J. Milton

112

THE TRUE BEAUTY

He that loves a rosy cheek
  Or a coral lip admires,
Or from star-like eyes doth seek
  Fuel to maintain his fires;
As old Time makes these decay,
So his flames must waste away.

But a smooth and steadfast mind,
    Gentle thoughts, and calm desires,
Hearts with equal love combined,
    Kindle never-dying fires: —
Where these are not, I despise
Lovely cheeks or lips or eyes.

T. Carew

113

TO DIANEME

Sweet, be not proud of those two eyes
Which starlike sparkle in their skies;
Nor be you proud, that you can see
All hearts your captives; yours yet free:
Be you not proud of that rich hair
Which wantons with the lovesick air;
Whenas that ruby which you wear,
Sunk from the tip of your soft ear,
Will last to be a precious stone
When all your world of beauty's gone.

R. Herrick

114

Love in thy youth, fair Maid, be wise;
    Old Time will make thee colder,
And though each morning new arise
    Yet we each day grow older.
Thou as Heaven art fair and young,
    Thine eyes like twin stars shining;
But ere another day be sprung
    All these will be declining.

Then winter comes with all his fears,
    And all thy sweets shall borrow;
Too late then wilt thou shower thy tears, —
    And I too late shall sorrow!

Anon.

115

    Go, lovely Rose!
Tell her, that wastes her time and me,
    That now she knows,
When I resemble her to thee,
How sweet and fair she seems to be.

    Tell her that's young
And shuns to have her graces spied,
    That hadst thou sprung
In deserts, where no men abide,
Thou must have uncommended died.

    Small is the worth
Of beauty from the light retired:
    Bid her come forth,
Suffer herself to be desired,
And not blush so to be admired.

    Then die! that she
The common fate of all things rare
    May read in thee:
How small a part of time they share
That are so wondrous sweet and fair!

E. Waller

116

TO CELIA

Drink to me only with thine eyes,
  And I will pledge with mine;
Or leave a kiss but in the cup
  And I'll not look for wine.
The thirst that from the soul doth rise
  Doth ask a drink divine;
But might I of Jove's nectar sup,
  I would not change for thine.

I sent thee late a rosy wreath,
  Not so much honouring thee
As giving it a hope that there
  It could not wither'd be;
But thou thereon didst only breathe
  And sent'st it back to me;
Since when it grows, and smells, I swear,
  Not of itself but thee!

B. Jonson

117

CHERRY-RIPE

There is a garden in her face
  Where roses and white lilies blow;
A heavenly paradise is that place,
  Wherein all pleasant fruits do grow;
There cherries grow that none may buy,
Till Cherry-Ripe themselves do cry.

BEN JONSON

Those cherries fairly do enclose
   Of orient pearl, a double row,
Which when her lovely laughter shows,
   They look like rose-buds fill'd with snow:
Yet them no peer nor prince may buy,
Till Cherry-Ripe themselves do cry.

Her eyes like angels watch them still;
   Her brows like bended bows do stand,
Threat'ning with piercing frowns to kill
   All that approach with eye or hand
These sacred cherries to come nigh,
Till Cherry-Ripe themselves do cry!

T. Campion

118

CORINNA'S MAYING

Get up, get up for shame! The blooming morn
Upon her wings presents the god unshorn.
   See how Aurora throws her fair
   Fresh-quilted colours through the air:
   Get up, sweet Slug-a-bed, and see
   The dew bespangling herb and tree.
Each flower has wept, and bow'd toward the east,
Above an hour since; yet you not drest,
   Nay! not so much as out of bed?
   When all the birds have matins said,
   And sung their thankful hymns: 'tis sin,
   Nay, profanation, to keep in, —
Whenas a thousand virgins on this day,
Spring, sooner than the lark, to fetch-in May.

15 Rise; and put on your foliage, and be seen
   To come forth, like the Spring-time, fresh and green
       And sweet as Flora. Take no care
       For jewels for your gown, or hair:
       Fear not; the leaves will strew
20   Gems in abundance upon you:
Besides, the childhood of the day has kept,
Against you come, some orient pearls unwept:
       Come, and receive them while the light
       Hangs on the dew-locks of the night:
25   And Titan on the eastern hill
       Retires himself, or else stands still
Till you come forth. Wash, dress, be brief in praying:
Few beads are best, when once we go a Maying.

Come, my Corinna, come; and coming, mark
30 How each field turns a street; each street a park
       Made green, and trimm'd with trees: see how
       Devotion gives each house a bough
       Or branch: Each porch, each door, ere this,
       An ark, a tabernacle is,
35 Made up of white-thorn neatly interwove;
As if here were those cooler shades of love.
       Can such delights be in the street,
       And open fields, and we not see't?
       Come we'll abroad: and let's obey
40   The proclamation made for May:
And sin no more, as we have done, by staying;
But, my Corinna, come, let's go a Maying.

There's not a budding boy, or girl, this day,
But is got up, and gone to bring in May.

    A deal of youth, ere this, is come
    Back, and with white-thorn laden home.
    Some have despatch'd their cakes and cream,
    Before that we have left to dream:
And some have wept, and woo'd, and plighted troth,
And chose their priest, ere we can cast off sloth:
    Many a green-gown has been given;
    Many a kiss, both odd and even:
    Many a glance too has been sent
    From out the eye, Love's firmament:
Many a jest told of the keys betraying
This night, and locks pick'd:—Yet we're not a Maying.

—Come, let us go, while we are in our prime;
And take the harmless folly of the time!
    We shall grow old apace, and die
    Before we know our liberty.
    Our life is short; and our days run
    As fast away as does the sun:—
And as a vapour, or a drop of rain
Once lost, can ne'er be found again:
    So when or you or I are made
    A fable, song, or fleeting shade;
    All love, all liking, all delight
    Lies drown'd with us in endless night.
Then while time serves, and we are but decaying,
Come, my Corinna! come, let's go a Maying.
                    R. Herrick

THE POETRY OF DRESS

i

A sweet disorder in the dress
Kindles in clothes a wantonness: —
A lawn about the shoulders thrown
Into a fine distraction, —
An erring lace, which here and there
Enthrals the crimson stomacher, —
A cuff neglectful, and thereby
Ribbands to flow confusedly, —
A winning wave, deserving note,
In the tempestuous petticoat, —
A careless shoe-string, in whose tie
I see a wild civility, —
Do more bewitch me, than when art
Is too precise in every part.

R. Herrick

ii

Whenas in silks my Julia goes
Then, then (methinks) how sweetly flows
That liquefaction of her clothes.

Next, when I cast mine eyes and see
That brave vibration each way free;
O how that glittering taketh me!

R. Herrick

121

iii

My love in her attire doth shew her wit,
   It doth so well become her:
For every season she hath dressings fit,
   For Winter, Spring, and Summer.
No beauty she doth miss
When all her robes are on:
But Beauty's self she is
When all her robes are gone.

Anon.

122

ON A GIRDLE

That which her slender waist confined
Shall now my joyful temples bind:
No monarch but would give his crown
His arms might do what this has done.

It was my Heaven's extremest sphere,
The pale which held that lovely deer:
My joy, my grief, my hope, my love
Did all within this circle move.

A narrow compass! and yet there
Dwelt all that's good, and all that's fair:
Give me but what this ribband bound,
Take all the rest the Sun goes round.

E. Waller

123

A MYSTICAL ECSTASY

E'en like two little bank-dividing brooks,
    That wash the pebbles with their wanton streams,
And having ranged and search'd a thousand nooks,
    Meet both at length in silver-breasted Thames,
      Where in a greater current they conjoin:
So I my Best-Belovéd's am; so He is mine.

E'en so we met; and after long pursuit,
    E'en so we join'd; we both became entire;
No need for either to renew a suit,
    For I was flax and he was flames of fire:
      Our firm-united souls did more than twine;
So I my Best-Belovéd's am; so He is mine.

If all those glittering Monarchs that command
    The servile quarters of this earthly ball,
Should tender, in exchange, their shares of land,
    I would not change my fortunes for them all:
      Their wealth is but a counter to my coin:
The world's but theirs; but my Belovéd's mine.

F. Quarles

124

TO ANTHEA WHO MAY COMMAND HIM ANY THING

Bid me to live, and I will live
    Thy Protestant to be:
Or bid me love, and I will give
    A loving heart to thee.

A heart as soft, a heart as kind,
    A heart as sound and free
As in the whole world thou canst find,
    That heart I'll give to thee.

Bid that heart stay, and it will stay,
    To honour thy decree:
Or bid it languish quite away,
    And't shall do so for thee.

Bid me to weep, and I will weep
    While I have eyes to see:
And having none, yet I will keep
    A heart to weep for thee.

Bid me despair, and I'll despair,
    Under that cypress tree:
Or bid me die, and I will dare
    E'en Death, to die for thee.

Thou art my life, my love, my heart,
    The very eyes of me,
And hast command of every part,
    To live and die for thee.

R. Herrick

Love not me for comely grace,
For my pleasing eye or face,
Nor for any outward part,
No, nor for my constant heart, —
    For those may fail, or turn to ill,
    So thou and I shall sever:

Keep therefore a true woman's eye,
And love me still, but know not why —
So hast thou the same reason still
    To doat upon me ever!

Anon.

126

Not, Celia, that I juster am
    Or better than the rest;
For I would change each hour, like them
    Were not my heart at rest.

But I am tied to very thee
    By every thought I have;
Thy face I only care to see,
    Thy heart I only crave.

All that in woman is adored
    In thy dear self I find —
For the whole sex can but afford
    The handsome and the kind.

Why then should I seek further store,
    And still make love anew?
When change itself can give no more,
    'Tis easy to be true.

Sir C. Sedley

127

TO ALTHEA FROM PRISON

When Love with unconfinéd wings
    Hovers within my gates,
And my divine Althea brings
    To whisper at the grates;

When I lie tangled in her hair
   And fetter'd to her eye,
The Gods that wanton in the air
   Know no such liberty.

When flowing cups run swiftly round
   With no allaying Thames,
Our careless heads with roses bound,
   Our hearts with loyal flames;
When thirsty grief in wine we steep,
   When healths and draughts go free —
Fishes that tipple in the deep
   Know no such liberty.

When, (like committed linnets), I
   With shriller throat shall sing
The sweetness, mercy, majesty
   And glories of my King;
When I shall voice aloud how good
   He is, how great should be,
Enlargéd winds, that curl the flood,
   Know no such liberty.

Stone walls do not a prison make,
  Nor iron bars a cage;
Minds innocent and quiet take
   That for an hermitage;
If I have freedom in my love
   And in my soul am free,
Angels alone, that soar above,
   Enjoy such liberty.

Colonel Lovelace

128

TO LUCASTA, ON GOING BEYOND THE SEAS

If to be absent were to be
    Away from thee;
    Or that when I am gone
    You or I were alone;
    Then, my Lucasta, might I crave
Pity from blustering wind, or swallowing wave.

But I'll not sigh one blast or gale
    To swell my sail,
    Or pay a tear to 'suage
    The foaming blue-god's rage;
    For whether he will let me pass
Or no, I'm still as happy as I was.

Though seas and land betwixt us both,
    Our faith and troth,
    Like separated souls,
    All time and space controls:
    Above the highest sphere we meet
Unseen, unknown, and greet as Angels greet.

So then we do anticipate
    Our after-fate,
    And are alive i' the skies,
    If thus our lips and eyes
    Can speak like spirits unconfined
In Heaven, their earthy bodies left behind.

Colonel Lovelace

129

ENCOURAGEMENTS TO A LOVER

Why so pale and wan, fond lover?
    Prythee, why so pale?
Will, if looking well can't move her,
    Looking ill prevail?
    Prythee, why so pale?   5

Why so dull and mute, young sinner?
    Prythee, why so mute?
Will, when speaking well can't win her,
    Saying nothing do't?
    Prythee, why so mute?   10

Quit, quit, for shame! this will not move,
    This cannot take her;
If of herself she will not love,
    Nothing can make her:
    The D—l take her!   15
                    Sir J. Suckling

130

A SUPPLICATION

Awake, awake, my Lyre!
And tell thy silent master's humble tale
    In sounds that may prevail;
Sounds that gentle thoughts inspire:
    Though so exalted she   5
    And I so lowly be
Tell her, such different notes make all thy harmony.

Hark, how the strings awake!
And, though the moving hand approach not near,
    Themselves with awful fear
  A kind of numerous trembling make.
    Now all thy forces try;
    Now all thy charms apply;
Revenge upon her ear the conquests of her eye.

    Weak Lyre! thy virtue sure
Is useless here, since thou art only found
    To cure, but not to wound,
  And she to wound, but not to cure.
    Too weak too wilt thou prove
    My passion to remove;
Physic to other ills, thou'rt nourishment to Love.

    Sleep, sleep again, my Lyre
For thou canst never tell my humble tale
    In sounds that will prevail,
  Nor gentle thoughts in her inspire;
    All thy vain mirth lay by,
    Bid thy strings silent lie,
Sleep, sleep again, my Lyre, and let thy master die.

A. Cowley

131

THE MANLY HEART

Shall I, wasting in despair,
Die because a woman's fair?
Or make pale my cheeks with care
'Cause another's rosy are?

Book Second

Be she fairer than the day
Or the flowery meads in May —
    If she think not well of me
    What care I how fair she be?

Shall my silly heart be pined
'Cause I see a woman kind;
Or a well disposéd nature
Joinéd with a lovely feature?
Be she meeker, kinder than
Turtle-dove or pelican,
    If she be not so to me
    What care I how kind she be?

Shall a woman's virtues move
Me to perish for her love?
Or her well-deservings known
Make me quite forget mine own?
Be she with that goodness blest
Which may merit name of Best;
    If she be not such to me,
    What care I how good she be?

'Cause her fortune seems too high,
Shall I play the fool and die?
She that bears a noble mind
If not outward helps she find,
Thinks what with them he would do
Who without them dares her woo;
    And unless that mind I see,
    What care I how great she be?

>   Great or good, or kind or fair,
>   I will ne'er the more despair;
>   If she love me, this believe,
>   I will die ere she shall grieve;
>   If she slight me when I woo,
>   I can scorn and let her go;
>   For if she be not for me,
>   What care I for whom she be?

G. Wither

132

MELANCHOLY

> Hence, all you vain delights,
> As short as are the nights
> Wherein you spend your folly:
> There's nought in this life sweet
> If man were wise to see't,
> But only melancholy,
> O sweetest Melancholy!
>
> Welcome, folded arms, and fixéd eyes,
> A sigh that piercing mortifies,
> A look that's fasten'd to the ground,
> A tongue chain'd up without a sound!
> Fountain-heads and pathless groves,
> Places which pale passion loves!
> Moonlight walks, when all the fowls
> Are warmly housed save bats and owls!
> A midnight bell, a parting groan!
> These are the sounds we feed upon;
> Then stretch our bones in a still gloomy valley;
> Nothing's so dainty sweet as lovely melancholy.

J. Fletcher

133
FORSAKEN

O waly waly up the bank,
   And waly waly down the brae,
And waly waly yon burn-side
Where I and my Love wont to gae!
I leant my back unto an aik,   5
   I thought it was a trusty tree;
But first it bow'd, and syne it brak,
   Sae my true Love did lichtly me.

O waly waly, but love be bonny
   A little time while it is new;   10
But when 'tis auld, it waxeth cauld
And fades awa' like morning dew.
O wherefore should I busk my head?
   Or wherefore should I kame my hair?
For my true Love has me forsook,   15
   And says he'll never loe me mair.

Now Arthur-seat sall be my bed;
   The sheets shall ne'er be prest by me:
Saint Anton's well sall be my drink,
   Since my true Love has forsaken me.   20
Marti'mas wind, when wilt thou blaw
   And shake the green leaves aff the tree?
O gentle Death, when wilt thou come?
   For of my life I am wearie.

25   'Tis not the frost, that freezes fell,
    Nor blawing snaw's inclemencie;
  'Tis not sic cauld that makes me cry,
    But my Love's heart grown cauld to me.
  When we came in by Glasgow town
30   We were a comely sight to see;
  My Love was clad in the black velvét,
    And I myself in cramasie.

  But had I wist, before I kist,
    That love had been sae ill to win;
35   I had lockt my heart in a case of gowd
    And pinn'd it with a siller pin.
  And, O! if my young babe were born,
    And set upon the nurse's knee,
  And I myself were dead and gane,
40   And the green grass growing over me!

Anon.

134

  Upon my lap my sovereign sits
  And sucks upon my breast;
  Meantime his love maintains my life
  And gives my sense her rest.
5   Sing lullaby, my little boy,
    Sing lullaby, mine only joy!

  When thou hast taken thy repast,
  Repose, my babe, on me;
  So may thy mother and thy nurse
10   Thy cradle also be.
    Sing lullaby, my little boy,
    Sing lullaby, mine only joy!

I grieve that duty doth not work
All that my wishing would,
Because I would not be to thee
But in the best I should.
  Sing lullaby, my little boy,
  Sing lullaby, mine only joy!

Yet as I am, and as I may,
I must and will be thine,
Though all too little for thyself
Vouchsafing to be mine.
  Sing lullaby, my little boy,
  Sing lullaby, mine only joy!

Anon.

135

FAIR HELEN

I wish I were where Helen lies;
Night and day on me she cries;
O that I were where Helen lies
  On fair Kirconnell lea!

Curst be the heart that thought the thought,
And curst the hand that fired the shot,
When in my arms burd Helen dropt,
  And died to succour me!

O think na but my heart was sair
When my Love dropt down and spak nae mair!
I laid her down wi' meikle care
  On fair Kirconnell lea.

As I went down the water-side,
None but my foe to be my guide,
None but my foe to be my guide,
    On fair Kirconnell lea;

I lighted down my sword to draw,
I hackéd him in pieces sma',
I hackéd him in pieces sma',
    For her sake that died for me.

O Helen fair, beyond compare!
I'll make a garland of thy hair
Shall bind my heart for evermair
    Until the day I die.

O that I were where Helen lies!
Night and day on me she cries;
Out of my bed she bids me rise,
    Says, ' Haste and come to me!'

O Helen fair! O Helen chaste!
If I were with thee, I were blest
Where thou lies low and takes thy rest
    On fair Kirconnell lea.

I wish my grave were growing green,
A winding-sheet drawn ower my een,
And I in Helen's arms lying,
    On fair Kirconnell lea.

I wish I were where Helen lies,
  Night and day on me she cries;
And I am weary of the skies,
    Since my Love died for me.   40

Anon.

136

THE TWA CORBIES

As I was walking all alane
I heard twa corbies making a mane;
The tane unto the t'other say,
' Where sall we gang and dine today?'

' — In behint yon auld fail dyke,   5
I wot there lies a new-slain Knight;
And naebody kens that he lies there,
But his hawk, his hound, and lady fair.

' His hound is to the hunting gane,
His hawk to fetch the wild-fowl hame,   10
His lady's ta'en another mate,
So we may mak our dinner sweet.

' Ye'll sit on his white hause-bane,
And I'll pick out his bonnie blue een:
Wi' ae lock o' his gowden hair   15
We'll theek our nest when it grows bare.

' Mony a one for him makes mane,
But nane sall ken where he is gane;
O'er his white banes, when they are bare,
The wind sall blaw for evermair.'   20

Anon.

137

ON THE DEATH OF MR. WILLIAM HERVEY

It was a dismal and a fearful night,—
Scarce could the Morn drive on th' unwilling light,
When sleep, death's image, left my troubled breast
    By something liker death possest.
My eyes with tears did uncommanded flow,
    And on my soul hung the dull weight
    Of some intolerable fate.
What bell was that? Ah me! Too much I know!

My sweet companion, and my gentle peer,
Why hast thou left me thus unkindly here,
Thy end for ever, and my life, to moan?
    O thou hast left me all alone!
Thy soul and body, when death's agony
    Besieged around thy noble heart,
    Did not with more reluctance part
Than I, my dearest friend, do part from thee.

Ye fields of Cambridge, our dear Cambridge, say,
Have ye not seen us, walking every day?
Was there a tree about which did not know
    The love betwixt us two?
Henceforth, ye gentle trees, for ever fade,
    Or your sad branches thicker join,
    And into darksome shades combine,
Dark as the grave wherein my friend is laid.

Large was his soul; as large a soul as e'er 25
Submitted to inform a body here;
High as the place 'twas shortly in Heaven to have,
    But low and humble as his grave;
So high that all the virtues there did come
      As to the chiefest seat 30
        Conspicuous, and great;
So low that for me too it made a room.

Knowledge he only sought, and so soon caught,
As if for him knowledge had rather sought;
Nor did more learning ever crowded lie 35
    In such a short mortality.
Whene'er the skilful youth discoursed or writ,
      Still did the notions throng
        About his eloquent tongue;
Nor could his ink flow faster than his wit. 40

His mirth was the pure spirits of various wit,
Yet never did his God or friends forget.
And when deep talk and wisdom came in view,
    Retired, and gave to them their due.
For the rich help of books he always took, 45
      Though his own searching mind before
        Was so with notions written o'er,
As if wise Nature had made that her book.

With as much zeal, devotion, piety,
He always lived, as other saints do die. 50
Still with his soul severe account he kept,
    Weeping all debts out ere he slept.

Then down in peace and innocence he lay,
    Like the sun's laborious light,
55   Which still in water sets at night,
Unsullied with his journey of the day.

A. Cowley

138

FRIENDS IN PARADISE

They are all gone into the world of light!
    And I alone sit lingering here;
Their very memory is fair and bright,
      And my sad thoughts doth clear: —

5 It glows and glitters in my cloudy breast,
    Like stars upon some gloomy grove,
Or those faint beams in which this hill is drest,
    After the sun's remove.

I see them walking in an air of glory,
10   Whose light doth trample on my days:
My days, which are at best but dull and hoary,
    Mere glimmering and decays.

O holy Hope! and high Humility,
    High as the Heavens above!
15 These are your walks, and you have shew'd them me,
    To kindle my cold love.

Dear, beauteous Death! the jewel of the just,
    Shining no where, but in the dark;
What mysteries do lie beyond thy dust,
20   Could man outlook that mark!

He that hath found some fledged bird's nest, may know
    At first sight, if the bird be flown;
But what fair well or grove he sings in now,
    That is to him unknown.

And yet, as Angels in some brighter dreams
    Call to the soul, when man doth sleep;
So some strange thoughts transcend our wonted themes,
    And into glory peep.

H. Vaughan

TO BLOSSOMS

Fair pledges of a fruitful tree,
    Why do ye fall so fast?
    Your date is not so past,
But you may stay yet here awhile
    To blush and gently smile,
    And go at last.

What, were ye born to be
    An hour or half's delight,
    And so to bid good-night?
'Twas pity Nature brought ye forth
    Merely to show your worth,
    And lose you quite.

But you are lovely leaves, where we
    May read how soon things have
    Their end, though ne'er so brave:

And after they have shown their pride
    Like you, awhile, they glide
        Into the grave.

                                    R. Herrick

140

TO DAFFODILS

Fair Daffodils, we weep to see
    You haste away so soon:
As yet the early-rising Sun
    Has not attain'd his noon.
        Stay, stay,
        Until the hasting day
            Has run
        But to the even-song;
And, having pray'd together, we
    Will go with you along.

We have short time to stay, as you,
    We have as short a Spring;
As quick a growth to meet decay
    As you, or any thing.
        We die,
        As your hours do, and dry
            Away
        Like the Summer's rain;
Or as the pearls of morning's dew
    Ne'er to be found again.

                                    R. Herrick

Book Second

THE GIRL DESCRIBES HER FAWN

With sweetest milk and sugar first
I it at my own fingers nursed;
And as it grew, so every day
It wax'd more white and sweet than they —
It had so sweet a breath! and oft
I blush'd to see its foot more soft
And white,—shall I say,—than my hand?
Nay, any lady's of the land!

It is a wondrous thing how fleet
'Twas on those little silver feet:
With what a pretty skipping grace
It oft would challenge me the race:—
And when't had left me far away
'Twould stay, and run again, and stay:
For it was nimbler much than hinds,
And trod as if on the four winds.

I have a garden of my own,
But so with roses overgrown
And lilies, that you would it guess
To be a little wilderness;
And all the spring-time of the year
It only lovéd to be there.
Have sought it oft, where it should lie;
Yet could not, till itself would rise,
Find it, although before mine eyes:—
For in the flaxen lilies' shade
It like a bank of lilies laid.

Upon the roses it would feed,
Until its lips e'en seem'd to bleed:
And then to me 'twould boldly trip,
And print those roses on my lip.
But all its chief delight was still
On roses thus itself to fill,
And its pure virgin limbs to fold
In whitest sheets of lilies cold;—
Had it lived long, it would have been
Lilies without—roses within.

A. Marvell

142

THOUGHTS IN A GARDEN

How vainly men themselves amaze
To win the palm, the oak, or bays,
And their uncessant labours see
Crown'd from some single herb or tree,
Whose short and narrow-vergéd shade
Does prudently their toils upbraid;
While all the flowers and trees do close
To weave the garlands of Repose.

Fair Quiet, have I found thee here,
And Innocence thy sister dear!
Mistaken long, I sought you then
In busy companies of men:
Your sacred plants, if here below,
Only among the plants will grow:
Society is all but rude
To this delicious solitude.

Book Second

No white nor red was ever seen
So amorous as this lovely green.
Fond lovers, cruel as their flame,
Cut in these trees their mistress' name: 20
Little, alas, they know or heed
How far these beauties hers exceed!
Fair trees! wheres'e'er your barks I wound,
No name shall but your own be found.

When we have run our passions' heat 25
Love hither makes his best retreat:
The gods, who mortal beauty chase,
Still in a tree did end their race;
Apollo hunted Daphne so
Only that she might laurel grow; 30
And Pan did after Syrinx speed
Not as a nymph, but for a reed.

What wondrous life is this I lead!
Ripe apples drop about my head;
The luscious clusters of the vine 35
Upon my mouth do crush their wine;
The nectarine and curious peach
Into my hands themselves do reach;
Stumbling on melons, as I pass,
Ensnared with flowers, I fall on grass. 40

Meanwhile the mind from pleasure less
Withdraws into its happiness;
The mind, that ocean where each kind
Does straight its own resemblance find;

45   Yet it creates, transcending these,
       Far other worlds, and other seas;
       Annihilating all that's made
       To a green thought in a green shade.

       Here at the fountain's sliding foot
50   Or at some fruit-tree's mossy root,
       Casting the body's vest aside
       My soul into the boughs does glide;
       There, like a bird, it sits and sings,
       Then whets and claps its silver wings,
55   And, till prepared for longer flight,
       Waves in its plumes the various light.

       Such was that happy Garden-state
       While man there walk'd without a mate.
       After a place so pure and sweet,
60   What other help could yet be meet!
       But 'twas beyond a mortal's share
       To wander solitary there:
       Two paradises 'twere in one,
       To live in paradise alone.

65   How well the skilful gardener drew
       Of flowers and herbs this dial new!
       Where, from above, the milder sun
       Does through a fragrant zodiac run:
       And, as it works, th' industrious bee
70   Computes its time as well as we.
       How could such sweet and wholesome hours
       Be reckon'd, but with herbs and flowers!

A. Marvell

143

FORTUNATI NIMIUM

Jack and Joan, they think no ill,
But loving live, and merry still;
Do their week-day's work, and pray
Devoutly on the holy-day:
Skip and trip it in the green,
And help to choose the Summer Queen;
Lash out at a country feast
Their silver penny with the best.

Well can they judge of nappy ale,
And tell at large a winter tale;
Climb up to the apple loft,
And turn the crabs till they be soft.
Tib is all the father's joy,
And little Tom the mother's boy:—
All their pleasure is, Content,
And care, to pay their yearly rent.

Joan can call by name her cows
And deck her windows with green boughs;
She can wreaths and tutties make,
And trim with plums a bridal cake.
Jack knows what brings gain or loss,
And his long flail can stoutly toss:
Makes the hedges which others break,
And ever thinks what he doth speak.

—Now, you courtly dames and knights
That study only strange delights,

Though you scorn the homespun gray,
And revel in your rich array;
Though your tongues dissemble deep
And can your heads from danger keep;
Yet, for all your pomp and train,
Securer lives the silly swain!

T. Campion

L'ALLEGRO

Hence, loathéd Melancholy,
  Of Cerberus and blackest Midnight born
In Stygian cave forlorn
  'Mongst horrid shapes, and shrieks, and sights unholy!
Find out some uncouth cell
  Where brooding Darkness spreads his jealous wings
And the night-raven sings;
  There under ebon shades, and low-brow'd rocks
As ragged as thy locks,
  In dark Cimmerian desert ever dwell.

But come, thou Goddess fair and free,
  In heaven yclept Euphrosyne,
And by men, heart-easing Mirth,
Whom lovely Venus at a birth
  With two sister Graces more
To ivy-crownéd Bacchus bore;
Or whether (as some sager sing)
The frolic wind that breathes the spring,

Book Second

Zephyr, with Aurora playing,
As he met her once a-Maying—
There on beds of violets blue
And fresh-blown roses wash'd in dew
Fill'd her with thee, a daughter fair,
So buxom, blithe, and debonair.

   Haste thee, Nymph, and bring with thee
Jest, and youthful jollity,
Quips, and cranks, and wanton wiles,
Nods, and becks, and wreathéd smiles
Such as hang on Hebe's cheek,
And love to live in dimple sleek;
Sport that wrinkled Care derides,
And Laughter holding both his sides:—
Come, and trip it as you go
On the light fantastic toe;
And in thy right hand lead with thee
The mountain-nymph, sweet Liberty;
And if I give thee honour due
Mirth, admit me of thy crew,
To live with her, and live with thee
In unreprovéd pleasures free;
To hear the lark begin his flight
And singing startle the dull night
From his watch-tower in the skies,
Till the dappled dawn doth rise;
Then to come, in spite of sorrow,
And at my window bid good-morrow
Through the sweetbriar, or the vine,
Or the twisted eglantine;
While the cock with lively din

50 Scatters the rear of darkness thin,
    And to the stack, or the barn-door,
    Stoutly struts his dames before:
    Oft listening how the hounds and horn
    Cheerly rouse the slumbering morn,
55 From the side of some hoar hill,
    Through the high wood echoing shrill:
    Sometime walking, not unseen,
    By hedge-row elms, on hillocks green,
    Right against the eastern gate
60 Where the great Sun begins his state
    Robed in flames and amber light,
    The clouds in thousand liveries dight;
    While the ploughman, near at hand,
    Whistles o'er the furrow'd land,
65 And the milkmaid singeth blithe,
    And the mower whets his scythe,
    And every shepherd tells his tale
    Under the hawthorn in the dale.
        Straight mine eye hath caught new pleasures
70 Whilst the landscape round it measures;
    Russet lawns, and fallows gray,
    Where the nibbling flocks do stray;
    Mountains, on whose barren breast
    The laboring clouds do often rest;
75 Meadows trim with daisies pied,
    Shallow brooks, and rivers wide;
    Towers and battlements it sees
    Bosom'd high in tufted trees,
    Where perhaps some Beauty lies,
80 The Cynosure of neighboring eyes.

Towers and batlements it sees
Bosom'd high in tufted trees.

Book Second

    Hard by, a cottage chimney smokes
From betwixt two aged oaks,
Where Corydon and Thyrsis, met,
Are at their savoury dinner set
Of herbs, and other country messes   85
Which the neat-handed Phillis dresses;
And then in haste her bower she leaves
With Thestylis to bind the sheaves;
Or, if the earlier season lead,
To the tann'd haycock in the mead.   90
    Sometimes with secure delight
The upland hamlets will invite,
When the merry bells ring round,
And the jocund rebecks sound
To many a youth and many a maid,   95
Dancing in the chequer'd shade;
And young and old come forth to play
On a sun-shine holyday,
Till the live-long day-light fail:
Then to the spicy nut-brown ale,   100
With stories told of many a feat,
How Faery Mab the junkets eat: —
She was pinch'd and pull'd, she said;
And he, by Friar's lantern led;
Tells how the drudging Goblin sweat   105
To earn his cream-bowl duly set,
When in one night, ere glimpse of morn,
His shadowy flail hath thresh'd the corn
That ten day labourers could not end;
Then lies him down the lubber fiend,   110
And, stretch'd out all the chimney's length,

    Basks at the fire his hairy strength;
And crop-full out of doors he flings,
Ere the first cock his matin rings.
    Thus done the tales, to bed they creep,
By whispering winds soon lull'd asleep.
    Tower'd cities please us then
And the busy hum of men,
Where throngs of knights and barons bold,
In weeds of peace, high triumphs hold,
With store of ladies, whose bright eyes
Rain influence, and judge the prize
Of wit or arms, while both contend
To win her grace, whom all commend.
There let Hymen oft appear
In saffron robe, with taper clear,
And pomp, and feast, and revelry,
With mask, and antique pageantry;
Such sights as youthful poets dream
On summer eves by haunted stream.
Then to the well-trod stage anon,
If Jonson's learned sock be on,
Or sweetest Shakespeare, Fancy's child,
Warble his native wood-notes wild.
    And ever against eating cares
Lap me in soft Lydian airs
Married to immortal verse,
Such as the meeting soul may pierce
In notes, with many a winding bout
Of linkéd sweetness long drawn out,
With wanton heed and giddy cunning,
The melting voice through mazes running,

Untwisting all the chains that tie
The hidden soul of harmony;
That Orpheus' self may heave his head 145
From golden slumber, on a bed
Of heap'd Elysian flowers, and hear
Such strains as would have won the ear
Of Pluto, to have quite set free
His half-regain'd Eurydice. 150

These delights if thou canst give,
Mirth, with thee I mean to live.
J. Milton

145

IL PENSEROSO

Hence, vain deluding Joys,
  The brood of Folly without father bred!
How little you bestead
  Or fill the fixéd mind with all your toys!
Dwell in some idle brain, 5
  And fancies fond with gaudy shapes possess
As thick and numberless
  As the gay motes that people the sunbeams,
Or likest hovering dreams,
  The fickle pensioners of Morpheus' train. 10

But hail, thou goddess sage and holy,
Hail, divinest Melancholy!
Whose saintly visage is too bright
To hit the sense of human sight,

15 And therefore to our weaker view
O'erlaid with black, staid Wisdom's hue;
Black, but such as in esteem
Prince Memnon's sister might beseem,
Or that starr'd Ethiop queen that strove
20 To set her beauty's praise above
The sea-nymphs, and their powers offended:
Yet thou art higher far descended:
Thee bright-hair'd Vesta, long of yore,
To solitary Saturn bore;
25 His daughter she; in Saturn's reign
Such mixture was not held a stain:
Oft in glimmering bowers and glades
He met her, and in secret shades
Of woody Ida's inmost grove,
30 While yet there saw no fear of Jove.

    Come, pensive Nun, devout and pure,
Sober, steadfast, and demure,
All in a robe of darkest grain
Flowing with majestic train,
35 And sable stole of Cipres lawn
Over thy decent shoulders drawn:
Come, but keep thy wonted state,
With even step, and musing gait,
And looks commercing with the skies,
40 Thy rapt soul sitting in thine eyes:
There, held in holy passion still,
Forget thyself to marble, till
With a sad leaden downward cast
Thou fix them on the earth as fast:
45 And join with thee calm Peace, and Quiet,

Spare Fast, that oft with gods doth diet,
And hears the Muses in a ring
Aye round about Jove's altar sing:
And add to these retired Leisure
That in trim gardens takes his pleasure:— 50
But first and chiefest, with thee bring
Him that yon soars on golden wing
Guiding the fiery-wheeléd throne,
The cherub Contemplatión;
And the mute Silence hist along, 55
'Less Philomel will deign a song
In her sweetest saddest plight
Smoothing the rugged brow of Night,
While Cynthia checks her dragon yoke
Gently o'er the accustom'd oak. 60
—Sweet bird, that shunn'st the noise of folly,
Most musical, most melancholy!
Thee, chauntress, oft, the woods among
I woo, to hear thy even-song;
And missing thee, I walk unseen 65
On the dry smooth-shaven green,
To behold the wandering Moon
Riding near her highest noon,
Like one that had been led astray
Through the heaven's wide pathless way, 70
And oft, as if her head she bow'd,
Stooping through a fleecy cloud.

Oft, on a plat of rising ground
I hear the far-off Curfeu sound
Over some wide-water'd shore, 75
Swinging slow with sullen roar:

  Or, if the air will not permit,
Some still removéd place will fit,
Where glowing embers through the room
Teach light to counterfeit a gloom;
Far from all resort of mirth,
Save the cricket on the hearth,
Or the bellman's drowsy charm
To bless the doors from nightly harm.
 Or let my lamp at midnight hour
Be seen in some high lonely tower,
Where I may oft out-watch the Bear
With thrice-great Hermes, or unsphere
The spirit of Plato, to unfold
What worlds or what vast regions hold
The immortal mind, that hath forsook
Her mansion in this fleshly nook:
And of those demons that are found
In fire, air, flood, or under ground,
Whose power hath a true consent
With planet, or with element.
Sometime let gorgeous Tragedy
In scepter'd pall come sweeping by,
Presenting Thebes, or Pelops' line,
Or the tale of Troy divine;
Or what (though rare) of later age
Ennobled hath the buskin'd stage.
 But, O sad Virgin, that thy power
Might raise Musaeus from his bower,
Or bid the soul of Orpheus sing
Such notes as, warbled to the string,
Drew iron tears down Pluto's cheek

And made Hell grant what Love did seek!
Or call up him that left half-told
The story of Cambuscan bold, 110
Of Camball, and of Algarsife,
And who had Canacé to wife
That own'd the virtuous ring and glass;
And of the wondrous horse of brass
On which the Tartar king did ride: 115
And if aught else great bards beside
In sage and solemn tunes have sung
Of turneys, and of trophies hung,
Of forests, and enchantments drear,
Where more is meant than meets the ear. 120
    Thus, Night, oft see me in thy pale career,
Till civil-suited Morn appear,
Not trick'd and frounced as she was wont
With the Attic Boy to hunt,
But kercheft in a comely cloud 125
While rocking winds are piping loud,
Or usher'd with a shower still,
When the gust hath blown his fill,
Ending on the rustling leaves
With minute drops from off the eaves. 130
And when the sun begins to fling
His flaring beams, me, goddess, bring
To archéd walks of twilight groves,
And shadows brown, that Sylvan loves,
Of pine, or monumental oak, 135
Where the rude axe, with heavéd stroke,
Was never heard the nymphs to daunt
Or fright them from their hallow'd haunt.

There in close covert by some brook
Where no profaner eye may look,
Hide me from day's garish eye,
While the bee with honey'd thigh
That at her flowery work doth sing,
And the waters murmuring,
With such consort as they keep
Entice the dewy-feather'd Sleep;
And let some strange mysterious dream
Wave at his wings in airy stream
Of lively portraiture display'd,
Softly on my eyelids laid:
And, as I wake, sweet music breathe
Above, about, or underneath,
Sent by some Spirit to mortals good,
Or the unseen Genius of the wood.

But let my due feet never fail
To walk the studious cloister's pale,
And love the high-embowéd roof,
With antique pillars massy-proof,
And storied windows richly dight
Casting a dim religious light.
There let the pealing organ blow
To the full-voiced quire below
In service high and anthems clear,
As may with sweetness, through mine ear
Dissolve me into ecstasies,
And bring all Heaven before mine eyes.

And may at last my weary age
Find out the peaceful hermitage,
The hairy gown and mossy cell

. . . *the high-embowèd roof,*
With antique pillars massy-proof.

Where I may sit and rightly spell
Of every star that heaven doth shew,
And every herb that sips the dew;
Till old experience do attain
To something like prophetic strain.

    These pleasures, Melancholy, give,
And I with thee will choose to live.

J. Milton

146

SONG OF THE EMIGRANTS IN BERMUDA

Where the remote Bermudas ride
In the ocean's bosom unespied,
From a small boat that row'd along
The listening winds received this song.
    'What should we do but sing His praise
That led us through the watery maze
Where He the huge sea-monsters wracks,
That lift the deep upon their backs,
Unto an isle so long unknown,
And yet far kinder than our own?
He lands us on a grassy stage,
Safe from the storms, and prelate's rage;
He gave us this eternal Spring
Which here enamels everything
And sends the fowls to us in care
On daily visits through the air.
He hangs in shades the orange bright
Like golden lamps in a green light,
And does in the pomegranates close
Jewels more rich than Ormus shows:

He makes the figs our mouths to meet
And throws the melons at our feet;
But apples plants of such a price,
No tree could ever bear them twice.
With cedars chosen by His hand
From Lebanon He stores the land;
And makes the hollow seas that roar
Proclaim the ambergris on shore.
He cast (of which we rather boast)
The gospel's pearl upon our coast;
And in these rocks for us did frame
A temple where to sound His name.
Oh! let our voice His praise exalt
Till it arrive at Heaven's valt,
Which thence (perhaps) rebounding may
Echo beyond the Mexique bay!'
— Thus sung they in the English boat
A holy and a cheerful note:
And all the way, to guide their chime,
With falling oars they kept the time.

A. Marvell

147

AT A SOLEMN MUSIC

Blest pair of Sirens, pledges of Heaven's joy,
Sphere-born harmonious Sisters, Voice and Verse!
Wed your divine sounds, and mixt power employ,
Dead things with inbreathed sense able to pierce;
And to our high-raised phantasy present
That undisturbed Song of pure concent

Aye sung before the sapphire-color'd throne
    To Him that sits thereon,
With saintly shout and solemn jubilee;
Where the bright Seraphim in burning row   10
Their loud uplifted angel-trumpets blow;
And the Cherubic host in thousand quires
Touch their immortal harps of golden wires,
With those just Spirits that wear victorious palms,
    Hymns devout and holy psalms   15
    Singing everlastingly:
That we on Earth, with undiscording voice
May rightly answer that melodious noise;
As once we did, till disproportion'd sin
Jarr'd against nature's chime, and with harsh din   20
Broke the fair music that all creatures made
To their great Lord, whose love their motion sway'd
In perfect diapason, whilst they stood
In first obedience, and their state of good.
O may we soon again renew that Song,   25
And keep in tune with Heaven, till God ere long
To His celestial consort us unite,
To live with Him, and sing in endless morn of light.
                        J. Milton

148

NOX NOCTI INDICAT SCIENTIAM

    When I survey the bright
      Celestial sphere:
So rich with jewels hung, that night
Doth like an Ethiop bride appear;

My soul her wings doth spread,
    And heaven-ward flies,
The Almighty's mysteries to read
In the large volumes of the skies.

For the bright firmament
    Shoots forth no flame
So silent, but is eloquent
In speaking the Creator's name.

No unregarded star
    Contracts its light
Into so small a character,
Removed far from our human sight,

But if we steadfast look,
    We shall discern
In it as in some holy book,
How man may heavenly knowledge learn.

It tells the Conqueror,
    That far-stretch'd power
Which his proud dangers traffic for,
Is but the triumph of an hour.

That from the farthest North
    Some nations may
Yet undiscover'd issue forth,
And o'er his new-got conquest sway.

Some nation yet shut in
    With hills of ice,
May be let out to scourge his sin,
Till they shall equal him in vice.

And then they likewise shall
    Their ruin have;
For as yourselves your Empires fall,   35
And every Kingdom hath a grave.

Thus those celestial fires,
    Though seeming mute,
The fallacy of our desires
And all the pride of life, confute.   40

For they have watch'd since first
    The world had birth:
And found sin in itself accursed,
And nothing permanent on earth.
W. Habington

149

HYMN TO DARKNESS

Hail thou most sacred venerable thing!
    What Muse is worthy thee to sing?
Thee, from whose pregnant universal womb
All things, ev'n Light, thy rival, first did come.
What dares he not attempt that sings of thee,   5
    Thou first and greatest mystery?
Who can the secrets of thy essence tell?
Thou, like the light of God, art inaccessible.

Before great Love this monument did raise
    This ample theatre of praise;   10

Before the folding circles of the sky
　　Were tuned by Him, Who is all harmony;
　Before the morning Stars their hymn began,
　　Before the council held for man,
15　　Before the birth of either time or place,
Thou reign'st unquestion'd monarch in the empty space.

Thy native lot thou didst to Light resign,
　　But still half of the globe is thine.
　Here with quiet, but yet awful hand,
20　　Like the best emperors thou dost command.
　To thee the stars above their brightness owe,
　　And mortals their repose below:
　To thy protection fear and sorrow flee,
And those that weary are of light, find rest in thee.
J. Norris of Bemerton

150

A VISION

I saw Eternity the other night,
　Like a great ring of pure and endless light,
　　All calm, as it was bright:—
　And round beneath it, Time, in hours, days, years,
5　　Driven by the spheres,
　Like a vast shadow moved; in which the World
　　And all her train were hurl'd.

H. Vaughan

151

ALEXANDER'S FEAST, OR, THE POWER OF MUSIC

'Twas at the royal feast for Persia won
  By Philip's warlike son—
  Aloft in awful state
  The godlike hero sate
  On his imperial throne;   5
His valiant peers were placed around,
Their brows with roses and with myrtles bound,
(So should desert in arms be crown'd);
  The lovely Thais by his side
  Sate like a blooming Eastern bride   10
  In flower of youth and beauty's pride:—
    Happy, happy, happy pair!
      None but the brave
      None but the brave
      None but the brave deserve the fair!   15

    Timotheus placed on high
Amid the tuneful quire
With flying fingers touch'd the lyre:
The trembling notes ascend the sky
And heavenly joys inspire.   20
  The song began from Jove
Who left his blissful seats above—
Such is the power of mighty love!
A dragon's fiery form belied the god;
Sublime on radiant spires he rode   25

When he to fair Olympia prest,
And while he sought her snowy breast,
Then round her slender waist he curl'd,
And stamp'd an image of himself, a sovereign of the world.
30 —The listening crowd admire the lofty sound;
A present deity! they shout around:
A present deity! the vaulted roofs rebound:
With ravish'd ears
The monarch hears,
35 Assumes the god;
Affects to nod
And seems to shake the spheres.

The praise of Bacchus then the sweet musician sung,
Of Bacchus ever fair and ever young:
40 The jolly god in triumph comes;
Sound the trumpets, beat the drums!
Flush'd with a purple grace
He shows his honest face:
Now give the hautboys breath; he comes, he comes!
45 Bacchus, ever fair and young,
Drinking joys did first ordain;
Bacchus' blessings are a treasure,
Drinking is the soldier's pleasure:
Rich the treasure,
50 Sweet the pleasure,
Sweet is pleasure after pain.

Soothed with the sound, the king grew vain;
Fought all his battles o'er again,

JOHN DRYDEN

And thrice he routed all his foes, and thrice he slew
    the slain!
The master saw the madness rise,
His glowing cheeks, his ardent eyes;
And while he Heaven and Earth defied
Changed his hand and check'd his pride.
He chose a mournful Muse
Soft pity to infuse:
He sung Darius great and good,
By too severe a fate
Fallen, fallen, fallen, fallen,
Fallen from his high estate.
And weltering in his blood;
Deserted at his utmost need
By those his former bounty fed;
  On the bare earth exposed he lies
  With not a friend to close his eyes.
— With downcast looks the joyless victor sate,
Revolving in his alter'd soul
The various turns of Chance below;
And now and then a sigh he stole,
And tears began to flow.

  The mighty master smiled to see
That love was in the next degree;
'Twas but a kindred-sound to move,
For pity melts the mind to love.
Softly sweet, in Lydian measures
Soon he soothed his soul to pleasures.
War, he sung, is toil and trouble,
Honour but an empty bubble;

  Never ending, still beginning,
  Fighting still, and still destroying;
85 If the world be worth thy winning,
  Think, O think, it worth enjoying:
  Lovely Thais sits beside thee,
  Take the good the gods provide thee!
— The many rend the skies with loud applause;
90 So Love was crown'd, but Music won the cause.
  The prince, unable to conceal his pain,
    Gazed on the fair
    Who caused his care,
  And sigh'd and look'd, sigh'd and look'd,
95 Sigh'd and look'd, and sigh'd again:
  At length with love and wine at once opprest
  The vanquish'd victor sunk upon her breast.

  Now strike the golden lyre again:
  A louder yet, and yet a louder strain!
100 Break his bands of sleep asunder
  And rouse him like a rattling peal of thunder.
    Hark, hark! the horrid sound
    Has raised up his head:
    As waked from the dead
105 And amazed he stares around.
  Revenge, revenge, Timotheus cries,
    See the Furies arise!
    See the snakes that they rear
    How they hiss in their hair,
110 And the sparkles that flash from their eyes!
    Behold a ghastly band,
    Each a torch in his hand!

Those are Grecian ghosts, that in battle were slain
And unburied remain
Inglorious on the plain: 115
Give the vengeance due
To the valiant crew!
Behold how they toss their torches on high,
How they point to the Persian abodes
And glittering temples of their hostile gods. 120
— The princes applaud with furious joy:
And the King seized a flambeau with zeal to destroy;
Thais led the way
To light him to his prey,
And like another Helen, fired another Troy! 125

— Thus, long ago,
Ere heaving bellows learn'd to blow,
While organs yet were mute,
Timotheus, to his breathing flute
And sounding lyre 130
Could swell the soul to rage, or kindle soft desire.
At last divine Cecilia came.
Inventress of the vocal frame;
The sweet enthusiast from sacred store
Enlarged the former narrow bounds, 135
And added length to solemn sounds,
With Nature's mother-wit, and arts unknown before.
— Let old Timotheus yield the prize
Or both divide the crown;
He raised a mortal to the skies; 140
She drew an angel down!   *J. Dryden*

Book Second

"Those are Grecian ghosts, that in battle were slain
  And unburied remain
    Inglorious on the plain:
      Give the vengeance due
        To the valiant crew!
Behold how they toss their torches on high,
  How they point to the Persian abode,
  And glittering temples of their hostile gods.
— The princes applaud with furious joy;
And the King seized a flambeau with zeal to destroy;
    Thaïs led the way,
    To light him to his prey,
And like another Helen, fired another Troy!

        Thus long ago,
  Ere heaving bellows learn'd to blow,
    While organs yet were mute,
    Timotheus, to his breathing flute
      And sounding lyre
Could swell the soul to rage, or kindle soft desire.
    At last divine Cecilia came,
    Inventress of the vocal frame;
The sweet enthusiast from sacred store
  Enlarged the former narrow bounds,
And added length to solemn sounds,
  With Nature's mother-wit, and arts unknown before.
    Let old Timotheus yield the prize
      Or both divide the crown:
      He raised a mortal to the skies;
      She drew an angel down."   J. Dryden.

BOOK THIRD

152

ODE ON THE PLEASURE ARISING FROM VICISSITUDE

Now the golden Morn aloft
  Waves her dew-bespangled wing,
With vermeil cheek and whisper soft
  She woos the tardy Spring:
Till April starts, and calls around   5
The sleeping fragrance from the ground,
And lightly o'er the living scene
Scatters his freshest, tenderest green.

New-born flocks, in rustic dance,
  Frisking ply their feeble feet;   10
Forgetful of their wintry trance
  The birds his presence greet:
But chief, the sky-lark warbles high
His trembling thrilling ecstasy;
And lessening from the dazzled sight,   15
Melts into air and liquid light.

Yesterday the sullen year
  Saw the snowy whirlwind fly;
Mute was the music of the air,
  The herd stood drooping by: 20

Their raptures now that wildly flow
No yesterday nor morrow know;
'Tis Man alone that joy descries
With forward and reverted eyes.

Smiles on past misfortune's brow
   Soft reflection's hand can trace,
And o'er the cheek of sorrow throw
   A melancholy grace;
While hope prolongs our happier hour,
Or deepest shades, that dimly lour
And blacken round our weary way,
Gilds with a gleam of distant day.

Still, where rosy pleasure leads,
   See a kindred grief pursue;
Behind the steps that misery treads
   Approaching comfort view:
The hues of bliss more brightly glow
Chastised by sabler tints of woe,
And blended form, with artful strife,
The strength and harmony of life.

See the wretch that long has tost
   On the thorny bed of pain,
At length repair his vigour lost
   And breathe and walk again:
The meanest floweret of the vale,
The simplest note that swells the gale,
The common sun, the air, the skies,
To him are opening Paradise.

T. Gray

153

ODE TO SIMPLICITY

O Thou, by Nature taught
To breathe her genuine thought
In numbers warmly pure, and sweetly strong;
  Who first, on mountains wild,
  In Fancy, loveliest child,
Thy babe, or Pleasure's, nursed the powers of song!

Thou, who with hermit heart,
Disdains't the wealth of art,
And gauds, and pageant weeds, and trailing pall,
  But com'st, a decent maid
  In Attic robe array'd,
O chaste, unboastful Nymph, to thee I call!

By all the honey'd store
On Hybla's thymy shore,
By all her blooms and mingled murmurs dear
  By her whose love-lorn woe
  In evening musings slow
Soothed sweetly sad Electra's poet's ear.

By old Cephisus deep,
Who spread his wavy sweep
In warbled wanderings round thy green retreat;
  On whose enamell'd side,
  When holy Freedom died,
No equal haunt allured thy future feet:—

  O sister meek of Truth,
  To my admiring youth

Thy sober aid and native charms infuse:
The flowers that sweetest breathe,
Though Beauty cull'd the wreath,
Still ask thy hand to range their order'd hues.

While Rome could none esteem
But Virtue's patriot theme,
You loved her hills, and led her laureat band;
But stay'd to sing alone
To one distinguish'd throne;
And turn'd thy face, and fled her alter'd land.

No more, in hall or bower,
The Passions own thy power;
Love, only Love, her forceless numbers mean:
For thou hast left her shrine;
Nor olive more, nor vine,
Shall gain thy feet to bless the servile scene.

Though taste, though genius, bless
To some divine excess.
Faints the cold work till thou inspire the whole;
What each, what all supply
May court, may charm our eye;
Thou, only thou, canst raise the meeting soul!

Of these let others ask
To aid some mighty task;
I only seek to find thy temperate vale;
Where oft my reed might sound
To maids and shepherds round,
And all thy sons, O Nature! learn my tale.

W. Collins

154

SOLITUDE

Happy the man, whose wish and care
A few paternal acres bound,
Content to breathe his native air
        In his own ground.

Whose herds with milk, whose fields with bread,
Whose flocks supply him with attire;
Whose trees in summer yield him shade,
        In winter fire.

Blest, who can unconcern'dly find
Hours, days, and years, slide soft away
In health of body, peace of mind,
        Quiet by day.

Sound sleep by night; study and ease
Together mixt, sweet recreation,
And innocence, which most does please
        With meditation.

Thus let me live, unseen, unknown;
Thus unlamented let me die;
Steal from the world, and not a stone
        Tell where I lie.

A. Pope

155

THE BLIND BOY

O say what is this thing call'd Light,
  Which I must ne'er enjoy;
What are the blessings of the sight,
  O tell your poor blind boy!

You talk of wondrous things you see,
  You say the sun shines bright;
I feel him warm, but how can he
  Or make it day or night?

My day or night myself I make
  Whene'er I sleep or play;
And could I ever keep awake
  With me 'twere always day.

With heavy sighs I often hear
  You mourn my hapless woe;
But sure with patience I can bear
  A loss I ne'er can know.

Then let not what I cannot have
  My cheer of mind destroy:
Whilst thus I sing, I am a king,
  Although a poor blind boy.

C. Cibber

156

ON A FAVOURITE CAT, DROWNED IN A TUB OF GOLD FISHES

'Twas on a lofty vase's side,
Where China's gayest art had dyed
The azure flowers that blow,
Demurest of the tabby kind
The pensive Selima, reclined,
Gazed on the lake below.

Her conscious tail her joy declared:
The fair round face, the snowy beard,
The velvet of her paws,
Her coat that with the tortoise vies,
Her ears of jet, and emerald eyes—
She saw, and purr'd applause.

Still had she gazed, but 'midst the tide
Two angel forms were seen to glide.
The Genii of the stream:
Their scaly armour's Tyrian hue
Through richest purple, to the view
Betray'd a golden gleam.

The hapless Nymph with wonder saw:
A whisker first, and then a claw
With many an ardent wish
She stretch'd, in vain, to reach the prize—
What female heart can gold despise?
What Cat's averse to fish?

25 Presumptuous maid! with looks intent
Again she stretch'd, again she bent,
Nor knew the gulf between—
Malignant Fate sat by and smiled—
The slippery verge her feet beguiled;
30 She tumbled headlong in!

Eight times emerging from the flood
She mew'd to every watery God
Some speedy aid to send:—
No Dolphin came, no Nereid stirred,
35 Nor cruel Tom nor Susan heard—
A favourite has no friend!

From hence, ye Beauties! undeceived
Know one false step is ne'er retrieved,
And be with caution bold:
40 Not all that tempts your wandering eyes
And heedless hearts, is lawful prize,
Nor all that glisters, gold!

T. Gray

157

TO CHARLOTTE PULTENEY

Timely blossom, Infant fair,
Fondling of a happy pair,
Every morn and every night
Their solicitous delight,
5 Sleeping, waking, still at ease,
Pleasing, without skill to please;
Little gossip, blithe and hale,
Tattling many a broken tale

Singing many a tuneless song,
Lavish of a heedless tongue;
Simple maiden, void of art,
Babbling out the very heart,
Yet abandon'd to thy will,
Yet imagining no ill,
Yet too innocent to blush;
Like the linnet in the bush
To the mother-linnet's note
Moduling her slender throat;
Chirping forth thy petty joys,
Wanton in the change of toys,
Like the linnet green, in May
Flitting to each bloomy spray;
Wearied then and glad of rest,
Like the linnet in the nest:—
This thy present happy lot
This, in time will be forgot:
Other pleasures, other cares,
Ever-busy Time prepares;
And thou shalt in thy daughter see,
This picture, once, resembled thee.

A. Philips

158

RULE BRITANNIA

When Britain first at Heaven's command
  Arose from out the azure main,
This was the charter of her land,
  And guardian angels sung this strain:

Rule, Britannia! rule the waves!
  Britons never will be slaves.

The nations not so blest as thee
  Must in their turn to tyrants fall,
Whilst thou shalt flourish great and free
  The dread and envy of them all.

Still more majestic shalt thou rise,
  More dreadful from each foreign stroke;
As the loud blast that tears the skies
  Serves but to root thy native oak.

Thee haughty tyrants ne'er shall tame;
  All their attempts to bend thee down
Will but arouse thy generous flame,
  And work their woe and thy renown.

To thee belongs the rural reign;
  Thy cities shall with commerce shine:
All thine shall be the subject main,
  And every shore it circles thine!

The Muses, still with Freedom found,
  Shall to thy happy coast repair;
Blest Isle, with matchless beauty crown'd
  And manly hearts to guard the fair:—
Rule, Britannia! rule the waves!
  Britons never will be slaves!

J. Thomson

159

THE BARD

Pindaric Ode

'Ruin seize thee, ruthless King!
  Confusion on thy banners wait;
Tho' fann'd by Conquest's crimson wing
  They mock the air with idle state.
Helm, nor hauberk's twisted mail,
Nor e'en thy virtues, Tyrant, shall avail
To save thy secret soul from nightly fears,
From Cambria's curse, from Cambria's tears!'
—Such were the sounds that o'er the crested pride
  Of the first Edward scatter'd wild dismay,
As down the steep of Snowdon's shaggy side
  He wound with toilsome march his long array:—
Stout Glo'ster stood aghast in speechless trance:
'To arms!' cried Mortimer, and couch'd his quivering
    lance.

  On a rock, whose haughty brow
Frowns o'er old Conway's foaming flood,
  Robed in the sable garb of woe
With haggard eyes the Poet stood;
(Loose his beard and hoary hair
Stream'd like a meteor to the troubled air)
And with a master's hand and prophet's fire
Struck the deep sorrows of his lyre:
  'Hark, how each giant-oak and desert-cave
Sighs to the torrent's awful voice beneath!

25 O'er thee, oh King! their hundred arms they wave,
　　Revenge on thee in hoarser murmurs breathe;
　Vocal no more, since Cambria's fatal day,
　To high-born Hoel's harp, or soft Llewellyn's lay.

　　'Cold is Cadwallo's tongue,
30　　That hush'd the stormy main:
　Brave Urien sleeps upon his craggy bed:
　　　Mountains, ye mourn in vain
　　　Modred, whose magic song
　Made huge Plinlimmon bow his cloud-topt head.
35　　On dreary Arvon's shore they lie
　Smear'd with gore and ghastly pale:
　Far, far aloof the affrighted ravens sail;
　　The famish'd eagle screams, and passes by.
　Dear lost companions of my tuneful art,
40　　Dear as the light that visits these sad eyes,
　Dear as the ruddy drops that warm my heart,
　　Ye died amidst your dying country's cries—
　No more I weep. They do not sleep;
　　On yonder cliffs, a griesly band,
45　I see them sit; they linger yet,
　　Avengers of their native land:
　With me in dreadful harmony they join,
　And weave with bloody hands the tissue of thy line.

　'*Weave the warp and weave the woof*
50　　*The winding sheet of Edward's race:*
　Give ample room and verge enough
　　The characters of hell to trace.
　Mark the year, and mark the night,
　When Severn shall re-echo with affright

THOMAS GRAY

The shrieks of death thro' Berkley's roof that ring,　　55
Shrieks of an agonizing king!
　　She-wolf of France, with unrelenting fangs
That tear'st the bowels of thy mangled mate,
　　From thee be born, who o'er thy country hangs
The scourge of heaven! What terrors round him wait!　60
Amazement in his van, with flight combined,
And sorrow's faded form, and solitude behind.

'*Mighty victor, mighty lord,*
　　Low on his funeral couch he lies!
No pitying heart, no eye afford　　65
　　A tear to grace his obsequies.
Is the sable warrior fled?
Thy son is gone. He rests among the dead.
The swarm that in thy noon-tide were born?
—Gone to salute the rising morn.　　70
Fair laughs the Morn, and soft the zephyr blows,
While proudly riding o'er the azure realm
In gallant trim the gilded vessel goes:
　　Youth on the prow, and Pleasure at the helm:
Regardless of the sweeping whirlwind's sway,　　75
That hush'd in grim repose expects his evening prey.

　　'*Fill high the sparkling bowl,*
The rich repast prepare;
　　Reft of a crown, he yet may share the feast:
Close by the regal chair　　80
　　Fell Thirst and Famine scowl
A baleful smile upon their baffled guest.
Heard ye the din of battle bray,

Lance to lance, and horse to horse?
Long years of havock urge their destined course,
And thro' the kindred squadrons mow their way.
Ye towers of Julius, London's lasting shame,
With many a foul and midnight murder fed,
Revere his consort's faith, his father's fame,
And spare the meek usurper's holy head!
Above, below, the rose of snow,
  Twined with her blushing foe, we spread:
The bristled boar in infant-gore
  Wallows beneath the thorny shade.
Now, brothers, bending o'er the accursèd loom,
Stamp we our vengeance deep, and ratify his doom.

'Edward, lo! to sudden fate
  (Weave we the woof; The thread is spun;)
Half of thy heart we consecrate.
  (The web is wove; The work is done.)
—Stay, oh stay! nor thus forlorn
Leave me unbless'd, unpitied, here to mourn:
In yon bright track that fires the western skies
They melt, they vanish from my eyes.
But oh! what solemn scenes on Snowdon's height
  Descending slow their glittering skirts unroll?
Visions of glory, spare my aching sight,
Ye unborn ages, crowd not on my soul!
No more our long-lost Arthur we bewail:—
All hail, ye genuine kings! Britannia's issue, hail!

'Girt with many a baron bold
Sublime their starry fronts they rear;

And gorgeous dames, and statesmen old
In bearded majesty, appear.
In the midst a form divine!   115
Her eye proclaims her of the Briton-line:
Her lion-port, her awe-commanding face
Attemper'd sweet to virgin-grace.
What strings symphonious tremble in the air,
    What strains of vocal transport round her play?   120
Hear from the grave, great Taliessin, hear;
    They breathe a soul to animate thy clay.
Bright Rapture calls, and soaring as she sings,
Waves in the eye of heaven her many-colour'd wings.

' The verse adorn again   125
    Fierce war, and faithful love,
And truth severe, by fairy fiction drest.
    In buskin'd measures move
Pale grief, and pleasing pain,
With horror, tyrant of the throbbing breast.   130
A voice as of the cherub-choir
    Gales from blooming Eden bear,
    And distant warblings lessen on my ear
That lost in long futurity expire.
Fond impious man, think'st thou yon sanguine cloud   135
    Raised by thy breath, has quench'd the orb of day?
To-morrow he repairs the golden flood
    And warms the nations with redoubled ray.
Enough for me: with joy I see
    The different doom our fates assign: 140
Be thine despair and sceptred care,
    To triumph and to die are mine.'

—He spoke, and headlong from the mountain's height
Deep in the roaring tide he plunged to endless night.

T. Gray

160

ODE WRITTEN IN 1746

How sleep the brave, who sink to rest
By all their country's wishes blest!
When Spring, with dewy fingers cold,
Returns to deck their hallow'd mould,
She there shall dress a sweeter sod
Than Fancy's feet have ever trod.

By fairy hands their knell is rung,
By forms unseen their dirge is sung:
There Honour comes, a pilgrim gray,
To bless the turf that wraps their clay;
And Freedom shall awhile repair
To dwell a weeping hermit there!

W. Collins

161

LAMENT FOR CULLODEN

The lovely lass o' Inverness,
Nae joy nor pleasure can she see;
For e'en and morn she cries, Alas!
And aye the saut tear blin's her ee:
Drumossie moor—Drumossie day—
A waefu' day it was to me!
For there I lost my father dear,
My father dear, and brethren three.

Their winding-sheet the bluidy clay,
Their graves are growing green to see:
And by them lies the dearest lad
That ever blest a woman's ee!
Now wae to thee, thou cruel lord,
A bluidy man I trow thou be;
For mony a heart thou hast made sair
That ne'er did wrang to thine or thee.

R. Burns

162

LAMENT FOR FLODDEN

I've heard them lilting at our ewe-milking,
    Lasses a' lilting before dawn o' day;
But now they are moaning on ilka green loaning—
    The Flowers of the Forest are a' wede away.

At bughts, in the morning, nae blythe lads are scorning,
    Lasses are lonely and dowie and wae;
Nae daffin', nae gabbin', but sighing and sabbing,
    Ilk ane lifts her leglin and hies her away.

In har'st, at the shearing, nae youths now are jeering,
    Bandsters are lyart, and runkled, and gray;
At fair or at preaching, nae wooing, nae fleeching—
    The Flowers of the Forest are a' wede away.

At e'en, in the gloaming, nae younkers are roaming
    'Bout stacks wi' the lasses at bogle to play;
But ilk ane sits drearie, lamenting her dearie—
    The Flowers of the Forest are wede away.

Dool and wae for the order, sent our lads to the Border!
  The English, for ance, by guile wan the day;
The Flowers of the Forest, that fought aye the foremost,
20   The prime of our land, are cauld in the clay.

We'll hear nae mair lilting at the ewe-milking;
  Women and bairns are heartless and wae;
Sighing and moaning on ilka green loaning—
  The Flowers of the Forest are a' wede away.

J. Elliott

163

THE BRAES OF YARROW

  Thy braes were bonny, Yarrow stream,
    When first on them I met my lover;
  Thy braes how dreary, Yarrow stream,
    When now thy waves his body cover!
5   For ever now, O Yarrow stream!
    Thou art to me a stream of sorrow;
  For never on thy banks shall I
    Behold my Love, the flower of Yarrow!

  He promised me a milk-white steed
10   To bear me to his father's bowers;
  He promised me a little page
    To squire me to his father's towers;
  He promised me a wedding-ring,—
    The wedding-day was fix'd to-morrow;—
15   Now he is wedded to his grave,
    Alas, his watery grave, in Yarrow!

Sweet were his words when last we met;
My passion I as freely told him;
Clasp'd in his arms, I little thought
That I should never more behold him! 20
Scarce was he gone, I saw his ghost;
It vanish'd with a shriek of sorrow;
Thrice did the water-wraith ascend,
And gave a doleful groan thro' Yarrow.

His mother from the window look'd 25
With all the longing of a mother;
His little sister weeping walk'd
The green-wood path to meet her brother;
They sought him east, they sought him west,
They sought him all the forest thorough; 30
They only saw the cloud of night,
They only heard the roar of Yarrow.

No longer from thy window look—
Thou hast no son, thou tender mother!
No longer walk, thou lovely maid; 35
Alas, thou hast no more a brother!
No longer seek him east or west
And search no more the forest thorough;
For, wandering in the night so dark,
He fell a lifeless corpse in Yarrow. 40

The tear shall never leave my cheek,
No other youth shall be my marrow—
I'll seek thy body in the stream,
And then with thee I'll sleep in Yarrow.

45   —The tear did never leave her cheek,
     No other youth became her marrow;
     She found his body in the stream,
     And now with him she sleeps in Yarrow.

J. Logan

164

WILLY DROWNED IN YARROW

     Down in yon garden sweet and gay
        Where bonnie grows the lily,
     I heard a fair maid sighing say,
        ' My wish be wi' sweet Willie!

5   ' Willie's rare, and Willie's fair,
        And Willie's wondrous bonny;
     And Willie hecht to marry me
        Gin e'er he married ony.

     ' O gentle wind, that bloweth south
10   From where my Love repaireth,
     Convey a kiss frae his dear mouth
        And tell me how he fareth!

     ' O tell sweet Willie to come doun
        And hear the mavis singing,
15   And see the birds on ilka bush
        And leaves around them hinging.

     ' The lav'rock there, wi' her white breast
        And gentle throat sae narrow;
     There's sport eneuch for gentlemen
20   On Leader haughs and Yarrow.

'O Leader haughs are wide and braid
    And Yarrow haughs are bonny;
There Willie hecht to marry me
    If e'er he married ony.

'But Willie's gone, whom I thought on,
    And does not hear me weeping;
Draws many a tear frae true love's e'e
    When other maids are sleeping.

'Yestreen I made my bed fu' braid,
    The night I'll mak' it narrow,
For a' the live-lang winter night
    I lie twined o' my marrow.

'O came ye by yon water-side?
    Pou'd you the rose or lily?
Or came you by yon meadow green,
    Or saw you my sweet Willie?'

She sought him up, she sought him down,
    She sought him braid and narrow;
Syne, in the cleaving of a craig,
    She found him drown'd in Yarrow!

Anon.

165

LOSS OF THE ROYAL GEORGE

Toll for the Brave!
The brave that are no more!
All sunk beneath the wave
Fast by their native shore!

Eight hundred of the brave
Whose courage well was tried,
Had made the vessel heel
And laid her on her side.

A land-breeze shook the shrouds
And she was overset;
Down went the Royal George,
With all her crew complete.

Toll for the brave!
Brave Kempenfelt is gone;
His last sea-fight is fought,
His work of glory done.

It was not in the battle;
No tempest gave the shock;
She sprang no fatal leak,
She ran upon no rock.

His sword was in its sheath,
His fingers held the pen,
When Kempenfelt went down
With twice four hundred men.

—Weigh the vessel up
Once dreaded by our foes!
And mingle with our cup
The tears that England owes.

Her timbers yet are sound,
And she may float again
Full charged with England's thunder,
And plough the distant main:

But Kempenfelt is gone,
  His victories are o'er;
And he and his eight hundred
  Shall plough the wave no more.

W. Cowper

166

BLACK-EYED SUSAN

All in the Downs the fleet was moor'd,
  The streamers waving in the wind,
When black-eyed Susan came aboard;
  'O! where shall I my true-love find?
Tell me, ye jovial sailors, tell me true
If my sweet William sails among the crew.'

William, who high upon the yard
  Rock'd with the billow to and fro,
Soon as her well-known voice he heard
  He sigh'd, and cast his eyes below:
The cord slides swiftly through his glowing hands,
And quick as lightning on the deck he stands.

So the sweet lark, high poised in air,
  Shuts close his pinions to his breast
If chance his mate's shrill call he hear,
  And drops at once into her nest:—
The noblest captain in the British fleet
Might envy William's lip those kisses sweet.

'O Susan, Susan, lovely dear,
  My vows shall ever true remain;

Let me kiss off that falling tear;
  We only part to meet again.
Change as ye list, ye winds; my heart shall be
The faithful compass that still points to thee.

25 ' Believe not what the landmen say
  Who tempt with doubts thy constant mind;
They'll tell thee, sailors, when away,
  In every port a mistress find:
Yes, yes, believe them when they tell thee so,
30 For thou art present wheresoe'er I go.

' If to fair India's coast we sail,
  Thy eyes are seen in diamonds bright,
Thy breath is Afric's spicy gale,
  Thy skin is ivory so white.
35 Thus every beauteous object that I view
Wakes in my soul some charm of lovely Sue.

' Though battle call me from thy arms
  Let not my pretty Susan mourn;
Though cannons roar, yet safe from harms
40 William shall to his Dear return.
Love turns aside the balls that round me fly,
Lest precious tears should drop from Susan's eye.'

The boatswain gave the dreadful word,
  The sails their swelling bosom spread,
45 No longer must she stay aboard;
  They kiss'd, she sigh'd, he hung his head.
Her lessening boat unwilling rows to land;
' Adieu!' she cries; and waved her lily hand.

J. Gay

Book Third

167

SALLY IN OUR ALLEY

Of all the girls that are so smart
  There's none like pretty Sally;
She is the darling of my heart,
  And she lives in our alley.
There is no lady in the land
  Is half so sweet as Sally;
She is the darling of my heart,
  And she lives in our alley.

Her father he makes cabbage-nets
  And through the streets does cry 'em;
Her mother she sells laces long
  To such as please to buy 'em:
But sure such folks could ne'er beget
  So sweet a girl as Sally!
She is the darling of my heart,
  And she lives in our alley.

When she is by, I leave my work,
  I love her so sincerely;
My master comes like any Turk,
  And bangs me most severely—
But let him bang his bellyful,
  I'll bear it all for Sally;
She is the darling of my heart,
  And she lives in our alley.

Of all the days that's in the week
  I dearly love but one day—

And that's the day that comes betwixt
  A Saturday and Monday;
For then I'm drest all in my best
  To walk abroad with Sally;
She is the darling of my heart,
  And she lives in our alley.

My master carries me to church,
  And often am I blamed
Because I leave him in the lurch
  As soon as text is named;
I leave the church in sermon-time
  And slink away to Sally;
She is the darling of my heart,
  And she lives in our alley.

When Christmas comes about again
  O then I shall have money;
I'll hoard it up, and box it all,
  I'll give it to my honey:
I would it were ten thousand pound,
  I'd give it all to Sally;
She is the darling of my heart,
  And she lives in our alley.

My master and the neighbours all
  Make game of me and Sally,
And, but for her, I'd better be
  A slave and row a galley;
But when my seven long years are out
  O then I'll marry Sally,—
O then we'll wed, and then we'll bed. . .
  But not in our alley!
                H. Carey

168

A FAREWELL

Go fetch to me a pint o' wine,
  An' fill it in a silver tassie;
That I may drink before I go
  A service to my bonnie lassie:
The boat rocks at the pier o' Leith,
  Fu' loud the winds blaws frae the Ferry,
The ship rides by the Berwick-law,
  And I maun leave my bonnie Mary.

The trumpets sound, the banners fly,
  The glittering spears are rankéd ready;
The shouts o' war are heard afar,
  The battle closes thick and bloody;
But it's not the roar o' sea or shore
  Wad make me langer wish to tarry;
Nor shout o' war that's heard afar—
  It's leaving thee, my bonnie Mary.

R. Burns

169

If doughty deeds my lady please
  Right soon I'll mount my steed;
And strong his arm, and fast his seat
  That bears frae me the meed.
I'll wear thy colours in my cap
  Thy picture at my heart;
And he that bends not to thine eye
  Shall rue it to his smart!

Then tell me how to woo thee, Love;
  O tell me how to woo thee!
For thy dear sake, nae care I'll take
  Tho' ne'er another trow me.

If gay attire delight thine eye
  I'll dight me in array;
I'll tend thy chamber door all night,
  And squire thee all the day.
If sweetest sounds can win thine ear,
  These sounds I'll strive to catch;
Thy voice I'll steal to woo thyself,
  That voice that nane can match.

But if fond love thy heart can gain,
  I never broke a vow;
Nae maiden lays her skaith to me,
  I never loved but you.
For you alone I ride the ring,
  For you I wear the blue;
For you alone I strive to sing,
  O tell me how to woo!
    Then tell me how to woo thee, Love;
      O tell me how to woo thee!
    For thy dear sake, nae care I'll take,
      Tho' ne'er another trow me.

R. Graham of Gartmore

170

TO A YOUNG LADY

Sweet stream, that winds through yonder glade,
Apt emblem of a virtuous maid—
Silent and chaste she steals along,
Far from the world's gay busy throng:
With gentle yet prevailing force,
Intent upon her destined course;
Graceful and useful all she does.
Blessing and blest where'er she goes;
Pure-bosom'd as that watery glass
And heaven reflected in her face.

W. Cowper

171

THE SLEEPING BEAUTY

Sleep on, and dream of Heaven awhile—
Tho' shut so close thy laughing eyes,
Thy rosy lips still wear a smile
And move, and breathe delicious sighs!

Ah, now soft blushes tinge her cheeks
And mantle o'er her neck of snow:
Ah, now she murmurs, now she speaks
What most I wish—and fear to know!

She starts, she trembles, and she weeps!
Her fair hands folded on her breast:
—And now, how like a saint she sleeps!
A seraph in the realms of rest!

Sleep on secure! Above controul
Thy thoughts belong to Heaven and thee:
And may the secret of thy soul
Remain within its sanctuary!

S. Rogers

172

For ever, Fortune, wilt thou prove
An unrelenting foe to Love,
And when we meet a mutual heart
Come in between, and bid us part?

Bid us sigh on from day to day,
And wish and wish the soul away;
Till youth and genial years are flown,
And all the life of life is gone?

But busy, busy, still art thou,
To bind the loveless joyless vow,
The heart from pleasure to delude,
To join the gentle to the rude.

For once, O Fortune, hear my prayer,
And I absolve thy future care;
All other blessings I resign,
Make but the dear Amanda mine.

J. Thomson

173

The merchant, to secure his treasure,
Conveys it in a borrow'd name:
Euphelia serves to grace my measure,
But Cloe is my real flame.

My softest verse, my darling lyre 5
Upon Euphelia's toilet lay—
When Cloe noted her desire
That I should sing, that I should play.

My lyre I tune, my voice I raise,
But with my numbers mix my sighs; 10
And whilst I sing Euphelia's praise,
I fix my soul on Cloe's eyes.

Fair Cloe blush'd: Euphelia frown'd:
I sung, and gazed; I play'd, and trembled:
And Venus to the Loves around 15
Remark'd how ill we all dissembled.

M. Prior

174

LOVE'S SECRET

Never seek to tell thy love,
  Love that never told can be;
For the gentle wind doth move
  Silently, invisibly.

I told my love, I told my love, 5
  I told her all my heart,
Trembling, cold, in ghastly fears:—
  Ah! she did depart.

Soon after she was gone from me
  A traveller came by, 10
Silently, invisibly:
  He took her with a sigh.

W. Blake

175

When lovely woman stoops to folly
And finds too late that men betray,—
What charm can soothe her melancholy,
What art can wash her guilt away?

The only art her guilt to cover,
To hide her shame from every eye,
To give repentance to her lover
And wring his bosom, is—to die.

O. Goldsmith

176

Ye banks and braes o' bonnie Doon
　How can ye blume sae fair!
How can ye chant, ye little birds,
　And I sae fu' o' care!

Thou'll break my heart, thou bonnie bird
　That sings upon the bough;
Thou minds me o' the happy days
　When my fause Luve was true.

Thou'll break my heart, thou bonnie bird
　That sings beside thy mate;
For sae I sat, and sae I sang,
　And wist na o' my fate.

Aft hae I roved by bonnie Doon
　To see the woodbine twine,
And ilka bird sang o' its love;
　And sae did I o' mine.

ROBERT BURNS

Robert Burns

Wi' lightsome heart I pu'd a rose,
  Frae aff its thorny tree;
And my fause luver staw the rose,
  But left the thorn wi' me.

                                R. Burns

177

THE PROGRESS OF POESY

A Pindaric Ode

Awake, Aeolian lyre, awake,
And give to rapture all thy trembling strings.
From Helicon's harmonious springs
  A thousand rills their mazy progress take;
The laughing flowers that round them blow
Drink life and fragrance as they flow.
Now the rich stream of music winds along
Deep, majestic, smooth, and strong,
Thro' verdant vales, and Ceres' golden reign;
Now rolling down the steep amain
Headlong, impetuous, see it pour:
The rocks and nodding groves re-bellow to the roar.

Oh! Sovereign of the willing soul,
Parent of sweet and solemn-breathing airs,
Enchanting shell! the sullen Cares
  And frantic Passions hear thy soft controul,
On Thracia's hills the Lord of War
Has curb'd the fury of his car
And dropt his thirsty lance at thy command.
Perching on the sceptred hand

Of Jove, thy magic lulls the feather'd king
With ruffled plumes, and flagging wing:
Quench'd in dark clouds of slumber lie
The terror of his beak, and lightnings of his eye.

25 Thee the voice, the dance, obey
Temper'd to thy warbled lay.
O'er Idalia's velvet-green
The rosy-crownéd Loves are seen
On Cytherea's day;
30 With antic Sport, and blue-eyed Pleasures,
Frisking light in frolic measures;
Now pursuing, now retreating,
　Now in circling troops they meet:
To brisk notes in cadence beating
35 　Glance their many-twinkling feet.
Slow melting strains their Queen's approach declare:
　Where'er she turns, the Graces homage pay:
With arms sublime that float upon the air
In gliding state she wins her easy way:
40 O'er her warm cheek and rising bosom move
The bloom of young Desire and purple light of Love.

Man's feeble race what ills await!
Labour, and Penury, the racks of Pain,
Disease, and Sorrow's weeping train,
45 　And Death, sad refuge from the storms of fate!
The fond complaint, my song, disprove,
And justify the laws of Jove.
Say, has he given in vain the heavenly Muse?
Night, and all her sickly dews,

Book Third

Her spectres wan, and birds of boding cry 50
He gives to range the dreary sky:
Till down the eastern cliffs afar
Hyperion's march they spy, and glittering shafts of war.

   In climes beyond the solar road
Where shaggy forms o'er ice-built mountains roam, 55
The Muse has broke the twilight gloom
   To cheer the shivering native's dull abode.
And oft, beneath the odorous shade
Of Chili's boundless forests laid,
She deigns to hear the savage youth repeat 60
In loose numbers wildly sweet
Their feather-cinctured chiefs, and dusky loves.
Her track, where'er the goddess roves,
Glory pursue, and generous Shame,
Th' unconquerable Mind, and Freedom's holy flame. 65

Woods, that wave o'er Delphi's steep,
Isles, that crown th' Aegean deep,
Fields that cool Ilissus laves,
Or where Maeander's amber waves
In lingering labyrinths creep, 70
How do your tuneful echoes languish,
Mute, but to the voice of anguish!
Where each old poetic mountain
   Inspiration breathed around;
Every shade and hallow'd fountain 75
   Murmur'd deep a solemn sound:
Till the sad Nine, in Greece's evil hour
   Left their Parnassus for the Latian plains.

Alike they scorn the pomp of tyrant Power,
80 And coward Vice, that revels in her chains.
When Latium had her lofty spirit lost,
They sought, oh Albion! next, thy sea-encircled coast.

Far from the sun and summer-gale
In thy green lap was Nature's Darling laid,
85 What time, where lucid Avon stray'd,
To him the mighty Mother did unveil
Her awful face: the dauntless child
Stretch'd forth his little arms, and smiled.
'This pencil take' (she said), 'whose colours clear
90 Richly paint the vernal year:
Thine, too, these golden keys, immortal Boy!
This can unlock the gates of joy;
Of horror that, and thrilling fears,
Or ope the sacred source of sympathetic tears.'

95 Nor second He, that rode sublime
Upon the seraph-wings of Extasy
The secrets of the abyss to spy:
He pass'd the flaming bounds of place and time:
The living Throne, the sapphire-blaze
100 Where angels tremble while they gaze,
He saw; but blasted with excess of light,
Closed his eyes in endless night.
Behold where Dryden's less presumptuous car
Wide o'er the fields of glory bear
105 Two coursers of ethereal race,
With necks in thunder clothed, and long-resounding pace.

Hark, his hands the lyre explore!
Bright-eyed Fancy, hovering o'er,
Scatters from her pictured urn
Thoughts that breathe, and words that burn.   110
But ah! 'tis heard no more—
Oh! lyre divine, what daring spirit
Wakes thee now? Tho' he inherit
Nor the pride, nor ample pinion,
   That the Theban eagle bear,   115
Sailing with supreme dominion
   Thro' the azure deep of air:
Yet oft before his infant eyes would run
   Such forms as glitter in the Muse's ray
With orient hues, unborrow'd of the sun: 120
   Yet shall he mount, and keep his distant way
Beyond the limits of a vulgar fate:
Beneath the Good how far—but far above the Great.

T. Gray

178

THE PASSIONS
An Ode for Music

  When Music, heavenly maid, was young,
  While yet in early Greece she sung,
  The Passions oft, to hear her shell,
  Throng'd around her magic cell
  Exulting, trembling, raging, fainting,   5
  Possest beyond the Muse's painting;
  By turns they felt the glowing mind
  Disturb'd, delighted, raised, refined:

'Till once, 'tis said, when all were fired,
Fill'd with fury, rapt, inspired,
From the supporting myrtles round
They snatch'd her instruments of sound,
And, as they oft had heard apart
Sweet lessons of her forceful art,
Each (for Madness ruled the hour)
Would prove his own expressive power.

First Fear his hand, its skill to try,
  Amid the chords bewilder'd laid,
And back recoil'd, he knew not why,
  E'en at the sound himself had made.

Next Anger rush'd, his eyes on fire,
  In lightnings, own'd his secret stings;
In one rude clash he struck the lyre
  And swept with hurried hand the strings.

With woeful measures wan Despair,
  Low sullen sounds, his grief beguiled;
A solemn, strange, and mingled air,
  'Twas sad by fits, by starts 'twas wild.

But thou, O Hope, with eyes so fair,
  What was thy delighted measure?
Still it whisper'd promised pleasure
  And bade the lovely scenes at distance hail!
Still would her touch the strain prolong;
  And from the rocks, the woods, the vale
She call'd on Echo still through all the song;

And, where her sweetest theme she chose,
　　A soft responsive voice was heard at every close;
And Hope enchanted smiled, and waved her golden hair;—

And longer had she sung:—but with a frown
　　Revenge impatient rose:
He threw his blood-stain'd sword in thunder down;
　　And with a withering look
　　The war-denouncing trumpet took
And blew a blast so loud and dread,
Were ne'er prophetic sounds so full of woe!
　　And ever and anon he beat
　　The doubling drum with furious heat;
And, though sometimes, each dreary pause between,
　　Dejected Pity at his side
　　Her soul-subduing voice applied,
　　Yet still he kept his wild unalter'd mien,
While each strain'd ball of sight seem'd bursting from his head.

Thy numbers, Jealousy, to nought were fix'd:
　　Sad proof of thy distressful state!
Of differing themes the veering song was mix'd;
　　And now it courted Love, now raving call'd on Hate.

With eyes up-raised, as one inspired,
Pale Melancholy sat retired;
And from her wild sequester'd seat,
In notes by distance made more sweet,
Pour'd through the mellow horn her pensive soul:

And dashing soft from rocks around
    Bubbling runnels join'd the sound;
Through glades and glooms the mingled measure stole,
65 Or, o'er some haunted stream, with fond delay,
    Round an holy calm diffusing,
    Love of peace, and lonely musing,
In hollow murmurs died away.

But O! how alter'd was its sprightlier tone
70 When Cheerfulness, a nymph of healthiest hue,
    Her bow across her shoulder flung,
    Her buskins gemm'd with morning dew,
Blew an inspiring air, that dale and thicket rung,
    The hunter's call to Faun and Dryad known!
75 The oak-crown'd Sisters and their chaste-eyed Queen,
    Satyrs and Sylvan Boys, were seen
    Peeping from forth their alleys green:
Brown Exercise rejoiced to hear;
And Sport leapt up, and seized his beechen spear.

80 Last came Joy's ecstatic trial:
    He, with viny crown advancing,
    First to the lively pipe his hand addrest:
But soon he saw the brisk awakening viol
    Whose sweet entrancing voice he loved the best:
85 They would have thought who heard the strain
    They saw, in Tempe's vale, her native maids
    Amidst the festal-sounding shades
To some unwearied minstrel dancing;
While, as his flying fingers kiss'd the strings,

Book Third

Love framed with Mirth a gay fantastic round: 90
Loose were her tresses seen, her zone unbound;
And he, amidst his frolic play,
As if he would the charming air repay,
Shook thousand odours from his dewy wings.

O Music! sphere-descended maid, 95
Friend of Pleasure, Wisdom's aid!
Why, goddess! why, to us denied,
Lay'st thou thy ancient lyre aside?
As in that loved Athenian bower
You learn'd an all-commanding power, 100
Thy mimic soul, O Nymph endear'd,
Can well recall what then it heard.
Where is thy native simple heart
Devote to Virtue, Fancy, Art?
Arise, as in that elder time, 105
Warm, energic, chaste, sublime!
Thy wonders, in that god-like age,
Fill thy recording Sister's page;—
'Tis said, and I believe the tale,
Thy humblest reed could more prevail, 110
Had more of strength, diviner rage,
Than all which charms this laggard age:
E'en all at once together found,
Cecilia's mingled world of sound:—
O bid our vain endeavours cease: 115
Revive the just designs of Greece:
Return in all thy simple state!
Confirm the tales her sons relate!

W. Collins

179

THE SONG OF DAVID

He sang of God, the mighty source
Of all things, the stupendous force
  On which all strength depends:
From Whose right arm, beneath Whose eyes,
All period, power, and enterprise
  Commences, reigns, and ends.

The world, the clustering spheres He made,
The glorious light, the soothing shade,
  Dale, champaign, grove and hill:
The multitudinous abyss,
Where secrecy remains in bliss,
  And wisdom hides her skill.

Tell them, I AM, Jehovah said
To Moses: while Earth heard in dread,
  And, smitten to the heart,
At once, above, beneath, around,
All Nature, without voice or sound,
  Replied, 'O Lord, THOU ART.'

C. Smart

180

INFANT JOY

'I have no name;
I am but two days old.'
—What shall I call thee?
'I happy am;
Joy is my name.'
—Sweet joy befall thee!

Pretty joy!
Sweet joy, but two days old;
Sweet joy I call thee:
Thou dost smile:
I sing the while,
Sweet joy befall thee!

W. Blake

181

A CRADLE SONG

Sleep, sleep, beauty bright,
Dreaming in the joys of night;
Sleep, sleep; in thy sleep
Little sorrows sit and weep.

Sweet babe, in thy face
Soft desires I can trace,
Secret joys and secret smiles,
Little pretty infant wiles.

As thy softest limbs I feel,
Smiles as of the morning steal
O'er thy cheek, and o'er thy breast
Where thy little heart doth rest.

Oh the cunning wiles that creep
In thy little heart asleep!
When thy little heart doth wake,
Then the dreadful light shall break.

W. Blake

182

ODE ON THE SPRING

Lo! where the rosy-bosom'd Hours,
    Fair Venus' train, appear,
Disclose the long-expecting flowers
    And wake the purple year!
The Attic warbler pours her throat
Responsive to the cuckoo's note,
The untaught harmony of Spring:
While, whispering pleasure as they fly,
Cool Zephyrs thro' the clear blue sky
    Their gather'd fragrance fling.

Where'er the oak's thick branches stretch
    A broader, browner shade,
Where'er the rude and moss-grown beech
    O'er-canopies the glade,
Beside some water's rushy brink
With me the Muse shall sit, and think
(At ease reclined in rustic state)
How vain the ardour of the crowd,
How low, how little are the proud,
    How indigent the great!

Still is the toiling hand of Care;
    The panting herds repose:
Yet hark, how thro' the peopled air
    The busy murmur glows!

The insect-youth are on the wing,
Eager to taste the honied spring
And float amid the liquid noon:
Some lightly o'er the current skim,
Some show their gaily-gilded trim
   Quick-glancing to the sun.

To Contemplation's sober eye
   Such is the race of Man:
And they that creep, and they that fly,
   Shall end where they began.
Alike the Busy and the Gay
But flutter thro' life's little day,
In Fortune's varying colours drest:
Brush'd by the hand of rough Mischance,
Or chill'd by Age, their airy dance
   They leave, in dust to rest.

Methinks I hear in accents low
   The sportive kind reply:
Poor moralist! and what art thou?
   A solitary fly!
Thy joys no glittering female meets,
No hive hast thou of hoarded sweets,
No painted plumage to display:
On hasty wings thy youth is flown;
Thy sun is set, thy spring is gone—
   We frolic while 'tis May.

T. Gray

183

THE POPLAR FIELD

The poplars are fell'd; farewell to the shade
And the whispering sound of the cool colonnade;
The winds play no longer and sing in the leaves,
Nor Ouse on his bosom their image receives.

Twelve years have elapsed since I first took a view
Of my favourite field, and the bank where they grew:
And now in the grass behold they are laid,
And the tree is my seat that once lent me a shade!

The blackbird has fled to another retreat
Where the hazels afford him a screen from the heat;
And the scene where his melody charm'd me before
Resounds with his sweet-flowing ditty no more.

My fugitive years are all hasting away,
And I must ere long lie as lowly as they,
With a turf on my breast and a stone at my head,
Ere another such grove shall arise in its stead.

The change both my heart and my fancy employs;
I reflect on the frailty of man and his joys:
Short-lived as we are, yet our pleasures, we see,
Have a still shorter date, and die sooner than we.

W. Cowper

184

TO A MOUSE

*On turning her up in her nest, with the plough,
November, 1785*

Wee, sleekit, cow'rin', tim'rous beastie,
O what a panic's in thy breastie!
Thou need na start awa sae hasty,
Wi' bickering brattle!
I wad be laith to rin an' chase thee   5
Wi' murd'ring pattle!

I'm truly sorry man's dominion
Has broken Nature's social union,
An' justifies that ill opinion
Which makes thee startle   10
At me, thy poor earth-born companion,
An' fellow-mortal!

I doubt na, whiles, but thou may thieve;
What then? poor beastie, thou maun live!
A daimen-icker in a thrave   15
'S a sma' request:
I'll get a blessin' wi' the lave,
And never miss't!

Thy wee bit housie, too, in ruin!
Its silly wa's the win's are strewin: 20
And naething, now, to big a new ane,
O' foggage green!

An' bleak December's winds ensuin'
Baith snell an' keen!

Thou saw the fields laid bare an' waste
An' weary winter comin' fast,
An' cozie here, beneath the blast,
Thou thought to dwell,
Till, crash! the cruel coulter past
Out thro' thy cell.

That wee bit heap o' leaves an' stibble
Has cost thee mony a weary nibble!
Now thou's turn'd out, for a' thy trouble,
But house or hald,
To thole the winter's sleety dribble
An' cranreuch cauld!

But, Mousie, thou art no thy lane
In proving foresight may be vain:
The best laid schemes o' mice an' men
Gang aft a-gley,
An' lea'e us nought but grief an' pain,
For promised joy.

Still thou art blest, compared wi' me!
The present only toucheth thee:
But, Och! I backward cast my e'e
On prospects drear!
An' forward, tho' I canna see,
I guess an' fear!

R. Burns

185

A WISH

Mine be a cot beside the hill;
A bee-hive's hum shall soothe my ear;
A willowy brook that turns a mill,
With many a fall shall linger near.

The swallow, oft, beneath my thatch 5
Shall twitter from her clay-built nest;
Oft shall the pilgrim lift the latch,
And share my meal, a welcome guest.

Around my ivied porch shall spring
Each fragrant flower that drinks the dew; 10
And Lucy, at her wheel, shall sing
In russet-gown and apron blue.

The village-church among the trees,
Where first our marriage-vows were given,
With merry peals shall swell the breeze 15
And point with taper spire to Heaven.

S. Rogers

186

ODE TO EVENING

If aught of oaten stop or pastoral song
May hope, O pensive Eve, to soothe thine ear
   Like thy own solemn springs,
    Thy springs, and dying gales;

5 O Nymph reserved,—while now the bright-hair'd sun
  Sits in yon western tent, whose cloudy skirts,
        With brede ethereal wove,
        O'erhang his wavy bed;

  Now air is hush'd, save where the weak-eyed bat
10 With short shrill shriek flits by on leathern wing,
        Or where the beetle winds
        His small but sullen horn,

  As oft he rises midst the twilight path,
  Against the pilgrim borne in heedless hum,—
15   Now teach me, maid composed,
        To breathe some soften'd strain

  Whose numbers, stealing through thy darkening vale,
  May not unseemly with its stillness suit;
        As, musing slow, I hail
20   Thy genial loved return.

  For when thy folding-star arising shows
  His paly circlet, at his warning lamp
        The fragrant Hours, and Elves
        Who slept in buds the day,

25 And many a Nymph who wreathes her brows with sedge
  And sheds the freshening dew, and, lovelier still,
        The pensive Pleasures sweet,
        Prepare thy shadowy car.

Then let me rove some wild and heathy scene;
Or find some ruin midst its dreary dells,
    Whose walls more awful nod
    By thy religious gleams.

Or, if chill blustering winds or driving rain
Prevent my willing feet, be mine the hut
    That, from the mountain's side,
    Views wilds, and swelling floods,

And hamlets brown, and dim-discover'd spires;
And hears their simple bell; and marks o'er all
    Thy dewy fingers draw
    The gradual dusky veil.

While Spring shall pour his showers, as oft he wont,
And bathe thy breathing tresses, meekest Eve!
    While Summer loves to sport
    Beneath thy lingering light;

While sallow Autumn fills thy lap with leaves;
Or Winter, yelling through the troublous air,
    Affrights thy shrinking train
    And rudely rends thy robes;

So long, regardful of thy quiet rule,
Shall Fancy, Friendship, Science, smiling Peace,
    Thy gentlest influence own,
    And love thy favourite name!

W. Collins

187

ELEGY WRITTEN IN A COUNTRY CHURCHYARD

The curfew tolls the knell of parting day,
The lowing herd wind slowly o'er the lea,
The ploughman homeward plods his weary way,
And leaves the world to darkness and to me.

5 Now fades the glimmering landscape on the sight,
And all the air a solemn stillness holds,
Save where the beetle wheels his droning flight,
And drowsy tinklings lull the distant folds:

Save that from yonder ivy-mantled tower
10 The moping owl does to the moon complain
Of such as, wandering near her secret bower,
Molest her ancient solitary reign.

Beneath those rugged elms, that yew-tree's shade
Where heaves the turf in many a mouldering heap,
15 Each in his narrow cell for ever laid,
The rude forefathers of the hamlet sleep.

The breezy call of incense-breathing morn,
The swallow twittering from the straw-built shed,
The cock's shrill clarion, or the echoing horn,
20 No more shall rouse them from their lowly bed.

For them no more the blazing hearth shall burn
Or busy housewife ply her evening care:
No children run to lisp their sire's return,
Or climb his knees the envied kiss to share.

... *from yonder ivy-mantled tower*
The moping owl does to the moon complain.

Oft did the harvest to their sickle yield, 25
Their furrow oft the stubborn glebe has broke;
How jocund did they drive their team afield!
How bow'd the woods beneath their sturdy stroke!

Let not ambition mock their useful toil,
Their homely joys, and destiny obscure; 30
Nor grandeur hear with a disdainful smile
The short and simple annals of the poor.

The boast of heraldry, the pomp of power,
And all that beauty, all that wealth e'er gave,
Awaits alike th' inevitable hour:— 35
The paths of glory lead but to the grave.

Nor you, ye proud, impute to these the fault
If memory o'er their tomb no trophies raise,
Where through the long-drawn aisle and fretted vault
The pealing anthem swells the note of praise. 40

Can storied urn or animated bust
Back to its mansion call the fleeting breath?
Can honour's voice provoke the silent dust,
Or flattery soothe the dull cold ear of death?

Perhaps in this neglected spot is laid 45
Some heart once pregnant with celestial fire;
Hands, that the rod of empire might have sway'd,
Or waked to extasy the living lyre:

But knowledge to their eyes her ample page
Rich with the spoils of time, did ne'er unroll; 50
Chill penury repress'd their noble rage,
And froze the genial current of the soul.

Full many a gem of purest ray serene
The dark unfathom'd caves of ocean bear:
Full many a flower is born to blush unseen,
And waste its sweetness on the desert air.

Some village-Hampden, that with dauntless breast
The little tyrant of his fields withstood,
Some mute inglorious Milton here may rest,
Some Cromwell, guiltless of his country's blood.

Th' applause of listening senates to command,
The threats of pain and ruin to despise,
To scatter plenty o'er a smiling land,
And read their history in a nation's eyes

Their lot forbad: nor circumscribed alone
Their growing virtues, but their crimes confined;
Forbad to wade thro' slaughter to a throne,
And shut the gates of mercy on mankind;

The struggling pangs of conscious truth to hide,
To quench the blushes of ingenuous shame,
Or heap the shrine of luxury and pride
With incense kindled at the Muse's flame.

Far from the madding crowd's ignoble strife,
Their sober wishes never learn'd to stray;
Along the cool sequester'd vale of life
They kept the noiseless tenour of their way.

Yet e'en these bones from insult to protect
Some frail memorial still erected nigh,
With uncouth rhymes and shapeless sculpture deck'd,
Implores the passing tribute of a sigh.

Their name, their years, spelt by th' unletter'd Muse,
The place of fame and elegy supply:
And many a holy text around she strews,
That teach the rustic moralist to die.

For who, to dumb forgetfulness a prey, 85
This pleasing anxious being e'er resign'd,
Left the warm precincts of the cheerful day,
Nor cast one longing lingering look behind?

On some fond breast the parting soul relies,
Some pious drops the closing eye requires; 90
E'en from the tomb the voice of nature cries,
E'en in our ashes live their wonted fires.

For thee, who, mindful of th' unhonour'd dead,
Dost in these lines their artless tale relate;
If chance, by lonely contemplation led, 95
Some kindred spirit shall enquire thy fate,—

Haply some hoary-headed swain may say,
'Oft have we seen him at the peep of dawn
Brushing with hasty steps the dews away,
To meet the sun upon the upland lawn; 100

'There at the foot of yonder nodding beech
That wreathes its old fantastic roots so high,
His listless length at noon-tide would he stretch,
And pore upon the brook that babbles by.

'Hard by yon wood, now smiling as in scorn, 105
Muttering his wayward fancies he would rove;
Now drooping, woeful-wan, like one forlorn,
Or crazed with care, or cross'd in hopeless love.

'One morn I miss'd him on the custom'd hill,
Along the heath, and near his favourite tree;
Another came; nor yet beside the rill,
Nor up the lawn, nor at the wood was he;

'The next with dirges due in sad array
Slow through the church-way path we saw him borne,—
Approach and read (for thou canst read) the lay
Graved on the stone beneath yon aged thorn.'

THE EPITAPH

Here rests his head upon the lap of earth
A youth, to fortune and to fame unknown;
Fair Science frown'd not on his humble birth
And melancholy mark'd him for her own.

Large was his bounty, and his soul sincere;
Heaven did a recompense as largely send:
He gave to misery (all he had) a tear,
He gain'd from Heaven ('twas all he wish'd) a friend.

No farther seek his merits to disclose,
Or draw his frailties from their dread abode,
(There they alike in trembling hope repose,)
The bosom of his Father and his God.

T. Gray

188

MARY MORISON

O Mary, at thy window be,
It is the wish'd, the trysted hour!
Those smiles and glances let me see
That make the miser's treasure poor:
How blithely wad I bid the stoure,
A weary slave frae sun to sun,
Could I the rich reward secure,
The lovely Mary Morison.

Yestreen when to the trembling string
The dance gaed thro' the lighted ha',
To thee my fancy took its wing,—
I sat, but neither heard nor saw:
Tho' this was fair, and that was braw,
And yon the toast of a' the town,
I sigh'd, and said amang them a',
' Ye are na Mary Morison.'

O Mary, canst thou wreck his peace
Wha for thy sake wad gladly dee?
Or canst thou break that heart of his
Whase only faut is loving thee?
If love for love thou wilt na gie,
At least be pity to me shown;
A thought ungentle canna be
The thought o' Mary Morison.

R. Burns

189

BONNIE LESLEY

O saw ye bonnie Lesley
  As she gaed o'er the border?
She's gane, like Alexander,
  To spread her conquests farther.

To see her is to love her,
  And love but her for ever;
For Nature made her what she is,
  And ne'er made sic anither!

Thou art a queen, Fair Lesley,
  Thy subjects we, before thee;
Thou art divine, Fair Lesley,
  The hearts o' men adore thee.

The Deil he could na scaith thee,
  Or aught that wad belang thee;
He'd look into thy bonnie face,
  And say 'I canna wrang thee!'

The Powers aboon will tent thee;
  Misfortune sha' na steer thee;
Thou 'rt like themselves sae lovely
  That ill they'll ne'er let near thee.

Return again, Fair Lesley,
  Return to Caledonie!
That we may brag we hae a lass
  There's nane again sae bonnie.

R. Burns

190

O my Luve's like a red, red rose
  That's newly sprung in June:
O my Luve's like the melodie
  That's sweetly play'd in tune.

As fair art thou, my bonnie lass,
  So deep in luve am I:
And I will luve thee still, my dear,
  Till a' the seas gang dry:

Till a' the seas gang dry, my dear,
  And the rocks melt wi' the sun;
I will luve thee still, my dear,
  While the sands o' life shall run.

And fare thee weel, my only Luve!
  And fare thee weel awhile;
And I will come again, my Luve,
  Tho' it were ten thousand mile.

R. Burns

191

HIGHLAND MARY

Ye banks and braes and streams around
  The castle o' Montgomery,
Green be your woods, and fair your flowers,
  Your waters never drumlie!
There simmer first unfauld her robes,
  And there the langest tarry;

For there I took the last fareweel
  O' my sweet Highland Mary.

How sweetly bloom'd the gay green birk,
  How rich the hawthorn's blossom,
As underneath their fragrant shade
  I clasp'd her to my bosom!
The golden hours on angel wings
  Flew o'er me and my dearie;
For dear to me as light and life
  Was my sweet Highland Mary.

Wi' mony a vow and lock'd embrace
  Our parting was fu' tender;
And pledging aft to meet again,
  We tore oursels asunder;
But, Oh! fell Death's untimely frost,
  That nipt my flower sae early!
Now green's the sod, and cauld's the clay,
  That wraps my Highland Mary!

O pale, pale now, those rosy lips,
  I aft hae kiss'd sae fondly;
And closed for aye the sparkling glance
  That dwelt on me sae kindly;
And mouldering now in silent dust
  That heart that lo'ed me dearly!
But still within my bosom's core
  Shall live my Highland Mary.

R. Burns

192

AULD ROBIN GRAY

When the sheep are in the fauld, and the kye at hame,
And a' the world to rest are gane,
The waes o' my heart fa' in showers frae my e'e,
While my gudeman lies sound by me.

Young Jamie lo'ed me weel, and sought me for his bride;
But saving a croun he had naething else beside:
To make the croun a pund, young Jamie gaed to sea;
And the croun and the pund were baith for me.

He hadna been awa' a week but only twa,
When my father brak his arm, and the cow was stown awa;
My mother she fell sick, and my Jamie at the sea—
And auld Robin Gray came a-courtin' me.

My father couldna work, and my mother couldna spin;
I toil'd day and night, but their bread I couldna win;
Auld Rob maintain'd them baith, and wi' tears in his e'e
Said, Jennie, for their sakes, O, marry me!

My heart it said nay; I look'd for Jamie back;
But the wind it blew high, and the ship it was a wrack;
His ship it was a wrack—why didna Jamie dee?
Or why do I live to cry, Wae's me?

My father urgit sair: my mother didna speak;
But she look'd in my face till my heart was like to break:
They gi'ed him my hand, but my heart was at the sea;
Sae auld Robin Gray he was gudeman to me.

25 I hadna been a wife a week but only four,
When mournfu' as I sat on the stane at the door,
I saw my Jamie's wraith, for I couldna think it he
Till he said, I'm come hame to marry thee.

O sair, sair did we greet, and muckle did we say;
30 We took but ae kiss, and I bad him gang away;
I wish that I were dead, but I'm no like to dee;
And why was I born to say, Wae's me!

I gang like a ghaist, and I carena to spin;
I daurna think on Jamie, for that wad be a sin;
35 But I'll do my best a gude wife aye to be,
For auld Robin Gray he is kind unto me.

Lady A. Lindsay

193

DUNCAN GRAY

Duncan Gray cam here to woo,
 Ha, ha, the wooing o't;
On blythe Yule night when we were fou,
 Ha, ha, the wooing o't:
5 Maggie coost her head fu' high,
 Look'd asklent and unco skeigh,
 Gart poor Duncan stand abeigh;
 Ha, ha, the wooing o't!

Duncan fleech'd, and Duncan pray'd;
Meg was deaf as Ailsa Craig; 10
Duncan sigh'd baith out and in,
Grat his een baith bleer't and blin',
Spak o' lowpin ower a linn!

Time and chance are but a tide,
Slighted love is sair to bide; 15
Shall I, like a fool, quoth he,
For a haughty hizzie dee?
She may gae to—France for me!

How it comes let doctors tell,
Meg grew sick—as he grew well; 20
Something in her bosom wrings,
For relief a sigh she brings!
And O, her een, they spak sic things!

Duncan was a lad o' grace;
Maggie's was a piteous case; 25
Duncan couldna be her death,
Swelling pity smoor'd his wrath;
Now they're crouse and canty baith:
    Ha, ha, the wooing o't!

R. Burns

194

THE SAILOR'S WIFE

And are ye sure the news is true?
    And are ye sure he's weel?
Is this the time to think o' wark?
    Ye jades, lay by your wheel;

Is this the time to spin a thread,
  When Colin's at the door?
Reach down my cloak, I'll to the quay,
  And see him come ashore,
For there's nae luck about the house,
  There's nae luck at a';
There's little pleasure in the house
  When our gudeman's awa'.

And gie to me my bigonet,
  My bishop's satin gown;
For I maun tell the baillie's wife
  That Colin's in the town.
My Turkey slippers maun gae on,
  My stockins pearly blue;
It's a' to pleasure our gudeman,
  For he's baith leal and true.

Rise, lass, and mak a clean fireside,
  Put on the muckle pot;
Gie little Kate her button gown
  And Jock his Sunday coat;
And mak their shoon as black as slaes,
  Their hose as white as snaw;
It's a' to please my ain gudeman,
  For he's been long awa'.

There's twa fat hens upo' the coop
  Been fed this month and mair;

Mak haste and thraw their necks about,
  That Colin weel may fare;
And spread the table neat and clean,
  Gar ilka thing look braw,
For wha can tell how Colin fared   35
  When he was far awa'?

Sae true his heart, sae smooth his speech,
  His breath like caller air;
His very foot has music in't
  As he comes up the stair—   40
And will I see his face again?
  And will I hear him speak?
I'm downright dizzy wi' the thought,
  In troth I'm like to greet!

If Colin's weel, and weel content,   45
  I hae nae mair to crave:
And gin I live to keep him sae,
  I'm blest aboon the lave:
And will I see his face again,
  And will I hear him speak?   50
I'm downright dizzy wi' the thought,
  In troth I'm like to greet.
For there's nae luck about the house,
  There's nae luck at a';
There's little pleasure in the house   55
  When our gudeman's awa'.

W. J. Mickle

195

ABSENCE

When I think on the happy days
    I spent wi' you, my dearie;
And now what lands between us lie,
    How can I be but eerie!

How slow ye move, ye heavy hours,
    As ye were wae and weary!
It was na sae ye glinted by
    When I was wi' my dearie!

Anon.

196

JEAN

Of a' the airts the wind can blaw
    I dearly like the West,
For there the bonnie lassie lives,
    The lassie I lo'e best:
There wild woods grow, and rivers row,
    And mony a hill between;
But day and night my fancy's flight
    Is ever wi' my Jean.

I see her in the dewy flowers,
    I see her sweet and fair:
I hear her in the tunefu' birds,
    I hear her charm the air:
There's not a bonnie flower that springs
    By fountain, shaw, or green,

There's not a bonnie bird that sings 15
  But minds me o' my Jean.

O blaw ye westlin winds, blaw saft
  Amang the leafy trees;
Wi' balmy gale, frae hill and dale
  Bring hame the laden bees; 20
And bring the lassie back to me
  That's aye sae neat and clean;
Ae smile o' her wad banish care,
  Sae charming is my Jean.

What sighs and vows amang the knowes 25
  Hae pass'd atween us twa!
How fond to meet, how wae to part
  That night she gaed awa!
The Powers aboon can only ken
  To whom the heart is seen, 30
That nane can be sae dear to me
  As my sweet lovely Jean!

R. Burns

197

JOHN ANDERSON

John Anderson my jo, John,
When we were first acquent
Your locks were like the raven,
Your bonnie brow was brent;
But now your brow is bald, John, 5
Your locks are like the snow;
But blessings on your frosty pow,
John Anderson my jo.

John Anderson my jo, John,
We clamb the hill thegither,
And mony a canty day, John,
We've had wi' ane anither:
Now we maun totter down, John,
But hand in hand we'll go,
And sleep thegither at the foot,
John Anderson my jo.

R. Burns

198

THE LAND O' THE LEAL

I'm wearing awa', Jean,
Like snaw when its thaw, Jean,
I'm wearing awa'
  To the land o' the leal.
There's nae sorrow there, Jean,
There's neither cauld nor care, Jean,
The day is aye fair
  In the land o' the leal.

Ye were aye leal and true, Jean,
Your task's ended noo, Jean,
And I'll welcome you
  To the land o' the leal.
Our bonnie bairn's there, Jean,
She was baith guid and fair, Jean;
O we grudged her right sair
  To the land o' the leal!

Ye distant spires, ye antique towers
That crown the watery glade

Then dry that tearfu' e'e, Jean,
   My soul langs to be free, Jean,
   And angels wait on me
      To the land o' the leal.
   Now fare ye weel, my ain Jean,
   This warld's care is vain, Jean;
   We'll meet and aye be fain
      In the land o' the leal!

                                   Lady Nairne

199

ODE ON A DISTANT PROSPECT OF ETON COLLEGE

Ye distant spires, ye antique towers
   That crown the watery glade,
Where grateful Science still adores
   Her Henry's holy shade;
And ye, that from the stately brow
Of Windsor's heights th' expanse below
Of grove, of lawn, of mead survey,
Whose turf, whose shade, whose flowers among
Wanders the hoary Thames along
   His silver-winding way:

Ah happy hills! ah pleasing shade!
   Ah fields beloved in vain!
Where once my careless childhood stray'd,
   A stranger yet to pain!
I feel the gales that from ye blow
A momentary bliss bestow,

As waving fresh their gladsome wing
My weary soul they seem to soothe,
And, redolent of joy and youth,
    To breathe a second spring.

Say, Father Thames, for thou hast seen
    Full many a sprightly race
Disporting on thy margent green
    The paths of pleasure trace;
Who foremost now delight to cleave
With pliant arm, thy glassy wave?
The captive linnet which enthral?
What idle progeny succeed
To chase the rolling circle's speed
    Or urge the flying ball?

While some on earnest business bent
    Their murmuring labours ply
'Gainst graver hours that bring constraint
    To sweeten liberty:
Some bold adventurers disdain
The limits of their little reign
And unknown regions dare descry:
Still as they run they look behind,
They hear a voice in every wind,
    And snatch a fearful joy.

Gay hope is theirs by fancy fed,
    Less pleasing when possest:
The tear forgot as soon as shed,
    The sunshine of the breast:

Theirs buxom health, of rosy hue,
Wild wit, invention ever new,
And lively cheer, of vigour born;
The thoughtless day, the easy night,
The spirits pure, the slumbers light
  That fly th' approach of morn.

Alas! regardless of their doom
  The little victims play;
No sense have they of ills to come
  Nor care beyond to-day:
Yet see how all around 'em wait
The ministers of human fate
And black Misfortune's baleful train!
Ah show them where in ambush stand
To seize their prey, the murderous band!
  Ah, tell them they are men!

These shall the fury Passions tear,
  The vultures of the mind,
Disdainful Anger, pallid Fear,
  And Shame that sculks behind,
Or pining Love shall waste their youth,
Or Jealousy with rankling tooth
That inly gnaws the secret heart,
And Envy wan, and faded Care,
Grim-visaged comfortless Despair,
  And Sorrow's piercing dart.

Ambition this shall tempt to rise,
  Then whirl the wretch from high

>   To bitter Scorn a sacrifice
>   And grinning Infamy.
> 75 The stings of Falsehood those shall try
>   And hard Unkindness' alter'd eye,
>   That mocks the tear it forced to flow;
>   And keen Remorse with blood defiled,
>   And moody Madness laughing wild
> 80   Amid severest woe.
>
>   Lo, in the vale of years beneath
>   A griesly troop are seen,
>   The painful family of Death,
>   More hideous than their queen:
> 85 This racks the joints, this fires the veins,
>   That every labouring sinew strains,
>   Those in the deeper vitals rage:
>   Lo! Poverty, to fill the band,
>   That numbs the soul with icy hand,
> 90   And slow-consuming Age.
>
>   To each his sufferings: all are men,
>   Condemn'd alike to groan;
>   The tender for another's pain,
>   Th' unfeeling for his own.
> 95 Yet, ah! why should they know their fate,
>   Since sorrow never comes too late,
>   And happiness too swiftly flies?
>   Thought would destroy their paradise.
>   No more;—where ignorance is bliss,
> 100   'Tis folly to be wise.

T. Gray

200

THE SHRUBBERY

O happy shades! to me unblest!
    Friendly to peace, but not to me!
How ill the scene that offers rest,
    And heart that cannot rest, agree!

This glassy stream, that spreading pine,   5
    Those alders quivering to the breeze,
Might soothe a soul less hurt than mine,
    And please, if anything could please.

But fix'd unalterable Care
    Foregoes not what she feels within,   10
Shows the same sadness everywhere,
    And slights the season and the scene.

For all that pleased in wood or lawn
    While Peace possess'd these silent bowers,
Her animating smile withdrawn,   15
    Has lost its beauties and its powers.

The saint or moralist should tread
    This moss-grown alley, musing, slow,
They seek like me the secret shade,
    But not, like me, to nourish woe!   20

Me, fruitful scenes and prospects waste
    Alike admonish not to roam;
These tell me of enjoyments past,
    And those of sorrows yet to come.

W. Cowper

201

HYMN TO ADVERSITY

Daughter of Jove, relentless power,
    Thou tamer of the human breast,
Whose iron scourge and torturing hour
    The bad affright, afflict the best!
5 Bound in thy adamantine chain
    The proud are taught to taste of pain,
And purple tyrants vainly groan
With pangs unfelt before, unpitied and alone.

When first thy Sire to send on earth
10   Virtue, his darling child, design'd,
To thee he gave the heavenly birth
    And bade to form her infant mind.
Stern, rugged nurse; thy rigid lore
With patience many a year she bore;
15 What sorrow was, thou bad'st her know,
And from her own she learn'd to melt at others' woe.

Scared at thy frown terrific, fly
    Self-pleasing Folly's idle brood,
Wild Laughter, Noise, and thoughtless Joy,
20   And leave us leisure to be good.
Light they disperse, and with them go
The summer friend, the flattering foe;
By vain Prosperity received,
To her they vow their truth, and are again believed.

25 Wisdom in sable garb array'd
    Immersed in rapturous thought profound,

And Melancholy, silent maid,
  With leaden eye, that loves the ground,
Still on thy solemn steps attend:
Warm Charity, the general friend,
With Justice, to herself severe,
And Pity dropping soft the sadly-pleasing tear.

Oh! gently on thy suppliant's head
  Dread goddess, lay thy chastening hand!
Not in thy Gorgon terrors clad,
  Nor circled with the vengeful band
(As by the impious thou art seen)
With thundering voice, and threatening mien,
With screaming Horror's funeral cry,
Despair, and fell Disease, and ghastly Poverty;—

Thy form benign, oh goddess, wear,
  Thy milder influence impart,
Thy philosophic train be there
  To soften, not to wound my heart.
The generous spark extinct revive,
Teach me to love and to forgive,
Exact my own defects to scan,
What others are to feel, and know myself a Man.

T. Gray

202

THE SOLITUDE OF ALEXANDER SELKIRK

I am monarch of all I survey;
My right there is none to dispute;
From the centre all round to the sea
I am lord of the fowl and the brute.

O Solitude! where are the charms
That sages have seen in thy face?
Better dwell in the midst of alarms,
Than reign in this horrible place.

I am out of humanity's reach,
I must finish my journey alone,
Never hear the sweet music of speech;
I start at the sound of my own.
The beasts that roam over the plain
My form with indifference see;
They are so unacquainted with man,
Their tameness is shocking to me.

Society, Friendship, and Love
Divinely bestow'd upon man,
Oh, had I the wings of a dove
How soon would I taste you again!
My sorrows I then might assuage
In the ways of religion and truth,
Might learn from the wisdom of age,
And be cheer'd by the sallies of youth.

Ye winds that have made me your sport,
Convey to this desolate shore
Some cordial endearing report
Of a land I shall visit no more:
My friends, do they now and then send
A wish or a thought after me?
O tell me I yet have a friend,
Though a friend I am never to see.

How fleet is a glance of the mind!
Compared with the speed of its flight,
The tempest itself lags behind, 35
And the swift-wingéd arrows of light.
When I think of my own native land
In a moment I seem to be there;
But alas! recollection at hand
Soon hurries me back to despair. 40

But the sea-fowl is gone to her nest,
The beast is laid down in his lair;
Even here is a season of rest,
And I to my cabin repair.
There's mercy in every place, 45
And mercy, encouraging thought!
Gives even affliction a grace
And reconciles man to his lot.

W. Cowper

203

TO MARY UNWIN

Mary! I want a lyre with other strings,
Such aid from Heaven as some have feign'd they drew,
An eloquence scarce given to mortals, new
And undebased by praise of meaner things,

That ere through age or woe I shed my wings 5
I may record thy worth with honour due,
In verse as musical as thou art true,
And that immortalizes whom it sings:—

But thou hast little need.　There is a Book
By seraphs writ with beams of heavenly light,
On which the eyes of God not rarely look,

A chronicle of actions just and bright—
There all thy deeds, my faithful Mary, shine;
And since thou own'st that praise, I spare thee mine.

W. Cowper

204

TO THE SAME

The twentieth year is well-nigh past
Since first our sky was overcast;
Ah would that this might be the last!
　　My Mary!

Thy spirits have a fainter flow,
I see thee daily weaker grow—
'Twas my distress that brought thee low,
　　My Mary!

Thy needles, once a shining store,
For my sake restless heretofore,
Now rust disused, and shine no more;
　　My Mary!

For though thou gladly wouldst fulfil
The same kind office for me still,
Thy sight now seconds not thy will,
　　My Mary!

But well thou play'st the housewife's part,
And all thy threads with magic art
Have wound themselves about this heart,
    My Mary!

Thy indistinct expressions seem
Like language utter'd in a dream;
Yet me they charm, whate'er the theme,
    My Mary!

Thy silver locks, once auburn bright,
Are still more lovely in my sight
Than golden beams of orient light,
    My Mary!

For could I view nor them nor thee,
What sight worth seeing could I see?
The sun would rise in vain for me,
    My Mary!

Partakers of thy sad decline
Thy hands their little force resign;
Yet, gently prest, press gently mine,
    My Mary!

Such feebleness of limbs thou prov'st
That now at every step thou mov'st
Upheld by two ; yet still thou lov'st,
    My Mary!

And still to love, though prest with ill,
In wintry age to feel no chill,
With me is to be lovely still,
    My Mary!

> But ah! by constant heed I know
> How oft the sadness that I show
> Transforms thy smiles to looks of woe,
>   My Mary!
>
> And should my future lot be cast
> With much resemblance of the past,
> Thy worn-out heart will break at last—
>   My Mary!

W. Cowper

205

THE CASTAWAY

> Obscurest night involved the sky,
>   The Atlantic billows roar'd
> When such a destined wretch as I,
>   Wash'd headlong from on board,
> Of friends, of hope, of all bereft,
> His floating home for ever left.
>
> No braver chief could Albion boast
>   Than he with whom he went,
> Nor ever ship left Albion's coast
>   With warmer wishes sent.
> He loved them both, but both in vain,
> Nor him beheld, nor her again.
>
> Not long beneath the whelming brine,
>   Expert to swim, he lay;
> Nor soon he felt his strength decline,
>   Or courage die away;

But waged with death a lasting strife,
Supported by despair of life.

He shouted: nor his friends had fail'd
   To check the vessel's course, 20
But so the furious blast prevail'd,
   That, pitiless perforce,
They left their outcast mate behind,
And scudded still before the wind.

Some succour yet they could afford; 25
   And such as storms allow,
The cask, the coop, the floated cord,
   Delay'd not to bestow.
But he (they knew) nor ship nor shore,
Whate'er they gave, should visit more. 30

Nor, cruel as it seem'd, could he
   Their haste himself condemn,
Aware that flight, in such a sea,
   Alone could rescue them;
Yet bitter felt it still to die 35
Deserted, and his friends so nigh.

He long survives, who lives an hour
   In ocean, self-upheld;
And so long he, with unspent power,
   His destiny repell'd; 40
And ever, as the minutes flew,
Entreated help, or cried 'Adieu!'

At length, his transient respite past,
   His comrades, who before
Had heard his voice in every blast,
   Could catch the sound no more;
For then, by toil subdued, he drank
The stifling wave, and then he sank.

No poet wept him; but the page
   Of narrative sincere,
That tells his name, his worth, his age,
   Is wet with Anson's tear:
And tears by bards or heroes shed
Alike immortalize the dead.

I therefore purpose not, or dream,
   Descanting on his fate,
To give the melancholy theme
   A more enduring date:
But misery still delights to trace
Its semblance in another's case.

No voice divine the storm allay'd,
   No light propitious shone,
When, snatch'd from all effectual aid,
   We perish'd, each alone:
But I beneath a rougher sea,
And whelm'd in deeper gulfs than he.

W. Cowper

206

TOMORROW

In the downhill of life, when I find I'm declining,
  May my fate no less fortunate be
Than a snug elbow-chair will afford for reclining,
  And a cot that o'erlooks the wide sea;
With an ambling pad-pony to pace o'er the lawn,
  While I carol away idle sorrow,
And blithe as the lark that each day hails the dawn
  Look forward with hope for Tomorrow.

With a porch at my door, both for shelter and shade too,
  As the sunshine or rain may prevail;
And a small spot of ground for the use of the spade too,
  With a barn for the use of the flail:
A cow for my dairy, a dog for my game,
  And a purse when a friend wants to borrow;
I'll envy no Nabob his riches or fame,
  Or what honours may wait him Tomorrow.

From the bleak northern blast may my cot be completely
  Secured by a neighbouring hill;
And at night may repose steal upon me more sweetly
  By the sound of a murmuring rill:
And while peace and plenty I find at my board,
  With a heart free from sickness and sorrow,
With my friends may I share what Today may afford,
  And let them spread the table Tomorrow.

25 And when I at last must throw off this frail cov'ring
    Which I've worn for three-score years and ten,
On the brink of the grave I'll not seek to keep hov'ring,
    Nor my thread wish to spin o'er again:
But my face in the glass I'll serenely survey,
30   And with smiles count each wrinkle and furrow;
As this old worn-out stuff, which is threadbare Today
    May become Everlasting Tomorrow.

J. Collins

207

Life! I know not what thou art,
    But know that thou and I must part;
And when, or how, or where we met
    I own to me's a secret yet.

5   Life! we've been long together
Through pleasant and through cloudy weather;
'Tis hard to part when friends are dear—
Perhaps 'twill cost a sigh, a tear;
—Then steal away, give little warning,
10   Choose thine own time;
Say not Good Night,—but in some brighter clime
    Bid me Good Morning.

A. L. Barbauld

BOOK FOURTH

208

TO THE MUSES

Whether on Ida's shady brow,
   Or in the chambers of the East,
The chambers of the sun, that now
   From ancient melody have ceased;

Whether in Heaven ye wander fair,
   Or the green corners of the earth,
Or the blue regions of the air,
   Where the melodious winds have birth;

Whether on crystal rocks ye rove
   Beneath the bosom of the sea,
Wandering in many a coral grove,—
   Fair Nine, forsaking Poetry;

How have you left the ancient love
   That bards of old enjoy'd in you!
The languid strings do scarcely move,
   The sound is forced, the notes are few.

W. Blake

209

ODE ON THE POETS

Bards of Passion and of Mirth
Ye have left your souls on earth!
Have ye souls in heaven too,
Double-lived in regions new?

—Yes, and those of heaven commune
With the spheres of sun and moon;
With the noise of fountains wond'rous
And the parle of voices thund'rous;
With the whisper of heaven's trees
And one another, in soft ease
Seated on Elysian lawns
Browsed by none but Dian's fawns;
Underneath large blue-bells tented,
Where the daisies are rose-scented,
And the rose herself has got
Perfume which on earth is not;
Where the nightingale doth sing
Not a senseless, trancéd thing,
But divine melodious truth;
Philosophic numbers smooth;
Tales and golden histories
Of heaven and its mysteries.

Thus ye live on high, and then
On the earth ye live again;
And the souls ye left behind you
Teach us, here, the way to find you,

JOHN KEATS

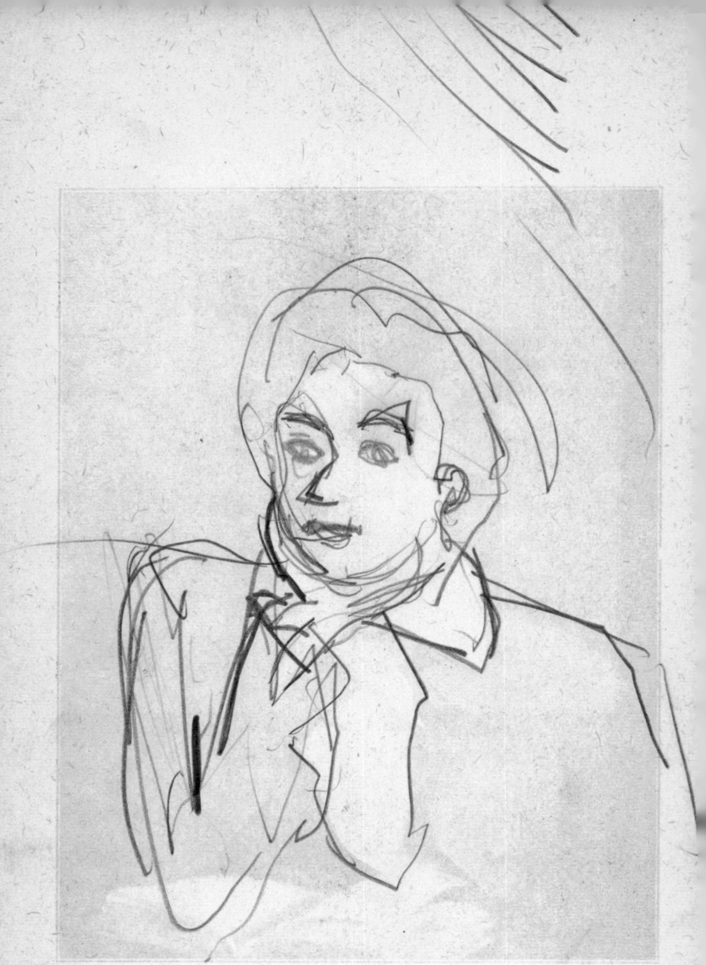

Book Fourth

Where your other souls are joying,
Never slumber'd, never cloying.
Here, your earth-born souls still speak
To mortals, of their little week; 30
Of their sorrows and delights;
Of their passions and their spites;
Of their glory and their shame;
What doth strengthen and what maim:—
Thus ye teach us, every day, 35
Wisdom, though fled far away.

Bards of Passion and of Mirth
Ye have left your souls on earth!
Ye have souls in heaven too,
Double-lived in regions new! 40

J. Keats

210

ON FIRST LOOKING INTO CHAPMAN'S HOMER

Much have I travell'd in the realms of gold
And many goodly states and kingdoms seen;
Round many western islands have I been
Which bards in fealty to Apollo hold.

Oft of one wide expanse had I been told 5
That deep-brow'd Homer ruled as his demesne:
Yet did I never breathe its pure serene
Till I heard Chapman speak out loud and bold:

The Golden Treasury

—Then felt I like some watcher of the skies
When a new planet swims into his ken;
Or like stout Cortez, when with eagle eyes

He stared at the Pacific—and all his men
Look'd at each other with a wild surmise—
Silent, upon a peak in Darien.

J. Keats

211

LOVE

All thoughts, all passions, all delights,
Whatever stirs this mortal frame,
All are but ministers of Love,
    And feed his sacred flame.

Oft in my waking dreams do I
Live o'er again that happy hour,
When mid-way on the mount I lay,
    Beside the ruin'd tower.

The moonshine stealing o'er the scene
Had blended with the lights of eve;
And she was there, my hope, my joy,
    My own dear Genevieve!

She lean'd against the arméd man,
The statue of the arméd knight;
She stood and listen'd to my lay,
    Amid the lingering light.

Few sorrows hath she of her own,
My hope! my joy! my Genevieve!
She loves me best, whene'er I sing
    The songs that make her grieve.

I play'd a soft and doleful air,
I sang an old and moving story—
An old rude song, that suited well
    That ruin wild and hoary.

She listen'd with a flitting blush,
With downcast eyes and modest grace;
For well she knew, I could not choose
    But gaze upon her face.

I told her of the Knight that wore
Upon his shield a burning brand;
And that for ten long years he woo'd
    The Lady of the Land.

I told her how he pined: and ah!
The deep, the low, the pleading tone
With which I sang another's love
    Interpreted my own.

She listen'd with a flitting blush,
With downcast eyes, and modest grace;
And she forgave me, that I gazed
    Too fondly on her face!

But when I told the cruel scorn
That crazed that bold and lovely Knight,
And that he cross'd the mountain-woods,
    Nor rested day nor night;

⁴⁵ That sometimes from the savage den,
And sometimes from the darksome shade,
And sometimes starting up at once
    In green and sunny glade,—

There came and look'd him in the face
⁵⁰ An angel beautiful and bright;
And that he knew it was a Fiend.
    This miserable Knight!

And that unknowing what he did,
He leap'd amid a murderous band,
⁵⁵ And saved from outrage worse than death
    The Lady of the Land;—

And how she wept, and clasp'd his knees;
And how she tended him in vain—
And ever strove to expiate
⁶⁰   The scorn that crazed his brain;—

And that she nursed him in a cave,
And how his madness went away,
When on the yellow forest-leaves
    A dying man he lay;—

⁶⁵ His dying words—but when I reach'd
That tenderest strain of all the ditty,
My faltering voice and pausing harp
    Disturb'd her soul with pity!

All impulses of soul and sense
⁷⁰ Had thrill'd my guileless Genevieve;

SAMUEL TAYLOR COLERIDGE

The music and the doleful tale,
    The rich and balmy eve;

And hopes, and fears that kindle hope,
An undistinguishable throng,
And gentle wishes long subdued,
    Subdued and cherish'd long!

She wept with pity and delight,
She blush'd with love, and virgin shame;
And like the murmur of a dream,
    I heard her breathe my name.

Her bosom heaved—she stepp'd aside,
As conscious of my look she stept—
Then suddenly, with timorous eye
    She fled to me and wept.

She half inclosed me with her arms,
She press'd me with a meek embrace;
And bending back her head, look'd up,
    And gazed upon my face.

'Twas partly love, and partly fear,
And partly 'twas a bashful art
That I might rather feel, than see,
    The swelling of her heart.

I calm'd her fears, and she was calm
And told her love with virgin pride;
And so I won my Genevieve,
    My bright and beauteous Bride.

S. T. Coleridge

212

ALL FOR LOVE

O talk not to me of a name great in story;
The days of our youth are the days of our glory;
And the myrtle and ivy of sweet two-and-twenty
Are worth all your laurels, though ever so plenty.

5 What are garlands and crowns to the brow that is wrinkled?
'Tis but as a dead flower with May-dew besprinkled:
Then away with all such from the head that is hoary—
What care I for the wreaths that can only give glory?

Oh fame!—if I e'er took delight in thy praises,
10 'Twas less for the sake of thy high-sounding phrases,
Than to see the bright eyes of the dear one discover
She thought that I was not unworthy to love her.

There chiefly I sought thee, there only I found thee;
Her glance was the best of the rays that surround thee;
15 When it sparkled o'er aught that was bright in my story,
I knew it was love, and I felt it was glory.

Lord Byron

213

THE OUTLAW

O Brignall banks are wild and fair,
   And Greta woods are green,
And you may gather garlands there
   Would grace a summer-queen.
And as I rode by Dalton-Hall,
   Beneath the turrets high,
A maiden on the castle-wall
   Was singing merrily:
'O Brignall banks are fresh and fair,
   And Greta woods are green;
I'd rather rove with Edmund there
   Than reign our English queen.'

'If, Maiden, thou wouldst wend with me,
   To leave both tower and town,
Thou first must guess what life lead we
   That dwell by dale and down.
And if thou canst that riddle read,
   As read full well you may,
Then to the greenwood shalt thou speed
   As blithe as Queen of May.'
Yet sung she, 'Brignall banks are fair,
   And Greta woods are green;
I'd rather rove with Edmund there
   Than reign our English queen.

'I read you, by your bugle-horn
   And by your palfrey good,

I read you for a ranger sworn
  To keep the king's greenwood.'
'A Ranger, lady, winds his horn,
  And 'tis at peep of light;
His blast is heard at merry morn,
  And mine at dead of night.'
Yet sung she, 'Brignall banks are fair,
  And Greta woods are gay;
I would I were with Edmund there
  To reign his Queen of May!

'With burnish'd brand and musketoon
  So gallantly you come,
I read you for a bold Dragoon
  That lists the tuck of drum.'
'I list no more the tuck of drum,
  No more the trumpet hear;
But when the beetle sounds his hum
  My comrades take the spear.
And O! though Brignall banks be fair
  And Greta woods be gay,
Yet mickle must the maiden dare
  Would reign my Queen of May!

'Maiden! a nameless life I lead,
  A nameless death I'll die;
The fiend whose lantern lights the mead
  Were better mate than I!
And when I'm with my comrades met
  Beneath the greenwood bough,—
What once we were we all forget,
  Nor think what we are now.'

Chorus

'Yet Brignall banks are fresh and fair,
  And Greta woods are green,
And you may gather garlands there
  Would grace a summer-queen.'

Sir W. Scott

214

There be none of Beauty's daughters
  With a magic like Thee;
And like music on the waters
  Is thy sweet voice to me:
When, as if its sound were causing
The charmed ocean's pausing,
The waves lie still and gleaming,
And the lull'd winds seem dreaming:
And the midnight moon is weaving
  Her bright chain o'er the deep,
Whose breast is gently heaving
  As an infant's asleep:
So the spirit bows before thee
To listen and adore thee:
With a full but soft emotion,
Like the swell of Summer's ocean.

Lord Byron

215

THE INDIAN SERENADE

I arise from dreams of Thee
In the first sweet sleep of night,
When the winds are breathing low
And the stars are shining bright:

I arise from dreams of thee,
And a spirit in my feet
Hath led me—who knows how?
To thy chamber-window, Sweet!

The wandering airs they faint
On the dark, the silent stream—
The champak odours fail
Like sweet thoughts in a dream;
The nightingale's complaint
It dies upon her heart,
As I must die on thine
O belovéd as thou art!

O lift me from the grass!
I die, I faint, I fail!
Let thy love in kisses rain
On my lips and eyelids pale.
My cheek is cold and white, alas!
My heart beats loud and fast;
Oh! press it close to thine again
Where it will break at last.

P. B. Shelley

216

She walks in beauty, like the night
Of cloudless climes and starry skies,
And all that's best of dark and bright
Meet in her aspect and her eyes;
Thus mellow'd to that tender light
Which heaven to gaudy day denies.

PERCY BYSSHE SHELLEY

One shade the more, one ray the less,
Had half impair'd the nameless grace
Which waves in every raven tress
Or softly lightens o'er her face,
Where thoughts serenely sweet express
How pure, how dear their dwelling-place.

And on that cheek and o'er that brow
So soft, so calm, yet eloquent,
The smiles that win, the tints that glow
But tell of days in goodness spent,—
A mind at peace with all below,
A heart whose love is innocent.

Lord Byron

217

She was a Phantom of delight
When first she gleam'd upon my sight;
A lovely Apparition, sent
To be a moment's ornament;
Her eyes as stars of twilight fair;
Like Twilight's too, her dusky hair;
But all things else about her drawn
From May-time and the cheerful dawn;
A dancing shape, an image gay,
To haunt, to startle, and waylay.

I saw her upon nearer view,
A Spirit, yet a Woman too!
Her household motions light and free,
And steps of virgin-liberty;
A countenance in which did meet
Sweet records, promises as sweet;

A creature not too bright or good
For human nature's daily food,
For transient sorrows, simple wiles,
Praise, blame, love, kisses, tears, and smiles.

And now I see with eye serene
The very pulse of the machine;
A being breathing thoughtful breath,
A traveller between life and death:
The reason firm, the temperate will,
Endurance, foresight, strength, and skill;
A perfect Woman, nobly plann'd
To warn, to comfort, and command;
And yet a Spirit still, and bright
With something of an angel-light.

W. Wordsworth

218

She is not fair to outward view
  As many maidens be;
Her loveliness I never knew
  Until she smiled on me.
O then I saw her eye was bright,
A well of love, a spring of light.

But now her looks are coy and cold,
  To mine they ne'er reply,
And yet I cease not to behold
  The love-light in her eye:
Her very frowns are fairer far
Than smiles of other maidens are.

H. Coleridge

219

I fear thy kisses, gentle maiden;
  Thou needest not fear mine;
My spirit is too deeply laden
  Ever to burthen thine.

I fear thy mien, thy tones, thy motion;
  Thou needest not fear mine;
Innocent is the heart's devotion
  With which I worship thine.

P. B. Shelley

220

She dwelt among the untrodden ways
  Beside the springs of Dove;
A maid whom there were none to praise,
  And very few to love.

A violet by a mossy stone
  Half-hidden from the eye!
—Fair as a star, when only one
  Is shining in the sky.

She lived unknown, and few could know
  When Lucy ceased to be;
But she is in her grave, and, oh,
  The difference to me!

W. Wordsworth

221

I travell'd among unknown men
  In lands beyond the sea;
Nor, England! did I know till then
  What love I bore to thee.

'Tis past, that melancholy dream!
  Nor will I quit thy shore
A second time; for still I seem
  To love thee more and more.

Among thy mountains did I feel
  The joy of my desire;
And she I cherish'd turn'd her wheel
  Beside an English fire.

Thy mornings show'd, thy nights conceal'd
  The bowers where Lucy play'd;
And thine too is the last green field
  That Lucy's eyes survey'd.

W. Wordsworth

222

THE EDUCATION OF NATURE

Three years she grew in sun and shower;
Then Nature said, 'A lovelier flower
On earth was never sown:
This child I to myself will take;
She shall be mine, and I will make
A lady of my own.

Book Fourth

'Myself will to my darling be
Both law and impulse: and with me
The girl, in rock and plain,
In earth and heaven, in glade and bower,
Shall feel an overseeing power
To kindle or restrain.

'She shall be sportive as the fawn
That wild with glee across the lawn
Or up the mountains springs;
And hers shall be the breathing balm,
And hers the silence and the calm
Of mute insensate things.

'The floating clouds their state shall lend
To her; for her the willow bend;
Nor shall she fail to see
Ev'n in the motions of the storm
Grace that shall mould the maiden's form
By silent sympathy.

'The stars of midnight shall be dear
To her; and she shall lean her ear
In many a secret place
Where rivulets dance their wayward round,
And beauty born of murmuring sound
Shall pass into her face.

'And vital feelings of delight
Shall rear her form to stately height,
Her virgin bosom swell;

Such thoughts to Lucy I will give
While she and I together live
Here in this happy dell.'

Thus Nature spake—The work was done—
How soon my Lucy's race was run!
She died, and left to me
This heath, this calm and quiet scene;
The memory of what has been,
And never more will be.

W. Wordsworth

223

A slumber did my spirit seal;
  I had no human fears:
She seem'd a thing that could not feel
  The touch of earthly years.

No motion has she now, no force;
  She neither hears nor sees;
Roll'd round in earth's diurnal course
  With rocks, and stones, and trees.

W. Wordsworth

224

A LOST LOVE

I meet thy pensive, moonlight face;
  Thy thrilling voice I hear;
And former hours and scenes retrace,
  Too fleeting, and too dear!

Then sighs and tears flow fast and free,
  Though none is nigh to share;
And life has nought beside for me
  So sweet is this despair.

There are crush'd hearts that will not break;
  And mine, methinks, is one;
Or thus I should not weep and wake,
  And thou to slumber gone.

I little thought it thus could be
  In days more sad and fair—
That earth could have a place for me,
  And thou no longer there.

Yet death cannot our hearts divide,
  Or make thee less my own:
'Twere sweeter sleeping at thy side
  Than watching here alone.

Yet never, never can we part,
  While Memory holds her reign:
Thine, thine is still this wither'd heart,
  Till we shall meet again.

H. F. Lyte

225

LORD ULLIN'S DAUGHTER

  A Chieftain to the Highlands bound
  Cries 'Boatman, do not tarry!
  And I'll give thee a silver pound
  To row us o'er the ferry!'

'Now who be ye, would cross Lochgyle
This dark and stormy water?'
'O I'm the chief of Ulva's isle,
And this, Lord Ullin's daughter.

'And fast before her father's men
Three days we've fled together,
For should he find us in the glen,
My blood would stain the heather.

'His horsemen hard behind us ride—
Should they our steps discover,
Then who will cheer my bonny bride,
When they have slain her lover?'

Out spoke the hardy Highland wight,
'I'll go, my chief, I'm ready:
It is not for your silver bright,
But for your winsome lady:—

'And by my word! the bonny bird
In danger shall not tarry;
So though the waves are raging white
I'll row you o'er the ferry.'

By this the storm grew loud apace,
The water-wraith was shrieking;
And in the scowl of Heaven each face
Grew dark as they were speaking.

But still as wilder blew the wind,
And as the night grew drearer,

Adown the glen rode arméd men,
Their trampling sounded nearer.

'O haste thee, haste!' the lady cries
'Though tempests round us gather;
I'll meet the raging of the skies,
But not an angry father.'

The boat has left a stormy land,
A stormy sea before her,—
When, oh! too strong for human hand
The tempest gather'd o'er her.

And still they row'd amidst the roar
Of waters fast prevailing:
Lord Ullin reach'd that fatal shore,—
His wrath was changed to wailing.

For, sore dismay'd, through storm and shade
His child he did discover;—
One lovely hand she stretch'd for aid,
And one was round her lover.

'Come back! come back!' he cried in grief
'Across this stormy water:
And I'll forgive your Highland chief,
My daughter!—Oh, my daughter!'

'Twas vain: the loud waves lash'd the shore,
Return or aid preventing:
The waters wild went o'er his child,
And he was left lamenting.

T. Campbell

LUCY GRAY

Oft I had heard of Lucy Gray:
And when I cross'd the wild,
I chanced to see at break of day;
The solitary child.

No mate, no comrade Lucy knew;
She dwelt on a wide moor,
The sweetest thing that ever grew
Beside a human door!

You yet may spy the fawn at play,
The hare upon the green;
But the sweet face of Lucy Gray
Will never more be seen.

'To-night will be a stormy night—
You to the town must go;
And take a lantern, Child, to light
Your mother through the snow.'

'That, Father! will I gladly do:
'Tis scarcely afternoon—
The minster-clock has just struck two,
And yonder is the moon!'

At this the father raised his hook,
And snapp'd a faggot-band;
He plied his work;—and Lucy took
The lantern in her hand.

WILLIAM WORDSWORTH

Not blither is the mountain roe:
With many a wanton stroke
Her feet disperse the powdery snow,
That rises up like smoke.

The storm came on before its time;
She wander'd up and down;
And many a hill did Lucy climb:
But never reach'd the town.

The wretched parents all that night;
Went shouting far and wide;
But there was neither sound nor sight
To serve them for a guide.

At day-break on a hill they stood;
That overlook'd the moor;
And thence they saw the bridge of wood
A furlong from their door.

They wept—and, turning homeward, cried
' In heaven we all shall meet!'
—When in the snow the mother spied
The print of Lucy's feet.

Then downwards from the steep hill's edge
They track'd the footmarks small;
And through the broken hawthorn hedge,
And by the long stone-wall:

And then an open field they cross'd:
The marks were still the same;

They track'd them on, nor ever lost;
And to the bridge they came:

They follow'd from the snowy bank
Those footmarks, one by one,
Into the middle of the plank;
And further there were none!

—Yet some maintain that to this day
She is a living child;
That you may see sweet Lucy Gray
Upon the lonesome wild.

O'er rough and smooth she trips along,
And never looks behind;
And sings a solitary song
That whistles in the wind.

W. Wordsworth

227

JOCK OF HAZELDEAN

'Why weep ye by the tide, ladie?
  Why weep ye by the tide?
I'll wed ye to my youngest son,
  And ye sall be his bride:
And ye sall be his bride, ladie,
  Sae comely to be seen '—

But aye she loot the tears down fa'
   For Jock of Hazeldean.

'Now let this wilfu' grief be done,
   And dry that cheek so pale;
Young Frank is chief of Errington
   And lord of Langleydale;
His step is first in peaceful ha',
   His sword in battle keen '—
But aye she loot the tears down fa'
   For Jock of Hazeldean.

'A chain of gold ye sall not lack,
   Nor braid to bind your hair,
Nor mettled hound, nor managed hawk,
   Nor palfrey fresh and fair;
And you the foremost o' them a'
   Shall ride our forest-queen '—
But aye she loot the tears down fa'
   For Jock of Hazeldean.

The kirk was deck'd at morning-tide,
   The tapers glimmer'd fair;
The priest and bridegroom wait the bride,
   And dame and knight are there:
They sought her baith by bower and ha';
   The ladie was not seen!
She's o'er the Border, and awa'
   Wi' Jock of Hazeldean.

Sir W. Scott

228

LOVE'S PHILOSOPHY

The fountains mingle with the river
  And the rivers with the ocean,
The winds of heaven mix for ever
  With a sweet emotion;
Nothing in the world is single,
  All things by a law divine
In one another's being mingle—
  Why not I with thine?

See the mountains kiss high heaven,
  And the waves clasp one another;
No sister-flower would be forgiven
  If it disdain'd its brother:
And the sunlight clasps the earth,
  And the moonbeams kiss the sea—
What are all these kissings worth,
  If thou kiss not me?

P. B. Shelley

229

ECHOES

How sweet the answer Echo makes
  To Music at night
When, roused by lute or horn, she wakes,
And far away o'er lawns and lakes
  Goes answering light!

Yet Love hath echoes truer far
   And far more sweet
Than e'er, beneath the moonlight's star,
Of horn or lute or soft guitar
   The songs repeat.

'Tis when the sigh,—in youth sincere
   And only then,
The sigh that's breathed for one to hear—
Is by that one, that only Dear
   Breathed back again.

T. Moore

230

A SERENADE

Ah! County Guy, the hour is nigh,
   The sun has left the lea,
The orange-flower perfumes the bower,
   The breeze is on the sea.
The lark, his lay who thrill'd all day,
   Sits hush'd his partner nigh;
Breeze, bird, and flower confess the hour,
   But where is County Guy?

The village maid steals through the shade
   Her shepherd's suit to hear;
To Beauty shy, by lattice high,
   Sings high-born Cavalier.
The star of Love, all stars above,
   Now reigns o'er earth and sky,
And high and low the influence know—
   But where is County Guy?

Sir W. Scott

231

TO THE EVENING STAR

    Gem of the crimson-colour'd Even,
    Companion of retiring day,
    Why at the closing gates of heaven,
    Beloved Star, dost thou delay?

    So fair thy pensile beauty burns
    When soft the tear of twilight flows;
    So due thy plighted love returns
    To chambers brighter than the rose;

    To Peace, to Pleasure, and to Love
    So kind a star thou seem'st to be,
    Sure some enamour'd orb above
    Descends and burns to meet with thee.

    Thine is the breathing, blushing hour
    When all unheavenly passions fly,
    Chased by the soul-subduing power
    Of Love's delicious witchery.

    O! sacred to the fall of day
    Queen of propitious stars, appear,
    And early rise, and long delay,
    When Caroline herself is here!

    Shine on her chosen green resort
    Whose trees the sunward summit crown,
    And wanton flowers, that well may court
    An angel's feet to tread them down:—

Shine on her sweetly scented road 25
Thou star of evening's purple dome,
That lead'st the nightingale abroad,
And guid'st the pilgrim to his home.

Shine where my charmer's sweeter breath
Embalms the soft exhaling dew, 30
Where dying winds a sigh bequeath
To kiss the cheek of rosy hue:—

Where, winnow'd by the gentle air,
Her silken tresses darkly flow
And fall upon her brow so fair, 35
Like shadows on the mountain snow.

Thus, ever thus, at day's decline
In converse sweet to wander far—
O bring with thee my Caroline,
And thou shalt be my Ruling Star! 40
T. Campbell

232

TO THE NIGHT

Swiftly walk over the western wave,
    Spirit of Night!
Out of the misty eastern cave
Where, all the long and lone daylight,
Thou wovest dreams of joy and fear 5
Which make thee terrible and dear,—
    Swift be thy flight!

           Wrap thy form in a mantle gray
                   Star-inwrought;
10   Blind with thine hair the eyes of Day,
       Kiss her until she be wearied out:
       Then wander o'er city and sea and land,
       Touching all with thine opiate wand—
                   Come, long-sought!

15   When I arose and saw the dawn,
                   I sigh'd for thee;
       When light rode high, and the dew was gone,
       And noon lay heavy on flower and tree,
       And the weary Day turn'd to his rest
20   Lingering like an unloved guest,
                   I sigh'd for thee.

       Thy brother Death came, and cried
                   Wouldst thou me?
       Thy sweet child Sleep, the filmy-eyed,
25   Murmur'd like a noon-tide bee
       Shall I nestle near thy side?
       Wouldst thou me?—And I replied
                   No, not thee!

       Death will come when thou art dead,
30   Soon, too soon—
       Sleep will come when thou art fled;
       Of neither would I ask the boon
       I ask of thee, belovéd Night—
       Swift be thine approaching flight,
35   Come soon, soon!

                                       P. B. Shelley

Book Fourth

233
TO A DISTANT FRIEND

Why art thou silent?   Is thy love a plant
Of such weak fibre that the treacherous air
Of absence withers what was once so fair?
Is there no debt to pay, no boon to grant?

Yet have my thoughts for thee been vigilant,
Bound to thy service with unceasing care—
The mind's least generous wish a mendicant
For nought but what thy happiness could spare.

Speak!—though this soft warm heart, once free to hold
A thousand tender pleasures, thine and mine,
Be left more desolate, more dreary cold

Than a forsaken bird's-nest fill'd with snow
'Mid its own bush of leafless eglantine—
Speak, that my torturing doubts their end may know!
                                        W. Wordsworth

234

When we two parted
In silence and tears,
Half broken-hearted,
To sever for years,
Pale grew thy cheek and cold,
Colder thy kiss;
Truly that hour foretold
Sorrow to this!

　　　　The dew of the morning
　　　　Sunk chill on my brow;
　　　　It felt like the warning
　　　　Of what I feel now.
　　　　Thy vows are all broken,
　　　　And light is thy fame:
　　　　I hear thy name spoken
　　　　And share in its shame.

　　　　They name thee before me,
　　　　A knell to mine ear;
　　　　A shudder comes o'er me—
　　　　Why wert thou so dear?
　　　　They know not I knew thee
　　　　Who knew thee too well:
　　　　Long, long shall I rue thee,
　　　　Too deeply to tell.

　　　　In secret we met:
　　　　In silence I grieve
　　　　That thy heart could forget,
　　　　Thy spirit deceive.
　　　　If I should meet thee
　　　　After long years,
　　　　How should I greet thee?—
　　　　With silence and tears.

Lord Byron

235

HAPPY INSENSIBILITY

In a drear-nighted December,
  Too happy, happy tree,
Thy branches ne'er remember
  Their green felicity:
The north cannot undo them
With a sleety whistle through them,
Nor frozen thawings glue them
  From budding at the prime.

In a drear-nighted December,
  Too happy, happy brook,
Thy bubblings ne'er remember
  Apollo's summer look;
But with a sweet forgetting
They stay their crystal fretting,
Never, never petting
  About the frozen time.

Ah! would 'twere so with many
  A gentle girl and boy!
But were there ever any
  Writhed not at passéd joy?
To know the change and feel it,
When there is none to heal it
Nor numbéd sense to steal it—
  Was never said in rhyme.

J. Keats

236

Where shall the lover rest
  Whom the fates sever
From his true maiden's breast,
  Parted for ever?
Where, through groves deep and high
  Sounds the far billow,
Where early violets die
  Under the willow.
    Eleu loro
  Soft shall be his pillow.

There through the summer day
  Cool streams are laving:
There, while the tempests sway,
  Scarce are boughs waving;
There thy rest shalt thou take,
  Parted for ever,
Never again to wake
  Never, O never!
    Eleu loro
  Never, O never!

Where shall the traitor rest,
  He, the deceiver,
Who could win maiden's breast,
  Ruin, and leave her?
In the lost battle,
  Borne down by the flying,
Where mingles war's rattle

SIR WALTER SCOTT

SIR WALTER SCOTT.

With groans of the dying;
  Eleu loro
There shall he be lying.

Her wing shall the eagle flap
  O'er the falsehearted;
His warm blood the wolf shall lap
  Ere life be parted:
Shame and dishonour sit
  By his grave ever;
Blessing shall hallow it
  Never, O never!
    Eleu loro
  Never, O never!

Sir W. Scott

237

LA BELLE DAME SANS MERCI

'O what can ail thee, knight-at-arms,
  Alone and palely loitering?
The sedge has wither'd from the lake,
  And no birds sing.

'O what can ail thee, knight-at-arms!
  So haggard and so woe-begone?
The squirrel's granary is full,
  And the harvest's done.

'I see a lily on thy brow
  With anguish moist and fever-dew,
And on thy cheeks a fading rose
  Fast withereth too.'

'I met a lady in the meads,
  Full beautiful—a faery's child,
Her hair was long, her foot was light,
  And her eyes were wild.

'I made a garland for her head,
  And bracelets too, and fragrant zone;
She look'd at me as she did love,
  And made sweet moan.

'I set her on my pacing steed
  And nothing else saw all day long,
For sidelong would she bend, and sing
  A faery's song.

'She found me roots of relish sweet,
  And honey wild and manna-dew,
And sure in language strange she said
  "I love thee true."

'She took me to her elfin grot,
  And there she wept and sigh'd full sore;
And there I shut her wild wild eyes
  With kisses four.

'And there she lullèd me asleep,
  And there I dream'd—Ah! woe betide!
The latest dream I ever dream'd
  On the cold hill's side.

'I saw pale kings and princes too,
  Pale warriors, death-pale were they all:

They cried—"La belle Dame sans Merci
    Hath thee in thrall!"

'I saw their starved lips in the gloam
    With horrid warning gapèd wide,
And I awoke and found me here
    On the cold hill's side.

'And this is why I sojourn here
    Alone and palely loitering,
Though the sedge is wither'd from the lake,
    And no birds sing.'

J. Keats

238

THE ROVER

A weary lot is thine, fair maid,
    A weary lot is thine!
To pull the thorn thy brow to braid,
    And press the rue for wine.
A lightsome eye, a soldier's mien,
    A feather of the blue,
A doublet of the Lincoln green—
    No more of me you knew—
            My Love!
No more of me you knew.

'This morn is merry June, I trow,
    The rose is budding fain:
But she shall bloom in winter snow
    Ere we two meet again.'

He turn'd his charger as he spake
  Upon the river shore,
He gave the bridle-reins a shake,
  Said 'Adieu for evermore
          My Love!
And adieu for evermore.'

Sir W. Scott

239
THE FLIGHT OF LOVE

When the lamp is shatter'd
  The light in the dust lies dead—
When the cloud is scatter'd,
  The rainbow's glory is shed.
When the lute is broken,
  Sweet tones are remember'd not;
When the lips have spoken,
  Loved accents are soon forgot.

As music and splendour
  Survive not the lamp and the lute,
The heart's echoes render
  No song when the spirit is mute—
No song but sad dirges,
  Like the wind through a ruin'd cell,
Or the mournful surges
  That ring the dead seaman's knell.

When hearts have once mingled,
  Love first leaves the well-built nest;
The weak one is singled
  To endure what it once possesst.

O Love! who bewailest
The frailty of all things here,
Why choose you the frailest
For your cradle, your home, and your bier?

Its passions will rock thee 25
As the storms rock the ravens on high;
Bright reason will mock thee
Like the sun from a wintry sky.
From thy nest every rafter
Will rot, and thine eagle home 30
Leave thee naked to laughter,
When leaves fall and cold winds come.

P. B. Shelley

240

THE MAID OF NEIDPATH

O lovers' eyes are sharp to see,
   And lovers' ears in hearing;
And love, in life's extremity,
   Can lend an hour of cheering.
Disease had been in Mary's bower 5
   And slow decay from mourning,
Though now she sits on Neidpath's tower
   To watch her Love's returning.

All sunk and dim her eyes so bright,
   Her form decay'd by pining, 10
Till through her wasted hand, at night,
   You saw the taper shining.

By fits a sultry hectic hue
  Across her cheek was flying;
By fits so ashy pale she grew
  Her maidens thought her dying.

Yet keenest powers to see and hear
  Seem'd in her frame residing;
Before the watch-dog prick'd his ear
  She heard her lover's riding;
Ere scarce a distant form was kenn'd
  She knew and waved to greet him,
And o'er the battlement did bend
  As on the wing to meet him.

He came—he pass'd—an heedless gaze
  As o'er some stranger glancing;
Her welcome, spoke in faltering phrase,
  Lost in his courser's prancing—
The castle-arch, whose hollow tone
  Returns each whisper spoken,
Could scarcely catch the feeble moan
  Which told her heart was broken.

Sir W. Scott

241

Earl March look'd on his dying child,
  And, smit with grief to view her—
The youth, he cried, whom I exiled
  Shall be restored to woo her.

She's at the window many an hour
    His coming to discover:
  And he look'd up to Ellen's bower
    And she look'd on her lover—

  But ah! so pale, he knew her not,
    Though her smile on him was dwelling—
  And am I then forgot—forgot?
    It broke the heart of Ellen.

  In vain he weeps, in vain he sighs,
    Her cheek is cold as ashes;
  Nor love's own kiss shall wake those eyes
    To lift their silken lashes.
              T. Campbell

242

Bright Star! would I were steadfast as thou art—
Not in lone splendour hung aloft the night,
And watching, with eternal lids apart,
Like Nature's patient sleepless Eremite,

The moving waters at their priestlike task
Of pure ablution round earth's human shores,
Or gazing on the new soft fallen mask
Of snow upon the mountains and the moors:—

No—yet still steadfast, still unchangeable,
Pillow'd upon my fair Love's ripening breast
To feel for ever its soft fall and swell,
Awake for ever in a sweet unrest;

Still, still to hear her tender-taken breath,
And so live ever,—or else swoon to death.

J. Keats

243

THE TERROR OF DEATH

When I have fears that I may cease to be
Before my pen has glean'd my teeming brain,
Before high-piléd books, in charact'ry
Hold like rich garners the full-ripen'd grain;

5 When I behold, upon the night's starr'd face,
Huge cloudy symbols of a high romance,
And think that I may never live to trace
Their shadows, with the magic hand of chance;

And when I feel, fair Creature of an hour!
10 That I shall never look upon thee more,
Never have relish in the faery power
Of unreflecting love—then on the shore

Of the wide world I stand alone, and think
Till Love and Fame to nothingness do sink.

J. Keats

244

DESIDERIA

Surprized by joy—impatient as the wind—
I turn'd to share the transport—Oh! with whom
But Thee—deep buried in the silent tomb,
That spot which no vicissitude can find?

Love, faithful love recall'd thee to my mind—
But how could I forget thee?   Through what power
Even for the least division of an hour
Have I been so beguiled as to be blind

To my most grievous loss!—That thought's return
Was the worst pang that sorrow ever bore
Save one, one only, when I stood forlorn,

Knowing my heart's best treasure was no more;
That neither present time, nor years unborn
Could to my sight that heavenly face restore.

W. Wordsworth

245

At the mid hour of night, when stars are weeping, I fly
To the lone vale we loved, when life shone warm in thine eye;
And I think oft, if spirits can steal from the regions of air
To revisit past scenes of delight, thou wilt come to me there
And tell me our love is remember'd, even in the sky!

Then I sing the wild song it once was rapture to hear
When our voices, commingling, breathed like one on the ear;
And as Echo far off through the vale my sad orison rolls,

I think, oh my Love! 'tis thy voice, from the Kingdom of Souls
Faintly answering still the notes that once were so dear.

T. Moore

246

ELEGY ON THYRZA

And thou art dead, as young and fair
   As aught of mortal birth;
And form so soft and charms so rare
   Too soon return'd to Earth!
Though Earth received them in her bed,
And o'er the spot the crowd may tread
   In carelessness or mirth,
There is an eye which could not brook
A moment on that grave to look.

I will not ask where thou liest low
   Nor gaze upon the spot;
There flowers or weeds at will may grow
   So I behold them not:
It is enough for me to prove
That what I loved, and long must love,
   Like common earth can rot;
To me there needs no stone to tell
'Tis Nothing that I loved so well.

Yet did I love thee to the last,
   As fervently as thou
Who didst not change through all the past
   And canst not alter now.

The love where Death has set his seal
Nor age can chill, nor rival steal,
  Nor falsehood disavow:
And, what were worse, thou canst not see
Or wrong, or change, or fault in me.

The better days of life were ours;
  The worst can be but mine:
The sun that cheers, the storm that lours,
  Shall never more be thine.
The silence of that dreamless sleep
I envy now too much to weep;
  Nor need I to repine
That all those charms have pass'd away
I might have watch'd through long decay.

The flower in ripen'd bloom unmatch'd
  Must fall the earliest prey;
Though by no hand untimely snatch'd
  The leaves must drop away.
And yet it were a greater grief
To watch it withering, leaf by leaf,
  Than see it pluck'd today;
Since earthly eye but ill can bear
To trace the change to foul from fair.

I know not if I could have borne
  To see thy beauties fade;
The night that follow'd such a morn
  Had worn a deeper shade:
Thy day without a cloud hath past,

And thou wert lovely to the last,
    Extinguish'd, not decay'd;
As stars that shoot along the sky
Shine brightest as they fall from high.

55   As once I wept, if I could weep,
    My tears might well be shed
To think I was not near, to keep
    One vigil o'er thy bed:
To gaze, how fondly! on thy face,
To fold thee in a faint embrace,
    Uphold thy drooping head;
And show that love, however vain,
Nor thou nor I can feel again.

Yet how much less it were to gain,
    Though thou hast left me free,
The loveliest things that still remain
    Than thus remember thee!
The all of thine that cannot die
Through dark and dread Eternity
    Returns again to me,
And more thy buried love endears
Than aught except its living years.

Lord Byron

247

One word is too often profaned
    For me to profane it,
One feeling too falsely disdain'd
    For thee to disdain it.

One hope is too like despair
  For prudence to smother,
And pity from thee more dear
  Than that from another.

I can give not what men call love;
  But wilt thou accept not
The worship the heart lifts above
  And the Heavens reject not:
The desire of the moth for the star,
  Of the night for the morrow,
The devotion to something afar
  From the sphere of our sorrow?
P. B. Shelley

248

GATHERING SONG OF DONALD THE BLACK

Pibroch of Donuil Dhu
  Pibroch of Donuil
Wake thy wild voice anew,
  Summon Clan Conuil.
Come away, come away,
  Hark to the summons!
Come in your war-array,
  Gentles and commons.

Come from deep glen, and
  From mountain so rocky;
The war-pipe and pennon
  Are at Inverlocky.

Come every hill-plaid, and
    True heart that wears one,
Come every steel blade, and
    Strong hand that bears one.

Leave untended the herd,
    The flock without shelter;
Leave the corpse uninterr'd,
    The bride at the altar;
Leave the deer, leave the steer,
    Leave nets and barges:
Come with your fighting gear,
    Broadswords and targes.

Come as the winds come, when
    Forests are rended,
Come as the waves come, when
    Navies are stranded:
Faster come, faster come,
    Faster and faster,
Chief, vassal, page and groom,
    Tenant and master.

Fast they come, fast they come;
    See how they gather!
Wide waves the eagle plume
    Blended with heather.
Cast your plaids, draw your blades,
    Forward each man set!
Pibroch of Donuil Dhu
    Knell for the onset!

Sir W. Scott

*A wet sheet and a flowing sea,
A wind that follows fast.*

249

A wet sheet and a flowing sea,
  A wind that follows fast
And fills the white and rustling sail
  And bends the gallant mast;
And bends the gallant mast, my boys,
  While like the eagle free
Away the good ship flies, and leaves
  Old England on the lee.

O for a soft and gentle wind!
  I heard a fair one cry;
But give to me the snoring breeze
  And white waves heaving high;
And white waves heaving high, my lads,
  The good ship tight and free—
The world of waters is our home,
  And merry men are we.

There's tempest in yon hornéd moon,
  And lightning in yon cloud;
But hark the music, mariners!
  The wind is piping loud;
The wind is piping loud, my boys,
  The lightning flashes free—
While the hollow oak our palace is,
  Our heritage the sea.

A. Cunningham

250

Ye Mariners of England
That guard our native seas!
Whose flag has braved, a thousand years,
The battle and the breeze!
Your glorious standard launch again
To match another foe:
And sweep through the deep,
While the stormy winds do blow;
While the battle rages loud and long
And the stormy winds do blow.

The spirits of your fathers
Shall start from every wave—
For the deck it was their field of fame,
And Ocean was their grave:
Where Blake and mighty Nelson fell
Your manly hearts shall glow,
As ye sweep through the deep,
While the stormy winds do blow;
While the battle rages loud and long
And the stormy winds do blow..

Britannia needs no bulwarks,
No towers along the steep;
Her march is o'er the mountain-waves,
Her home is on the deep.
With thunders from her native oak
She quells the floods below—
As they roar on the shore,
When the stormy winds do blow;

When the battle rages loud and long,
And the stormy winds do blow.

The meteor flag of England
Shall yet terrific burn;
Till danger's troubled night depart
And the star of peace return.
Then, then, ye ocean-warriors!
Our song and feast shall flow
To the fame of your name,
When the storm has ceased to blow;
When the fiery fight is heard no more,
And the storm has ceased to blow.

T. Campbell

251

BATTLE OF THE BALTIC

Of Nelson and the North
Sing the glorious day's renown,
When to battle fierce came forth
All the might of Denmark's crown,
And her arms along the deep proudly shone;
By each gun the lighted brand
In a bold determined hand,
And the Prince of all the land
Led them on.

Like leviathans afloat
Lay their bulwarks on the brine;
While the sign of battle flew
On the lofty British line:

It was ten of April morn by the chime:
As they drifted on their path
There was silence deep as death;
And the boldest held his breath
For a time.

But the might of England flush'd
To anticipate the scene;
And her van the fleeter rush'd
O'er the deadly space between.
'Hearts of Oak!' our captains cried, when each gun
From its adamantine lips
Spread a death-shade round the ships,
Like the hurricane eclipse
Of the sun.

Again! again! again!
And the havoc did not slack,
Till a feeble cheer the Dane
To our cheering sent us back;—
Their shots along the deep slowly boom:—
Then ceased—and all is wail,
As they strike the shatter'd sail;
Or in conflagration pale
Light the gloom.

Out spoke the victor then
As he hail'd them o'er the wave,
'Ye are brothers! ye are men!
And we conquer but to save:—
So peace instead of death let us bring:
But yield, proud foe, thy fleet
With the crews, at England's feet,

And make submission meet
To our King.'

Then Denmark bless'd our chief
That he gave her wounds repose;
And the sounds of joy and grief
From her people wildly rose,
As death withdrew his shades from the day.
While the sun look'd smiling bright
O'er a wide and woeful sight,
Where the fires of funeral light
Died away.

Now joy, old England, raise!
For the tidings of thy might,
By the festal cities' blaze,
Whilst the wine-cup shines in light;
And yet amidst that joy and uproar,
Let us think of them that sleep
Full many a fathom deep
By thy wild and stormy steep,
Elsinore!

Brave hearts! to Britain's pride
Once so faithful and so true,
On the deck of fame that died
With the gallant good Riou:
Soft sigh the winds of Heaven o'er their grave!
While the billow mournful rolls
And the mermaid's song condoles
Singing glory to the souls
Of the brave!

T. Campbell

252

ODE TO DUTY

Stern Daughter of the Voice of God!
O Duty! if that name thou love
Who art a light to guide, a rod
To check the erring, and reprove;
Thou who art victory and law
When empty terrors overawe;
From vain temptations dost set free,
And calm'st the weary strife of frail humanity!

There are who ask not if thine eye
Be on them; who, in love and truth
Where no misgiving is, rely
Upon the genial sense of youth:
Glad hearts! without reproach or blot,
Who do thy work, and know it not:
Oh! if through confidence misplaced
They fail, thy saving arms, dread Power! around them cast.

Serene will be our days and bright
And happy will our nature be
When love is an unerring light,
And joy its own security.
And they a blissful course may hold
Ev'n now, who, not unwisely bold,
Live in the spirit of this creed;
Yet seek thy firm support, according to their need.

I, loving freedom, and untried,
    No sport of every random gust,
Yet being to myself a guide,
    Too blindly have reposed my trust:
And oft, when in my heart was heard
Thy timely mandate, I deferr'd
The task, in smoother walks to stray;
But thee I now would serve more strictly, if I may.

Through no disturbance of my soul
    Or strong compunction in me wrought,
I supplicate for thy control,
    But in the quietness of thought:
Me this uncharter'd freedom tires;
I feel the weight of chance-desires:
My hopes no more must change their name;
I long for a repose that ever is the same.

Stern Lawgiver! yet thou dost wear
    The Godhead's most benignant grace;
Nor know we anything so fair
    As is the smile upon thy face:
Flowers laugh before thee on their beds,
And fragrance in thy footing treads;
Thou dost preserve the Stars from wrong;
And the most ancient Heavens, through Thee, are fresh and strong.

To humbler functions, awful Power!
    I call thee: I myself commend
Unto thy guidance from this hour;
    Oh let my weakness have an end!

Give unto me, made lowly wise,
The spirit of self-sacrifice;
The confidence of reason give;
And in the light of truth thy Bondman let me live.

W. Wordsworth

253

ON THE CASTLE OF CHILLON

Eternal Spirit of the chainless Mind!
Brightest in dungeons, Liberty! thou art,
For there thy habitation is the heart—
The heart which love of Thee alone can bind;

And when thy sons to fetters are consign'd,
To fetters, and the damp vault's dayless gloom,
Their country conquers with their martyrdom,
And Freedom's fame finds wings on every wind.

Chillon! thy prison is a holy place
And thy sad floor an altar, for 'twas trod,
Until his very steps have left a trace

Worn as if thy cold pavement were a sod,
By Bonnivard! May none those marks efface!
For they appeal from tyranny to God.

Lord Byron

254

ENGLAND AND SWITZERLAND, 1802

Two Voices are there; one is of the Sea,
One of the Mountains; each a mighty voice:
In both from age to age thou didst rejoice,
They were thy chosen music, Liberty!

There came a tyrant, and with holy glee
Thou fought'st against him,—but hast vainly striven:
Thou from thy Alpine holds at length art driven,
Where not a torrent murmurs heard by thee.

—Of one deep bliss thine ear hath been bereft;
Then cleave, O cleave to that which still is left—
For, high-soul'd Maid, what sorrow would it be

That Mountain floods should thunder as before,
And Ocean bellow from his rocky shore,
And neither awful Voice be heard by Thee!

W. Wordsworth

255

ON THE EXTINCTION OF THE VENETIAN REPUBLIC

Once did She hold the gorgeous East in fee
And was the safeguard of the West; the worth
Of Venice did not fall below her birth,
Venice, the eldest child of Liberty.

She was a maiden city, bright and free;
No guile seduced, no force could violate;
And when she took unto herself a mate,
She must espouse the everlasting Sea.

And what if she had seen those glories fade,
Those titles vanish, and that strength decay,
Yet shall some tribute of regret be paid

When her long life hath reach'd its final day:
Men are we, and must grieve when even the shade
Of that which once was great is pass'd away.

W. Wordsworth

256

LONDON, 1802

O Friend! I know not which way I must look
For comfort, being, as I am, opprest
To think that now our life is only drest
For show; mean handy-work of craftsman, cook,

5 Or groom!—We must run glittering like a brook
In the open sunshine, or we are unblest;
The wealthiest man among us is the best:
No grandeur now in nature or in book

Delights us. Rapine, avarice, expense,
10 This is idolatry; and these we adore:
Plain living and high thinking are no more:

The homely beauty of the good old cause
Is gone; our peace, our fearful innocence,
And pure religion breathing household laws.

W. Wordsworth

257

THE SAME

Milton! thou shouldst be living at this hour:
England hath need of thee: she is a fen
Of stagnant waters: altar, sword, and pen,
Fireside, the heroic wealth of hall and bower,

Book Fourth

Have forfeited their ancient English dower
Of inward happiness.   We are selfish men:
Oh! raise us up, return to us again;
And give us manners, virtue, freedom, power.

Thy soul was like a Star, and dwelt apart:
Thou hadst a voice whose sound was like a sea,
Pure as the naked heavens, majestic, free;

So didst thou travel on life's common way
In cheerful godliness; and yet thy heart
The lowliest duties on herself did lay.

W. Wordsworth

258

When I have borne in memory what has tamed
Great nations; how ennobling thoughts depart
When men change swords for ledgers, and desert
The student's bower for gold,—some fears unnamed

I had, my Country!—am I to be blamed?
Now, when I think of thee, and what thou art,
Verily, in the bottom of my heart
Of those unfilial fears I am ashamed.

For dearly must we prize thee; we who find
In thee a bulwark for the cause of men;
And I by my affection was beguiled:

What wonder if a Poet now and then,
Among the many movements of his mind,
Felt for thee as a lover or a child!

W. Wordsworth

259

HOHENLINDEN

On Linden, when the sun was low,
All bloodless lay the untrodden snow;
And dark as winter was the flow
    Of Iser, rolling rapidly.

But Linden saw another sight,
When the drum beat at dead of night
Commanding fires of death to light
    The darkness of her scenery.

By torch and trumpet fast array'd
Each horseman drew his battle-blade,
And furious every charger neigh'd
    To join the dreadful revelry.

Then shook the hills with thunder riven;
Then rush'd the steed, to battle driven;
And louder than the bolts of Heaven
    Far flash'd the red artillery.

But redder yet that light shall glow
On Linden's hills of stainéd snow;
And bloodier yet the torrent flow
    Of Iser, rolling rapidly.

'Tis morn; but scarce yon level sun
Can pierce the war-clouds rolling dun,
Where furious Frank and fiery Hun
    Shout in their sulphurous canopy.

The combat deepens. On, ye Brave   25
Who rush to glory, or the grave!
Wave, Munich! all thy banners wave,
    And charge with all thy chivalry!

Few, few shall part, where many meet!
The snow shall be their winding-sheet,   30
And every turf beneath their feet
    Shall be a soldier's sepulchre.

T. Campbell

260

AFTER BLENHEIM

It was a summer evening,
  Old Kaspar's work was done,
And he before his cottage door
  Was sitting in the sun;
And by him sported on the green   5
His little grandchild Wilhelmine.

She saw her brother Peterkin
  Roll something large and round
Which he beside the rivulet
  In playing there had found;   10
He came to ask what he had found
That was so large and smooth and round.

Old Kaspar took it from the boy
  Who stood expectant by;
And then the old man shook his head,   15
  And with a natural sigh
''Tis some poor fellow's skull,' said he,
'Who fell in the great victory.

'I find them in the garden,
    For there's many here about;
And often when I go to plough
    The ploughshare turns them out.
For many thousand men,' said he,
'Were slain in that great victory.'

'Now tell us what 'twas all about,'
    Young Peterkin he cries;
And little Wilhelmine looks up
    With wonder-waiting eyes;
'Now tell us all about the war,
And what they fought each other for.'

'It was the English,' Kaspar cried,
    'Who put the French to rout;
But what they fought each other for
    I could not well make out.
But everybody said,' quoth he,
'That 'twas a famous victory.

'My father lived at Blenheim then,
    Yon little stream hard by;
They burnt his dwelling to the ground,
    And he was forced to fly:
So with his wife and child he fled,
Nor had he where to rest his head.

'With fire and sword the country round
    Was wasted far and wide,
And many a childing mother then
    And newborn baby died:

But things like that, you know, must be
At every famous victory.

'They say it was a shocking sight
  After the field was won;
For many thousand bodies here
  Lay rotting in the sun:
But things like that, you know, must be
After a famous victory.

'Great praise the Duke of Marlbro' won
  And our good Prince Eugene;'
'Why 'twas a very wicked thing!'
  Said little Wilhelmine;
'Nay . . nay . . my little girl,' quoth he,
'It was a famous victory.

'And everybody praised the Duke
  Who this great fight did win.'
'But what good came of it at last?'
  Quoth little Peterkin:—
'Why that I cannot tell,' said he,
'But 'twas a famous victory.'

R. Southey

261

PRO PATRIA MORI

When he who adores thee has left but the name
  Of his fault and his sorrows behind,
Oh! say wilt thou weep, when they darken the fame
  Of a life that for thee was resign'd!

5 Yes, weep, and however my foes may condemn,
 Thy tears shall efface their decree;
For, Heaven can witness, though guilty to them,
 I have been but too faithful to thee.

With thee were the dreams of my earliest love;
10 Every thought of my reason was thine:
In my last humble prayer to the Spirit above
 Thy name shall be mingled with mine!
Oh! blest are the lovers and friends who shall live
 The days of thy glory to see;
15 But the next dearest blessing that Heaven can give
 Is the pride of thus dying for thee.

T. Moore

262

THE BURIAL OF SIR JOHN MOORE AT CORUNNA

Not a drum was heard, not a funeral note,
 As his corpse to the rampart we hurried;
Not a soldier discharged his farewell shot
 O'er the grave where our hero we buried.

5 We buried him darkly at dead of night,
 The sods with our bayonets turning;
By the struggling moonbeam's misty light
 And the lantern dimly burning.

No useless coffin enclosed his breast,
10 Not in sheet or in shroud we wound him;
But he lay like a warrior taking his rest,
 With his martial cloak around him.

Few and short were the prayers we said,
   And we spoke not a word of sorrow;
But we steadfastly gazed on the face that was dead,
   And we bitterly thought of the morrow.

We thought, as we hollow'd his narrow bed
   And smoothed down his lonely pillow,
That the foe and the stranger would tread o'er his head,
   And we far away on the billow!

Lightly they'll talk of the spirit that's gone
   And o'er his cold ashes upbraid him,—
But little he'll reck, if they let him sleep on
   In the grave where a Briton has laid him.

But half of our heavy task was done
   When the clock struck the hour for retiring:
And we heard the distant and random gun
   That the foe was sullenly firing.

Slowly and sadly we laid him down,
   From the field of his fame fresh and gory;
We carved not a line, and we raised not a stone,
   But we left him alone with his glory.

C. Wolfe

263
SIMON LEE THE OLD HUNTSMAN

   In the sweet shire of Cardigan,
     Not far from pleasant Ivor Hall,
   An old man dwells, a little man,—
     'Tis said he once was tall.

Full five-and-thirty years he lived
    A running huntsman merry;
And still the centre of his cheek
    Is red as a ripe cherry.

No man like him the horn could sound,
    And hill and valley rang with glee,
When Echo bandied, round and round,
    The halloo of Simon Lee.
In those proud days he little cared
    For husbandry or tillage;
To blither tasks did Simon rouse
    The sleepers of the village.

He all the country could outrun,
    Could leave both man and horse behind;
And often, ere the chase was done
    He reel'd and was stone-blind.
And still there's something in the world
    At which his heart rejoices;
For when the chiming hounds are out,
    He dearly loves their voices.

But oh the heavy change!—bereft
    Of health, strength, friends and kindred, see!
Old Simon to the world is left
    In liveried poverty:—
His master's dead, and no one now
    Dwells in the Hall of Ivor;
Men, dogs, and horses, all are dead;
    He is the sole survivor.

And he is lean and he is sick,
  His body, dwindled and awry,
Rests upon ankles swoln and thick;
  His legs are thin and dry.
One prop he has, and only one,—
  His wife, an aged woman,
Lives with him, near the waterfall,
  Upon the village common.

Beside their moss-grown hut of clay,
  Not twenty paces from the door,
A scrap of land they have, but they
  Are poorest of the poor.
This scrap of land he from the heath
  Enclosed when he was stronger;
But what to them avails the land
  Which he can till no longer?

Oft, working by her husband's side,
  Ruth does what Simon cannot do;
For she, with scanty cause for pride,
  Is stouter of the two.
And, though you with your utmost skill
  From labour could not wean them,
'Tis little, very little, all
  That they can do between them.

Few months of life has he in store
  As he to you will tell,
For still, the more he works, the more
  Do his weak ankles swell.

My gentle Reader, I perceive
  How patiently you've waited,
And now I fear that you expect
  Some tale will be related.

O Reader! had you in your mind
  Such stores as silent thought can bring,
O gentle Reader! you would find
  A tale in every thing.
What more I have to say is short,
  And you must kindly take it:
It is no tale; but, should you think,
  Perhaps a tale you'll make it.

One summer-day I chanced to see
  This old Man doing all he could
To unearth the root of an old tree,
  A stump of rotten wood.
The mattock totter'd in his hand:
  So vain was his endeavour
That at the root of the old tree
  He might have work'd for ever.

'You're overtask'd, good Simon Lee,
  Give me your tool,' to him I said;
And at the word right gladly he
  Received my proffer'd aid.
I struck, and with a single blow
  The tangled root I sever'd,
At which the poor old man so long
  And vainly had endeavour'd.

The tears into his eyes were brought,
   And thanks and praises seem'd to run
So fast out of his heart, I thought
   They never would have done.
—I've heard of hearts unkind, kind deeds
   With coldness still returning;
Alas! the gratitude of men
   Hath oftener left me mourning.

W. Wordsworth

264

THE OLD FAMILIAR FACES

I have had playmates, I have had companions,
In my days of childhood, in my joyful school-days;
All, all are gone, the old familiar faces.

I have been laughing, I have been carousing,
Drinking late, sitting late, with my bosom cronies;
All, all are gone, the old familiar faces.

I loved a Love once, fairest among women:
Closed are her doors on me, I must not see her—
All, all are gone, the old familiar faces.

I have a friend, a kinder friend has no man:
Like an ingrate, I left my friend abruptly;
Left him, to muse on the old familiar faces.

Ghost-like I paced round the haunts of my childhood,
Earth seem'd a desert I was bound to traverse,
Seeking to find the old familiar faces.

Friend of my bosom, thou more than a brother,
Why wert not thou born in my father's dwelling?
So might we talk of the old familiar faces,

How some they have died, and some they have left me,
20 And some are taken from me; all are departed;
All, all are gone, the old familiar faces.

C. Lamb

265

THE JOURNEY ONWARDS

As slow our ship her foamy track
    Against the wind was cleaving,
Her trembling pennant still look'd back
    To that dear isle 'twas leaving.
5   So loth we part from all we love,
    From all the links that bind us;
So turn our hearts, as on we rove,
    To those we've left behind us!

When, round the bowl, of vanish'd years
10   We talk with joyous seeming—
With smiles that might as well be tears,
    So faint, so sad their beaming;
While memory brings us back again
    Each early tie that twined us,
15   Oh, sweet's the cup that circles then
    To those we've left behind us!

And when, in other climes, we meet
    Some isle or vale enchanting,

> Where all looks flowery, wild, and sweet,
>   And nought but love is wanting;
> We think how great had been our bliss
>   If Heaven had but assign'd us
> To live and die in scenes like this,
>   With some we've left behind us!
>
> As travellers oft look back at eve
>   When eastward darkly going,
> To gaze upon that light they leave
>   Still faint behind them glowing,—
> So, when the close of pleasure's day
>   To gloom hath near consign'd us,
> We turn to catch one fading ray
>   Of joy that's left behind us.

T. Moore

266

YOUTH AND AGE

There's not a joy the world can give like that it takes away
When the glow of early thought declines in feeling's dull decay;
'Tis not on youth's smooth cheek the blush alone, which fades so fast,
But the tender bloom of heart is gone, ere youth itself be past.

Then the few whose spirits float above the wreck of happiness
Are driven o'er the shoals of guilt, or ocean of excess;

The magnet of their course is gone, or only points in vain
The shore to which their shiver'd sail shall never stretch again.

Then the mortal coldness of the soul like death itself comes down;
It cannot feel for others' woes, it dare not dream its own;
That heavy chill has frozen o'er the fountain of our tears,
And though the eye may sparkle still, 'tis where the ice appears.

Though wit may flash from fluent lips, and mirth distract the breast,
Through midnight hours that yield no more their former hope of rest;
'Tis but as ivy-leaves around the ruin'd turret wreathe,
All green and wildly fresh without, but worn and gray beneath.

Oh could I feel as I have felt, or be what I have been,
Or weep as I could once have wept o'er many a vanish'd scene,—
As springs in deserts found seem sweet, all brackish though they be,
So midst the wither'd waste of life, those tears would flow to me!

Lord Byron

LORD BYRON

267

A LESSON

There is a Flower, the lesser Celandine,
That shrinks like many more from cold and rain,
And the first moment that the sun may shine,
Bright as the sun himself, 'tis out again!

When hailstones have been falling, swarm on swarm, 5
Or blasts the green field and the trees distrest,
Oft have I seen it muffled up from harm
In close self-shelter, like a thing at rest.

But lately, one rough day, this Flower I past,
And recognized it, though an alter'd form, 10
Now standing forth an offering to the blast,
And buffeted at will by rain and storm.

I stopp'd and said, with inly-mutter'd voice,
'It doth not love the shower, nor seek the cold;
This neither is its courage nor its choice, 15
But its necessity in being old.

'The sunshine may not cheer it, nor the dew;
It cannot help itself in its decay;
Stiff in its members, wither'd, changed of hue,'—
And, in my spleen, I smiled that it was gray. 20

To be a prodigal's favourite—then, worse truth,
A miser's pensioner—behold our lot!
O Man! that from thy fair and shining youth
Age might but take the things Youth needed not!

W. Wordsworth

268

PAST AND PRESENT

I remember, I remember
The house where I was born,
The little window where the sun
Came peeping in at morn;
He never came a wink too soon
Nor brought too long a day;
But now, I often wish the night
Had borne my breath away.

I remember, I remember
The roses, red and white,
The violets, and the lily-cups—
Those flowers made of light!
The lilacs where the robin built,
And where my brother set
The laburnum on his birth-day,—
The tree is living yet!

I remember, I remember
Where I was used to swing,
And thought the air must rush as fresh
To swallows on the wing;
My spirit flew in feathers then
That is so heavy now,
And summer pools could hardly cool
The fever on my brow.

I remember, I remember 25
The fir trees dark and high;
I used to think their slender tops
Were close against the sky:
It was a childish ignorance,
But now 'tis little joy 30
To know I'm farther off from Heaven
Than when I was a boy.

T. Hood

THE LIGHT OF OTHER DAYS

Oft in the stilly night
  Ere slumber's chain has bound me,
Fond Memory brings the light
  Of other days around me:
    The smiles, the tears 5
      Of boyhood's years,
    The words of love then spoken;
      The eyes that shone,
      Now dimm'd and gone,
    The cheerful hearts now broken! 10
Thus in the stilly night
  Ere slumber's chain has bound me,
Sad Memory brings the light
  Of other days around me.

When I remember all 15
  The friends so link'd together
I've seen around me fall
  Like leaves in wintry weather,

>   I feel like one
>   Who treads alone
>   Some banquet-hall deserted,
>   Whose lights are fled
>   Whose garlands dead,
>   And all but he departed!
>   Thus in the stilly night
>   Ere slumber's chain has bound me,
>   Sad Memory brings the light
>   Of other days around me.

T. Moore

270

STANZAS WRITTEN IN DEJECTION NEAR NAPLES

> The sun is warm, the sky is clear,
> The waves are dancing fast and bright,
> Blue isles and snowy mountains wear
> The purple noon's transparent might:
> The breath of the moist earth is light
> Around its unexpanded buds;
> Like many a voice of one delight—
> The winds, the birds, the ocean-floods—
> The city's voice itself is soft like Solitude's.
>
> I see the deep's untrampled floor
> With green and purple sea-weeds strown;
> I see the waves upon the shore
> Like light dissolved in star-showers thrown:
> I sit upon the sands alone;

The lightning of the noon-tide ocean
Is flashing round me, and a tone
Arises from its measured motion—
How sweet! did any heart now share in my emotion.

Alas! I have nor hope nor health,
Nor peace within nor calm around,
Nor that content, surpassing wealth,
The sage in meditation found,
And walk'd with inward glory crown'd—
Nor fame, nor power, nor love, nor leisure;
Others I see whom these surround—
Smiling they live, and call life pleasure;
To me that cup has been dealt in another measure.

Yet now despair itself is mild
Even as the winds and waters are;
I could lie down like a tired child,
And weep away the life of care
Which I have borne, and yet must bear,—
Till death like sleep might steal on me,
And I might feel in the warm air
My cheek grow cold, and hear the sea
Breathe o'er my dying brain its last monotony.

P. B. Shelley

271

THE SCHOLAR

My days among the Dead are past;
Around me I behold,
Where'er these casual eyes are cast,
The mighty minds of old:

My never-failing friends are they,
With whom I converse day by day.

With them I take delight in weal
And seek relief in woe:
And while I understand and feel
How much to them I owe,
My cheeks have often been bedew'd
With tears of thoughtful gratitude.

My thoughts are with the Dead; with them
I live in long-past years,
Their virtues love, their faults condemn,
Partake their hopes and fears,
And from their lessons seek and find
Instructions with an humble mind.

My hopes are with the Dead; anon
My place with them will be,
And I with them shall travel on
Through all Futurity;
Yet leaving here a name, I trust,
That will not perish in the dust.

R. Southey

272

THE MERMAID TAVERN

Souls of Poets dead and gone,
What Elysium have ye known,
Happy fields or mossy cavern,
Choicer than the Mermaid Tavern?

Have ye tippled drink more fine
Than mine host's Canary wine?
Or are fruits of Paradise
Sweeter than those dainty pies
Of venison? O generous food!
Drest as though bold Robin Hood
Would, with his Maid Marian,
Sup and bowse from horn and can.

I have heard that on a day
Mine host's sign-board flew away
Nobody knew whither till
An astrologer's old quill
To a sheepskin gave the story,
Said he saw you in your glory,
Underneath a new-old sign
Sipping beverage divine,
And pledging with contented smack
The Mermaid in the Zodiac.

Souls of Poets dead and gone,
What Elysium have ye known,
Happy fields or mossy cavern,
Choicer than the Mermaid Tavern?

J. Keats

273

THE PRIDE OF YOUTH

Proud Maisie is in the wood,
    Walking so early;
Sweet Robin sits on the bush,
    Singing so rarely.

'Tell me, thou bonny bird,
  When shall I marry me?'
—'When six braw gentlemen
  Kirkward shall carry ye.'

'Who makes the bridal bed,
  Birdie, say truly?'
—'The gray-headed sexton
  That delves the grave duly.

'The glow-worm o'er grave and stone
  Shall light thee steady;
The owl from the steeple sing
  Welcome, proud lady.'

Sir W. Scott

274

THE BRIDGE OF SIGHS

One more Unfortunate
Weary of breath
Rashly importunate,
Gone to her death!
Take her up tenderly,
Lift her with care;
Fashion'd so slenderly,
Young, and so fair!

Look at her garments
Clinging like cerements;
Whilst the wave constantly
Drips from her clothing;
Take her up instantly,
Loving, not loathing.

Touch her not scornfully,
Think of her mournfully,
Gently and humanly;
Not of the stains of her—
All that remains of her
Now is pure womanly.

Make no deep scrutiny
Into her mutiny
Rash and undutiful:
Past all dishonour,
Death has left on her
Only the beautiful.

Still, for all slips of hers,
One of Eve's family—
Wipe those poor lips of hers
Oozing so clammily.
Loop up her tresses
Escaped from the comb,
Her fair auburn tresses;
Whilst wonderment guesses
Where was her home?

Who was her father?
Who was her mother?
Had she a sister?
Had she a brother?
Or was there a dearer one
Still, and a nearer one;
Yet, than all other?

Alas! for the rarity
Of Christian charity
Under the sun!
Oh! it was pitiful!
Near a whole city full,
Home she had none.

Sisterly, brotherly,
Fatherly, motherly
Feelings had changed:
Love, by harsh evidence,
Thrown from its eminence;
Even God's providence
Seeming estranged.

Where the lamps quiver
So far in the river,
With many a light
From window and casement,
From garret to basement,
She stood with amazement,
Houseless by night.

The bleak wind of March
Made her tremble and shiver
But not the dark arch,
Or the black flowing river:
Mad from life's history,
Glad to death's mystery
Swift to be hurl'd—
Any where, any where
Out of the world!

Book Fourth

In she plunged boldy,
No matter how coldly
The rough river ran,—
Over the brink of it,   75
Picture it—think of it,
Dissolute Man!
Lave in it, drink of it,
Then, if you can!

Take her up tenderly,   80
Lift her with care;
Fashion'd so slenderly,
Young, and so fair!

Ere her limbs frigidly
Stiffen too rigidly,   85
Decently, kindly,
Smooth and compose them,
And her eyes, close them,
Staring so blindly!

Dreadfully staring   90
Thro' muddy impurity,
As when with the daring
Last look of despairing
Fix'd on futurity.

Perishing gloomily,   95
Spurr'd by contumely,
Cold inhumanity,
Burning insanity,

                    Into her rest.
　　　　　—Cross her hands humbly
　　　　　As if praying dumbly,
　　　　　Over her breast!

　　　　　Owning her weakness,
　　　　　Her evil behaviour,
　　　　　And leaving, with meekness,
　　　　　Her sins to her Saviour.
                                           T. Hood

275

ELEGY

　　Oh snatch'd away in beauty's bloom!
　　On thee shall press no ponderous tomb;
　　But on thy turf shall roses rear
　　Their leaves, the earliest of the year,
And the wild cypress wave in tender gloom:

　　And oft by yon blue gushing stream
　　Shall Sorrow lean her drooping head,
　　And feed deep thought with many a dream,
　　And lingering pause and lightly tread;
Fond wretch! as if her step disturb'd the dead!

　　Away! we know that tears are vain,
　　That Death nor heeds nor hears distress:
　　Will this unteach us to complain?
　　Or make one mourner weep the less?
　　And thou, who tell'st me to forget,
Thy looks are wan, thine eyes are wet.
                                        Lord Byron

276

HESTER

When maidens such as Hester die
Their place ye may not well supply,
Though ye among a thousand try
    With vain endeavour.
A month or more hath she been dead,
Yet cannot I by force be led
To think upon the wormy bed
    And her together.

A springy motion in her gait,
A rising step did indicate
Of pride and joy no common rate
    That flush'd her spirit:
I know not by what name beside
I shall it call: 'twas not pride,
It was a joy to that allied
    She did inherit.

Her parents held the Quaker rule,
Which doth the human feeling cool;
But she was train'd in Nature's school,
    Nature had blest her.
A waking eye, a prying mind,
A heart that stirs, is hard to bind;
A hawk's keen sight ye cannot blind,
    Ye could not Hester.

My sprightly neighbor! gone before
To that unknown and silent shore,
Shall we not meet, as heretofore
    Some summer morning—
When from thy cheerful eyes a ray
Hath struck a bliss upon the day,
A bliss that would not go away,
    A sweet fore-warning?

C. Lamb

277

TO MARY

If I had thought thou couldst have died,
    I might not weep for thee;
But I forgot, when by thy side,
    That thou couldst mortal be:
It never through my mind had past
    The time would e'er be o'er,
And I on thee should look my last,
    And thou shouldst smile no more!

And still upon that face I look,
    And think 'twill smile again;
And still the thought I will not brook
    That I must look in vain!
But when I speak—thou dost not say
    What thou ne'er left'st unsaid;
And now I feel, as well I may,
    Sweet Mary! thou art dead!

If thou wouldst stay, e'en as thou art,
    All cold and all serene—
I still might press thy silent heart,
    And where thy smiles have been.
While e'en thy chill, bleak corse I have,
    Thou seemest still mine own;
But there I lay thee in thy grave—
    And I am now alone!

I do not think, where'er thou art,
    Thou hast forgotten me;
And I, perhaps, may soothe this heart,
    In thinking too of thee:
Yet there was round thee such a dawn
    Of light ne'er seen before,
As fancy never could have drawn,
    And never can restore!

C. Wolfe

278

CORONACH

He is gone on the mountain,
    He is lost to the forest,
Like a summer-dried fountain,
    When our need was the sorest.
The font reappearing
    From the raindrops shall borrow,
But to us comes no cheering,
    To Duncan no morrow!

The hand of the reaper
    Takes the ears that are hoary,
But the voice of the weeper
    Wails manhood in glory.
The autumn winds rushing
    Waft the leaves that are searest,
But our flower was in flushing
    When blighting was nearest.

Fleet foot on the correi,
    Sage counsel in cumber,
Red hand in the foray,
    How sound is thy slumber!
Like the dew on the mountain,
    Like the foam on the river,
Like the bubble on the fountain,
    Thou art gone; and for ever!

Sir W. Scott

279

THE DEATH BED

We watch'd her breathing thro' the night,
    Her breathing soft and low,
As in her breast the wave of life
    Kept heaving to and fro.

So silently we seem'd to speak,
    So slowly moved about,
As we had lent her half our powers
    To eke her living out.

Our very hopes belied our fears,
  Our fears our hopes belied—
We thought her dying when she slept,
  And sleeping when she died.

For when the morn came dim and sad
  And chill with early showers,
Her quiet eyelids closed—she had
  Another morn than ours.

T. Hood

280

AGNES

I saw her in childhood—
  A bright, gentle thing,
Like the dawn of the morn,
  Or the dews of the spring:
The daisies and hare-bells
  Her playmates all day;
Herself as light-hearted
  And artless as they.

I saw her again—
  A fair girl of eighteen,
Fresh glittering with graces
  Of mind and of mien.
Her speech was all music;
  Like moonlight she shone;
The envy of many,
  The glory of one.

Years, years fleeted over—
    I stood at her foot:
The bud had grown blossom,
    The blossom was fruit.
A dignified mother,
    Her infant she bore;
And look'd, I thought, fairer
    Than ever before.

I saw her once more—
    'Twas the day that she died;
Heaven's light was around her,
    And God at her side;
No wants to distress her,
    No fears to appal—
O then, I felt, then
    She was fairest of all!

H. F. Lyte

281

ROSABELLE

O listen, listen, ladies gay!
    No haughty feat of arms I tell;
Soft is the note, and sad the lay
    That mourns the lovely Rosabelle.

'Moor, moor the barge, ye gallant crew!
    And, gentle ladye, deign to stay!
Rest thee in Castle Ravensheuch,
    Nor tempt the stormy firth to-day.

'The blackening wave is edged with white;
  To inch and rock the sea-mews fly;
The fishers have heard the Water-Sprite,
  Whose screams forebode that wreck is nigh.

'Last night the gifted Seer did view
  A wet shroud swathed round ladye gay;
Then stay thee, Fair, in Ravensheuch;
  Why cross the gloomy firth to-day?'

'Tis not because Lord Lindesay's heir
  To-night at Roslin leads the ball,
But that my ladye-mother there
  Sits lonely in her castle-hall.

''Tis not because the ring they ride,
  And Lindesay at the ring rides well,
But that my sire the wine will chide
  If 'tis not fill'd by Rosabelle.'

—O'er Roslin all that dreary night
  A wondrous blaze was seen to gleam;
'Twas broader than the watch-fire's light,
  And redder than the bright moonbeam.

It glared on Roslin's castled rock,
  It ruddied all the copse-wood glen;
'Twas seen from Dryden's groves of oak,
  And seen from cavern'd Hawthornden.

Seem'd all on fire that chapel proud
  Where Roslin's chiefs uncoffin'd lie,
Each Baron, for a sable shroud,
  Sheathed in his iron panoply.

Seem'd all on fire within, around,
  Deep sacristy and altar's pale;
Shone every pillar foliage-bound,
  And glimmer'd all the dead men's mail.

Blazed battlement and pinnet high,
  Blazed every rose-carved buttress fair—
So still they blaze, when fate is nigh
  The lordly line of high Saint Clair.

There are twenty of Roslin's barons bold—
  Lie buried within that proud chapelle;
Each one the holy vault doth hold—
  But the sea holds lovely Rosabelle.

And each Saint Clair was buried there,
  With candle, with book, and with knell;
But the sea-caves rung, and the wild winds sung
  The dirge of lovely Rosabelle.

Sir W. Scott

282

ON AN INFANT DYING AS SOON AS BORN

I saw wherein the shroud did lurk
A curious frame of Nature's work;
A flow'ret crushèd in the bud,
A nameless piece of Babyhood,
Was in her cradle-coffin lying;
Extinct, with scarce the sense of dying:
So soon to exchange the imprisoning womb
For darker closets of the tomb!
She did but ope an eye, and put
A clear beam forth, then straight up shut

ROSLIN CHAPEL

Shone every pillar foliage-bound.

For the long dark: ne'er more to see
Through glasses of mortality.
Riddle of destiny, who can show
What thy short visit meant, or know
What thy errand here below? 15
Shall we say, that Nature blind
Check'd her hand, and changed her mind
Just when she had exactly wrought
A finish'd pattern without fault?
Could she flag, or could she tire, 20
Or lack'd she the Promethean fire
(With her nine moons' long workings sicken'd)
That should thy little limbs have quicken'd?
Limbs so firm, they seem'd to assure
Life of health, and days mature: 25
Woman's self in miniature!
Limbs so fair, they might supply
(Themselves now but cold imagery)
The sculptor to make Beauty by.
Or did the stern-eyed Fate descry 30
That babe or mother, one must die;
So in mercy left the stock
And cut the branch; to save the shock
Of young years widow'd, and the pain
When Single State comes back again 35
To the lone man who, reft of wife,
Thenceforward drags a maiméd life?
The economy of Heaven is dark,
And the wisest clerks have miss'd the mark
Why human buds, like this, should fall, 40
More brief than fly ephemeral

    That has his day; while shrivell'd crones
    Stiffen with age to stocks and stones;
    And crabbéd use the conscience sears
45 In sinners of an hundred years.
    Mother's prattle, mother's kiss,
    Baby fond, thou ne'er wilt miss:
    Rites, which custom does impose,
    Silver bells, and baby clothes;
50 Coral redder than those lips
    Which pale death did late eclipse;
    Music framed for infants' glee,
    Whistle never tuned for thee;
    Though thou want'st not, thou shalt have them,
55 Loving hearts were they which gave them.
    Let not one be missing; nurse,
    See them laid upon the hearse
    Of infant slain by doom perverse.
    Why should kings and nobles have
60 Pictured trophies to their grave,
    And we, churls, to thee deny
    Thy pretty toys with thee to lie—
    A more harmless vanity?

C. Lamb

283

IN MEMORIAM

A child's a plaything for an hour;
    Its pretty tricks we try
For that or for a longer space,—
    Then tire, and lay it by.

But I knew one that to itself
  All seasons could control;
That would have mock'd the sense of pain
  Out of a grievéd soul.

Thou straggler into loving arms,
  Young climber up of knees,
When I forget thy thousand ways
  Then life and all shall cease!

M. Lamb

284

THE AFFLICTION OF MARGARET

Where art thou, my beloved Son,
Where art thou, worse to me than dead?
Oh find me, prosperous or undone!
Or if the grave be now thy bed,
Why am I ignorant of the same
That I may rest; and neither blame
Nor sorrow may attend thy name?

Seven years, alas! to have received
No tidings of an only child—
To have despair'd, have hoped, believed,
And been for ever more beguiled,—
Sometimes with thoughts of very bliss!
I catch at them, and then I miss;
Was ever darkness like to this?

He was among the prime in worth,
An object beauteous to behold;

Well born, well bred; I sent him forth
Ingenuous, innocent, and bold:
If things ensued that wanted grace
As hath been said, they were not base;
And never blush was on my face.

Ah! little doth the young-one dream
When full of play and childish cares,
What power is in his wildest scream
Heard by his mother unawares!
He knows it not, he cannot guess;
Years to a mother bring distress;
But do not make her love the less.

Neglect me! no, I suffer'd long
From that ill thought; and being blind
Said 'Pride shall help me in my wrong:
Kind mother have I been, as kind
As ever breathed:' and that is true;
I've wet my path with tears like dew,
Weeping for him when no one knew.

My Son, if thou be humbled, poor,
Hopeless of honour and of gain,
Oh! do not dread thy mother's door;
Think not of me with grief and pain:
I now can see with better eyes;
And worldly grandeur I despise
And fortune with her gifts and lies.

Alas! the fowls of heaven have wings,
And blasts of heaven will aid their flight;

They mount—how short a voyage brings 45
The wanderers back to their delight!
Chains tie us down by land and sea;
And wishes, vain as mine, may be
All that is left to comfort thee.

Perhaps some dungeon hears thee groan 50
Maim'd, mangled by inhuman men;
Or thou upon a desert thrown
Inheritest the lion's den;
Or hast been summon'd to the deep
Thou, thou, and all thy mates to keep 55
An incommunicable sleep.

I look for ghosts: but none will force
Their way to me; 'tis falsely said
That there was ever intercourse
Between the living and the dead; 60
For surely then I should have sight
Of him I wait for day and night
With love and longing infinite.

My apprehensions come in crowds;
I dread the rustling of the grass; 65
The very shadows of the clouds
Have power to shake me as they pass:
I question things, and do not find
One that will answer to my mind;
And all the world appears unkind. 70

Beyond participation lie
My troubles, and beyond relief:

If any chance to heave a sigh
They pity me, and not my grief.
Then come to me, my Son, or send
Some tidings that my woes may end!
I have no other earthly friend.

W. Wordsworth

285

HUNTING SONG

Waken, lords and ladies gay,
On the mountain dawns the day;
All the jolly chase is here
With hawk and horse and hunting-spear;
Hounds are in their couples yelling,
Hawks are whistling, horns are knelling,
Merrily merrily mingle they,
'Waken, lords and ladies gay.'

Waken, lords and ladies gay,
The mist has left the mountain gray,
Springlets in the dawn are steaming,
Diamonds on the brake are gleaming;
And foresters have busy been
To track the buck in thicket green;
Now we come to chant our lay
'Waken, lords and ladies gay.'

Waken, lords and ladies gay,
To the greenwood haste away;
We can show you where he lies,
Fleet of foot and tall of size;

We can show the marks he made
When 'gainst the oak his antlers fray'd;
You shall see him brought to bay;
'Waken, lords and ladies gay.'

Louder, louder chant the lay   25
Waken, lords and ladies gay!
Tell them youth and mirth and glee
Run a course as well as we;
Time, stern huntsman! who can baulk,
Stanch as hound and fleet as hawk;   30
Think of this, and rise with day,
Gentle lords and ladies gay!

Sir W. Scott

286

TO THE SKYLARK

Ethereal minstrel! pilgrim of the sky!
Dost thou despise the earth where cares abound?
Or while the wings aspire, are heart and eye
Both with thy nest upon the dewy ground?
Thy nest which thou canst drop into at will,   5
Those quivering wings composed, that music still!

To the last point of vision, and beyond
Mount, daring warbler!—that love-prompted strain
—'Twixt thee and thine a never-failing bond—
Thrills not the less the bosom of the plain: 10
Yet might'st thou seem, proud privilege! to sing
All independent of the leafy Spring.

Leave to the nightingale her shady wood;
A privacy of glorious light is thine,
Whence thou dost pour upon the world a flood
Of harmony, with instinct more divine;
Type of the wise, who soar, but never roam—
True to the kindred points of Heaven and Home.

W. Wordsworth

288

TO A SKYLARK

Hail to thee, blithe Spirit!
    Bird thou never wert,
That from heaven, or near it
    Pourest thy full heart
In profuse strains of unpremeditated art.

Higher still and higher
    From the earth thou springest,
Like a cloud of fire,
    The blue deep thou wingest,
And singing still dost soar, and soaring ever singest.

In the golden lightning
    Of the sunken sun
O'er which clouds are brightening,
    Thou dost float and run,
Like an unbodied joy whose race is just begun.

The pale purple even
    Melts around thy flight;
Like a star of heaven
    In the broad daylight
Thou art unseen, but yet I hear thy shrill delight:

Keen as are the arrows
  Of that silver sphere,
Whose intense lamp narrows
  In the white dawn clear
Until we hardly see, we feel that it is there.

All the earth and air
  With thy voice is loud,
As, when night is bare,
  From one lonely cloud
The moon rains out her beams, and heaven is overflow'd.

What thou art we know not;
  What is most like thee?
From rainbow clouds there flow not
  Drops so bright to see
As from thy presence showers a rain of melody;—

Like a poet hidden
  In the light of thought,
Singing hymns unbidden,
  Till the world is wrought
To sympathy with hopes and fears it heeded not:

Like a high-born maiden
  In a palace tower,
Soothing her love-laden
  Soul in secret hour
With music sweet as love, which overflows her bower:

Like a glow-worm golden
  In a dell of dew,
Scattering unbeholden
  Its aerial hue
50 Among the flowers and grass, which screen it from the view:

Like a rose embower'd
  In its own green leaves,
By warm winds deflower'd,
  Till the scent it gives
55 Makes faint with too much sweet these heavy-wingéd thieves.

Sound of vernal showers
  On the twinkling grass,
Rain-awaken'd flowers,
  All that ever was
60 Joyous, and clear, and fresh, thy music doth surpass.

Teach us, sprite or bird,
  What sweet thoughts are thine:
I have never heard
  Praise of love or wine
65 That panted forth a flood of rapture so divine.

Chorus hymeneal
  Or triumphal chaunt
Match'd with thine, would be all
  But an empty vaunt—
70 A thing wherein we feel there is some hidden want.

What objects are the fountains
    Of thy happy strain?
What fields, or waves, or mountains?
    What shapes of sky or plain?
What love of thine own kind? what ignorance of pain? 75

With thy clear keen joyance
    Languor cannot be:
Shadow of annoyance
    Never came near thee:
Thou lovest; but ne'er knew love's sad satiety.   80

Waking or asleep
    Thou of death must deem
Things more true and deep
    Than we mortals dream,
Or how could thy notes flow in such a crystal stream? 85

We look before and after,
    And pine for what is not:
Our sincerest laughter
    With some pain is fraught;
Our sweetest songs are those that tell of saddest thought. 90

Yet if we could scorn
    Hate, and pride, and fear;
If we were things born
    Not to shed a tear,
I know not how thy joy we ever should come near.   95

  Better than all measures
   Of delightful sound,
  Better than all treasures
   That in books are found,
100 Thy skill to poet were, thou scorner of the ground!

  Teach me half the gladness
   That thy brain must know,
  Such harmonious madness
   From my lips would flow,
105 The world should listen then, as I am listening now!
         P. B. Shelley

288
THE GREEN LINNET

 Beneath these fruit-tree boughs that shed
 Their snow-white blossoms on my head,
 With brightest sunshine round me spread
  Of Spring's unclouded weather,
5 In this sequester'd nook how sweet
  To sit upon my orchard-seat!
 And flowers and birds once more to greet,
  My last year's friends together.

 One have I mark'd, the happiest guest
10 In all this covert of the blest:
 Hail to Thee, far above the rest
  In joy of voice and pinion!
 Thou, Linnet! in thy green array
 Presiding Spirit here to-day

Dost lead the revels of the May; 15
And this is thy dominion.

While birds, and butterflies, and flowers,
Make all one band of paramours,
Thou, ranging up and down the bowers,
Art sole in thy employment; 20
A Life, a Presence like the air,
Scattering thy gladness without care,
Too blest with any one to pair;
Thyself thy own enjoyment.

Amid yon tuft of hazel trees 25
That twinkle to the gusty breeze,
Behold him perch'd in ecstasies
Yet seeming still to hover;
There! where the flutter of his wings
Upon his back and body flings 30
Shadows and sunny glimmerings,
That cover him all over.

My dazzled sight he oft deceives—
A brother of the dancing leaves;
Then flits, and from the cottage-eaves 35
Pours forth his song in gushes;
As if by that exulting strain
He mock'd and treated with disdain
The voiceless Form he chose to feign,
While fluttering in the bushes. 40

W. Wordsworth

289

TO THE CUCKOO

O blithe new-comer! I have heard,
I hear thee and rejoice:
O Cuckoo! shall I call thee Bird,
Or but a wandering Voice?

While I am lying on the grass
Thy twofold shout I hear;
From hill to hill it seems to pass,
At once far off and near.

Though babbling only to the vale
Of sunshine and of flowers,
Thou bringest unto me a tale
Of visionary hours.

Thrice welcome, darling of the Spring!
Even yet thou art to me
No bird, but an invisible thing,
A voice, a mystery;

The same whom in my school-boy days
I listen'd to; that Cry
Which made me look a thousand ways
In bush, and tree, and sky.

To seek thee did I often rove
Through woods and on the green;
And thou wert still a hope, a love;
Still long'd for, never seen!

And I can listen to thee yet; 25
Can lie upon the plain
And listen, till I do beget
That golden time again.

O blesséd Bird! the earth we pace
Again appears to be 30
An unsubstantial, faery place,
That is fit home for Thee!

W. Wordsworth

290

ODE TO A NIGHTINGALE

My heart aches, and a drowsy numbness pains
  My sense, as though of hemlock I had drunk,
Or emptied some dull opiate to the drains
  One minute past, and Lethe-wards had sunk:
'Tis not through envy of thy happy lot, 5
  But being too happy in thine happiness,—
    That thou, light-wingéd Dryad of the trees,
      In some melodious plot
Of beechen green, and shadows numberless,
  Singest of summer in full-throated ease. 10

O, for a draught of vintage! that hath been
  Cool'd a long age in the deep-delvéd earth,
Tasting of Flora and the country green,
  Dance, and Provençal song, and sunburnt mirth!
O for a beaker full of the warm South, 15
  Full of the true, the blushful Hippocrene,

With beaded bubbles winking at the brim,
  And purple-stainéd mouth;
That I might drink, and leave the world unseen,
  And with thee fade away into the forest dim:

Fade far away, dissolve, and quite forget
  What thou among the leaves hast never known,
The weariness, the fever, and the fret
  Here, where men sit and hear each other groan;
Where palsy shakes a few, sad, last gray hairs,
  Where youth grows pale, and spectre-thin, and dies,
    Where but to think is to be full of sorrow
      And leaden-eyed despairs;
Where Beauty cannot keep her lustrous eyes,
  Or new Love pine at them beyond to-morrow.

Away! away! for I will fly to thee,
  Not charioted by Bacchus and his pards,
But on the viewless wings of Poesy,
  Though the dull brain perplexes and retards:
Already with thee! tender is the night,
  And haply the Queen-Moon is on her throne,
    Cluster'd around by all her starry Fays;
      But here there is no light,
Save what from heaven is with the breezes blown
  Through verdurous glooms and winding mossy ways.

I cannot see what flowers are at my feet,
  Nor what soft incense hangs upon the boughs,
But, in embalméd darkness, guess each sweet
  Wherewith the seasonable month endows

The grass, the thicket, and the fruit-tree wild; 45
  White hawthorn, and the pastoral eglantine;
    Fast fading violets cover'd up in leaves;
      And mid-May's eldest child,
    The coming musk-rose, full of dewy wine,
      The murmurous haunt of flies on summer eves. 50

Darkling I listen; and for many a time
  I have been half in love with easeful Death,
Call'd him soft names in many a muséd rhyme,
  To take into the air my quiet breath;
Now more than ever seems it rich to die, 55
  To cease upon the midnight with no pain,
    While thou art pouring forth thy soul abroad
      In such an ecstasy!
    Still wouldst thou sing, and I have ears in vain—
      To thy high requiem become a sod. 60

Thou wast not born for death, immortal Bird!
  No hungry generations tread thee down;
The voice I hear this passing night was heard
  In ancient days by emperor and clown:
Perhaps the self-same song that found a path 65
  Through the sad heart of Ruth, when, sick for home,
    She stood in tears amid the alien corn;
      The same that oft-times hath
    Charm'd magic casements, opening on the foam
      Of perilous seas, in faery lands forlorn. 70

Forlorn! the very word is like a bell
  To toll me back from thee to my sole self!

Adieu! the fancy cannot cheat so well
  As she is famed to do, deceiving elf.
Adieu! adieu! thy plaintive anthem fades
  Past the near meadows, over the still stream,
    Up the hill-side; and now 'tis buried deep
      In the next valley-glades:
Was it a vision, or a waking dream?
  Fled is that music:—Do I wake or sleep?

J. Keats

291

UPON WESTMINSTER BRIDGE,
SEPT. 3, 1802

Earth has not anything to show more fair:
Dull would he be of soul who could pass by
A sight so touching in its majesty:
This City now doth like a garment wear

The beauty of the morning: silent, bare,
Ships, towers, domes, theatres, and temples lie
Open unto the fields, and to the sky,—
All bright and glittering in the smokeless air.

Never did sun more beautifully steep
In his first splendour valley, rock, or hill;
Ne'er saw I, never felt, a calm so deep!

The river glideth at its own sweet will:
Dear God! the very houses seem asleep;
And all that mighty heart is lying still!

W. Wordsworth

292

To one who has been long in city pent,
'Tis very sweet to look into the fair
And open face of heaven,—to breathe a prayer
Full in the smile of the blue firmament.

Who is more happy, when, with heart's content, 5
Fatigued he sinks into some pleasant lair
Of wavy grass, and reads a debonair
And gentle tale of love and languishment?

Returning home at evening, with an ear
Catching the notes of Philomel,—an eye 10
Watching the sailing cloudlet's bright career,

He mourns that day so soon has glided by:
E'en like the passage of an angel's tear
That falls through the clear ether silently.

J. Keats

293

OZYMANDIAS OF EGYPT

I met a traveller from an antique land
Who said: Two vast and trunkless legs of stone
Stand in the desert. Near them on the sand,
Half sunk, a shatter'd visage lies, whose frown

And wrinkled lip and sneer of cold command 5
Tell that its sculptor well those passions read
Which yet survive, stamp'd on these lifeless things,
The hand that mock'd them and the heart that fed;

And on the pedestal these words appear:
'My name is Ozymandias, king of kings:
Look on my works, ye Mighty, and despair!'

Nothing beside remains. Round the decay
Of that colossal wreck, boundless and bare,
The lone and level sands stretch far away.

P. B. Shelley

294

COMPOSED AT NEIDPATH CASTLE, THE PROPERTY OF LORD QUEENSBERRY, 1803

Degenerate Douglas! oh, the unworthy lord!
Whom mere despite of heart could so far please
And love of havoc, (for with such disease
Fame taxes him,) that he could send forth word

To level with the dust a noble horde,
A brotherhood of venerable trees,
Leaving an ancient dome, and towers like these,
Beggar'd and outraged!—Many hearts deplored

The fate of those old trees; and oft with pain
The traveller at this day will stop and gaze
On wrongs, which Nature scarcely seems to heed:

For shelter'd places, bosoms, nooks, and bays,
And the pure mountains, and the gentle Tweed,
And the green silent pastures, yet remain.

W. Wordsworth

295
THE BEECH TREE'S PETITION

O leave this barren spot to me!
Spare, woodman, spare the beechen tree!
Though bush or floweret never grow
My dark unwarming shade below;
Nor summer bud perfume the dew 5
Of rosy blush, or yellow hue;
Nor fruits of autumn, blossom-born,
My green and glossy leaves adorn;
Nor murmuring tribes from me derive
Th' ambrosial amber of the hive; 10
Yet leave this barren spot to me:
Spare, woodman, spare the beechen tree!

    Thrice twenty summers I have seen
The sky grow bright, the forest green;
And many a wintry wind have stood 15
In bloomless, fruitless solitude,
Since childhood in my pleasant bower
First spent its sweet and sportive hour;
Since youthful lovers in my shade
Their vows of truth and rapture made, 20
And on my trunk's surviving frame
Carved many a long-forgotten name.
Oh! by the sighs of gentle sound,
First breathed upon this sacred ground;
By all that Love has whisper'd here, 25
Or Beauty heard with ravish'd ear;
As Love's own altar honour me:
Spare, woodman, spare the beechen tree!

                        T. Campbell

296

ADMONITION TO A TRAVELLER

Yes, there is holy pleasure in thine eye!
—The lovely Cottage in the guardian nook
Hath stirr'd thee deeply; with its own dear brook,
Its own small pasture, almost its own sky!

But covet not the abode; forbear to sigh
As many do, repining while they look;
Intruders—who would tear from Nature's book
This precious leaf with harsh impiety.

—Think what the home must be if it were thine,
Even thine, though few thy wants!—Roof, window, door,
The very flowers are sacred to the Poor,

The roses to the porch which they entwine:
Yea, all that now enchants thee, from the day
On which it should be touch'd, would melt away!

W. Wordsworth

297

TO THE HIGHLAND GIRL OF INVERSNEYDE

Sweet Highland Girl, a very shower
Of beauty is thy earthly dower!
Twice seven consenting years have shed
Their utmost bounty on thy head:
And these gray rocks, that household lawn,
Those trees—a veil just half withdrawn,

This fall of water that doth make
A murmur near the silent lake,
This little bay, a quiet road
That holds in shelter thy abode;   10
In truth together ye do seem
Like something fashion'd in a dream;
Such forms as from their covert peep
When earthly cares are laid asleep!
But O fair Creature! in the light   15
Of common day, so heavenly bright,
I bless Thee, Vision as thou art,
I bless thee with a human heart:
God shield thee to thy latest years!
Thee neither know I nor thy peers: 20
And yet my eyes are fill'd with tears.

With earnest feeling I shall pray
For thee when I am far away;
For never saw I mien or face
In which more plainly I could trace   25
Benignity and home-bred sense
Ripening in perfect innocence.
Here scatter'd, like a random seed,
Remote from men, Thou dost not need
The embarrass'd look of shy distress,   30
And maidenly shamefacédness:
Thou wear'st upon thy forehead clear
The freedom of a Mountaineer:
A face with gladness overspread;
Soft smiles, by human kindness bred;   35
And seemliness complete, that sways

Thy courtesies, about thee plays;
With no restraint, but such as springs
From quick and eager visitings
Of thoughts that lie beyond the reach
Of thy few words of English speech:
A bondage sweetly brook'd, a strife
That gives thy gestures grace and life!
So have I, not unmoved in mind,
Seen birds of tempest-loving kind—
Thus beating up against the wind.

What hand but would a garland cull
For thee who art so beautiful?
O happy pleasure! here to dwell
Beside thee in some heathy dell;
Adopt your homely ways and dress,
A shepherd, thou a shepherdess!
But I could frame a wish for thee
More like a grave reality:
Thou art to me but as a wave
Of the wild sea: and I would have
Some claim upon thee, if I could,
Though but of common neighbourhood.
What joy to hear thee, and to see!
Thy elder brother I would be,
Thy father—anything to thee.

Now thanks to Heaven! that of its grace
Hath led me to this lonely place;
Joy have I had; and going hence
I bear away my recompence.

In spots like these it is we prize
Our Memory, feel that she hath eyes:
Then why should I be loth to stir?
I feel this place was made for her;
To give new pleasure like the past,   70
Continued long as life shall last.
Nor am I loth, though pleased at heart,
Sweet Highland Girl! from thee to part;
For I, methinks, till I grow old
As fair before me shall behold   75
As I do now, the cabin small,
The lake, the bay, the waterfall;
And Thee, the Spirit of them all!

W. Wordsworth

298

THE REAPER

Behold her, single in the field,
Yon solitary Highland Lass!
Reaping and singing by herself;
Stop here, or gently pass!
Alone she cuts and binds the grain,   5
And sings a melancholy strain;
O listen! for the vale profound
Is overflowing with the sound.

No nightingale did ever chaunt
More welcome notes to weary bands   10
Of travellers in some shady haunt,
Among Arabian sands:

A voice so thrilling ne'er was heard
In spring-time from the cuckoo-bird,
Breaking the silence of the seas
Among the farthest Hebrides.

Will no one tell me what she sings?
Perhaps the plaintive numbers flow
For old, unhappy, far-off things,
And battles long ago:
Or is it some more humble lay,
Familiar matter of to-day?
Some natural sorrow, loss, or pain,
That has been, and may be again!

Whate'er the theme, the maiden sang
As if her song could have no ending;
I saw her singing at her work,
And o'er the sickle bending;—
I listen'd, motionless and still;
And, as I mounted up the hill,
The music in my heart I bore
Long after it was heard no more.

W. Wordsworth

THE REVERIE OF POOR SUSAN

At the corner of Wood Street, when daylight appears,
Hangs a Thrush that sings loud, it has sung for three years:
Poor Susan has pass'd by the spot, and has heard
In the silence of morning the song of the bird.

'Tis a note of enchantment; what ails her? She sees
A mountain ascending, a vision of trees;
Bright volumes of vapour through Lothbury glide,
And a river flows on through the vale of Cheapside.

Green pastures she views in the midst of the dale
Down which she so often has tripp'd with her pail;
And a single small cottage, a nest like a dove's,
The one only dwelling on earth that she loves.

She looks, and her heart is in heaven: but they fade,
The mist and the river, the hill and the shade;
The stream will not flow, and the hill will not rise,
And the colours have all pass'd away from her eyes!

W. Wordsworth

300

TO A LADY, WITH A GUITAR

Ariel to Miranda:—Take
This slave of music, for the sake
Of him, who is the slave of thee;
And teach it all the harmony
In which thou canst, and only thou,
Make the delighted spirit glow,
Till joy denies itself again
And too intense, is turn'd to pain.
For by permission and command
Of thine own Prince Ferdinand,
Poor Ariel sends this silent token
Of more than ever can be spoken;
Your guardian spirit, Ariel, who
From life to life must still pursue

    Your happiness, for thus alone
Can Ariel ever find his own.
From Prospero's enchanted cell,
As the mighty verses tell,
To the throne of Naples he
Lit you o'er the trackless sea,
Flitting on, your prow before,
Like a living meteor.
When you die, the silent Moon
In her interlunar swoon
Is not sadder in her cell
Than deserted Ariel:—
When you live again on earth,
Like an unseen Star of birth
Ariel guides you o'er the sea
Of life from your nativity:—
Many changes have been run
Since Ferdinand and you begun
Your course of love, and Ariel still
Has track'd your steps and served your will.
Now in humbler, happier lot,
This is all remember'd not;
And now, alas! the poor Sprite is
Imprison'd for some fault of his
In a body like a grave—
From you he only dares to crave,
For his service and his sorrow
A smile to-day, a song to-morrow.

The artist who this idol wrought
To echo all harmonious thought,

Fell'd a tree, while on the steep,   45
The woods were in their winter sleep,
Rock'd in that repose divine
On the wind-swept Apennine;
And dreaming, some of Autumn past,
And some of Spring approaching fast,   50
And some of April buds and showers,
And some of songs in July bowers,
And all of love: And so this tree,—
Oh that such our death may be!—
Died in sleep, and felt no pain,   55
To live in happier form again:
From which, beneath heaven's fairest star,
The artist wrought this loved Guitar;
And taught it justly to reply
To all who question skilfully   60
In language gentle as thine own;
Whispering in enamour'd tone
Sweet oracles of woods and dells,
And summer winds in sylvan cells:
—For it had learnt all harmonies   65
Of the plains and of the skies,
Of the forests and the mountains,
And the many-voicéd fountains;
The clearest echoes of the hills,
The softest notes of falling rills,   70
The melodies of birds and bees,
The murmuring of summer seas,
And pattering rain, and breathing dew,
And airs of evening; and it knew
That seldom-heard mysterious sound   75

Which, driven on its diurnal round,
As it floats through boundless day,
Our world enkindles on its way:
—All this it knows, but will not tell
To those who cannot question well
The Spirit that inhabits it;
It talks according to the wit
Of its companions; and no more
Is heard than has been felt before
By those who tempt it to betray
These secrets of an elder day.
But, sweetly as its answers will
Flatter hands of perfect skill,
It keeps its highest holiest tone
For our beloved Friend alone.

P. B. Shelley

301

THE DAFFODILS

I wander'd lonely as a cloud
That floats on high o'er vales and hills,
When all at once I saw a crowd,
A host of golden daffodils,
Beside the lake, beneath the trees,
Fluttering and dancing in the breeze.

Continuous as the stars that shine
And twinkle on the milky way,
They stretch'd in never-ending line
Along the margin of a bay:
Ten thousand saw I at a glance
Tossing their heads in sprightly dance.

The waves beside them danced, but they
Out-did the sparkling waves in glee:—
A Poet could not but be gay
In such a jocund company!
I gazed—and gazed—but little thought
What wealth the show to me had brought;

For oft, when on my couch I lie
In vacant or in pensive mood,
They flash upon that inward eye
Which is the bliss of solitude;
And then my heart with pleasure fills,
And dances with the daffodils.

W. Wordsworth

302

TO THE DAISY

With little here to do or see
Of things that in the great world be,
Sweet Daisy! oft I talk to thee
    For thou art worthy,
Thou unassuming Common-place
Of Nature, with that homely face,
And yet with something of a grace
    Which Love makes for thee!

Oft on the dappled turf at ease
I sit and play with similes,
Loose types of things through all degrees,
    Thoughts of thy raising;
And many a fond and idle name

I give to thee, for praise or blame
  As is the humour of the game,
      While I am gazing.

  A nun demure, of lowly port;
  Or sprightly maiden, of Love's court,
  In thy simplicity the sport
      Of all temptations;
  A queen in crown of rubies drest;
  A starveling in a scanty vest;
  Are all, as seems to suit thee best,
      Thy appellations.

  A little Cyclops, with one eye
  Staring to threaten and defy,
  That thought comes next—and instantly
      The freak is over,
  The shape will vanish, and behold!
  A silver shield with boss of gold
  That spreads itself, some faery bold
      In fight to cover.

  I see thee glittering from afar—
  And then thou art a pretty star,
  Not quite so fair as many are
      In heaven above thee!
  Yet like a star, with glittering crest,
  Self-poised in air thou seem'st to rest;—
  May peace come never to his nest
      Who shall reprove thee!

Sweet Flower! for by that name at last
When all my reveries are past
I call thee, and to that cleave fast,
    Sweet silent Creature!
That breath'st with me in sun and air,   45
Do thou, as thou art wont, repair
My heart with gladness, and a share
    Of thy meek nature!

W. Wordsworth

303

ODE TO AUTUMN

Season of mists and mellow fruitfulness,
Close bosom-friend of the maturing sun;
Conspiring with him how to load and bless
With fruit the vines that round the thatch-eaves run;
To bend with apples the moss'd cottage-trees,   5
And fill all fruit with ripeness to the core;
To swell the gourd, and plump the hazel shells
With a sweet kernel; to set budding more,
And still more, later flowers for the bees,
Until they think warm days will never cease;   10
For Summer has o'erbrimm'd their clammy cells.

Who hath not seen thee oft amid thy store?
Sometimes whoever seeks abroad may find
Thee sitting careless on a granary floor,
Thy hair soft-lifted by the winnowing wind;   15
Or on a half-reap'd furrow sound asleep,
Drowsed with the fume of poppies, while thy hook
Spares the next swath and all its twinéd flowers:

And sometimes like a gleaner thou dost keep
Steady thy laden head across a brook;
Or by a cyder-press, with patient look,
Thou watchest the last oozings, hours by hours.

Where are the songs of Spring? Ay, where are they?
Think not of them, thou hast thy music too,—
While barréd clouds bloom the soft-dying day
And touch the stubble-plains with rosy hue;
Then in a wailful choir the small gnats mourn
Among the river-sallows, borne aloft
Or sinking as the light wind lives or dies;
And full-grown lambs loud bleat from hilly bourn;
Hedge-crickets sing; and now with treble soft
The red-breast whistles from a garden-croft;
And gathering swallows twitter in the skies.

J. Keats

304

ODE TO WINTER

Germany, December, 1800

When first the fiery-mantled Sun
His heavenly race began to run,
Round the earth and ocean blue
His children four the Seasons flew.
    First, in green apparel dancing.
The young Spring smiled with angel-grace;
Rosy Summer next advancing,
Rush'd into her sire's embrace—

Her bright-hair'd sire, who bade her keep
    For ever nearest to his smiles,   10
On Calpe's olive-shaded steep
    Or India's citron-cover'd isles:
More remote, and buxom-brown,
    The Queen of vintage bow'd before his throne;
A rich pomegranate gemm'd her crown,   15
    A ripe sheaf bound her zone.

But howling Winter fled afar
To hills that prop the polar star;
And loves on deer-borne car to ride
With barren darkness by his side,   20
Round the shore where loud Lofoden
    Whirls to death the roaring whale,
Round the hall where Runic Odin
    Howls his war-song to the gale;
Save when adown the ravaged globe   25
    He travels on his native storm,
Deflowering Nature's grassy robe
    And trampling on her faded form:—
Till light's returning Lord assume
    The shaft that drives him to his polar field,   30
Of power to pierce his raven plume
    And crystal-cover'd shield.

Oh, sire of storms! whose savage ear
The Lapland drum delights to hear,
When Frenzy with her blood-shot eye   35
Implores thy dreadful deity—
Archangel! Power of desolation!

>   Fast descending as thou art,
> Say, hath mortal invocation
>   Spells to touch thy stony heart?
> Then, sullen Winter! hear my prayer,
> And gently rule the ruin'd year;
> Nor chill the wanderer's bosom bare
> Nor freeze the wretch's falling tear:
> To shuddering Want's unmantled bed
>   Thy horror-breathing agues cease to lend,
> And gently on the orphan head
>   Of Innocence descend.
>
> But chiefly spare, O king of clouds!
> The sailor on his airy shrouds,
> When wrecks and beacons strew the steep,
> And spectres walk along the deep.
> Milder yet thy snowy breezes
>   Pour on yonder tented shores,
> Where the Rhine's broad billow freezes,
>   Or the dark-brown Danube roars.
> Oh, winds of Winter! list ye there
>   To many a deep and dying groan?
> Or start, ye demons of the midnight air,
>   At shrieks and thunders louder than your own?
> Alas! ev'n your unhallow'd breath
>   May spare the victim fallen low;
> But Man will ask no truce to death,—
>   No bounds to human woe.

T. Campbell

305

YARROW UNVISITED

1803

From Stirling Castle we had seen
The mazy Forth unravell'd,
Had trod the banks of Clyde and Tay
And with the Tweed had travell'd;
And when we came to Clovenford,   5
Then said my 'winsome Marrow,'
'Whate'er betide, we'll turn aside,
And see the Braes of Yarrow.'

'Let Yarrow folk, frae Selkirk town,
Who have been buying, selling,   10
Go back to Yarrow, 'tis their own,
Each maiden to her dwelling!
On Yarrow's banks let herons feed,
Hares couch, and rabbits burrow;
But we will downward with the Tweed,   15
Nor turn aside to Yarrow.

'There's Gala Water, Leader Haughs,
Both lying right before us;
And Dryburgh, where with chiming Tweed
The lintwhites sing in chorus;   20
There's pleasant Tivot-dale, a land
Made blithe with plough and harrow;
Why throw away a needful day
To go in search of Yarrow?

25 'What's Yarrow but a river bare
That glides the dark hills under?
There are a thousand such elsewhere
As worthy of your wonder.'
—Strange words they seem'd of slight and scorn
30 My True-love sigh'd for sorrow,
And look'd me in the face, to think
I thus could speak of Yarrow!

'O green,' said I, 'are Yarrow's holms,
And sweet is Yarrow flowing!
35 Fair hangs the apple frae the rock,
But we will leave it growing.
O'er hilly path and open strath
We'll wander Scotland thorough;
But, though so near, we will not turn
40 Into the dale of Yarrow.

'Let beeves and home-bred kine partake
The sweets of Burn-mill meadow;
The swan on still Saint Mary's Lake
Float double, swan and shadow!
45 We will not see them; will not go
To-day, nor yet to-morrow;
Enough if in our hearts we know
There's such a place as Yarrow.

'Be Yarrow stream unseen, unknown!
50 It must, or we shall rue it:
We have a vision of our own,
Ah! why should we undo it?

The treasured dreams of times long past,
We'll keep them, winsome Marrow!
For when we're there, although 'tis fair,
'Twill be another Yarrow!

'If Care with freezing years should come
And wandering seem but folly,—
Should we be loth to stir from home,
And yet be melancholy;
Should life be dull, and spirits low,
'Twill soothe us in our sorrow
That earth has something yet to show,
The bonny holms of Yarrow!'

W. Wordsworth

306

YARROW VISITED

September, 1814

And is this—Yarrow?—This the stream
Of which my fancy cherish'd
So faithfully, a waking dream,
An image that hath perish'd?
O that some minstrel's harp were near
To utter notes of gladness
And chase this silence from the air,
That fills my heart with sadness!

Yet why?—a silvery current flows
With uncontroll'd meanderings;
Nor have these eyes by greener hills
Been soothed, in all my wanderings.

And, through her depths, Saint Mary's Lake
Is visibly delighted;
For not a feature of those hills
Is in the mirror slighted.

A blue sky bends o'er Yarrow Vale,
Save where that pearly whiteness
Is round the rising sun diffused,
A tender hazy brightness;
Mild dawn of promise! that excludes
All profitless dejection;
Though not unwilling here to admit
A pensive recollection.

Where was it that the famous Flower
Of Yarrow Vale lay bleeding?
His bed perchance was yon smooth mound
On which the herd is feeding:
And haply from this crystal pool,
Now peaceful as the morning,
The Water-wraith ascended thrice,
And gave his doleful warning.

Delicious is the lay that sings
The haunts of happy lovers,
The path that leads them to the grove,
The leafy grove that covers:
And pity sanctifies the verse
That paints, by strength of sorrow,
The unconquerable strength of love;
Bear witness, rueful Yarrow!

Book Fourth

But thou that didst appear so fair
To fond imagination,
Dost rival in the light of day
Her delicate creation:
Meek loveliness is round thee spread, 45
A softness still and holy:
The grace of forest charms decay'd,
And pastoral melancholy.

That region left, the vale unfolds
Rich groves of lofty stature, 50
With Yarrow winding through the pomp
Of cultivated nature;
And rising from those lofty groves
Behold a ruin hoary,
The shatter'd front of Newark's towers, 55
Renown'd in Border story.

Fair scenes for childhood's opening bloom,
For sportive youth to stray in,
For manhood to enjoy his strength,
And age to wear away in! 60
Yon cottage seems a bower of bliss,
A covert for protection
Of tender thoughts that nestle there —
The brood of chaste affection.

How sweet on this autumnal day 65
The wild-wood fruits to gather,
And on my True-love's forehead plant
A crest of blooming heather!

And what if I enwreathed my own?
'Twere no offence to reason;
The sober hills thus deck their brows
To meet the wintry season.

I see — but not by sight alone,
Loved Yarrow, have I won thee;
A ray of Fancy still survives —
Her sunshine plays upon thee!
Thy ever-youthful waters keep
A course of lively pleasure;
And gladsome notes my lips can breathe
Accordant to the measure.

The vapours linger round the heights,
They melt, and soon must vanish;
One hour is theirs, nor more is mine —
Sad thought! which I would banish,
But that I know, where'er I go,
Thy genuine image, Yarrow!
Will dwell with me, to heighten joy,
And cheer my mind in sorrow.

W. Wordsworth

307

THE INVITATION

Best and brightest, come away,—
Fairer far than this fair Day,
Which, like thee, to those in sorrow
Comes to bid a sweet good-morrow

To the rough year just awake
In its cradle on the brake.
The brightest hour of unborn Spring
Through the winter wandering,
Found, it seems, the halcyon morn
To hoar February born;
Bending from heaven, in azure mirth,
It kiss'd the forehead of the earth,
And smiled upon the silent sea,
And bade the frozen streams be free,
And waked to music all their fountains,
And breathed upon the frozen mountains,
And like a prophetess of May
Strew'd flowers upon the barren way,
Making the wintry world appear
Like one on whom thou smilest, dear.

   Away, away, from men and towns,
To the wild wood and the downs —
To the silent wilderness
Where the soul need not repress
Its music, lest it should not find
An echo in another's mind,
While the touch of Nature's art
Harmonizes heart to heart.

   Radiant Sister of the Day,
Awake! arise! and come away!
To the wild woods and the plains,
To the pools where winter rains
Image all their roof of leaves,
Where the pine its garland weaves

    Of sapless green, and ivy dun,
    Round stems that never kiss the sun;
    Where the lawns and pastures be
    And the sandhills of the sea;
    Where the melting hoar-frost wets
    The daisy-star that never sets,
    And wind-flowers and violets
    Which yet join not scent to hue
    Crown the pale year weak and new;
    When the night is left behind
    In the deep east, dun and blind,
    And the blue noon is over us,
    And the multitudinous
    Billows murmur at our feet,
    Where the earth and ocean meet,
    And all things seem only one
    In the universal Sun.

P. B. Shelley

308

THE RECOLLECTION

Now the last day of many days
All beautiful and bright as thou,
The loveliest and the last, is dead:
Rise, Memory, and write its praise!
Up—to thy wonted work! come, trace
The epitaph of glory fled,
For now the earth has changed its face,
A frown is on the heaven's brow.

Book Fourth

We wander'd to the Pine Forest
    That skirts the Ocean's foam;
The lightest wind was in its nest,
    The tempest in its home.
The whispering waves were half asleep,
    The clouds were gone to play,
And on the bosom of the deep
    The smile of heaven lay;
It seem'd as if the hour were one
    Sent from beyond the skies
Which scatter'd from above the sun
    A light of Paradise!

We paused amid the pines that stood
    The giants of the waste,
Tortured by storms to shapes as rude
    As serpents interlaced,—
And soothed by every azure breath
    That under heaven is blown,
To harmonies and hues beneath,
    As tender as its own:
Now all the tree-tops lay asleep
    Like green waves on the sea,
As still as in the silent deep
    The ocean-woods may be.

How calm it was!—The silence there
    By such a chain was bound,
That even the busy woodpecker
    Made stiller with her sound
The inviolable quietness;

>   The breath of peace we drew
>   With its soft motion made not less
>   The calm that round us grew.
>   There seem'd, from the remotest seat
>   Of the white mountain waste
>   To the soft flower beneath our feet,
>   A magic circle traced,—
>   A spirit interfused around,
>   A thrilling silent life;
>   To momentary peace it bound
>   Our mortal nature's strife;—
>   And still I felt the centre of
>   The magic circle there
>   Was one fair form that fill'd with love
>   The lifeless atmosphere.
>
>   We paused beside the pools that lie
>   Under the forest bough;
>   Each seem'd as 'twere a little sky
>   Gulf'd in a world below;
>   A firmament of purple light
>   Which in the dark earth lay,
>   More boundless than the depth of night
>   And purer than the day—
>   In which the lovely forests grew
>   As in the upper air,
>   More perfect both in shape and hue
>   Than any spreading there.
>   There lay the glade and neighbouring lawn,
>   And through the dark-green wood
>   The white sun twinkling like the dawn

Book Fourth

    Out of a speckled cloud.
Sweet views which in our world above
    Can never well be seen
Were imaged in the water's love
    Of that fair forest green:
And all was interfused beneath
    With an Elysian glow,
An atmosphere without a breath,
    A softer day below.
Like one beloved, the scene had lent
    To the dark water's breast
Its every leaf and lineament
    With more than truth exprest;
Until an envious wind crept by,
    Like an unwelcome thought
Which from the mind's too faithful eye
    Blots one dear image out.
—Though thou art ever fair and kind,
    The forests ever green,
Less oft is peace in Shelley's mind
    Than calm in waters seen!

P. B. Shelley

309

BY THE SEA

It is a beauteous evening, calm and free;
The holy time is quiet as a Nun
Breathless with adoration; the broad sun
Is sinking down in its tranquillity;

The gentleness of heaven is on the Sea:
Listen! the mighty Being is awake,
And doth with his eternal motion make
A sound like thunder—everlastingly.

Dear child! dear girl! that walkest with me here,
If thou appear untouch'd by solemn thought
Thy nature is not therefore less divine:

Thou liest in Abraham's bosom all the year,
And worship'st at the Temple's inner shrine,
God being with thee when we know it not.

W. Wordsworth

310

SONG TO THE EVENING STAR

Star that bringest home the bee,
And sett'st the weary labourer free!
If any star shed peace, 'tis Thou
   That send'st it from above,
Appearing when Heaven's breath and brow
   Are sweet as hers we love.

Come to the luxuriant skies,
Whilst the landscape's odours rise,
Whilst far off lowing herds are heard
   And songs when toil is done,
From cottages whose smoke unstirr'd
   Curls yellow in the sun.

Star of love's soft interviews,
Parted lovers on thee muse:

The sun upon the lake is low.

> Their remembrancer in Heaven
>   Of thrilling vows thou art,
> Too delicious to be riven
>   By absence from the heart.
>
> *T. Campbell*

311

DATUR HORA QUIETI

The sun upon the lake is low,
  The wild birds hush their song,
The hills have evening's deepest glow,
  Yet Leonard tarries long.
Now all whom varied toil and care
  From home and love divide,
In the calm sunset may repair
  Each to the loved one's side.

The noble dame, on turret high,
  Who waits her gallant knight,
Looks to the western beam to spy
  The flash of armour bright.
The village maid, with hand on brow
  The level ray to shade,
Upon the footpath watches now
  For Colin's darkening plaid.

Now to their mates the wild swans row,
  By day they swam apart,
And to the thicket wanders slow
  The hind beside the hart.

> The woodlark at his partner's side
> Twitters his closing song—
> All meet whom day and care divide,
> But Leonard tarries long!

Sir W. Scott

312

TO THE MOON

> Art thou pale for weariness
> Of climbing heaven, and gazing on the earth,
> Wandering companionless
> Among the stars that have a different birth,—
> And ever-changing, like a joyless eye
> That finds no object worth its constancy?

P. B. Shelley

313

TO SLEEP

> A flock of sheep that leisurely pass by
> One after one; the sound of rain, and bees
> Murmuring; the fall of rivers, winds, and seas,
> Smooth fields, white sheets of water, and pure sky;
>
> I've thought of all by turns, and yet do lie
> Sleepless; and soon the small birds' melodies
> Must hear, first utter'd from my orchard trees,
> And the first cuckoo's melancholy cry.
>
> Even thus last night, and two nights more I lay,
> And could not win thee, Sleep! by any stealth:
> So do not let me wear to-night away:

Without Thee what is all the morning's wealth?
Come, blessèd barrier between day and day,
Dear mother of fresh thoughts and joyous health.
W. Wordsworth

314

THE SOLDIER'S DREAM

Our bugles sang truce, for the night-cloud had lower'd
  And the sentinel stars set their watch in the sky;
And thousands had sunk on the ground overpower'd,
  The weary to sleep, and the wounded to die.

When reposing that night on my pallet of straw
  By the wolf-scaring faggot that guarded the slain,
At the dead of the night a sweet Vision I saw;
  And thrice ere the morning I dreamt it again.

Methought from the battle-field's dreadful array
  Far, far, I had roam'd on a desolate track:
'Twas Autumn,—and sunshine arose on the way
  To the home of my fathers, that welcomed me back.

I flew to the pleasant fields traversed so oft
  In life's morning march, when my bosom was young,
I heard my own mountain-goats bleating aloft,
  And knew the sweet strain that the corn-reapers sung.

Then pledged we the wine-cup, and fondly I swore
  From my home and my weeping friends never to part;
My little ones kiss'd me a thousand times o'er,
  And my wife sobb'd aloud in her fulness of heart.

'Stay—stay with us!—rest!—thou art weary and worn!'—
  And fain was their war-broken soldier to stay;—
But sorrow return'd with the dawning of morn,
  And the voice in my dreaming ear melted away.

T. Campbell

315

A DREAM OF THE UNKNOWN

I dream'd that as I wander'd by the way
  Bare Winter suddenly was changed to Spring,
And gentle odours led my steps astray,
  Mix'd with a sound of waters murmuring
Along a shelving bank of turf, which lay
  Under a copse, and hardly dared to fling
Its green arms round the bosom of the stream,
But kiss'd it and then fled, as Thou mightest in dream.

There grew pied wind-flowers and violets,
  Daisies, those pearl'd Arcturi of the earth,
The constellated flower that never sets;
  Faint oxlips; tender blue-bells, at whose birth
The sod scarce heaved; and that tall flower that wets —
  Like a child, half in tenderness and mirth —
Its mother's face with heaven-collected tears,
When the low wind, its playmate's voice, it hears.

And in the warm hedge grew lush eglantine,
  Green cow-bind and the moonlight-colour'd May,
And cherry-blossoms, and white cups, whose wine
  Was the bright dew yet drain'd not by the day;

And wild roses, and ivy serpentine
  With its dark buds and leaves, wandering astray;
And flowers azure, black, and streak'd with gold,
Fairer than any waken'd eyes behold.

And nearer to the river's trembling edge
  There grew broad flag-flowers, purple prank'd with white,
And starry river-buds among the sedge,
  And floating water-lilies, broad and bright,
Which lit the oak that overhung the hedge
  With moonlight beams of their own watery light;
And bulrushes, and reeds of such deep green
As soothed and dazzled eye with sober sheen.

Methought that of these visionary flowers
  I made a nosegay, bound in such a way
That the same hues, which in their natural bowers
  Were mingled or opposed, the like array
Kept these imprison'd children of the Hours
  Within my hand,—and then, elate and gay,
I hasten'd to the spot whence I had come
That I might there present it—O! to Whom?
P. B. Shelley

316

KUBLA KHAN

In Xanadu did Kubla Khan
A stately pleasure-dome decree:
Where Alph, the sacred river, ran
Through caverns measureless to man
  Down to a sunless sea.

So twice five miles of fertile ground
With walls and towers were girdled round:
And there were gardens bright with sinuous rills
Where blossom'd many an incense-bearing tree;
10 And here were forests ancient as the hills,
Enfolding sunny spots of greenery.

But oh! that deep romantic chasm which slanted
Down the green hill athwart a cedarn cover!
A savage place! as holy and enchanted
15 As e'er beneath a waning moon was haunted
By woman wailing for her demon-lover!
And from this chasm, with ceaseless turmoil seething
As if this earth in fast thick pants were breathing,
A mighty fountain momently was forced:
20 Amid whose swift half-intermitted burst
Huge fragments vaulted like rebounding hail,
Or chaffy grain beneath the thresher's flail:
And mid these dancing rocks at once and ever
It flung up momently the sacred river.
25 Five miles meandering with a mazy motion
Through wood and dale the sacred river ran,
Then reach'd the caverns measureless to man,
And sank in tumult to a lifeless ocean:
And 'mid this tumult Kubla heard from far
30 Ancestral voices prophesying war!

The shadow of the dome of pleasure
Floated midway on the waves;
Where was heard the mingled measure
From the fountain and the caves.

It was a miracle of rare device,
A sunny pleasure-dome with caves of ice!
   A damsel with a dulcimer
   In a vision once I saw:
   It was an Abyssinian maid,
   And on her dulcimer she play'd,
     Singing of Mount Abora.
   Could I revive within me
     Her symphony and song,
To such a deep delight 'twould win me
     That with music loud and long,
I would build that dome in air,
That sunny dome! those caves of ice!
And all who heard should see them there,
And all should cry, Beware! Beware!
His flashing eyes, his floating hair!
Weave a circle round him thrice,
And close your eyes with holy dread,
For he on honey-dew hath fed,
And drunk the milk of Paradise.

                         S. T. Coleridge

317
THE INNER VISION

Most sweet it is with unuplifted eyes
To pace the ground, if path be there or none,
While a fair region round the traveller lies
Which he forbears again to look upon;

Pleased rather with some soft ideal scene,
The work of Fancy, or some happy tone

Of meditation, slipping in between
The beauty coming and the beauty gone.

—If Thought and Love desert us, from that day
Let us break off all commerce with the Muse:
With Thought and Love companions of our way—

Whate'er the senses take or may refuse,—
The Mind's internal heaven shall shed her dews
Of inspiration on the humblest lay.

W. Wordsworth

318

THE REALM OF FANCY

Ever let the Fancy roam;
Pleasure never is at home:
At a touch sweet Pleasure melteth,
Like to bubbles when rain pelteth;
Then let wingéd Fancy wander
Through the thought still spread beyond her:
Open wide the mind's cage-door,
She'll dart forth, and cloudward soar.
O sweet Fancy! let her loose;
Summer's joys are spoilt by use,
And the enjoying of the Spring
Fades as does its blossoming;
Autumn's red-lipp'd fruitage too,
Blushing through the mist and dew,
Cloys with tasting: What do then?
Sit thee by the ingle, when
The sear faggot blazes bright,
Spirit of a winter's night;

Book Fourth 401

When the soundless earth is muffled,
And the cakéd snow is shuffled
From the ploughboy's heavy shoon;
When the Night doth meet the Noon
In a dark conspiracy
To banish Even from her sky.
Sit thee there, and send abroad,
With a mind self-overaw'd,
Fancy, high-commission'd:—send her!
She has vassals to attend her:
She will bring, in spite of frost,
Beauties that the earth hath lost;
She will bring thee, all together,
All delights of summer weather;
All the buds and bells of May,
From dewy sward or thorny spray;
All the heapéd Autumn's wealth,
With a still, mysterious stealth:
She will mix these pleasures up
Like three fit wines in a cup,
And thou shalt quaff it:—thou shalt hear
Distant harvest-carols clear;
Rustle of the reapéd corn;
Sweet birds antheming the morn:
And, in the same moment—hark!
'Tis the early April lark,
Or the rooks, with busy caw,
Foraging for sticks and straw.
Thou shalt, at one glance, behold
The daisy and the marigold;
White-plumed lilies, and the first

50 Hedge-grown primrose that hath burst;
Shaded hyacinth, alway
Sapphire queen of the mid-May;
And every leaf, and every flower
Pearlèd with the self-same shower.
55 Thou shalt see the field-mouse peep
Meagre from its cellèd sleep;
And the snake all winter-thin
Cast on sunny bank its skin;
Freckled nest-eggs thou shalt see
60 Hatching in the hawthorn-tree,
When the hen-bird's wing doth rest
Quiet on her mossy nest;
Then the hurry and alarm
When the bee-hive casts its swarm;
65 Acorns ripe down-pattering,
While the autumn breezes sing.

Oh, sweet Fancy! let her loose;
Everything is spoilt by use:
Where's the cheek that doth not fade,
70 Too much gazed at? Where's the maid
Whose lip mature is ever new?
Where's the eye, however blue,
Doth not weary? Where's the face
One would meet in every place?
75 Where's the voice, however soft,
One would hear so very oft?
At a touch sweet Pleasure melteth
Like to bubbles when rain pelteth.
Let then wingèd Fancy find

Thee a mistress to thy mind: 80
Dulcet-eyed as Ceres' daughter,
Ere the God of Torment taught her
How to frown and how to chide;
With a waist and with a side
White as Hebe's, when her zone 85
Slipt its golden clasp, and down
Fell her kirtle to her feet,
While she held the goblet sweet,
And Jove grew languid.—Break the mesh
Of the Fancy's silken leash; 90
Quickly break her prison-string,
And such joys as these she'll bring,
—Let the wingéd Fancy roam,
Pleasure never is at home.

J. Keats

319

WRITTEN IN EARLY SPRING

I heard a thousand blended notes
While in a grove I sate reclined,
In that sweet mood when pleasant thoughts
Bring sad thoughts to the mind.

To her fair works did Nature link 5
The human soul that through me ran;
And much it grieved my heart to think
What Man has made of Man.

Through primrose tufts, in that sweet bower,
The periwinkle trail'd its wreaths; 10

And 'tis my faith that every flower
Enjoys the air it breathes.

The birds around me hopp'd and play'd,
Their thoughts I cannot measure,—
But the least motion which they made
It seem'd a thrill of pleasure.

The budding twigs spread out their fan
To catch the breezy air;
And I must think, do all I can,
That there was pleasure there.

If this belief from heaven be sent,
If such be Nature's holy plan,
Have I not reason to lament
What Man has made of Man?

W. Wordsworth

320

RUTH: OR THE INFLUENCES OF NATURE

When Ruth was left half desolate
Her father took another mate;
And Ruth, not seven years old,
A slighted child, at her own will
Went wandering over dale and hill,
In thoughtless freedom, bold.

And she had made a pipe of straw,
And music from that pipe could draw
Like sounds of winds and floods;

Had built a bower upon the green,
As if she from her birth had been
An infant of the woods.

Beneath her father's roof, alone
She seem'd to live; her thoughts her own;
Herself her own delight:
Pleased with herself, nor sad nor gay;
And passing thus the live-long day,
She grew to woman's height.

There came a youth from Georgia's shore—
A military casque he wore
With splendid feathers drest;
He brought them from the Cherokees;
The feathers nodded in the breeze
And made a gallant crest.

From Indian blood you deem him sprung:
But no! he spake the English tongue
And bore a soldier's name;
And, when America was free
From battle and from jeopardy,
He 'cross the ocean came.

With hues of genius on his cheek,
In finest tones the youth could speak:
—While he was yet a boy
The moon, the glory of the sun,
And streams that murmur as they run
Had been his dearest joy.

He was a lovely youth! I guess
The panther in the wilderness
Was not so fair as he;
And when he chose to sport and play,
No dolphin ever was so gay
Upon the tropic sea.

Among the Indians he had fought;
And with him many tales he brought
Of pleasure and of fear;
Such tales as, told to any maid
By such a youth, in the green shade,
Were perilous to hear.

He told of girls, a happy rout!
Who quit their fold with dance and shout,
Their pleasant Indian town,
To gather strawberries all day long;
Returning with a choral song
When daylight is gone down.

He spake of plants that hourly change
Their blossoms, through a boundless range
Of intermingling hues;
With budding, fading, faded flowers,
They stand the wonder of the bowers
From morn to evening dews.

He told of the magnolia, spread
High as a cloud, high over head!
The cypress and her spire;

—Of flowers that with one scarlet gleam
Cover a hundred leagues, and seem 65
To set the hills on fire.

The youth of green savannahs spake,
And many an endless, endless lake
With all its fairy crowds
Of islands, that together lie 70
As quietly as spots of sky
Among the evening clouds.

'How pleasant,' then he said, 'it were
A fisher or a hunter there,
In sunshine or in shade 75
To wander with an easy mind,
And build a household fire, and find
A home in every glade!

'What days and what bright years! Ah me!
Our life were life indeed, with thee 80
So pass'd in quiet bliss;
And all the while,' said he, 'to know
That we were in a world of woe,
On such an earth as this!'

And then he sometimes interwove 85
Fond thoughts about a father's love,
'For there,' said he, 'are spun
Around the heart such tender ties,
That our own children to our eyes
Are dearer than the sun. 90

'Sweet Ruth! and could you go with me
My helpmate in the woods to be,
Our shed at night to rear;
Or run, my own adopted bride,
A sylvan huntress at my side,
And drive the flying deer!

'Beloved Ruth!'—No more he said.
The wakeful Ruth at midnight shed
A solitary tear:
She thought again—and did agree
With him to sail across the sea,
And drive the flying deer.

'And now, as fitting is and right,
We in the church our faith will plight,
A husband and a wife.'
Even so they did; and I may say
That to sweet Ruth that happy day
Was more than human life.

Through dream and vision did she sink,
Delighted all the while to think
That, on those lonesome floods
And green savannahs, she should share
His board with lawful joy, and bear
His name in the wild woods.

But, as you have before been told,
This Stripling, sportive, gay, and bold,
And with his dancing crest

So beautiful, through savage lands
Had roam'd about, with vagrant bands
Of Indians in the West. 120

The wind, the tempest roaring high,
The tumult of a tropic sky
Might well be dangerous food
For him, a youth to whom was given
So much of earth—so much of heaven, 125
And such impetuous blood.

Whatever in those climes he found
Irregular in sight or sound
Did to his mind impart
A kindred impulse, seem'd allied 130
To his own powers, and justified
The workings of his heart.

Nor less, to feed voluptuous thought,
The beauteous forms of Nature wrought,—
Fair trees and gorgeous flowers; 135
The breezes their own languor lent;
The stars had feelings, which they sent
Into those favour'd bowers.

Yet, in his worst pursuits, I ween
That sometimes there did intervene 140
Pure hopes of high intent:
For passions link'd to forms so fair
And stately, needs must have their share
Of noble sentiment.

145 But ill he lived, much evil saw,
With men to whom no better law
Nor better life was known;
Deliberately and undeceived
Those wild men's vices he received,
150 And gave them back his own.

His genius and his moral frame
Were thus impair'd, and he became
The slave of low desires:
A man who without self-control
155 Would seek what the degraded soul
Unworthily admires.

And yet he with no feign'd delight
Had woo'd the maiden, day and night
Had loved her, night and morn:
160 What could he less than love a maid
Whose heart with so much nature play'd—
So kind and so forlorn?

Sometimes most earnestly he said,
'O Ruth! I have been worse than dead;
165 False thoughts, thoughts bold and vain
Encompass'd me on every side
When I, in confidence and pride,
Had cross'd the Atlantic main.

'Before me shone a glorious world
170 Fresh as a banner bright, unfurl'd
To music suddenly:

Book Fourth

I look'd upon those hills and plains,
And seem'd as if let loose from chains
To live at liberty!

'No more of this—for now, by thee,   175
Dear Ruth! more happily set free,
With nobler zeal I burn;
My soul from darkness is released
Like the whole sky when to the east
The morning doth return.'   180

Full soon that better mind was gone;
No hope, no wish remain'd, not one,—
They stirr'd him now no more;
New objects did new pleasure give,
And once again he wish'd to live   185
As lawless as before.

Meanwhile, as thus with him it fared,
They for the voyage were prepared,
And went to the sea-shore:
But, when they thither came, the youth   190
Deserted his poor bride, and Ruth
Could never find him more.

God help thee, Ruth!—Such pains she had
That she in half a year was mad
And in a prison housed;   195
And there, with many a doleful song
Made of wild words, her cup of wrong
She fearfully caroused.

Yet sometimes milder hours she knew,
Nor wanted sun, nor rain, nor dew,
Nor pastimes of the May,
—They all were with her in her cell;
And a clear brook with cheerful knell
Did o'er the pebbles play.

When Ruth three seasons thus had lain,
There came a respite to her pain;
She from her prison fled;
But of the Vagrant none took thought;
And where it liked her best she sought
Her shelter and her bread.

Among the fields she breathed again:
The master-current of her brain
Ran permanent and free;
And, coming to the banks of Tone,
There did she rest; and dwell alone
Under the greenwood tree.

The engines of her pain, the tools
That shaped her sorrow, rocks and pools,
And airs that gently stir
The vernal leaves—she loved them still,
Nor ever tax'd them with the ill
Which had been done to her.

A barn her Winter bed supplies;
But, till the warmth of Summer skies
And Summer days is gone,

(And all do in this tale agree)
She sleeps beneath the greenwood tree,
And other home hath none.

An innocent life, yet far astray!
And Ruth will, long before her day,   230
Be broken down and old.
Sore aches she needs must have! but less
Of mind, than body's wretchedness,
From damp, and rain, and cold.

If she is prest by want of food   235
She from her dwelling in the wood
Repairs to a road-side;
And there she begs at one steep place,
Where up and down with easy pace
The horsemen-travellers ride.   240

That oaten pipe of hers is mute
Or thrown away: but with a flute
Her loneliness she cheers;
This flute, made of a hemlock stalk,
At evening in his homeward walk   245
The Quantock woodman hears.

I, too, have pass'd her on the hills
Setting her little water-mills
By spouts and fountains wild—
Such small machinery as she turn'd   250
Ere she had wept, ere she had mourn'd,—
A young and happy child!

Farewell! and when thy days are told,
Ill-fated Ruth! in hallow'd mould
Thy corpse shall buried be;
For thee a funeral bell shall ring,
And all the congregation sing
A Christian psalm for thee.

W. Wordsworth

321

WRITTEN AMONG THE EUGANEAN HILLS

Many a green isle needs must be
In the deep wide sea of Misery,
Or the mariner, worn and wan,
Never thus could voyage on
Day and night, and night and day,
Drifting on his dreary way,
With the solid darkness black
Closing round his vessel's track;
Whilst above, the sunless sky
Big with clouds, hangs heavily,
And behind the tempest fleet
Hurries on with lightning feet,
Riving sail, and cord, and plank,
Till the ship has almost drank
Death from the o'er-brimming deep;
And sinks down, down, like that sleep
When the dreamer seems to be
Weltering through eternity;

And the dim low line before
Of a dark and distant shore
Still recedes, as ever still
Longing with divided will,
But no power to seek or shun,
He is ever drifted on
O'er the unreposing wave,
To the haven of the grave.

Ah, many flowering islands lie
In the waters of wide Agony:
To such a one this morn was led
My bark, by soft winds piloted.
—'Mid the mountains Euganean
I stood listening to the paean
With which the legion'd rooks did hail
The Sun's uprise majestical:
Gathering round with wings all hoar,
Through the dewy mist they soar
Like gray shades, till eastern heaven
Bursts; and then,—as clouds of even
Fleck'd with fire and azure, lie
In the unfathomable sky,—
So their plumes of purple grain
Starr'd with drops of golden rain
Gleam above the sunlight woods,
As in silent multitudes
On the morning's fitful gale
Through the broken mist they sail
And the vapours cloven and gleaming
Follow down the dark steep streaming,

Till all is bright, and clear, and still
Round the solitary hill.

Beneath is spread like a green sea
The waveless plain of Lombardy,
Bounded by the vaporous air,
Islanded by cities fair;
Underneath Day's azure eyes,
Ocean's nursling, Venice lies,—
A peopled labyrinth of walls,
Amphitrite's destined halls,
Which her hoary sire now paves
With his blue and beaming waves.
Lo! the sun upsprings behind,
Broad, red, radiant, half-reclined
On the level quivering line
Of the waters crystalline,
And before that chasm of light,
As within a furnace bright,
Column, tower, and dome, and spire,
Shine like obelisks of fire,
Pointing with inconstant motion
From the altar of dark ocean
To the sapphire-tinted skies;
As the flames of sacrifice
From the marble shrines did rise
As to pierce the dome of gold
Where Apollo spoke of old.

Sun-girt City! thou hast been
Ocean's child, and then his queen;

Book Fourth

Now is come a darker day,
And thou soon must be his prey,
If the power that raised thee here 80
Hallow so thy watery bier.
A less drear ruin then than now,
With thy conquest-branded brow
Stooping to the slave of slaves
From thy throne among the waves 85
Wilt thou be,—when the sea-mew
Flies, as once before it flew,
O'er thine isles depopulate,
And all is in its ancient state,
Save where many a palace-gate 90
With green sea-flowers overgrown
Like a rock of ocean's own,
Topples o'er the abandon'd sea
As the tides change sullenly.
The fisher on his watery way 95
Wandering at the close of day,
Will spread his sail and seize his oar
Till he pass the gloomy shore,
Lest thy dead should, from their sleep,
Bursting o'er the starlight deep, 100
Lead a rapid masque of death
O'er the waters of his path.

 Noon descends around me now:
'Tis the noon of autumn's glow,
When a soft and purple mist 105
Like a vaporous amethyst,

Or an air-dissolvéd star
Mingling light and fragrance, far
From the curved horizon's bound
To the point of heaven's profound,
Fills the overflowing sky;
And the plains that silent lie
Underneath; the leaves unsodden
Where the infant Frost has trodden
With his morning-wingéd feet
Whose bright print is gleaming yet;
And the red and golden vines
Piercing with their trellised lines
The rough, dark-skirted wilderness;
The dun and bladed grass no less,
Pointing from this hoary tower
In the windless air; the flower
Glimmering at my feet; the line
Of the olive-sandall'd Apennine
In the south dimly islanded;
And the Alps, whose snows are spread
High between the clouds and sun;
And of living things each one;
And my spirit, which so long
Darken'd this swift stream of song,—
Interpenetrated lie
By the glory of the sky;
Be it love, light, harmony,
Odour, or the soul of all
Which from heaven like dew doth fall,
Or the mind which feeds this verse,
Peopling the lone universe.

Book Fourth

Noon descends, and after noon
Autumn's evening meets me soon,
Leading the infantine moon   140
And that one star, which to her
Almost seems to minister
Half the crimson light she brings
From the sunset's radiant springs:
And the soft dreams of the morn   145
(Which like wingéd winds had borne
To that silent isle, which lies
'Mid remember'd agonies,
The frail bark of this lone being),
Pass, to other sufferers fleeing,   150
And its ancient pilot, Pain,
Sits beside the helm again.

Other flowering isles must be
In the sea of Life and Agony:
Other spirits float and flee   155
O'er that gulf: Ev'n now, perhaps,
On some rock the wild wave wraps,
With folded wings they waiting sit
For my bark, to pilot it
To some calm and blooming cove;   160
Where for me, and those I love,
May a windless bower be built,
Far from passion, pain, and guilt,
In a dell 'mid lawny hills
Which the wild sea-murmur fills,   165
And soft sunshine, and the sound
Of old forests echoing round,

And the light and smell divine
Of all flowers that breathe and shine,
— We may live so happy there,
That the Spirits of the Air
Envying us, may ev'n entice
To our healing paradise
The polluting multitude:
But their rage would be subdued
By that clime divine and calm,
And the winds whose wings rain balm
On the uplifted soul, and leaves
Under which the bright sea heaves;
While each breathless interval
In their whisperings musical
The inspired soul supplies
With its own deep melodies;
And the Love which heals all strife
Circling, like the breath of life,
All things in that sweet abode
With its own mild brotherhood:—
They, not it, would change; and soon
Every sprite beneath the moon
Would repent its envy vain,
And the Earth grow young again.

P. B. Shelley

322

ODE TO THE WEST WIND

O wild West Wind, thou breath of Autumn's being,
Thou, from whose unseen presence the leaves dead
Are driven, like ghosts from an enchanter fleeing,

Yellow, and black, and pale, and hectic red,
Pestilence-stricken multitudes! O thou
Who chariotest to their dark wintry bed
The wingéd seeds, where they lie cold and low,
Each like a corpse within its grave, until
Thine azure sister of the Spring shall blow
Her clarion o'er the dreaming earth, and fill
(Driving sweet buds like flocks to feed in air)
With living hues and odours plain and hill:
Wild Spirit, which art moving everywhere;
Destroyer and Preserver; Hear, oh hear!

  Thou on whose stream, 'mid the steep sky's commotion,
Loose clouds like earth's decaying leaves are shed,
Shook from the tangled boughs of heaven and ocean,
Angels of rain and lightning! there are spread
On the blue surface of thine airy surge,
Like the bright hair uplifted from the head
Of some fierce Maenad, ev'n from the dim verge
Of the horizon to the zenith's height—
The locks of the approaching storm. Thou dirge
Of the dying year, to which this closing night
Will be the dome of a vast sepulchre,
Vaulted with all thy congregated might
Of vapours, from whose solid atmosphere
Black rain, and fire, and hail, will burst: Oh hear!

  Thou who didst waken from his summer-dreams
The blue Mediterranean, where he lay,
Lull'd by the coil of his crystalline streams,
Beside a pumice isle in Baiae's bay,

And saw in sleep old palaces and towers
Quivering within the wave's intenser day,
All overgrown with azure moss, and flowers
So sweet, the sense faints picturing them! Thou
For whose path the Atlantic's level powers
Cleave themselves into chasms, while far below
The sea-blooms and the oozy woods which wear
The sapless foliage of the ocean, know
Thy voice, and suddenly grow gray with fear
And tremble and despoil themselves: Oh hear!

If I were a dead leaf thou mightest bear;
If I were a swift cloud to fly with thee;
A wave to pant beneath thy power, and share
The impulse of thy strength, only less free
Than Thou, O uncontrollable! If even
I were as in my boyhood, and could be
The comrade of thy wanderings over heaven,
As then, when to outstrip thy skiey speed
Scarce seem'd a vision,—I would ne'er have striven
As thus with thee in prayer in my sore need.
Oh! lift me as a wave, a leaf, a cloud!
I fall upon the thorns of life! I bleed!
A heavy weight of hours has chain'd and bow'd
One too like thee—tameless, and swift, and proud.

Make me thy lyre, ev'n as the forest is:
What if my leaves are falling like its own!
The tumult of thy mighty harmonies
Will take from both a deep autumnal tone,
Sweet though in sadness. Be thou, Spirit fierce,

My spirit! be thou me, impetuous one!
Drive my dead thoughts over the universe,
Like wither'd leaves, to quicken a new birth;
And, by the incantation of this verse, 65
Scatter, as from an unextinguish'd hearth
Ashes and sparks, my words among mankind!
Be through my lips to unawaken'd earth
The trumpet of a prophecy! O Wind,
If Winter comes, can Spring be far behind? 70

P. B. Shelley

323

NATURE AND THE POET

Suggested by a Picture of Peele Castle in a Storm, painted by Sir George Beaumont

I was thy neighbour once, thou rugged Pile!
Four summer weeks I dwelt in sight of thee:
I saw thee every day; and all the while
Thy Form was sleeping on a glassy sea.

So pure the sky, so quiet was the air! 5
So like, so very like, was day to day!
Whene'er I look'd, thy image still was there;
It trembled, but it never pass'd away.

How perfect was the calm! It seem'd no sleep,
No mood, which season takes away, or brings: 10
I could have fancied that the mighty Deep
Was even the gentlest of all gentle things.

Ah! then — if mine had been the painter's hand
To express what then I saw; and add the gleam,
15 The light that never was on sea or land,
The consecration, and the Poet's dream, —

I would have planted thee, thou hoary pile,
Amid a world how different from this!
Beside a sea that could not cease to smile;
20 On tranquil land, beneath a sky of bliss.

Thou shouldst have seem'd a treasure-house divine
Of peaceful years; a chronicle of heaven; —
Of all the sunbeams that did ever shine
The very sweetest had to thee been given.

25 A picture had it been of lasting ease,
Elysian quiet, without toil or strife;
No motion but the moving tide; a breeze;
Or merely silent Nature's breathing life.

Such, in the fond illusion of my heart,
30 Such picture would I at that time have made·
And seen the soul of truth in every part,
A steadfast peace that might not be betray'd.

So once it would have been, — 'tis so no more;
I have submitted to a new control:
35 A power is gone, which nothing can restore;
A deep distress hath humanized my soul.

Not for a moment could I now behold
A smiling sea, and be what I have been:
The feeling of my loss will ne'er be old;
40 This, which I know, I speak with mind serene.

Then, Beaumont, Friend! who would have been the friend
If he had lived, of Him whom I deplore,
This work of thine I blame not, but commend;
This sea in anger, and that dismal shore.

O 'tis a passionate work! — yet wise and well, 45
Well chosen is the spirit that is here;
That hulk which labours in the deadly swell,
This rueful sky, this pageantry of fear!

And this huge Castle, standing here sublime,
I love to see the look with which it braves, 50
— Cased in the unfeeling armour of old time —
The lightning, the fierce wind, and trampling waves.

— Farewell, farewell the heart that lives alone,
Housed in a dream, at distance from the Kind!
Such happiness, wherever it be known, 55
Is to be pitied; for 'tis surely blind.

But welcome fortitude, and patient cheer,
And frequent sights of what is to be borne!
Such sights, or worse, as are before me here: —
Not without hope we suffer and we mourn. 60

W. Wordsworth

THE POET'S DREAM

On a Poet's lips I slept
Dreaming like a love-adept
In the sound his breathing kept;

Nor seeks nor finds he mortal blisses,
But feeds on the aerial kisses
Of shapes that haunt Thought's wildernesses.
He will watch from dawn to gloom
The lake-reflected sun illume
The yellow bees in the ivy-bloom,
Nor heed nor see what things they be —
But from these create he can
Forms more real than living Man,
    Nurslings of Immortality!

P. B. Shelley

325

GLEN-ALMAIN, THE NARROW GLEN

In this still place, remote from men,
Sleeps Ossian, in the Narrow Glen;
In this still place, where murmurs on
But one meek streamlet, only one:
He sang of battles, and the breath
Of stormy war, and violent death;
And should, methinks, when all was past,
Have rightfully been laid at last
Where rocks were rudely heap'd, and rent
As by a spirit turbulent;
Where sights were rough, and sounds were wild,
And everything unreconciled;
In some complaining, dim retreat,
For fear and melancholy meet;
But this is calm; there cannot be
A more entire tranquillity.

Book Fourth

Does then the Bard sleep here indeed?
Or is it but a groundless creed?
What matters it? — I blame them not
Whose fancy in this lonely spot
Was moved; and in such way express'd
Their notion of its perfect rest.
A convent, even a hermit's cell,
Would break the silence of this Dell:
It is not quiet, is not ease;
But something deeper far than these:
The separation that is here
Is of the grave; and of austere
Yet happy feelings of the dead:
And, therefore, was it rightly said
That Ossian, last of all his race!
Lies buried in this lonely place.

W. Wordsworth

326

The World is too much with us; late and soon,
Getting and spending, we lay waste our powers;
Little we see in Nature that is ours;
We have given our hearts away, a sordid boon!

This Sea that bares her bosom to the moon,
The winds that will be howling at all hours
And are up-gather'd now like sleeping flowers,
For this, for everything, we are out of tune;

It moves us not. — Great God! I'd rather be
A Pagan suckled in a creed outworn, —
So might I, standing on this pleasant lea,

Have glimpses that would make me less forlorn;
Have sight of Proteus rising from the sea;
Or hear old Triton blow his wreathéd horn.

W. Wordsworth

327

WITHIN KING'S COLLEGE CHAPEL, CAMBRIDGE

Tax not the royal Saint with vain expense,
With ill-match'd aims the Architect who plann'd
(Albeit labouring for a scanty band
Of white-robed Scholars only) this immense

5 And glorious work of fine intelligence!
— Give all thou canst; high Heaven rejects the lore
Of nicely-calculated less or more: —
So deem'd the man who fashion'd for the sense

These lofty pillars, spread that branching roof
10 Self-poised, and scoop'd into ten thousand cells
Where light and shade repose, where music dwells

Lingering — and wandering on as loth to die;
Like thoughts whose very sweetness yieldeth proof
That they were born for immortality.

W. Wordsworth

328

ODE ON A GRECIAN URN

Thou still unravish'd bride of quietness,
  Thou foster-child of silence and slow time,
Sylvan historian, who canst thus express
  A flowery tale more sweetly than our rhyme:

*. . . that branching roof
Self-poised.*

Book Fourth

What leaf-fringed legend haunts about thy shape
  Of deities or mortals, or of both,
    In Tempé or the dales of Arcady?
What men or gods are these? What maidens loth?
  What mad pursuit? What struggle to escape?
    What pipes and timbrels? What wild ecstasy?

Heard melodies are sweet, but those unheard
  Are sweeter; therefore, ye soft pipes, play on;
Not to the sensual ear, but, more endear'd,
  Pipe to the spirit ditties of no tone:
Fair youth, beneath the trees, thou canst not leave
  Thy song, nor ever can those trees be bare;
    Bold Lover, never, never canst thou kiss,
Though winning near the goal — yet, do not grieve;
  She cannot fade, though thou hast not thy bliss,
    For ever wilt thou love, and she be fair!

Ah, happy, happy boughs! that cannot shed
  Your leaves, nor ever bid the Spring adieu;
And, happy melodist, unwearièd,
  For ever piping songs for ever new;
More happy love! more happy, happy love!
    For ever warm and still to be enjoy'd,
    For ever panting, and for ever young;
All breathing human passion far above,
  That leaves a heart high-sorrowful and cloy'd,
    A burning forehead, and a parching tongue.

Who are these coming to the sacrifice?
  To what green altar, O mysterious priest,

Lead'st thou that heifer lowing at the skies,
  And all her silken flanks with garlands drest?
What little town by river or sea shore,
  Or mountain-built with peaceful citadel,
    Is emptied of this folk, this pious morn?
And, little town, thy streets for evermore
  Will silent be; and not a soul to tell
    Why thou art desolate, can e'er return.

O Attic shape! Fair attitude! with brede
  Of marble men and maidens overwrought,
With forest branches and the trodden weed;
  Thou, silent form, dost tease us out of thought
As doth eternity: Cold Pastoral!
  When old age shall this generation waste,
    Thou shalt remain, in midst of other woe
Than ours, a friend to man, to whom thou say'st,
  'Beauty is truth, truth beauty,' — that is all
    Ye know on earth, and all ye need to know.

J. Keats

329

YOUTH AND AGE

Verse, a breeze 'mid blossoms straying,
  Where Hope clung feeding, like a bee —
Both were mine! Life went a-maying
  With Nature, Hope and Poesy,
    When I was young!
When I was young? — Ah, woful when!
Ah! for the change 'twixt Now and Then!
This breathing house not built with hands,

This body that does me grievous wrong,
O'er aery cliffs and glittering sands
How lightly then it flash'd along:
Like those trim skiffs, unknown of yore,
On winding lakes and rivers wide,
That ask no aid of sail or oar,
That fear no spite of wind or tide!
Nought cared this body for wind or weather
When Youth and I lived in't together.

   Flowers are lovely; Love is flower-like;
Friendship is a sheltering tree;
O! the joys, that came down shower-like,
Of Friendship, Love, and Liberty,
        Ere I was old!
Ere I was old? Ah woful Ere,
Which tells me, Youth's no longer here!
O Youth! for years so many and sweet,
'Tis known that Thou and I were one,
I'll think it but a fond conceit —
It cannot be, that Thou art gone!
Thy vesper-bell hath not yet toll'd: —
And thou wert aye a masker bold!
What strange disguise hast now put on
To make believe that Thou art gone?
I see these locks in silvery slips,
This drooping gait, this alter'd size:
But Springtide blossoms on thy lips,
And tears take sunshine from thine eyes!
Life is but Thought: so think I will
That Youth and I are house-mates still.

Dew-drops are the gems of morning,
But the tears of mournful eve!
Where no hope is, life's a warning
That only serves to make us grieve
    When we are old:
— That only serves to make us grieve
With oft and tedious taking-leave,
Like some poor nigh-related guest
That may not rudely be dismist,
Yet hath out-stay'd his welcome while,
And tells the jest without the smile.
                      S. T. Coleridge

330

THE TWO APRIL MORNINGS

We walk'd along, while bright and red
Uprose the morning sun;
And Matthew stopp'd, he look'd, and said
'The will of God be done!'

A village schoolmaster was he,
With hair of glittering gray;
As blithe a man as you could see
On a spring holiday.

And on that morning, through the grass
And by the steaming rills
We travell'd merrily, to pass
A day among the hills.

'Our work,' said I, 'was well begun;
Then, from thy breast what thought,

Book Fourth

Beneath so beautiful a sun,
So sad a sigh has brought?'

A second time did Matthew stop;
And fixing still his eye
Upon the eastern mountain-top,
To me he made reply:

'Yon cloud with that long purple cleft
Brings fresh into my mind
A day like this, which I have left
Full thirty years behind.

'And just above yon slope of corn
Such colours, and no other,
Were in the sky that April morn,
Of this the very brother.

'With rod and line I sued the sport
Which that sweet season gave,
And to the church-yard come, stopp'd short
Beside my daughter's grave.

'Nine summers had she scarcely seen,
The pride of all the vale;
And then she sang, — she would have been
A very nightingale.

'Six feet in earth my Emma lay;
And yet I loved her more —
For so it seem'd, — than till that day
I e'er had loved before.

'And turning from her grave, I met,
  Beside the churchyard yew,
A blooming Girl, whose hair was wet
  With points of morning dew.

'A basket on her head she bare;
  Her brow was smooth and white:
To see a child so very fair,
  It was a pure delight!

'No fountain from its rocky cave
  E'er tripp'd with foot so free;
She seem'd as happy as a wave
  That dances on the sea.

'There came from me a sigh of pain
  Which I could ill confine;
I look'd at her, and look'd again:
  And did not wish her mine!'

— Matthew is in his grave, yet now
  Methinks I see him stand
As at that moment, with a bough
  Of wilding in his hand.

W. Wordsworth

331

THE FOUNTAIN

A Conversation

We talk'd with open heart, and tongue
  Affectionate and true,
A pair of friends, though I was young,
  And Matthew seventy-two.

Book Fourth

We lay beneath a spreading oak,
Beside a mossy seat;
And from the turf a fountain broke
And gurgled at our feet.

'Now, Matthew!' said I, 'let us match
This water's pleasant tune
With some old border-song, or catch
That suits a summer's noon;

' Or of the church-clock and the chimes
Sing here beneath the shade
That half-mad thing of witty rhymes
Which you last April made!'

In silence Matthew lay, and eyed
The spring beneath the tree;
And thus the dear old man replied,
The gray-hair'd man of glee:

'No check, no stay, this Streamlet fears,
How merrily it goes!
'Twill murmur on a thousand years
And flow as now it flows.

'And here, on this delightful day,
I cannot choose but think
How oft, a vigorous man, I lay
Beside this fountain's brink.

'My eyes are dim with childish tears,
My heart is idly stirr'd,
For the same sound is in my ears
Which in those days I heard.

'Thus fares it still in our decay:
And yet the wiser mind
Mourns less for what Age takes away,
Than what it leaves behind.

'The blackbird amid leafy trees,
The lark above the hill,
Let loose their carols when they please,
Are quiet when they will.

'With Nature never do they wage
A foolish strife; they see
A happy youth, and their old age
Is beautiful and free:

'But we are press'd by heavy laws;
And often, glad no more,
We wear a face of joy, because
We have been glad of yore.

'If there be one who need bemoan
His kindred laid in earth,
The household hearts that were his own,—
It is the man of mirth.

'My days, my friend, are almost gone,
My life has been approved,
And many love me; but by none
Am I enough beloved.'

'Now both himself and me he wrongs,
The man who thus complains!
I live and sing my idle songs
Upon these happy plains:

'And Matthew, for thy children dead
I'll be a son to thee!'
At this he grasp'd my hand and said,
'Alas! that cannot be.'

— We rose up from the fountain-side;
And down the smooth descent
Of the green sheep-track did we glide;
And through the wood we went;

And ere we came to Leonard's rock
He sang those witty rhymes
About the crazy old church-clock,
And the bewilder'd chimes.

W. Wordsworth

332

THE RIVER OF LIFE

The more we live, more brief appear
  Our life's succeeding stages:
A day to childhood seems a year,
  And years like passing ages.

The gladsome current of our youth,
  Ere passion yet disorders,
Steals lingering like a river smooth
  Along its grassy borders.

But as the care-worn cheek grows wan,
  And sorrow's shafts fly thicker,
Ye Stars, that measure life to man,
  Why seem your courses quicker?

When joys have lost their bloom and breath
    And life itself is vapid,
Why, as we reach the Falls of Death,
    Feel we its tide more rapid?

It may be strange — yet who would change
    Time's course to slower speeding,
When one by one our friends have gone
    And left our bosoms bleeding?

Heaven gives our years of fading strength
    Indemnifying fleetness;
And those of youth, a seeming length,
    Proportion'd to their sweetness.

T. Campbell

333

THE HUMAN SEASONS

Four Seasons fill the measure of the year;
There are four seasons in the mind of man:
He has his lusty Spring, when fancy clear
Takes in all beauty with an easy span:

He has his Summer, when luxuriously
Spring's honey'd cud of youthful thought he loves
To ruminate, and by such dreaming high
Is nearest unto heaven: quiet coves

His soul has in its Autumn, when his wings
He furleth close; contented so to look
On mists in idleness — to let fair things
Pass by unheeded as a threshold brook.

He has his Winter too of pale misfeature,
Or else he would forego his mortal nature.

J. Keats

334

A DIRGE

Rough wind, that moanest loud
  Grief too sad for song;
Wild wind, when sullen cloud
  Knells all the night long;
Sad storm whose tears are vain,
Bare woods whose branches stain,
Deep caves and dreary main, —
  Wail for the world's wrong!

P. B. Shelley

335

THRENOS

O World! O Life! O Time!
On whose last steps I climb,
  Trembling at that where I had stood before;
When will return the glory of your prime?
  No more — Oh, never more!

Out of the day and night
A joy has taken flight:
  Fresh spring, and summer, and winter hoar
Move my faint heart with grief, but with delight
  No more — Oh, never more!

P. B. Shelley

336

THE TROSACHS

There's not a nook within this solemn Pass,
But were an apt confessional for One
Taught by his summer spent, his autumn gone,
That Life is but a tale of morning grass
Wither'd at eve.   From scenes of art which chase
That thought away, turn, and with watchful eyes
Feed it 'mid Nature's old felicities,
Rocks, rivers, and smooth lakes more clear than glass

Untouch'd, unbreathed upon:— Thrice happy guest,
If from a golden perch of aspen spray
(October's workmanship to rival May),

The pensive warbler of the ruddy breast
That moral sweeten by a heaven-taught lay,
Lulling the year, with all its cares, to rest!

W. Wordsworth

337

My heart leaps up when I behold
   A rainbow in the sky:
So was it when my life began,
So is it now I am a man,
   So be it when I shall grow old
      Or let me die!
The Child is father of the Man:
And I could wish my days to be
Bound each to each by natural piety.

W. Wordsworth

Book Fourth

338

ODE ON INTIMATIONS OF IMMORTALITY FROM RECOLLECTIONS OF EARLY CHILDHOOD

There was a time when meadow, grove, and stream
The earth, and every common sight
    To me did seem
Apparell'd in celestial light,
The glory and the freshness of a dream.   5
It is not now as it hath been of yore;—
    Turn wheresoe'er I may,
      By night or day,
The things which I have seen I now can see no more.

    The rainbow comes and goes,   10
    And lovely is the rose;
    The moon doth with delight
Look round her when the heavens are bare;
    Waters on a starry night
    Are beautiful and fair;   15
    The sunshine is a glorious birth;
    But yet I know, where'er I go,
That there hath past away a glory from the earth.

Now, while the birds thus sing a joyous song,
    And while the young lambs bound   20
      As to the tabor's sound,
To me alone there came a thought of grief:
A timely utterance gave that thought relief,
    And I again am strong.

25 The cataracts blow their trumpets from the steep;
　No more shall grief of mine the season wrong:
　I hear the echoes through the mountains throng,
　The winds come to me from the fields of sleep,
　　　　And all the earth is gay;
30　　　　　　Land and sea
　　　Give themselves up to jollity,
　　　　And with the heart of May
　　Doth every beast keep holiday;—
　　　　　Thou child of joy
35 Shout round me, let me hear thy shouts, thou happy Shepherd-boy!

　Ye blessèd Creatures, I have heard the call
　　　Ye to each other make; I see
　The heavens laugh with you in your jubilee;
　　　My heart is at your festival,
40　　　　My head hath its coronal,
　The fulness of your bliss, I feel—I feel it all.
　　　Oh evil day! if I were sullen
　　　While Earth herself is adorning
　　　　　This sweet May-morning;
45　　　　And the children are culling
　　　　　　On every side
　　　In a thousand valleys far and wide,
　　Fresh flowers; while the sun shines warm,
　And the babe leaps up on his mother's arm:—
50　　　I hear, I hear, with joy I hear!
　　—But there's a tree, of many, one,
　A single field which I have look'd upon,
　Both of them speak of something that is gone:

*I hear the echoes through the mountains throng,
The winds come to me from the fields of sleep.*

>   The pansy at my feet
>   Doth the same tale repeat: 55
> Whither is fled the visionary gleam?
> Where is it now, the glory and the dream?
>
> Our birth is but a sleep and a forgetting;
> The Soul that rises with us, our life's Star,
>   Hath had elsewhere its setting 60
>   And cometh from afar:
>   Not in entire forgetfulness,
>   And not in utter nakedness,
> But trailing clouds of glory do we come
>   From God, who is our home: 65
> Heaven lies about us in our infancy!
> Shades of the prison-house begin to close
>   Upon the growing Boy,
> But he beholds the light, and whence it flows,
>   He sees it in his joy; 70
> The Youth, who daily farther from the east
>   Must travel, still is Nature's priest,
>   And by the vision splendid
>   Is on his way attended;
> At length the Man perceives it die away, 75
> And fade into the light of common day.
>
> Earth fills her lap with pleasures of her own;
> Yearnings she hath in her own natural kind,
> And, even with something of a mother's mind
>   And no unworthy aim, 80
>   The homely nurse doth all she can

To make her foster-child, her inmate, Man,
    Forget the glories he hath known
And that imperial palace whence he came.

85 Behold the Child among his new-born blisses,
A six years' darling of a pigmy size!
See, where 'mid work of his own hand he lies,
Fretted by sallies of his mother's kisses,
With light upon him from his father's eyes!
90 See, at his feet, some little plan or chart,
Some fragment from his dream of human life,
Shaped by himself with newly-learnéd art;
    A wedding or a festival,
    A mourning or a funeral;
95   And this hath now his heart,
    And unto this he frames his song:
    Then will he fit his tongue
To dialogues of business, love, or strife;
    But it will not be long
100   Ere this be thrown aside,
    And with new joy and pride
The little actor cons another part;
Filling from time to time his 'humorous stage'
With all the Persons, down to palsied Age,
105 That life brings with her in her equipage;
    As if his whole vocation
    Were endless imitation.

Thou, whose exterior semblance doth belie
    Thy soul's immensity;
110 Thou best philosopher, who yet dost keep

Thy heritage, thou eye among the blind,
That, deaf and silent, read'st the eternal deep,
Haunted for ever by the eternal Mind, —
　　　Mighty Prophet! Seer blest!
　　　　On whom those truths do rest　　　　　115
Which we are toiling all our lives to find,
In darkness lost, the darkness of the grave;
Thou, over whom thy Immortality
Broods like the day, a master o'er a slave,
A Presence which is not to be put by;　　　　120
Thou little child, yet glorious in the might
Of heaven-born freedom on thy being's height,
Why with such earnest pains dost thou provoke
The years to bring the inevitable yoke,
Thus blindly with thy blessedness at strife?　　125
Full soon thy soul shall have her earthly freight,
And custom lie upon thee with a weight
Heavy as frost, and deep almost as life!

　　　O joy! that in our embers
　　　Is something that doth live,　　　　　130
　　　That Nature yet remembers
　　　What was so fugitive!
The thought of our past years in me doth breed
Perpetual benediction: not indeed
For that which is most worthy to be blest,　　　135
Delight and liberty, and simple creed
Of Childhood, whether busy or at rest,
With new-fledged hope still fluttering in his breast: —
　　　— Not for these I raise
　　　The song of thanks and praise;　　　　140

But for those obstinate questionings
Of sense and outward things,
Fallings from us, vanishings;
Blank misgivings of a creature
Moving about in worlds not realized,
High instincts, before which our mortal nature
Did tremble like a guilty thing surprized:
But for those first affections,
Those shadowy recollections,
Which, be they what they may,
Are yet the fountain-light of all our day,
Are yet a master-light of all our seeing;
Uphold us, cherish, and have power to make
Our noisy years seem moments in the being
Of the eternal Silence: truths that wake,
To perish never;
Which neither listlessness, nor mad endeavour,
Nor man nor boy
Nor all that is at enmity with joy,
Can utterly abolish or destroy!
Hence, in a season of calm weather
Though inland far we be,
Our souls have sight of that immortal sea
Which brought us hither;
Can in a moment travel thither—
And see the children sport upon the shore,
And hear the mighty waters rolling evermore.

Then, sing ye birds, sing, sing a joyous song!
And let the young lambs bound
As to the tabor's sound!

Book Fourth

      We, in thought, will join your throng
        Ye that pipe and ye that play,
        Ye that through your hearts to-day
        Feel the gladness of the May!
What though the radiance which was once so bright   175
Be now for ever taken from my sight,
      Though nothing can bring back the hour
Of splendour in the grass, of glory in the flower;
        We will grieve not, rather find
        Strength in what remains behind;   180
        In the primal sympathy
        Which having been must ever be;
        In soothing thoughts that spring
        Out of human suffering;
        In the faith that looks through death,   185
In years that bring the philosophic mind.

And O, ye Fountains, Meadows, Hills, and Groves,
Forbode not any severing of our loves!
Yet in my heart of hearts I feel your might;
I only have relinquish'd one delight   190
To live beneath your more habitual sway:
I love the brooks which down their channels fret
Even more than when I tripp'd lightly as they;
The innocent brightness of a new-born day
            Is lovely yet;   195
The clouds that gather round the setting sun
Do take a sober colouring from an eye
That hath kept watch o'er man's mortality;
Another race hath been, and other palms are won.
Thanks to the human heart by which we live,   200

Thanks to its tenderness, its joys, and fears,
To me the meanest flower that blows can give
Thoughts that do often lie too deep for tears.
W. Wordsworth

339

Music, when soft voices die,
Vibrates in the memory —
Odours, when sweet violets sicken,
Live within the sense they quicken.

5 Rose leaves, when the rose is dead,
Are heap'd for the beloved's bed;
And so thy thoughts, when Thou art gone,
Love itself shall slumber on.
P. B. Shelley

APPENDIX

THE STUDY OF POETRY

Value of Palgrave's *Golden Treasury*. The value of the *Golden Treasury* is both historical and aesthetic. The historical value lies in the fact that it contains representative lyrics from the poetry of the three centuries from 1550 to 1850. The aesthetic value — the appeal to our taste — is found in the high literary quality of these lyrics, chosen as they were by two trained critics — Palgrave and Tennyson. Since its first publication, in 1861, the collection has become a standard. No other anthology has met so satisfactorily the test of time and use; no other forms so sound an introduction to the study of poetry in general.

The Nature of Poetry. The poet Keats began his *Endymion* with these words:

> "A thing of beauty is a joy for ever;
> Its loveliness increases; it will never
> Pass into nothingness; but still will keep
> A bower quiet for us, and a sleep
> Full of sweet dreams, and health, and quiet breathing."

There is a truth here that applies to all great poetry. In reading a collection like the present, it should be our aim to see the beauty and to understand the "loveliness," so that these may enter in some degree into our own experience. For the book contains, as Palgrave says, "treasures more golden than gold, leading us in higher and healthier ways than those of the world." Now, it is true of poetry, as of all great art, that full enjoyment is based upon full understanding. In proportion as we grasp the poet's meaning, just so far shall we appreciate the beauty which he tries to reveal. To gain such an understanding, we must look somewhat closely into the nature and technique of poetry.

A Criticism of Life. Matthew Arnold, one of the wisest of literary critics, said that the highest function of poetry was to act as "a criticism of life." What this means is, that all good poetry reflects in some manner the joys and sorrows of men and women on their way through the world. From our own experience we know that the poet speaks truth; he for his part helps us, or pleases us, or consoles us, by interpreting these experiences in a new light. A very brief reading in our book will enable us to see how true this is. Turn, for example, to Shakespeare's sonnet beginning "When to the sessions of sweet silent thought" (39), or Milton's noble lines on his blindness (94), or Burns's familiar love-song (190), or Hood's touching little dirge (279). These poems express in a beautiful way thoughts which come within the experience of many, and the comprehension of all.

Again, poetry tends to free us from what Wordsworth called the "preponderance of machinery" in life. He wrote, in words which are even more appropriate today than when they were written,

> "The world is too much with us; late and soon,
> Getting and spending, we lay waste our powers...
> We have given our hearts away, a sordid boon."

A real love for poetry will draw away the thoughts for a little while from the mere "machinery," and turn them to the permanent things which no machinery affects. Forgetting the petty details of everyday life, we may fix our minds on wider and more helpful ideas, — to quote Wordsworth again, on "the operations of the elements and the appearances of the visible universe, on cold and heat, on loss of friends and kindred, on injuries and resentments, on gratitude and hope, on fear and sorrow." Under such influences, the mind will be guided towards the "truths that perish never."

Beauty an End in Itself. At the same time, we must not think that poetry is written primarily to teach a lesson, or to instil a moral. Some poetry, indeed, — that which we term "didactic" — does just this. But when the poet deliberately tries to teach, he becomes a preacher; and while he may be a good preacher, he is usually a very poor poet. The great poets are concerned first of all with presenting, in the most beautiful and appropriate form possible, a thought worthy of poetical treatment.

Hence, we have poems like Shakespeare's *Full Fathom Five* (65), or Milton's *L'Allegro* (144); like Burns's *To a Mouse* (184), or Wordsworth's *The Reaper* (298). These certainly teach no lesson, but delight us because of their beauty or their pathos. We cannot "learn" anything from Keats's *Ode to a Nightingale* (290); yet really to appreciate that poem is to gain a pleasure which goes deep into the texture of living. No "lessons" can be pointed out in Shakespeare's *Fidele* (64) or in Shelley's *Art Thou Pale for Weariness* (312), yet who would be willing to forego the pure charm of idea and expression which they contain? The aim of our study of poetry is to increase in every way that we possibly can, our enjoyment of "the best that has been thought and said in the world."

Kinds of Poetry. Poetry is divided into three classes — Narrative, Dramatic, and Lyric. We shall have occasion to speak of the last at considerable length; the others may be touched upon more briefly.

Narrative Poetry: the Epic. Narrative Poetry is that which tells a story. Its tone is "objective"; that is, the interest lies in the story, rather than in the author himself. Under this division are grouped the *Epic*, the *Ballad*, the *Tale*, the *Romance*, and the *Idyl*. The most important example of the type is the Epic. It may best be described as a long poem which tells, in stately verse, about the real or imaginary exploits of great personages, heroes, or gods. It consists of a series of episodes, loosely strung together, and unified by the one strong central character. Thus, in Homer's *Iliad* we are told of "the wrath of Achilles" and its results; in the *Odyssey*, of the voyagings of Odysseus, the "far-wanderer." The most important epic poems, besides those just mentioned, are the *Aeneid* of Virgil, the *Divine Comedy* of Dante, the German *Nibelungenlied*, the early English poem *Beowulf*, and Milton's *Paradise Lost*.

Ballad, Romance, Idyl. The Ballad is a short story in verse. It is told very simply, deals with persons or events of popular interest, and follows a traditional verse-form. Familiar examples of the old ballad are *Sir Patrick Spens* and the *Robin Hood* cycle; of the modern type, Coleridge's *Rhyme of the Ancient Mariner* and Kipling's *Ballad of East and West*. The term Romance is somewhat loosely used. Originally it signified the long rhymed romantic story of the middle ages; in modern times it is represented by such work as Scott's *Marmion*, or *The Lady of the Lake*, or Morris's *The Earthly Paradise*. The Tale may be considered as simpler and truer to life than the Romance. Good examples are found in some of Chaucer's *Canterbury Tales*. For the Idyl, one naturally turns to Tennyson's *Idylls of the King*, or to the same poet's country idyls, *Enoch Arden*, or *Dora*.

Dramatic Poetry. Dramatic Poetry comprises the great body of verse written for the stage. It is composed primarily to be acted, and for this reason differs in several ways from the other types of poetry — in the rapid interchange of conversation, for instance, and the development of character, and the swift movement to a definite climax. The greatest examples of dramatic poetry are found in Shakespeare's plays. The "dramatic monologue" is a comparatively short poem wherein there is only one speaker, the presence of others being implied by the nature of the monologue. Browning's *My Last Duchess* is an excellent example of the type.

LYRIC POETRY

A Definition. The Lyric, in the original Greek meaning of the term, was a short poem intended to be sung to the lyre. Unlike Narrative Poetry, it is "subjective" — it records the personal feelings of the author. For the selections in this book, Palgrave laid down a simple rule that has been generally received as the best indication of what this kind of poetry should be. "Lyrical," he said, "has been held here essentially to mean that each poem should turn upon some single thought, feeling, or situation." This excludes, as he pointed out, narrative, descriptive, and didactic poems, as well as those of a strictly personal nature. If one had to define the limits of the true lyric, it would be difficult to use a better method.

Emotion. A lyric must have what Palgrave calls "the coloring of human passion." That is, it must touch the heart, rather than the intellect; we do not ask what it "means" but what is the impression produced upon us. Beautiful poetry is like beautiful music or beautiful painting. We do not search for the meaning or the message in a piece of magnificent operatic music, or in a superb picture; we simply enjoy the beauty that is in them. So with lyrical poetry; it appeals to our emotions, in all the various manifestations of joy or sorrow and through the emotional side of our nature we understand what the lyric has to tell us. And since our emotions are limited only by the extent of our imagination, the appeal of lyric poetry is wider than that of any other kind.

The Personal Appeal. The emotion of the lyric, as we have seen, is expressed in a personal way. And the personal emotion through the interpretation of the poet conveys so much of general truth that it becomes a "criticism of life." Thus, Shakespeare's experience is personal in the sonnet which opens,

> "When in disgrace with fortune and men's eyes,
> I all alone beweep my outcast state . . ."

Wordsworth records a personal feeling in the closing lines of the *Ode on Intimations of Immortality:*

> "Thanks to the human heart by which we live,
> Thanks to its tenderness, its joys, its fears,
> To me the meanest flower that blows can give
> Thoughts that do often lie too deep for tears."

And Shelley does the same in his *Threnos:*

> "Fresh spring, and summer, and winter hoar
> Move my faint heart with grief, but with delight
> No more — Oh, never more!"

But in each case the thought reaches out beyond the individual to a wider interest and significance. The personal emotion becomes universally true.

The " Singing " Quality. The lyric is primarily a song, and one of its characteristics has always been the " singing " quality of rhythm and metre. In some cases this quality is more strongly marked than in others, but we shall invariably find it present, whether in greater or less degree. Some lyrics are songs pure and simple — as Shakespeare's " O Mistress mine," " Under the greenwood tree," etc. Others are most familiar in their musical form, as Jonson's " Drink to me only with thine eyes," or Moore's " Oft in the stilly night." The musical settings to lyrics in *The Golden Treasury* are discussed in another place.

Must not tell a Story. We may wonder at the omission, from this collection, of poems like Coleridge's *Ancient Mariner* or Keats's *Eve of Saint Agnes* — poems which possess in the highest degree imaginative power and beauty of expression. The reason is that they tell a story, and the true lyric, as Palgrave defines it, stands apart from the ballad and other purely narrative work. Why, then, it may be asked, does he include such poems as *The Battle of the Baltic* (251), or *The Burial of Sir John Moore* (262), or *La Belle Dame sans Merci* (237), each of which is in some degree narrative? Because their interest lies distinctly not in the story but in the emotions stirred thereby. They are expressions of mood — not story-poems; the imaginative power deals with more purely emotional issues than is the case with the ballads. The lyrics in our collection touch upon love and death, on life, and friendship, on the beautiful things of earth and sea and sky. But none of these is embodied in a story, because that is not what a lyric is supposed to be.

Must be Short. Lastly, we see that the lyric is a " short " poem. A limited length is necessary to the effect which the lyric seeks to produce — the thought, the feeling, or the situation, seized at the moment of its greatest intensity. Even

Appendix

where the poem is not, literally speaking, short — as in *Lycidas*, for instance — there is preserved the essential unity of appeal.

RHYTHM AND METRE

Rhythm. In our study of lyric poetry we must know something about the form in which it finds expression. Since poetry, like music, is written for the ear, we cannot expect to read a poem with proper understanding unless we have some knowledge of the medium in which it is set forth. We come first, then, to "rhythm," the movement of verse. In the lyric, rhythmical effect is capable of the widest possible variation, and is always significant of the thought.

This movement may be quick and sprightly, as in the Elizabethan songs in Book I, or it may be slow-moving and solemn, as in Milton's *Lycidas* (89), or Gray's *Elegy* (187). Again, it may show the rapid interchange which is found in Dryden's *Alexander's Feast* (151), or be purely martial like Campbell's *Battle of the Baltic* (251), or nobly dignified, as in Wordsworth's *Ode to Duty* (252). There is something dainty and subtle in the rhythm of Herrick's *To Daffodils* (140), something indescribably etherial in Shelley's *To a Skylark* (287). The appreciation of the quality of rhythm in these and the other lyrics of *The Golden Treasury*, where all is of the first degree of excellence, forms a constant source of pleasure.

Metre. When regularly measured and defined, rhythm is called "metre." In the study of metre, we deal with strict rules which were evolved very early in the history of poetry, and which have been followed by all the great poets from Homer down to Wordsworth. It should be borne in mind that the masters of the poetic art have worked out with the utmost care the metrical forms which are most appropriate for the expression of their ideas. We shall now briefly consider these forms.

The Foot. The metre of any poem is determined by the way in which the accented syllables are disposed in the line.

The unit of the poetic line is the "foot." Each foot is made up of one accented syllable, with one or two unaccented. Four kinds of feet are generally recognized in English poetry:

Iambus ($\smile\angle$), two syllables with the accent on the second: awáy.
Anapest ($\smile\smile\angle$), three syllables with the accent on the last: interfére.
Trochee ($\angle\smile$), two syllables with the accent on the first: dóuble.
Dactyl ($\angle\smile\smile$), three syllables with the accent on the first: ténderly.

These are the feet most commonly used. There are other combinations of accented and unaccented syllables, but they may best be regarded, in our present discussion, as variations from the standard types.

Variations. If all the lines of a poem were based upon one unvarying foot we should soon find it tiresome. Hence the poet seeks to vary his metre. Metrical variety is secured in several ways — by substituting one foot for another, or by adding or omitting syllables. Thus, iambic and anapestic feet are frequently interchanged, as also are trochaic and dactyllic. The trochee is often substituted for the iambus. A simple example may be given from Scott's *Hunting Song* (285). The unit of metre here is the trochee:

> "Waken, lords and ladies gay,
>   On the mountain dawns the day;
>   All the jolly chase is here
>   With hawk and horse and hunting-spear;
>   Hounds are in their couples yelling,
>   Hawks are whistling, horns are knelling,
>   Merrily, merrily, mingle they,
>   'Waken, lords and ladies gay.'"

The good reader will unconsciously adjust himself to the variations from the normal which occur in all poetry. He will realize the added beauty which comes from such "variety in unity." A single line may be too irregular to be assignable to the regular metre of the poem in which it stands, but the succession of normal lines will establish the definite rhythm.

The Line. The lines of a poem may comprise any number of feet, from one to eight. They are named from the number and kind of feet which they contain, and the nomenclature, although a little difficult to remember, forms a very conven-

Appendix

ient way of describing the type of line employed in any poem. A line, then, is named as follows, according to the number of feet which it contains: *monometer*, one foot; *dimeter*, two feet; *trimeter*, three; *tetrameter*, four; *pentameter*, five; *hexameter*, six; *heptameter*, seven; *octameter*, eight. The last-named is really a double form of the tetrameter. The system may be illustrated by the following table:

Iambic monometer: A⌣wáy.

Iambic dimeter: | I ⌣lóve | thee ⌣trúe. |

Dactylic dimeter: | Óne more ⌣un⌣ | fórtu⌣nate. |

Iambic trimeter: | But ⌣hére | there ⌣ís | no ⌣líght. |

Anapestic trimeter: | I am ⌣⌣mónarch of ⌣⌣áll | I sur⌣⌣véy. |

Iambic tetrameter: | We ⌣paúsed | a⌣míd | the ⌣pínes | that ⌣stoód. |

Trochaic tetrameter: | Whére the | daísies | are róse | scénted. |

Anapestic tetrameter: | And the ⌣⌣sén | tinel ⌣⌣stárs | set their ⌣⌣wátch | in the ⌣ský. |

Iambic pentameter: | And ⌣quést | ioned ⌣év | ery ⌣gúst | of ⌣rúg | ged wíngs. |

Dactylic hexameter: | Thís is the | fórest prim | éval, the | múrmuring pínes and the | hémlocks. |

Iambic hexameter: | Our ⌣sweét | est ⌣sóngs | are ⌣thóse | which ⌣téll | of ⌣sád- | dest ⌣thoúght. |

Iambic heptameter: | There's ⌣nót | a ⌣jóy | the ⌣wórld | can ⌣gíve | like ⌣thát | it ⌣tákes | a⌣wáy. |

Important Metres. Some of the metrical types are seldom used, but there are others which have proved especially well adapted to the needs of English poetry. The dactylic hexameter, for instance, is rare; on the other hand, the iambic tetrameter and the iambic pentameter are very common. The former is familiar in Scott's romances, *The Lady of the Lake* and the others. The iambic pentameter, in the unrhymed form known as "blank verse," is one of the most widely used of all metres. Shakespeare's plays, Milton's *Paradise Lost*, and Tennyson's *Idylls of the King*, are all written in iambic pentameter. Many examples of the metre in its rhymed form will be found in this book; notably the sonnets of Shakespeare, Milton, and Wordsworth.

Variations in Metrical Effect. It is interesting to note that while the basis of rhythm is metre, yet of two poems written in the same metre, the rhythm may produce a totally different effect in each. If we compare, for example, Gray's *On a Favorite Cat* (156) with Wordsworth's *Education of Nature* (222), we shall observe that the metre of the poems is exactly alike, but that there is a very marked difference in the rhythm. The point may be illustrated by taking a stanza from each:

(*a*) Gray:

"The hapless Nymph with wonder saw:
   A whisker first, and then a claw
   With many an ardent wish
She stretched, in vain, to reach the prize —
What female heart can gold despise?
   What cat's averse to fish?"

(*b*) Wordsworth:

"The stars of midnight shall be dear
To her; and she shall lean her ear
   In many a secret place
Where rivulets dance their wayward round,
And beauty born of murmuring sound
   Shall pass into her face."

Metrical Subtleties. The subtlety of rhythm forms one of the most interesting and beautiful features of lyric poetry. Like the deeper qualities of any art, it will not reveal itself without careful study; but a rich reward awaits the student who gains a true knowledge of its possibilities. A few examples will show how much may be conferred by the rhythmic charm of great poets:

> "I hear the far-off Curfew sound
> Over some wide-water'd shore,
> Swinging slow with sullen roar."

> "Now fades the glimmering landscape on the sight,
> And all the air a solemn stillness holds."

> "The same that ofttimes hath
> Charmed magic casements, opening on the foam
> Of perilous seas, in faery lands forlorn."

> "Thou dost preserve the stars from wrong,
> And the most ancient heavens, through thee, are fresh and strong."

> "Music, when soft voices die,
> Vibrates in the memory."

The Stanza. Another important part of the technique of poetry is the "stanza," or line-group into which most poems are divided. It has a function somewhat similar to the paragraph in prose. It is the unit of the poem, as the foot is the unit of the line. Stanzas are of varying length, adapting themselves to the needs of the poems. They vary from two lines, as in the closing couplet of any of Shakespeare's sonnets, to eight as in Scott's *Datur Hora Quieti* (311), fourteen, as in Shelley's *Ode to the West Wind* (322), or an indeterminate and variable length as in Wordsworth's *Ode on Intimations of Immortality* (338).

Stanza Forms. The "heroic couplet," composed of two rhyming iambic pentameter lines, although not strictly a stanza form, may be mentioned because it is found in so large a body of eighteenth century verse. Lacking metrical variation, and hence monotonous in effect, it possessed almost invariable neatness of phrasing, with occasional brilliant epigrammatic passages. An example may be taken from Pope's *Essay on Criticism*:

> "In words, as fashions, the same rule will hold;
> Alike fantastic, if too new or old;
> Be not the first by whom the new are tried,
> Nor yet the last to lay the old aside."

Occasionally a stanza of three lines is found, as in Crashaw's *Wishes for the Supposed Mistress* (103) or Lamb's *Old Familiar*

Appendix

Faces (264). The "ballad stanza," of four lines, is very common. Originating with the old English ballads of the fourteenth and fifteenth centuries, its simplicity has made it universally popular. It is adaptable, furthermore, to many moods; as may be seen by such widely different instances as *The Twa Corbies* (136), *Rosabelle* (281), and *Lord Ullin's Daughter* (225). Another common stanza is that of eight lines; for example, Burns's *Highland Mary* (191) or Scott's *Serenade* (230).

The Spenserian Stanza. Noteworthy among the longer forms is the famous "Spenserian Stanza." As the name implies, it was first used by Spenser in *The Faerie Queene*. It consists of eight iambic pentameter lines, followed by an iambic hexameter, or "Alexandrine." It has proved finely adaptable to the expression of various emotional situations, and has been employed by many great poets. There are no examples in this collection, but the reader would be interested in looking up the two best modern instances — Keats's *Eve of St. Agnes* and Shelley's *Adonais*.

Fitness of the Stanza Form. In his choice of stanza form, the poet is always influenced by the needs of what he has to say. No better exercise in judging the appropriateness of the form to the thought could be found than an investigation of the lyrics in this book. As a beginning, look up the following numbers: 73, 129, 165, 290. In each case, judge why the particular stanza form was chosen.

Fixed Stanza Forms: the Sonnet. Some types of lyric poetry are cast in definite forms, from which they cannot vary. The most familiar of these is the "sonnet." It must consist of fourteen iambic pentameter lines, arranged in certain ways. The sonnet was introduced into England from Italy about the middle of the sixteenth century, and occupies a very important place in English poetry. All great poets have used this form, and have invariably found it worthy to enshrine the loftiest thought. There are two kinds of sonnet — the "Italianate" and the "Shakespearean." The Italianate follows the original Italian model; it is made up of an "octave," or group of eight lines, followed by a "sestet" of six lines. The Shakespearean is the modification adopted by Shakespeare and other Elizabethan poets. It employs three "quatrains," or four-line stanzas, followed by a couplet. If we indicate the rhyme-sounds by letters, the rhyme-system can easily be shown. Thus, the Italianate would be: *abbaabba, cdcdcd* or *cdecde;* the Shakespearean: *abab, cdcd, efef, gg.* For the typical Italianate sonnet, read Milton's *On His Blindness* (94), and Wordsworth's *London, 1802* (256); for the Shakespearean Drayton's *Love's Farewell* (49), and Shakespeare's *True Love* (31).

If we examine the emotional appeal of the two types, we note a difference. In the Italianate, the octave introduces a problem, a doubt, a reflection; the sestet "eases the load, resolves the problem or doubt, answers the query." The height of the feeling usually comes at the end of the octave. The Shakespearean sonnet, on the other hand, states a thought or mood, and reaches a climax in the couplet, which is often epigrammatic. Most modern sonnets follow the Italianate form.

The Ode. Another lyric type of great interest is the "ode." A number of examples occur in *The Golden Treasury;* notably Gray's two "Pindaric" odes, and Wordsworth's *On Intimations of Immortality.* An ode has been defined as "any strain of enthusiastic and exalted lyric verse, directed to a fixed purpose and dealing progressively with one dignified theme." The English ode is derived from two different sources: the Greek, or "Pindaric" ode, of which the poet Pindar was the originator; and the Latin, or "Horatian" ode, as written by Horace. Of the latter, excellent examples are to be found in Marvell's *Horatian Ode* (88), and Collins's *Ode to Evening* (186). The Greek type is more complicated. It was written for choral singing. The chorus sang one part, called the "strophe," while moving across in front of the stage; the "antistrophe" as they returned; and the "epode" when they stood still. The metre of the first two movements was iambic; of the last, trochaic. Gray's *The Bard* (159) and *The Progress of Poesy* (177) are the two best examples of the English Pindaric ode.

The Greek form, however, was not adapted to English poetry. We find that, although the idea of the ode as an expression of "exaltation and enthusiasm" persists, the poets tend to move away from the rigid requirements of the Pindaric model. Formality is preserved, indeed; but the stanza type approximating to the Greek model tends to disappear. It is highly suggestive to compare the odes of Dryden and Gray with such a group as the following: Milton's *Nativity Ode* (85), Collins's *How Sleep the Brave* (160), Keats's *On a Grecian Urn* (328), and Wordsworth's *Ode to Duty* (252). Eventually the English ode comes to represent an adaptation of the Greek and Latin forms to the requirements of English thought and style. The form is determined by the mood within the poem, and not by rules from without.

The Elegy. The elegy is a poem which touches on death, with reflections on the sorrow and loss common to all human beings, and the higher note of consolation in the face of grief. The two great examples in our collection are Milton's *Lycidas* (89) and Gray's *Elegy Written in a Country Churchyard* (187). *Lycidas* belongs to the type known as "pastoral elegy," a form originating in Greek literature which has proved well adapted to English usage. Besides Milton's poem, there are three other great pastoral elegies: Shelley's *Adonais*, Arnold's *Thyrsis*, and Swinburne's *Ave atque Vale*. All of these sing a personal sorrow. Gray's poem is impersonal; as is also another famous elegy — Tennyson's *In Memoriam*, of which he said: "It is the cry of the whole human race rather than mine." In Palgrave we have one example from each of the two great divisions of elegiac poetry.

Diction. Turning now from the form in which poetry is cast, we may speak for a moment about "diction," or the choice of words. The subject is one of very wide extent, and in this place can be touched upon only very briefly. As we look through the poems in our collection we see not only that the

Appendix

language is clear and forceful, but also that the words are most carefully chosen, and are, in many instances, beautiful in themselves. It is a fascinating study to follow out the theory of the "inevitable phrase"; to note how the poet's skill has enabled him to select the words or expressions which are most appropriate to the subject which he is writing about. Here are a few instances — culled from a great many — which will help us to understand what words may mean in the mind of a poet.

> "O how shall summer's honey breath hold out
> Against the wreckful siege of battering days."

> "And questioned every gust of rugged wings
> That blows from off each beakéd promontory."

> "The breezy call of incense-breathing morn,
> The swallow twittering from the straw-built shed."

> "Will no one tell me what she sings?
> Perhaps the plaintive numbers flow
> From old, unhappy, far-off things,
>   And battles long ago."

> "Round the decay
> Of that colossal wreck, boundless and bare,
> The lone and level sands stretch far away."

> "And here were forests ancient as the hills,
> Enfolding sunny spots of greenery."

> "In the golden lightning
>   Of the sunken sun
> O'er which clouds are brightening,
>   Thou dost float and run,
> Like an unbodied joy whose race is just begun."

Make your own selections; hunt for passages which seem to have unusual beauty. The exercise will prove a real adventure in poetry, and will do much to enlarge your knowledge and judgment. The true poet never writes carelessly or at random; hence the study of poetic diction forms a subject of deep and abiding interest.

Figures of Speech. Appeal to the imagination in poetry is made largely through the use of picturesque material, to enforce or to beautify the thought. Such material may be condensed into a single phrase, or elaborated through an extended passage. The chief devices by which the desired effects are gained we term "figures of speech." There are a great many of these; though they are not all of equal importance. A few of those most frequently used may be briefly explained and illustrated.

Simile. A simile is a comparison, definitely expressed.

"Like as the waves make towards the pebbled shore
  So do our minutes hasten to their end."

"O my luve's like a red, red rose
  That's newly sprung in June."

"Before me shone a glorious world
  Fresh as a banner bright, unfurl'd
  To music suddenly."

Metaphor. A metaphor is a comparison which is implied, not fully expressed. It is one of the most widely used of all figures of speech.

"Care-charmer Sleep, son of the sable Night.
  Brother to Death, in silent darkness born."

"Although a Lion in the field,
  A Lamb in town thou shalt him find."

"Fleet foot in the correi,
  Sage counsel in cumber,
  Red hand in the foray —
    How sound is thy slumber!"

"The cataracts blow their trumpets from the steep."

Personification is the figure in which things without life, or abstract ideas, are given the qualities of living persons.

"Night like a drunkard reels
  Beyond the hills, to shun his flaming wheels."

"Sport that wrinkled Care derides
  And Laughter holding both his sides."

"There Honour comes, a pilgrim gray,
  To bless the turf that wraps their clay."

"How sweet the answer Echo makes
    To Music at night
  When, roused by lute or horn, she wakes,
  And far away o'er lawns and lakes
    Goes answering light!"

Apostrophe is a poetical form of direct address.

> "With how sad steps, O Moon, thou climb'st the skies."

> "Milton! thou shouldst be living at this hour:
> England hath need of thee."

> "The combat deepens. On, ye Brave
> Who rush to glory, or the grave!
> Wave, Munich, all thy banners wave,
>   And charge with all thy chivalry!"

Onomatopeia is the employment of words in such a way that the sound helps the sense. It is sometimes used with very subtle effect.

> "Calm was the day, and through the trembling air
> Sweet-breathing Zephyrus did gently play."

> "Yet first, to those ychain'd in sleep
> The wakeful trump of doom must thunder through the deep."

> "Save where the beetle wheels his droning flight,
> And drowsy tinklings lull the distant folds."

> "The coming musk-rose, full of dewy wine,
>   The murmurous haunts of flies on summer eves."

HOW TO STUDY PALGRAVE

Methods of "Approach." It will be clear from what has been said, that the reading and understanding of poetry call for an alert mind, a sympathetic attitude, and a readiness to receive impressions that have been drawn from many different sources. Poetry interprets life; it gives us "by means of the imagination noble grounds for noble emotions." *The Golden Treasury* contains only the best of lyric verse; there is nothing that is weak, or ill-conceived, or based upon wrong ideals. The wisest way to read is to read aloud; this method not only emphasizes the rare melodies inherent in all good poetry, but also develops the inner significance of the poem. The ear will help the eye; the mind will more justly apprehend, the taste more surely appreciate what poetry has to give.

A practical "approach" to the real knowledge and enjoyment of poetry can be illustrated by some definite examples.

Appendix

Let us take for brief consideration a poem from each of the four books. In each case, a first reading will raise various questions: Is the poem easy to understand? What is the general meaning? To what class does it belong? What are the metre, stanza-form, etc.? In what way does it appeal to our sense of beauty, or to our imagination?

A Shakespeare Sonnet. Let us first turn our attention to the sonnet by Shakespeare in Book I which begins, " Let me not to the marriage of true minds " (31). We see at once that it is the typical Elizabethan form, with quatrains and couplet. The thought is the strength of true love, and it goes deeper than the conventional love-song. Time may bring changes; life may alter as the years go by. But " Love's not Time's fool," though time takes away youth and beauty and joy; Love is stronger than old age or death. In the splendid imagery of the poet,

> "It is an ever-fixéd mark
> That looks on tempests and is never shaken;
> It is the star to every wand'ring bark."

And we feel that here is a grand conception, finely expressed, of the noblest quality in human nature. We are led to the thought that if such conceptions were found in Elizabethan poetry, there must have been much that was excellent in the life of the time.

To Lucasta. From Book II we may take Lovelace's little poem *To Lucasta* (109). This is, in one sense, a trifle. But in its own field it has a special charm, and it represents a striking phase of seventeenth century literature. Lovelace was one of the " Cavalier Poets "; his poem, in simple and graceful ballad metre, embodies a lofty ideal. A soldier is summoned away to war; he must leave his lady-love behind him. This is hard; but it is not " unkind." Duty is more than love; he owes to his honor the higher allegiance. The charming lines close upon a noble thought —

> "I could not love thee, Dear, so much,
> Loved I not Honour more."

Ode Written in 1746. In Book III we find a characteristic bit of work in Collins's ode beginning "How Sleep the Brave" (160). It has, we see, a kind of stately simplicity which conveys at the same time a feeling of restrained pathos. Its clearness and purity are enhanced by the plain six-line stanzas. The personification, a familiar figure of the eighteenth century, seems here to be appropriately keyed to the tone of the thought.

Ode to the West Wind. The immense variety of the poetry in the fourth book makes it difficult to choose a poem that is "typical" except in so far as it represents the imaginative fervor which distinguished all the work of the period. We may take, however, Shelley's *Ode to the West Wind* (322), a lyric which possesses remarkable qualities. The first impressions we get upon reading this poem are a sense of beauty and a sense of power. There is the sweep of the wind, and the haunting pathos of the refrain — "Hear, O hear!" We note too the charm of the intricate stanza structure, with its interlocking rhyme — the "terza rima," as it is called — *aba bcb cdc ded ee.*

Then we observe the wonderful pictures — the driven leaves, "yellow, and black, and pale, and hectic red"; "Thine azure sister of the spring"; "Angels of rain and lightning"; "the steep sky's commotion"; "the blue surface of thine airy surge." There are lines which have a pure beauty which is difficult to analyze:

> "Driving sweet buds like flocks to feed in air."

> "The blue Mediterranean, where he lay
> Lull'd by the coil of his crystalline streams."

> "The tumult of thy mighty harmonies."

The poem, as we further see, has a deep spiritual significance. The leaves, the clouds, the waves, all driven by the wild West Wind, stir the poet to think that, like them, he too would fain feel "the impulse of thy strength." The exquisite imagery is touched with a note of pathos:

> "Oh, lift me as a wave, a leaf, a cloud!
> I fall upon the thorns of life! I bleed!
> A heavy weight of hours has chained and bowed
> One too like thee — tameless, and swift, and proud."

Yet the emotion, though keenly felt, is restrained, and the poem closes with a thought of hope:

> "O Wind,
> If Winter comes, can Spring be far behind?"

Group Study. The study of single poems, thus briefly indicated, can be followed by the study of groups. Every kind of subject may be found in Palgrave's collection: nature poems, love poems, lyrics of war and of the sea, of death, of the various sorrows that flesh is heir to. Humorous poems are few, probably because humor, as an unmixed element, does not lend itself to that "high seriousness" which characterizes the best verse. The poems which deal with these subjects may be correlated in various ways, so as to be thoroughly enjoyable.

1. Compile a collection of nature poems from all the books. Wherein do they seem to you especially beautiful or true? To what extent do they stir an echo in your own experience?

2. Take one or two nature poems from each book, and trace the course of development. If we compare, for instance, a poem such as Milton's *L'Allegro* (144) with Shelley's *Lines Written among the Euganean Hills* (321), we notice that Milton illustrates the spiritual by the material. Shelley, on the other hand, is more ethereal; he seeks a spirit behind nature; he interprets the spiritual by the more finely spiritual. Compare Nash's *Spring* (1) with Wordsworth's *Lines Written in Early Spring* (319). Here are two poems which are separated by a space of some three hundred years. In form, at least, they show a similar simplicity; are they alike in simplicity of thought?

3. Palgrave speaks of instances where the "purple light of love" is shadowed by a spirit of sterner reflection. It is interesting to contrast the innocent tenderness of Marlowe's "Come live with me" (7) or Shakespeare's "O mistress mine" (35) with the passion of Burns's "O my Luve's like a red, red rose" (190), or the intensity of Shelley's "I arise from dreams of Thee" (215). With these in turn may be compared the frank straightforward note of Scott's *Jock of Hazeldean* (227).

4. Of the many moods touched on in the lyrics we may suggest the thought of death as affording many examples of lyrical utterances of the greatest beauty. Shelley says "Our sweetest songs are those which tell of saddest thought"; how far can we find that this is true? Read the remarkable group in Book I, from 64 to 68. In Book II *Lycidas* (89) stands supreme in the glory of its language and the "sure and certain"

note of its consolation for the mourner. Book III offers Gray's *Elegy* (187) supreme in its own field, and the exquisite Scotch lyrics — *Highland Mary* (191) and *The Land o' the Leal* (198). The range of Book IV is, as we have seen, wider than any of the others, and from many poems which find inspiration in the sorrows of earth we may take two. Scott's *Coronach* (278) has a sort of grim pathos which is well sustained in the metre. Byron's *Elegy on Thyrza* (246) shows a sincerity which was not always at his command. In these and like poems — and many more might be cited — which seem to us the most beautiful? Which touch most deeply the springs of our own feeling?

Individual Types. Keats's *Nightingale* (290) is rightly thought of as his greatest emotional poem. With its richness and melancholy compare two other songs about the nightingale from Book I, the poems of Barnefield and Sidney (45 and 47). Shelley and Wordsworth both wrote lyrics on the skylark (287 and 286). How far may these be considered characteristic of the respective authors? We may turn, further, to poems about sleep, and find in Book I the lovely sonnet of Daniel, "Care-charmer Sleep" (46), or the equally beautiful lines by Sidney, "Come Sleep, O Sleep." (40). Different in general tone, and interestingly varied within itself, is the group in Book IV including 313, 314, and 315.

Palgrave's Grouping. One of the most striking things about *The Golden Treasury* is the arrangement. Palgrave has not followed chronological order, as is usually the case with anthologies, but has attempted, as he says himself, to arrange the poems within each book "in gradations of feeling or subject." It is not possible here to consider at length this very interesting subject, or to discuss in detail the skill of Palgrave's judgment in placing the poems. Two examples, however, will help to make the matter clear, and serve as a guide for further investigation. Take the group beginning with Collins's *Ode* (160). The sadness therein contained is supplemented by the *Lament for Culloden* and that in turn by the mournful *Lament for Flodden*, an earlier and equally terrible battle. These expressions of general grief lead to the special sorrow of the two Yarrow poems. There is a very subtle transition to the *Loss of the Royal George* — "Toll for the Brave!" — and the thought of the Fleet brings, perhaps as dramatic relief, the delightfully conventional song of *Black eyed Susan* and her sailor lover. From such a theme it is a natural step to Carey's pleasant little ballad of *Sally in Our Alley*.

The other example comes in Book IV — the group from 309 to 318. Wordsworth, in his sonnet *By the Sea*, expresses the calm and beauty of evening; this is followed by the twilight lyrics of Campbell and Scott. Then we have in turn the lines of Shelley *To the Moon*, Wordsworth's sonnet *To Sleep*, and three dream poems, culminating in the highly imaginative *Kubla Khan*. A subtle transition brings us to the thought of Wordsworth on "the mind's internal heaven," and this leads on very beautifully to *The Realm of Fancy*. The group fitly closes with the lines,

"Let the wingéd Fancy roam,
Pleasure never is at home."

The transitions are sometimes very subtle; it is a test of critical judgment to find out why certain poems are placed in juxtaposition. A further study may be made of Palgrave's titles. Many of the names given to the poems were originated either by him or by Tennyson; which of the two was chiefly responsible cannot now be known. The choice is, however, invariably wise and suggestive; *The Fairy Life*, for example, or *Frustra*, or *The World's Way*.

Metrical Effects and Stanza Forms. The form and the thought of a lyric are inseparable, hence the investigation of metre and stanza should make up some part of our study. Throughout the collection will be found all the ordinary types of metre, and some that are unusual. The most important of the latter are *Lament for Flodden* (162), *Auld Robin Gray* (192), *The Land o' the Leal* (198), and *The Old Familiar Faces* (264). An example of interest is the anonymous *Song for Music* (22). The stanza form here has been called the perfection of song-writing; the lyric is a slumber-song, and the movement softens down from the longer lines of the first part to the hushed and gentle close:

> "While She lies sleeping
> Softly, now softly lies,
> Sleeping."

A glance at Shakespeare's songs will suffice to show his easy mastery of metrical forms. Something of the folk-song clings to "When icicles hang by the wall" (37); an old-time sweetness marks such lyrics as "O Mistress mine, where are you roaming?" (35), or "Take, O take those lips away" (48). We note the delicacy of the fairy song "Come unto these yellow sands" (3); the dainty sadness of "Full fathom five thy father lies" (65), and of "Come away, come away, Death" (62). He produces his effects within limited space — "infinite riches in a little room." No one, as a critic has pointed out, has been able to imitate his style; his songs have no counterpart in all the verse that has been written since his day.

Herrick, a maker of Christmas songs and glees, wrote charmingly of girls and flowers. No better example of his metrical skill can be found than the two lyrics *To Blossoms* (139) and *To Daffodils* (140). The latter has a strange elusive beauty that almost defies criticism. In Book III we come upon the very unusual unrhymed lyric, Collins's *Ode to Evening* (186). The stanza-form has a richness that satisfies the ear with perfect modulations; as when the poet sees from his hut

> "hamlets brown and dim-discover'd spires;
> And hears their simple bell; and marks o'er all
> Thy dewy fingers draw
> The gradual dusky veil."

The variety of Book IV is seen in metrical differences no less than in subject. Among the original forms are Shelley's *To the Night* (232) and Scott's *Where Shall the Lover Rest?* (236). Byron's *When We Two Parted* (234) has a simple directness which is well expressed by the stanza-form; nor should we overlook Hood's highly successful use of the difficult dactylic measure in *The Bridge of Sighs* (274).

The supreme metrical effects are found in the poems of Shelley, Wordsworth, and Keats, which at their highest are only equalled by Shakespeare's lyrics, and the poems of Milton in Book II. These attain a technical excellence which has never been surpassed in English poetry.

Study a Means to Enjoyment. There is no doubt that it is harder to read a good poem intelligently than to glance through the latest novel or to follow the most recent play. The thought, the feeling, and the imagination must all be trained to appreciate what the poet has to give. Such training, however, is pleasant in itself, because it keeps us continually in touch with fine and beautiful things. And by such training a way is opened for us to the keenest intellectual enjoyment.

Suggestive Questions. Some questions will be helpful as a guide towards the appreciation of the lyrics in this book. A few are given here, of a type which may be indefinitely extended. They are adapted from various sources, and have been found to be of practical benefit.

What kind of poem is it — what metre, etc.? Is the purpose to convey emotion? to amuse? to instruct? Does it seem to need careful study?

Is the language simple, or involved? Is the expression figurative, or literal? Are the figures effective? Why? Are the words unusual (Books I and II)? employed in an unusual sense (Books III and IV)?

Does it appeal to the imagination, or to the intellect? Compare Books I and IV in this respect. Is the thought difficult to understand? Is the meaning clear or veiled? Does the poem leave a unified impression?

Is the poem easy to read aloud? melodious? What lines or stanzas seem to you especially musical? or the reverse? Do you find instances of onomatopeia? Are you more impressed by the art of the poet, or by his thought?

Does the poem reveal anything about the author? Should you be able to judge, from reading the poem, whether he was emotional? religious? sentimental? intellectual? optimistic? humorous? Should you think he was more interested in nature, or in human nature — or in his own feelings and the expression of them? Do you want to know more about him?

As we become more familiar with the general field, other points will naturally be taken up. Our further investigation may take the form indicated below.

Implication. Many poems are highly suggestive, and produce their effect by what is implied as much as by what is said. Search, then, for what lies behind the printed word. Nothing will help so much towards a right judgment of values; nothing, moreover, will so effectually check the bad habit of absorbing merely surface impressions — a habit which is fatal to literary appreciation.

Structure. Stanza division and metre may seem in themselves subjects that are mechanical and uninteresting. We must remember, however, that the verse which moves so easily, the line which seizes so exactly the fleeting thought, embodies the result of most careful observation and experiment — "for a good poet's made as well as born." Then comes the question, *why* is this type of stanza used, instead of some other? *Why* is this particular metre selected? These questions, and others like them, take us directly into the workshop.

Criticism. We may further direct our attention to the telling words and phrases; noting how the poet selects the "ultimate word," the one best phrase, for the expression of his thought. We may ask *why* this phrase, or that word, so emphatically serves the purpose. We may then formulate our own opinions about the poem.

In any such statement, however, two things are important: we must be honest with ourselves, and we must be just with the poet. It is useless to offer any opinion unless we really understand what we are talking about. There is too much criticism nowadays which is conditioned either by indolence or ignorance. Criticism — to apply Matthew Arnold's famous definition — is a disinterested endeavor to learn and propagate the best. Our ultimate aim should be nothing less than this.

Correlation. It is interesting and profitable to see how some thought, or some picture, or the poem as a whole, resembles some experience of our own. What, for instance, is our personal reaction to *A Consolation* (16), or *The Retreat* (98), or *To a Mouse* (184), or *Upon Westminster Bridge* (291)? Can we interpret the poem in terms of our own inner lives? Does it mean more to us because of what we have seen or done? Or, again, can we correlate what we read with other pieces of literature already known to us?

What We Shall Gain.

A genuine love of good poetry will mean more to us than we are sometimes disposed to think. In it we find the enduring record of high thoughts, clothed in noble language. It reveals the beauty of the world we live in; it enlarges our views of life, and broadens our sympathies. As we read, we shall gain power from men who write strongly and wisely; solace from men who have experienced our own troubles and sorrows. A knowledge of great poetry will store our minds with splendid memories, which in time of need will

> "flash upon that inward eye
> Which is the bliss of solitude."

Appendix

SUGGESTIONS FOR ORAL WORK

Reading Aloud. Poetry was written to be read aloud. Like music, it is intended for the ear, and the importance of definite oral work can hardly be overestimated. Only in this way, indeed, is it possible to find expression for the true values of rhythm and of diction. Silent reading has its place; it may show the charm of the picture or the significance of the ideas. But silent reading can never reveal the finer qualities of noble language. In the study of poetry the form as well as the substance must be considered: the form expresses the substance in beautiful and well-chosen words, and these best convey the thought that lies behind them when interpreted by the speaking voice.

The poems contained in *The Golden Treasury* offer valuable opportunities for oral work. They all have that "singing" quality which is characteristic of the true lyric, and which has a special charm when read aloud. The younger pupil will find plenty of material which is simple enough for his needs, while the older boy or girl may turn to poetry of a maturer type. For all alike the habit of reading aloud, once formed, will remain as a sure test of the ability to understand and to interpret, and as a constant source of service and pleasure. A few practical suggestions are offered here, which will be found useful for teacher and student.

The Reading Voice. The essential thing in all oral work — especially in poetry — is good enunciation. No amount of exact knowledge or facile speech, no degree of histrionic skill, can compensate for bad accent, slovenly phrasing, or muffled voice. Harsh tones and careless slurring of words are faults very common in our schools. The utmost effort should be made to teach, by precept and example, the necessity of a clear and pleasing delivery. A well-modulated voice, trained to competent expression, is of the greatest importance whether one reads for one's own pleasure, or for the enjoyment of other people. It has, too, a value in the general scheme of education which may not lightly be set aside.

Appendix

Reciting from Memory. The kind of oral work which is most practically helpful in the study of poetry is the memorized recitation. By this, there are various advantages to be gained. In the first place, the pupil is freed from the tyranny of the printed page — the need, that is, of keeping his eyes more or less upon a fixed point. In the second place, he must master every detail of the poet's phraseology; from the first word to the last his memory must hold true. But it is not enough that he be letter-perfect; the mere learning of the words is only the beginning. He must touch the spirit of the whole; he must fully understand and sympathetically interpret the thought and emotion of the poem. To this end he must control not only the material in hand, but the means of expression also; he must know how to employ his voice to the best advantage.

There are, then, real difficulties to be coped with, and there is an insistent demand for a high degree of excellence both in knowing and in doing. It is here — in the definite problems and the demand for excellence in solving these problems — that we find the peculiar value of reciting from memory. The manner in which this shall be done lies, of course, in the province of the individual teacher; but Shakespeare's words in *Hamlet* have a broad significance today. Hamlet gives sound advice to the Players:

> "Speak the speech, I pray you, as I pronounced it to you, trippingly on the tongue: but if you mouth it, as many of your players do, I had as lief the town-crier spoke my lines. Nor do not saw the air too much with your hand, thus, but use all gently. . . . Be not too tame, neither, but let your own discretion be your tutor: suit the action to the word, the word to the action."

The memorized recitation should be jealously watched and carefully developed. If wisely handled, it is capable of the most valuable results.

Poems Suggested. There are a number of poems in the book which should be left until the student has had some practice in memorizing. They demand a high degree of skill, based upon a deep appreciation of their noble qualities.

Appendix

Among such poems are Spenser's *Prothalamion*, Milton's *Lycidas*, Gray's *Elegy*, Shelley's *West Wind*, Keats's *Ode to a Nightingale*, and Wordsworth's *Ode to Duty* and *On Intimations of Immortality* — to mention no others. All these, in thought and expression, represent — each in its own way — the best that it is given poetry to attain; only by careful study can the student hope to appreciate the significance that underlies their beauty.

Many other poems, however, lend themselves excellently well to the purpose in view; they have sound emotional content, and appealing charm of phrase. A list will be helpful. This is divided according to Books, since it is important that the original grouping should be preserved in any study of the volume. Oral assignments may be used as the best approach to a complete study of the poetry contained in the book.

Book I. 1, 2 and 3; 7; 9, 10, 11; 35, 37, 53, 56, 64, 65 and 66, 73.
Sonnets: 16, 39, 40, 46, 49, 84.
Book II. 90, 92, 96, 104, 108, 109, 116, 119, 120, 129, 131, 135 and 136, 139, 140.
Sonnets: 87, 94.
Book III. 160, 162, 165, 167, 174, 175, 176, 180 and 181, 184, 197, 207.
Book IV. Wordsworth: 220, 223, 289, 298, 301.
Coleridge: 316, 329.
Scott: 213, 230, 248, 273, 278, 281, 285, 311.
Byron: 234, 275.
Shelley: 232, 239, 287, 334, 335, 339.
Keats: 235, 237, 303.
Miscellaneous: 229, 249, 250, 251, 259, 260, 262, 269, 279, 314.
Sonnets: 257, 326; 210, 242; 293.

It will be understood that this list is suggestive, rather than final. All the poems mentioned, however, have been tested by actual classroom experience. Some background instruction will be needed; in each case, for instance, the life of the author should be in some measure correlated with his work. For it is true of all great poetry that fuller understanding invariably brings deeper enjoyment.

Clearness and Sincerity. In oral recitation, whether memorized or not, the chief stress should be laid on two things: clearness of utterance, and sincerity of feeling. A simple, straightforward presentation based on an honest liking and a real understanding of the poem selected, will go far towards arousing both in speaker and hearer the spirit of genuine appreciation. And to those who truthfully read and truthfully hear, the message of the poet will never come in vain.

MUSICAL SETTINGS TO THE POEMS

The English lyric, until comparatively recent times, was intimately associated with music. No study of the subject is complete without some knowledge of the airs which so closely reflect the tone of the poetry. These airs have been published in collections from the period of Shakespeare, and earlier, down to our own time. Many of them have unfortunately disappeared; others survive, however, so that it is possible to hear settings today which go far back into the past; while there are numerous later settings of great beauty. In the case of the older lyrics, the words are more important than the music; our modern tendency is to reverse this order, and to set attractive music to words which, to say the least, have no literary value whatever. Hence it is refreshing to turn back to the lyrics of *The Golden Treasury*, where we find

> "airs
> Married to immortal verse,
> Such as the meeting soul may pierce
> In notes, with many a winding bout
> Of linkéd sweetness long drawn out."

In Shakespeare's day a knowledge of music was considered to be part of a liberal education. Indeed, so common was the love of good music, and so general the ability to sing and even to write airs, madrigals, or glees, that the lack of feeling for this art was regarded as a serious weakness. We remember Lorenzo's comment, in *The Merchant of Venice*:

> "The man who has no music in his soul
> Is fit for treasons, stratagems, and spoils;
> Let no such man be trusted."

Milton was an accomplished musician, and a skilful player on the organ. Dryden wrote two famous odes for a celebrated London musical society. Herrick and the Cavalier poets composed their lyrics for music; and the haunting melody of Ben Jonson's "Drink to me only with thine eyes" is inseparable from the words of the poem. Burns wrote words to many lovely old Scotch airs; Moore, in his long series of *Irish Melodies*, set his words to the lilt and pathos of tunes well known in Ireland.

A full discussion of these settings, old and new, would be apart from the general purposes of this book. What has been said may serve to indicate the extent and interest of the subject. The following lists, however, have been prepared in order to afford an opportunity to correlate the literary and musical aspects of the lyric. The first contains the titles of song collections; the others, lyrics from *The Golden Treasury* which may be found in these books. Reference is made by letter. A knowledge of the airs noted will add much to the pleasure of the classroom period.

A. *English Melodies from the Thirteenth to the Eighteenth Centuries.* V. Jackson. J. M. Dent and Sons, London.
B. *Our Familiar Songs.* H. K. Johnson. Henry Holt and Company, New York.
C. *Standard English Glees.* Boosey and Company, London.
D. *Songs of Scotland.* Boosey and Company, London.
E. *Songs of Ireland.* Boosey and Company, London.
F. *Songs of Burns.* H. Frowde, London.
G. *Songs of the North*, Vol. I. Schuberth, New York.
H. *Minstrelsy of Scotland.* Augener and Company, London.
I. *Genuine Scottish Melodies.* Wiley and Sons, New York.

Appendix

J. *Scottish Minstrel*, Vols. I–VIII. R. Purdie, Edinburgh.
K. *Melodies of Scotland*, Vols. I–III. Thomson, Edinburgh.
L. *The Songs of England*, Vols. I–III. Boosey, New York.
M. *English Minstrelsie*, Vols. I–VIII. T. C. Jack, Edinburgh.
N. *The Book of British Song.* Vols. I–II. Virtue, London.
O. *Musical Illustrations of Percy's " Reliques."* Cramer, Beal and Company, London.
P. *Cantos, Songs, and Fancies.* A. Gardner, Paisley.
Q. *English Songs.* Augener and Company, London.
R. *Thirty Songs.* Cecil Mackie and Company, London.
S. *Keats's Album.* Novello and Company, London.
T. *Secular Vocal Scores.* Novello and Company, London.
U. *Old Songs.* E. Riley, New York.
V. *Album of English Songs.* C. W. Thompson, Boston, Mass.
W. *Secular Songs.* Novello and Company, London.
X. *Songs from Oratorios.* Novello and Company, London.

For general reference :

Alphabetical Catalogue of Vocal Composition. Novello and Company, London.
Song Index. H. W. Wilson Company, New York.
Popular Music of the Olden Time. W. Chappell. Chappell and Company, London.

The publications of Novello and Company may be obtained from The H. W. Gray Company, New York, their authorized agents in this country.

Book I

As it fell upon a day (45) C
Blow, blow, thou winter wind (56) A
Come away, come away, Death (62) W
Come live with me and be my Love (7) A
Come unto these yellow sands (3) N, Vol. I
Crabbed Age and Youth (9) C
Cupid and my Campaspe (72) Q
Fear no more the heat o' the sun (64) W

Full fathom five (65) Q
Happy were he could finish forth his fate (83) W
It was a lover and his lass (11) A
Lady, when I behold the roses sprouting (70) R
Let me not to the marriage of true minds (31) W
My true love hath my heart and I have his (32) R
No longer mourn for me when I am dead (68) W
O Mistress mine, where are you roaming (35) A
O never say that I was false of heart (17) W
Pack, clouds, away, and welcome day (73) W
Take, O take those lips away (48) W
Tell me where is Fancy bred (69) P
Under the greenwood tree (10) L, Vol. I
Weep you no more, sad fountains (22) A
When icicles hang by the wall (37) W
Where the bee sucks, there suck I (2) M, Vol. I

Book II

Ah, Chloris, could I now but sit (106) X
Alexander's Feast (151) X
 Music by Händel.
As I was walking all alane (136) G
Bid me to live, and I will live (124) M, Vol. VIII
Blest pair of Sirens, pledges of Heaven's joy (147) T
Drink to me only with thine eyes (116) A
Fair pledges of a fruitful tree (139) W
From Harmony, from heavenly Harmony (86) W
Gather ye rosebuds while ye may (108) A
He that loves a rosy cheek (112) A
I cannot change as others do (107) W
I wish I were where Helen lies (135) H
L'Allegro *and* Il Penseroso (144, 145) X
 Composed by Händel in 1740.
O waly, waly up the bank (133) A
Over the mountains (104) A
Shall I, wasting in despair (131) X
Tell me not, Sweet, I am unkind (109) W

Appendix

The glories of our blood and state (92) R
There is a garden in her face (117) W
Upon my lap my sovereign sits (134) L, Vol. I
Victorious men of earth, no more (91) O
Whenas in silks my Julia goes (120) F
When love, with confinéd wings (127) O
Why so pale and wan, fond lover (129) O
You meaner beauties of the night (110) F

Book III

All in the Downs the Fleet was moored (166) A
And are ye sure the news is true (194) B
Awake, Æolian lyre, awake (177) C
Down in yon garden sweet and gay (164) I
Duncan Gray cam here to woo (193) B
Go fetch to me a pint of wine (168) D
How sleep the Brave who sink to rest (160) C
I'm wearin' awa', Jean (198) D
In the downhill of life (206) X
I saw Eternity the other night (150) A
I've heard them lilting at our ewe milking (162) B
John Anderson, my jo, John (197) B
Never seek to tell thy love (174) W
Of a' the airts the wind can blaw (196) D
Of all the girls that are so smart (167) A
O Mary, at thy window be (188) F
Obscurest night involved the sky (205) W
O my luve's like a red, red rose (190) D
O saw ye bonnie Lesley (189) D
Sleep on, and dream of Heaven awhile (171) A
Sleep, sleep, beauty bright (181) A
The lovely lass o' Inverness (161) F
Thy braes were bonny, Yarrow stream (163) M, Vol. VIII
When Britain first, at Heaven's command (158) A
When I think on the happy days (195) W
When the sheep are in the fauld (192) B

Ye banks and braes and streams around (191) B
Ye banks and braes o' bonnie Doon (176) B

Book IV

A Chieftain to the Highlands bound (225) B
A child's a plaything for an hour (283) W
Ah, County Guy, the hour is nigh (230) B
As slow our ship her foamy track (245) E
A weary lot is thine, fair maid (238) R
A wet sheet and a flowing sea (249) B
Bright Star! would I were stedfast as thou art (242) W
Ever let the Fancy roam (318) S
How sweet the answer Echo makes (229) S
I arise from dreams of Thee (215) V
I fear thy kisses, gentle maiden (219) W
In a drear-nighted December (235) W
I remember, I remember (268) B
Music when soft voices die (339) W
My heart aches, and a drowsy numbness pains (290) W
Not a drum was heard, not a funeral note (262) J
O blithe new-comer! I have heard (289) W
O Brignall banks are wild and fair (213) U
O Friend, I know not which way I should look (256) W
O listen, listen, Ladies gay (261) W
O what can ail thee, knight-at-arms (237) W
Of Nelson and the North (251) B
Oft in the stilly night (269) B
On a poet's lips I slept (324) R
One word is too often profaned (247) R
Our bugles sang truce, for the night-cloud had lower'd (314) B
Pibroch of Donuil Dhu (248) D
Proud Maisie is in the wood (273) G
She dwelt among the untrodden ways (220) W
She is not fair to outward view (218) R
She walks in beauty, like the night (216) R
She was a phantom of delight (217) K
The fountains mingle with the river (228) W

Appendix

There be none of beauty's daughters (214) R
Waken, lords and ladies gay (285) K
We talked with open heart and tongue (331) W
When he who adores thee has left but the name (261) E
When we two parted (234) W
Where shall the lover rest (236) W
When I have fears that I may cease to be (243) S
Why weep ye by the tide, ladie (227) B
Ye mariners of England (250) A

Phonographic Records. Interesting results can be obtained by the use of the phonograph. The records listed here have been found well-adapted to supplement the study of lyrical forms. They are published by the Victor Talking Machine Company of Camden, N. J.

Book I

Under the greenwood tree (10) 17623
Blow, blow, thou winter wind (56) 17717
It was a lover and his lass (11) 17634
Take, O take those lips away (48) 17662
Tell me where is Fancy bred (69) 55060
Come unto these yellow sands (3) 17724
Full fathom five thy father lies (65) 17702
Where the bee sucks, there suck I (2) 17702
O Mistress mine, where are you roaming? (35) 17662
Come away, come away, Death (62) 17762

Book II

Drink to me only with thine eyes (116) 74077, 74204
L'Allegro, (144) 18123, 35623
Il Penseroso (145) 35623, 88068

Book III

John Anderson my jo, John (197) 17366
O my Luve's like a red, red rose (190) 64321
Ye banks and braes of bonnie Doon (176) 87062

Of all the girls that are so smart (167) 64501
When Britain first, at Heaven's command (158) 16134

Book IV

Oft in the stilly night (269) 55065
He is gone on the mountain (278) 17987
Why weep ye by the tide, ladie (227) 16961

EXPLANATORY NOTES

(*Numerals in boldface type refer to poems; those in lightface, to lines. The original Palgrave notes are inclosed in square brackets.*)

BOOK FIRST

[The Elizabethan poetry, as it is rather vaguely termed, forms the substance of this Book, which contains pieces from Wyatt, under Henry VIII, to Shakespeare midway through the reign of James I, and Drummond, who carried on the early manner to a still later period. There is here a wide range of style, — from simplicity expressed in a language hardly yet broken-in to verse, through the pastoral fancies and Italian conceits of the strictly Elizabethan time, to the passionate reality of Shakespeare; yet a general uniformity of tone prevails. Few readers can fail to observe the natural sweetness of the verse, the single-hearted straightforwardness of the thoughts; nor less, the limitation of subject to the many phases of one passion, which then characterized our lyrical poetry, unless when, as in especial with Shakespeare, the " purple light of love " is tempered by a spirit of sterner reflection. For the didactic verse of the century, although lyrical in form, yet very rarely rises to the pervading emotion, the golden cadence, proper to the lyric.

It should be observed that this and the following summaries apply in the main to the collection here presented, in which (besides its restriction to lyrical poetry) a strictly representative or historical anthology has not been aimed at. Great excellence, in human art as in human character, has from the beginning of things been even more uniform than mediocrity, by virtue of the closeness of its approach to nature; and so far as the standard of excellence kept in view has been attained in this volume, a comparative absence of extreme contemporary phases in style, a similarity of tone and manner, will be found throughout, — something neither modern nor ancient, but true and speaking to the heart of man alike throughout all ages.]

1. Note the extreme simplicity of this pretty little lyric, which was sung in Nash's comedy, *Summer's Last Will and Testament*. The refrain is a conventional representation of bird notes.

5. **palm and may**: the "palm," so-called because it was used to decorate churches on Palm Sunday, is the same as the American pussy-willow; the "may" is the white hawthorn.

2. Sung by Ariel in Shakespeare's *The Tempest*, Act V, Scene 1.

3. Sung by Ariel in *The Tempest*, Act I, Scene 2. The "burthen," or chorus, was sung by boys' voices off stage.
4. **whist**: hushed, quieted.   5. **featly**: daintily.

4. This poem contains several of the references to mythology of which Elizabethan poets were so fond. We must be careful not to regard such references, here and in other poems, as in any degree affected; familiarity with mythology and with the great classical stories was taken for granted at the time.

4. [**Rouse Memnon's mother**: awaken the Dawn from the dark earth and the clouds, where she is resting. Aurora in the old mythology is the mother of Memnon (the East), and wife of Tithonus (the appearances of Earth and Sky during the last hours of night). She leaves him every morning in renewed youth, to prepare the way for Phoebus (the Sun), while Tithonus remains in perpetual old age and grayness.] Tennyson touches upon this legend in his beautiful poem, *Tithonus*.   11. **decore**: decorate, adorn.   18. **cruel stars**: an allusion to the belief that the destiny of man was controlled by the stars under which he was born. This belief was called

Notes 487

" astrology," and references to the influence of the stars are innumerable in English poetry. 20. **purely white**: there was an old Roman custom that a lucky day should be marked by a white stone. 27. [**Peneus' streams**: Phoebus loved the nymph Daphne, whom he met by the river Peneus in the vale of Tempe.] 29. **Flora**: goddess of flowers. 31. **Amphion's lyre**: Amphion, a master of music, caused the walls of Thebes to rise at the sound of his playing. 33. **Zephyr**: the west wind. 36. **chair**: chariot. 42. **orient**: bright, shining.

5. Shakespeare wrote 154 Sonnets, of which this is No. 64. They were first published in 1609, but were written much earlier — probably between 1590 and 1599. Palgrave gave the titles to the sonnets and songs of Shakespeare as printed in *The Golden Treasury*.

1. **fell**: cruel. 2. **cost**: glory, splendor. 3. **sometime**: once. 4. **eternal**: modifies "brass." **mortal rage**: the fury of death. 10. **state itself**, etc.: that is, the fixed condition not only interchanging (like the sea and the shore) but altogether disappearing.

6. Sonnet 65. The idea of the preceding poem is carried further. The general thought is that his friend's beauty and youth, although subject to death, may yet survive in the poet's verse.

3. **hold a plea**: make any defense — as in a law-court. 10. **Time's best jewel**: the poet's friend, whom Time must some day gather up into his "chest" with other "spoils of beauty." Lines 11 and 14 are instances of the Elizabethan fondness for antithesis.

7. This poem first appeared in a collection called *The Passionate Pilgrim* (1599) and was republished a year later in another anthology — *England's Helicon*. [A fine example of the high-wrought and conventional Elizabethan pastoralism, which it would be absurd to criticize on the ground of the unshepherdlike or unreal character of the images presented.] In the title, " passionate " means " loving," or " in love."

8. madrigals: songs, melodies. Literally, a part-song for five or six voices — a type very popular in those days.

Sir Walter Raleigh wrote an amusing answer to this lyric, beginning:

> "If all the world and love were young,
> And truth in every shepherd's tongue,
> These pretty pleasures might me move
> To live with thee and be thy love."

8. [This beautiful lyric is one of several recovered from the very rare Elizabethan song-books.] The title means: "(Love) conquers all things."

9. From *The Passionate Pilgrim*. It is not certain that Shakespeare was the author.

3. **pleasance**: enjoyment, pleasure. 7. **brave**: finely arrayed, fair to see. 20. **stay'st**: delayest.

10. Sung by Amiens in *As You Like It*, Act II, Scene 5. Music for this, as for many other Shakespeare songs, was composed by Dr. Arne, about 1730.

3. **turn**: adapt.

11. From *As You Like It*, Act V, Scene 3. It is sung by two pages — "both in a tune, like two gipsies on a horse." The music was composed at the time by Thomas Morley.

2. **With a hey and a ho**, etc.: a meaningless refrain, put in to carry the air. Such refrains were common in songs of the period. 3. **corn-field**: It may not be necessary to point out that "corn" in England is the same as "wheat" in America. 4. **ring-time**: time for giving wedding-rings. 13. **prime**: supreme happiness, period of perfection.

12. From a collection of 1602, *A Poetical Rhapsodie*, where it was printed anonymously. Palgrave points out that one stanza has been omitted, in accordance with the principles of selection in *The Golden Treasury*, and that similar omissions have been made in Crashaw's *Wishes* (103) and Shelley's *Euganean Hills* (321).

4. **for alteration**: to make me change. 5. **mettle**: temper, quality. 6. **settle**: make constant.

13. [Sidney's poetry is singularly unequal. At times he is heavy and even prosaic; his simplicity is rude and bare; his verse unmelodious. These, however, are the "defects of his merits." In a certain depth and chivalry of feeling, — in the rare and noble quality of disinterestedness (to put it in one word), — he has no superior, hardly perhaps an equal, amongst our poets; and after or beside Shakespeare's *Sonnets*, his *Astrophel and Stella*, in the Editor's judgment, offers the most intense and powerful picture of the passion of love in the whole range of poetry.] This sonnet is from his "sonnet-sequence" entitled *Astrophel and Stella;* the title is Palgrave's, and means "the way of love."

1. **Parnassus**: in mythology, a mountain in Greece famed as the abode of Apollo and the Muses. 3. **Tempers her words**, etc.: Sidney was a soldier as well as a poet.

14. Sonnet 57. The poet's friend has gone away. The warmth of friendship shown in this and other sonnets was characteristic of the age.

5. **world-without-end-hour**: a typical Elizabethan combination. 10. **your affairs suppose**: wonder what you are doing. 13–14. **in your will**, etc.: he thinks that, whatever you do, your intentions are always good.

15. Sonnet 97. Here the poet has been away from his friend.

5. **This time removed**: absence, time of separation. 7. **prime**: spring. 13. **cheer**: the word literally meant face, or expression; here, it has the secondary meaning of "feeling," "mood." Compare the phrase: "be of good cheer."

16. Sonnet 29. The power of friendship to help and console in time of depression.

3. **bootless**: useless, unavailing. 6. **Featured**: formed, endowed — perhaps referring to life rather than to appear-

ance. 7. **art**: skill in doing his work. **scope**: opportunity to carry out his plans. 8. **With what I most enjoy**, etc.: disgusted with the occupations which usually give me the greatest pleasure. Note the intense human feeling in the depression here pictured.

17. Sonnet 109. Continuing the topic of 14 and 15, above. The poet's heart has never changed, in spite of his absence. 2. **flame**: love, affection. **qualify**: diminish, lessen. 7. **just**: punctually, promptly. **exchanged**: altered, changed. 10. **all kinds of blood**: every different kind of temperament or disposition. 12. **to leave**: as to leave. 14. **my rose**: the word is used by Shakespeare to denote the perfection, the "fine flower," of character. Ophelia refers to Hamlet as "the expectancy and rose of the fair state."

18. Sonnet 104. The thought of the passing of beauty and youth before the assaults of time was very common in Elizabethan poetry.

2. The end of this line is an example of the play upon words which seems to have pleased the writers of the age. 4. **shook**: form for past participle frequently used in Elizabethan English. 8. **which**: common usage for "who." 9. **dial-hand**: shadow on a sun-dial. 10. **hue**: beauty. 11. **still**: here, an adjective.

19. This song is taken from Lodge's tale, *Rosalynde, Euphues Golden Legacy* (1590), which suggested to Shakespeare the plot of *As You Like It*. [Readers who have visited Italy will be reminded of more than one picture by this gorgeous Vision of Beauty. Lodge wrote it on a voyage to "the Islands of Terceras and the Canaries"; and he seems to have caught, in those southern seas, no small portion of the qualities which marked the contemporary Art of Venice. From the same romance is No. 71, — a charming picture in the purest style of the later Renaissance.]

1. **the clear in highest sphere**: the brightness; [the crystalline or outermost heaven of the old cosmography.] 8. **whenas they glow**: when they sparkle. 31. **orient**:

Notes

originally "eastern," then "brilliant." 43. **Since for a fair**, etc.: if you want a beauty, there is none more beautiful than she.

20. From *England's Helicon*; perhaps written by Anthony Munday.

12. **fond**: foolish.

21. 5. **That will**: that will pierce. 8. **thou art woe-begone thee**: a confusion of two constructions; the meaning is, " thou wilt be woe-begone."

22. This is an example of the freedom of metrical treatment which was so marked a feature of Elizabethan poetry. It has been called " the perfection of song writing"; note how the longer lines change into a shorter form, until the voice seems to die away. Compare this little song with the sonnets on sleep — such as 40, or 46.

2. **What**: why.

23. Sonnet 18. 7. **every fair from fair**, etc.: every beautiful thing will some time lose its beauty. 8. **untrimm'd**: stripped of adornment. 10. **that fair thou owest**: that beauty which you own.

24. Sonnet 106. All writers of the past, sings the poet, merely foretold your beauty; we of the present lack the skill to praise you as you deserve.

1. **wasted**: past, gone by. 2. **wights**: persons, beings. 5. **blazon**: celebration, praise. 8. **master**: own, possess. 11. **for**: since, because.

25. [From one of the three song-books of T. Campion, who appears to have been the author of the words which he set to music. His merit as a lyrical poet (recognized in his own time, but since then forgotten) has been again brought to light.] The title means "kisses."

5. **still**: always, ever.

26. 5. **as discontent**: as if discontented.

27. From *Love's Labour's Lost*, Act IV, Scene 3. It was reprinted in the *Passionate Pilgrim* and *England's Helicon*.

4. **wanton**: playful, sportive. 7. **That**: so that. 9–10. "The air can touch thy cheek; would that I might do so." 16. **forsworn**: to have broken an oath. In the play, the singer had vowed to see no woman for three years; he now finds it impossible to keep the vow. 19. **deny himself**, etc.: deny that he was Jove.

28. This is considered to be Wyatt's masterpiece. Note the simplicity and directness of the language, expressing a very deep emotion. It belongs to an earlier period than the other poems in this book.

1. **tried intent**: the proved purpose of my true devotion. 3. **travail**: toil. 6–7. **since whan**, etc.: (forget not) how long I have been your suitor, and paid you service which none can tell. 9. **assays**: trials. 17. **thine own approved**: him whom thou hast tested.

29. 2. **prejudge thy bliss**: prejudice thy happiness by not coming to me. 7. **transform'd in me**: made one with me.

30. The title means, "In tears." 3. **keep**: live, abide. 6. **parts**: qualities.

31. Sonnet 116. A noble poem of true love: "many waters cannot quench love, neither can the floods drown it." Youth and beauty may pass, but love remains.

1. **Let me not**, etc.: May I never admit that there are, etc. 4. **bends with the remover**, etc.: tends to draw back because the other draws back. 5. **mark**: a sea-mark, set on a rock. 7. **It is the star**, etc.: *i.e.*, the star will serve as guide to the sailor at sea who calculates its height above the horizon, but knows nothing of its worth as an influence upon his life. There is a reference to the familiar belief in astrology. 9. **Time's fool**: the victim or dupe of time. 12. **bears it out**, etc.: endures until the very end.

32. [This lovely song appears, as here given, in Puttenham's *Arte of English Poetrie*, 1589. A longer and inferior form was published in Sidney's *Arcadia*, 1590.]

Notes

33. 6–7. Compare *Macbeth*, I, 5, 63–4:

" Your face, my thane, is like a book where men
May read strange matters."

34. A sonnet of great passion and beauty. Note especially the thought of the third quatrain.

35. Sung by the Clown in *Twelfth Night*, Act II, Scene 3. The title means, " make the most of to-day."

11. **Sweet-and-twenty**: probably, as one critic has said, " a pretty term for a pretty age." Or it may mean " sweet and twenty times as sweet," a form quite in keeping with Elizabethan usage.

36. Autolycus is the peddler in Shakespeare's *A Winter's Tale*.

1. **brave**: fine-looking, showy. 10. **orient'st**: brightest.

37. Sung by Winter in *Love's Labour's Lost*, Act V, Scene 2. A fine bit of country realism.

2. **blows his nail**: blows on his fingers to warm them. 8. **keel**: cool by stirring. 11. **saw**: trite saying (in his sermon). 14. **crabs**: crab-apples.

38. Sonnet 73. The thought is of age and the approach of death. We are reminded of the passage in *Macbeth*, Act V, Scene 3, lines 22, 23:

" I have lived long enough: my way of life
Is fall'n into the sear, the yellow leaf."

10. **his**: its. 12. **Consum'd with that**, etc.: *i.e.*, the fire disappears with the fuel that fed it.

39. Sonnet 30. 1. **sessions . . . summon**: law terms — memory is called to bear witness. 4. **with old woes**, etc.: renew my old lamentations over the waste of my precious time. 6. **dateless**: endless, everlasting. 8. **moan**: mourn. **expense**: loss. 9. **foregone**: past, gone before. 10. **tell**: count.

40. One of the most beautiful of all the sonnets on sleep. Compare Daniel's sonnet, 46, and Wordsworth's, 313.

2. **baiting-place**: place for rest and refreshment.
4. **indifferent**: impartial. 5. **shield of proof**: tried, or tested, shield. **prease**: press. 10. **deaf of noise**, etc.: quiet and dark. 13. **heavy grace**: tardily granted favor. 14. **livelier**: more life-like, more real.

41. Sonnet 60. The subject is the change wrought by time upon youth and beauty.

4. **sequent**: successive, following one another. 5. [**Nativity, once in the main of light**: when a star has risen and entered on the full stream of light: — another of the astrological phrases no longer familiar.] The references to astrology here would be readily understood by the Elizabethans. We are born, says the poet, under lucky stars and slowly grow to maturity; but then troubles assail us, and everything goes awry; time gave us good, and now time takes it away. 7. **Crooked eclipses**: eclipses were considered unlucky. 9. **transfix the flourish**: pierce the beauty and strength of youth. 11. **Feeds on the rarities**, etc.: devours the finest qualities of nature's handiwork. 13. **times in hope**: ages yet to come.

42. Sonnet 87. A sad word of farewell; the poet feels himself unworthy of the love which he has enjoyed.

3. **charter of thy worth**: her own worthiness gives her the right to release herself. 4. **determinate**: cancelled, expired. 8. **my patent**: the right I held to your love. 11. [**upon misprision growing**: either, granted in error, or, upon the growth of contempt.] She had "misprized" him, and now knows better.

43. Sonnet 94. Those who possess strength and beauty, and yet have complete self-control, these men rightly enjoy the favors of heaven. Others hold these gifts like stewards, not like rightful heirs. Even if they are self-centered, they give pleasure; but if they become corrupt, they are all the more odious. [With the tone of this Sonnet compare Hamlet's "Give me that man that is not passion's slave," etc (*Hamlet*, III, 2, 60–71). Shakespeare's writings show the

Notes 495

deepest sensitiveness to passion; hence the attraction he felt in the contrasting effects of apathy.]

6. **husband**: guard. **expense**: waste. 11. **base infection**: taint of decay. 12. **outbraves**: outshines, surpasses.

44. Another example of the direct simplicity of Wyatt's verse. See 28.

3. **To save thee**, etc.: save thyself from being blamed for my grief and sorrow. [Renaissance influences long impeded the return of English poets to the charming realism of this and a few other poems by Wyatt.]

45. You would find it interesting to compare the poems on the nightingale contained in this collection. There is invariable reference to the sadness, as well as the beauty, of the bird's song.

3. **Sitting**: as I was sitting. 7. **moan**: sorrow. 10. **uptill a thorn**: against a thorn. There was an old belief that the nightingale could sing only when in pain. 12. **That**: so that. 17. **lively**: vividly, clearly. 23. **King Pandion**: In Greek mythology, king of Athens and the father of two beautiful daughters, Procne and Philomela. Procne married Tereus, king of Thrace. The story should be read in any good book on mythology. 24. **lapp'd in lead**: enclosed in leaden coffins.

46. The poet calls upon sleep to bring him peace and happiness.

3. **languish**: weariness, sorrow. **restore the light**: *i.e.*, the waking world was dark to him. 6. **ill-adventur'd youth**: youth which had carried out a disastrous venture in the voyage of life. 9. **Cease, dreams**, etc.: cease to repeat to me by night the sorrows that I must suffer by day. 11. **approve**: prove. 13. **Still**: always.

47. [In the old legend it is now Philomela, now Procne (the swallow) who suffers violence from Tereus. This song has a fascination in its calm intensity of passion; that "sad earnestness and vivid exactness" which Cardinal Newman ascribes to the masterpieces of ancient poetry.]

12. **Thy thorn without,** etc.: thy thorn is outside thee, but my grief is in my heart.　14. **wroken**: wreaked — obsolete form.

48. From *Measure for Measure*, Act IV, Scene 1. The title means, "In vain." This has been called the most passionate of Shakespeare's songs. Note his power of expressing pathos and deep emotion in very little space.

49. This is one of the finest of all our sonnets. The sudden outburst of the real feeling which comes in the last six lines — the change from pretence to reality — is handled in a masterly way.

4. **cleanly**: wholly, entirely.

50. The title means: "Man walketh in a vain shadow," and is taken from *Psalms*, xxxix, 6.

14. **a luckless night**: death.

51. Sonnet 148. This is one of the two which Palgrave took from the Second Series of Shakespeare's sonnets. The poet is struggling against a love which he feels to be unworthy.

4. **censures**: judges.

52. [Exquisite in its equably-balanced metrical flow.]

7. **charm'd**: placed under a spell.　**secure**: free from care.

53. [Judging from its style, this beautiful example of old simplicity and feeling may perhaps be referred to the earlier years of Elizabeth.] It is taken from *Songs of Sundry Nature*, a collection of part-songs published in 1589 with music by William Byrd. The refrain imitates the monotonous notes of the shepherd's pipe.

3. **late forgot**: lately forgotten by his lady-love.　28. **surpassing glad**: very happy. The shepherd is decidedly philosophic about his loss.

54. 11. **Self-proof**: your own experience.　13. **Cassandra-like**: Cassandra was the prophetess in the *Iliad* whose fate it was to make predictions which, though true, were never believed.

Notes 497

55. Another of Campion's clever and pleasing songs. 3. **mere**: pure. 11. **a woman right**: a true woman.

56. Sung by Amiens in *As You Like It*, Act II, Scene 7. It is a pessimistic song of the ingratitude of man. Note the irony of the last line in each verse.

2. **unkind**: unnatural. 7. **Heigh-ho**: an expression of weariness or melancholy, like a sigh. 8. **mere**: utter. 12. **so nigh**: so deeply. 13. **benefits forgot**: kindnesses forgotten. 14. **warp**: freeze. 16. **friend remember'd not**: unfaithful friendship.

57. [Printed in a little Anthology by Nicholas Breton, 1597. It is, however, a stronger and finer piece of work than any known to be his.]

1. **silly**: simple, innocent. 3. **as doubt**: as I fear. **dole**: grief. 5. **lap**: wrap. [15. **If there be any**, etc.: obscure: perhaps, if there be any who speak harshly of thee, thy pain may plead for pity from Fate.] 21. **grace**: favor. 39. **rascal**: base-born.

58. With this compare Shelley's lines *To the Moon* (312). What is the underlying thought in each?

4. **That busy archer**: Cupid. 5. **if that**: if. 7. **languish'd grace**: unhappy condition. 8. **descries**: points out. 9. **of**: on account of. 10. **constant**: faithful. 14. "Do they call ungratefulness, there, a virtue?"

59. The title means "O cruel love." 3. **engirt thee round**: surround thee. 6. **hell can move**: can charm the world of the dead.

60. From *Menaphon*, a romance by Robert Greene, published in 1589.

1. **wanton**: playful little child; a term of endearment, like **wag** in line 3. 7. **woe**: sad. 13. **stint**: cease. 15. **by course**: without ceasing, continuously. 16. **that**: so that.

61. 7. **caitiffs**: those who are unhappy or miserable. The word originally meant "captives"; finally, it came to have a connotation of wickedness or cowardice. **blest**: happy, fortunate.

Notes

62. Sung by the Clown in *Twelfth Night*, Act II, Scene 4.

2. **cypres**: probably referring to the cypress tree, from which coffins were made. Some critics think it refers to the fabric known as "cypress," a kind of crape material. See Milton's *Il Penseroso* (145), 19-20:

> "And sable stole of Cipres lawn
> Over thy decent shoulders drawn."

10. **black**: covered with a black funeral pall.

63. lute: a stringed instrument, somewhat resembling a guitar.

3. **immelodious**: unmelodious. 4. **ramage**: confused noise of singing. 6. **wont**: was accustomed. 8. **harbinger**: forerunner. 14. **turtle**: turtle-dove, frequently taken by poets as a symbol of constancy. **still her loss complain**: continually mourn for her loss.

64. Sung by Guiderius and Arviragus in *Cymbeline*, Act IV, Scene 2, as they laid Fidele in the grave.

5. **Golden**: used to express beauty or value. 6. **as**: the same as. 14. **thunder-stone**: thunderbolt. 16. **moan**: grief, sorrow. 18. **consign to thee**: be bound by the same fate with thee.

65. Sung by Ariel in *The Tempest*, Act I, Scene 2.

1. **Full fathom five**: a "fathom" is six feet, but the term here is used merely to express great depth.

66. This dirge is from Webster's play, *The White Devil*, which was one of his best works. ["I never saw anything like this funeral dirge," says Charles Lamb, "except the ditty which reminds Ferdinand of his drowned father in *The Tempest*." As that is of the water, watery; so this is of the earth, earthy. Both have that intenseness of feeling which seems to resolve itself into the element which it contemplates.]

5. **dole**: lament, mourning.

67. Sonnet 32. Remember me, after I am gone, not for my verse but for our old friendship.

Notes 499

1. **well-contented**: a "transferred epithet" — the day of his death will find him content to die.   4. **lover**: friend, a frequent usage in Shakespeare.   7. **Reserve**: keep, preserve.   8. **the height of happier men**: the achievement of men more fortunately endowed.   12. **better equipage**: finer poetic equipment.

68. Sonnet 71. The same thought, cast in a different mould. Do not remember me when I am dead, if thinking about me should make you sorrowful.

8. **woe**: sorrowful.   10. **compounded**: mingled.   13. **wise world**: a touch of irony: the world is too wise to grieve over the past.

69. From *The Merchant of Venice*, Act III, Scene 2 — the famous Casket Scene.

1. **Fancy**: love.

70. This little song is paraphrased from an Italian madrigal. It forms an excellent example of the Elizabethan "conceit," or highly elaborated thought.

71. From Lodge's romance, *Rosalynde, Euphues Golden Legacy*. See 19.

18. **Whist**: be quiet.   34. **I like of thee**, etc.: I like thee, if thou wilt pity me.

72. Lyly was the author of a number of plays to be acted by young boys. This song is from his *Alexander and Campaspe*, which appeared in 1584.

4. **His mother's doves**: the dove, the sparrow, and the swallow were all sacred to Venus.   8. **crystal**: fairness, clearness.   11. **set**: staked, betted.

73. From a play, *The Rape of Lucrece*, acted about 1608. Note the cheerful, open-air quality of the song.

7. **prune**: preen, smooth.   16. **stare**: starling.

74. A "Prothalamion" is a wedding hymn. [Written in honour of the Ladies Elizabeth and Katharine Somerset.

Nowhere has Spenser more emphatically displayed himself as the very poet of Beauty: the Renaissance impulse in England is here seen at its highest and purest. The genius of Spenser, like Chaucer's, does itself justice only in poems of some length. Hence it is impossible to represent it in this volume by other pieces of equal merit, but impracticable dimensions.] The poem was written in 1596; at the time Spenser was living in London with the Earl of Essex, and the marriage was the double wedding of the two daughters of the Earl of Worcester. The elaborate stanza form is beautifully sustained throughout, and never becomes monotonous, owing to the admirable choice of words and the singular charm of the refrain.

2. **Zephyrus**: the west wind. 4. **Titan**: the sun. 6. **long fruitless stay**: Spenser tried vainly more than once to get a position at the court of Queen Elizabeth. 12. **rutty**: marked with water-tracks, where little brooks run into the main river. The word may also mean "rooty"; that is, the roots of trees and shrubs showed all along the edge. 13. **painted**: adorned. **variable**: various, many-colored. 16. **paramours**: lovers. 17. **Against**: in preparation for. **is not long**: is close at hand. 21. **the flood thereby**: the neighboring river. 23. **As each**, etc.: it was a custom of the time for brides to go to church with their hair hanging loose. 25. **entrailéd curiously**: skilfully entwined. 26. **flasket**: a long, shallow basket, carried slung over the arm. 27. **full featously**: very neatly, skilfully. 33. **vermeil**: red, vermillion. 34. **posies**: bouquets.

38. **lee**: here used for stream, or current. See also line 115 below. 40. **Pindus**: a mountain range in northern Greece. 44. **Leda**: the story can be found in any classical dictionary. 55. **Eftsoons**: At once. **flowers their fill**: as many flowers as they wanted. 60. **Them seem'd**: it seemed to them. 63. **team**: chariot. 78. **Peneus**: a river of Thrace, running through the beautiful Vale of Tempe. Flowers were scattered upon its waters at the feast of Apollo. 100. **assoil**: dispel. 106. **redound**: overflow. 110. **undersong**: refrain. 121. **Cynthia**: the moon. **shend**: put to shame, outshine. 128. **my**

Notes 501

most kindly nurse: Spenser is said to have been born in East Smithfield, near the Tower of London. 130. **from another place**: he here claims relationship with the ancient family of Spencer in Althorp, Northamptonshire.

132. **those bricky towers**: a section of London, on the Thames, where the Knights Templar settled in 1185. In 1330 it was given to the law students. To-day it is known as the Inner Temple and the Middle Temple, two of the "Inns of Court," or lodgings for barristers. 135. **whilome wont**: formerly were accustomed. 136. **Till they decayed through pride**: The Order of the Knights Templar was founded in 1118 to guard pilgrims to Palestine. Originally humble, they eventually became so strong that they were a menace to the government and were suppressed in 1308. Look up the interesting descriptions in Scott's *Ivanhoe*. 137. **a stately place**: Essex House, seat of the Earl of Leicester, a favorite of Queen Elizabeth. Sir Philip Sidney, his nephew, introduced Spenser to him. 140. Leicester had died in 1588. 145. **a noble peer**: Robert Devereux, Earl of Essex. At this time he was at the height of his power, having just taken Cadiz. 148. **Hercules' two pillars**: the headlands on either side of the Straits of Gibraltar were anciently so named. 153. **endless happiness**: this "happiness" was not to last very long. Essex was executed for rebellion in 1601. 157. **Elisa's**: Queen Elizabeth's. 164. **Hesper**: Hesperus, the evening star. Compare Milton's *Lycidas* (89), lines 167–170. 166. **to the river's open viewing**: to where he could get a clear view of the river. 167. **ensuing**: following. 169. **Two gentle knights**: the two bridegrooms. 173. **twins of Jove**: Castor and Pollux. 174. **the baldric of the Heavens bright**: a baldric was a richly decorated belt; here it refers to the Zodiac, studded with stars. "Bright" modifies "baldric." 177. **tide**: time, season.

75. Taken from *The Pleasant Comodie of Patient Grissill*, acted in 1603. It is a little sermon on contentment.

6. **golden numbers**: great sums of gold. 11. **crispéd**: ruffled by the wind.

Notes

76. The title means: "thus it passes." Note the play upon words throughout; the form is typical of the age. 9. **dispossest**: "put out of commission."

77. A familiar simile, gracefully wrought out. 11. **in a thought**: in a flash. 12. **erst**: first, once.

78. Sonnet 146. 1. **earth**: body. 2. This line has never been arranged to the satisfaction of the critics, because of a misprint in the first issue of the sonnet. Various readings of the first two words are: Foil'd by, Fool'd by, Starved by. **array**: adorn, deck out. 5–9. The meaning seems to be: "Shall all this expenditure of yours be for the benefit of the worms?" 10. **aggravate**: increase. 11. **terms**: periods of time. 13–14. See *I Corinthians*, xv, 54: "Then shall be brought to pass the saying that is written, Death is swallowed up in victory."

79. This is a fine paraphrase of Horace's famous Ode, *Integer vitae*. For a poem generally similar in thought, see 95.

23. **sober**: serene, calm, tranquil.

80. 3. **of Him**: these words depend on "art and wisdom." 8. **period of**: end of, limit to. 9–14. These lines bear a very close resemblance to part of one of Sidney's sonnets, published in 1591:

> "For like a child, that some fair book doth find,
>   With gilded leaves or gilded vellum plays,
>   Or, at the most, on some fine picture stays,
> But never heeds the fruit of reader's mind."

11. **Fair dangling ribbands**: the bookmarkers, which were often richly decorated.

81. This sonnet, and the one which follows, are related in their general thought. The problem in both "is at least as old as the Book of Job; virtuous people do suffer, as it seems to us undeservedly. No one has ever satisfactorily accounted for it, but the most helpful comment on the fact is certainly that of the Stoics, who taught that from all adversity the wise man could gain advantage." (Wheeler.)

5–6. Those souls which are most blinded by the sullen mists of vice are the ones which are most helped by blind Fortune.

8. **Ply**: move to and fro.

82. Sonnet 66. Like the preceding, a despondent poem.

1. **all these**: these that follow. 2. **As**: for example. **desert**: worthiness. 3. **trimm'd**: adorned. **needy nothing**, etc.: some empty-headed nonentity finely decked out. 4. **unhappily forsworn**: forced by hard fate to forfeit its honor. 5. riches and honor lavished on unworthy persons. 8. A man of great ability held back by some weakling in authority. Pronounce "disabled" as of four syllables. 9. Perhaps a reference to the narrow-minded edicts against the theatres, from which Shakespeare suffered more than once. 11. **simplicity**: foolishness, silliness, lack of intelligence.

83. The author is the "noble peer" mentioned in Spenser's *Prothalamion*, see lines 145–162. Do you think he is sincere in his wish as expressed in this poem?

1. **he**: he who. 2. **unhaunted desert**: some lonely place, unfrequented by men. 4. **secure**: free from care. 6. **hip, etc.**: field fruits and field flowers.

84. For the thought, see *St. Matthew*, iii, 1–4.

6. **virgin hives**: hives of wild bees, never touched by man.

Questions and Topics for Discussion

1. Make a list of the classical myths and traditions which are touched upon in the various poems.

2. Select some poems which seem to you especially typical of the period covered by the Book. What qualities do they possess which do not characterize modern poetry?

3. Look up the context of the Songs from Shakespeare's plays, and comment upon their dramatic value.

4. Select passages which seem to you especially significant as regards pathos, pure beauty, or the mere "joy of living." Comment upon the manner in which the thought is presented.

5. Spenser has been called "the apostle of beauty," and "the poet's poet." Can you see how his *Prothalamion* justifies such expressions?

6. Study the grouping of the poems, and investigate Palgrave's method of arrangement.

7. Group the sonnets according to their subject.

8. Which of the poems shows the greatest simplicity? the most elaborate form? In each case, comment upon the effect upon the reader.

9. Select three or four poems which deal with different emotions. Comment upon the elements of power and appeal as shown in each.

10. Make a list of passages which seem to you especially well adapted for oral recitation.

BIOGRAPHICAL SKETCHES

FRANCIS TURNER PALGRAVE, compiler of *The Golden Treasury*, was born at Great Yarmouth on September 28, 1824. He was the son of Sir Francis Palgrave, a famous historian, and was educated at Charterhouse School and Oxford University. After leaving the University he took up literary and educational work, and from 1884 to 1897 was professor of poetry at Oxford. He died on October 24, 1897. His great anthology was published in 1861. Some years before this time he had met Tennyson, and a close friendship sprang up between them. To him Palgrave naturally turned for advice and assistance. "I had put the scheme of my *Golden Treasury* before him during a walk near the Land's End in the late summer of 1860, and he encouraged me to proceed, barring only any poems by himself from insertion. . . And at the Christmastide following, the gathered materials already submitted to the judgment of two friends of taste, were laid before Tennyson for final judgment."

Notes

Sir William Alexander was a Scotchman and a friend of King James I, who made him a large grant of land in North America. Sir William named it "Nova Scotia"; the name and the grant (somewhat reduced) survive in the Canadian Province of to-day. He was a scholar and courtier, and eventually became Secretary of State for Scotland. He lived from 1567 to 1640.

Richard Barnefield (1574–1627) was educated at Oxford University. The poem chosen by Palgrave (45) appeared in *The Passionate Pilgrim*, an important Elizabethan anthology. It was there attributed to Shakespeare, but is found in Barnefield's collection called *Poems in Divers Humors* (1598). In this form it was printed in another anthology, *England's Helicon* (1600), with the signature "Ignoto" — the "unknown."

Thomas Campion was a musician and a writer of "airs," or short songs. The words and music of the *First Book of Airs*, published in 1601, were almost entirely his work. He was a Cambridge University man and a friend of Thomas Nash. He wrote several masques — plays characterized by beautiful music and fine scenery — but was best known as a song-writer. In 1602 he published an important piece of criticism, *Observations on the Art of English Poesy*. The date of his birth is unknown; he died in 1619.

Samuel Daniel, famed for the charm of his verse, was one of a musical family. Born at Taunton in 1562, he went to Magdalen College, Oxford, and enjoyed many honors during his lifetime. He succeeded Spenser as Poet Laureate. He died in 1619.

Thomas Dekker wrote many plays, the most famous being *The Shoemaker's Holiday*, a vivid picture of London life. He went to the Merchant Taylor's School in London, and later became a "hack" writer under the famous theatrical manager Philip Henslowe. Dekker was born in 1570 and died in London about 1641.

Robert Devereux, Earl of Essex was a famous and picturesque figure in the reign of Queen Elizabeth. He was born in 1566, went to Cambridge University, and had a brilliant career as a soldier, a protégé of the Queen, and a friend of Shakespeare. He captured Cadiz in 1596, and three years later was made Governor General of Ireland. He fell into disfavor with the Queen, and tried to start a rebellion against her. On February 25, 1601, he was beheaded for high treason.

JOHN DONNE (1573-1631) attended both Oxford and Cambridge Universities, though he never took a degree. He entered the Church, won fame as a preacher, and eventually became Dean of St. Paul's Cathedral. Ben Jonson said that "he was the first poet in the world for some things," but that he would probably perish "for not being understood."

MICHAEL DRAYTON lived from 1563 to 1631. His most famous poem is the splendid ballad called *The Battle of Agincourt;* his greatest work a gigantic historical poem, *Polyolbion*, which embodies many of the early legends of England.

WILLIAM DRUMMOND was born at Hawthornden, Scotland, in 1585. He was educated at Edinburgh University and travelled on the Continent. He took part in the Civil War on the side of King Charles, and died in 1649. Ben Jonson visited him at Hawthornden in 1618. The record of their conversations on contemporary poets is a highly interesting literary document.

ROBERT GREENE is chiefly remembered because of his bitter attack on Shakespeare in a pamphlet entitled *A Groatsworth of Wit Bought with a Million of Repentance*. Born in 1558, he died in extreme poverty in London in 1592. He was educated at Oxford and Cambridge Universities, travelled on the Continent, and settled in London, where he won fame as a writer of romances and dramas. He deeply repented what he himself called a vicious life.

THOMAS HEYWOOD wrote many lyrics of great musical beauty; the one here given (73) is among his best. He wrote a number of plays, the most successful being *A Woman Killed with Kindness*. He was born about 1575; he died about 1648.

Notes

THOMAS LODGE, educated at Oxford University, made several sea voyages. On one of them he wrote a romance called *Rosalynde, Euphues' Golden Legacy*, which was the source of Shakespeare's *As You Like It*. He also was known as a writer of plays. He lived from 1558 till 1625.

JOHN LYLY was born in 1553, and educated at Charterhouse School and Oxford University. He is best known as the author of *Euphues and his England* (1579-80), which had an important effect upon Elizabethan prose style. He also composed plays for the "Children's Companies" — the Children of Saint Paul's and the Children of the Chapel Royal — and his influence may be traced in some of the early plays of Shakespeare. He died in 1606.

CHRISTOPHER MARLOWE was the most important dramatic writer before Shakespeare. Born in 1564, he was the son of a Canterbury shoemaker, and received a good education at King's School and Cambridge University. He died in a tavern brawl in 1593. He was the author of four important plays: *Tamburlane, Doctor Faustus, The Jew of Malta*, and *Edward II*. His influence on Shakespeare was marked; his genius showed wonderful possibilities which were cut short by his untimely death. He was a master of beautiful verse, as is seen not only in the blank verse of his dramas ("Marlowe's mighty line"), but in the musical quality of his famous poem, *Hero and Leander*.

THOMAS NASH was a Cambridge man and a friend of Marlowe and Greene, to both of whom he did some service in defending them against the attacks of pamphleteers. Like most educated Elizabethans, he wrote freely; his best known work being a play, *Summer's Last Will and Testament* (1600). His life: 1567-1601.

THE SHEPHERD TONIE. Generally supposed to be the pen name of Anthony Munday, of whom very little is known. He was a writer for Henslowe, and the approximate dates of his life were 1553-1633.

WILLIAM SHAKESPEARE, the greatest English dramatist, was born at Stratford-on-Avon, April 23, 1564. The details of his life are obscure, yet we know as much about him as we do about any other writer of the time. He attended the village school; married early; went up to London at the age of eighteen; and by the year 1592 was well-known as an actor and playwright. He rose

Shakespeare's Birthplace, Stratford-on-Avon

to the greatest heights as a dramatist, became shareholder in two theatres, and retired to his native town, where he died on April 23, 1616. The best short account of his life is found in *The Facts about Shakespeare*, by Neilson and Thorndike; the standard biography is the *Life* by Sir Sidney Lee. The poems in the *Golden Treasury* were taken from his plays and from *The Passionate Pilgrim*. The sonnets were chosen from the edition of 1609.

SIR PHILIP SIDNEY came of a noble family and was born at Penshurst, Kent, in 1554. He went to Shrewsbury School and studied at Oxford University. After travel on the Continent, he attended the court of the Queen, where his remarkable gifts of person, mind, and character won him many friends. He died on the battlefield of Zutphen, in the Netherlands, in 1586. Sidney did well everything he undertook to do; as soldier, courtier, poet, romance-writer, and critic, he was equally successful. His writings were: *Astrophel and Stella*, a sonnet-sequence; *Arcadia*, a romance; and *An Apologie for Poesy*, a critical essay. By his contemporaries Sidney was considered the type of a perfect gentleman.

EDMUND SPENSER, "the poets' poet," was born in London in 1552. Educated at Cambridge, he soon went to Court, where for a time he was in high favor. His first work, *The Shephearde's Calendar*, appeared in 1579. He was sent to Ireland in 1580 as Secretary to the Lord Deputy. The first three books of *The Faery Queene*, his great allegorical poem, were issued in 1590; the next three in 1596. The poem was never finished. Among his other works were *Colin Clout's Come Home Again*, and the *Amoretti*, a sonnet-sequence. He suffered great sorrow and loss in Ireland, and returned to London, where he died, poor and lonely, in 1599. He was a close friend of Sir Walter Raleigh.

JOSHUA SYLVESTER, a native of Kent, lived from 1563 to 1618. He was a successful business man, and won some fame by his translations from the French. He spent his latter years at the Court of King James I.

JOHN WEBSTER was one of the chief dramatic writers after Shakespeare. His two great tragedies were *The White Devil* and *The Duchess of Malfi*. In their sheer horror, these plays stand alone; his less powerful dramas were written in collaboration with Dekker, Drayton, and others. The dates of his life are uncertain; those usually assigned are 1580–1625.

SIR THOMAS WYATT, with the Earl of Surrey, was the first of the Elizabethan poets. He introduced the sonnet into English literature. His poems were published in the important collection known as *Tottel's Miscellany* (1557). Wyatt was born in Kent, (1503?) studied at Cambridge, travelled on the Continent, and became a courtier at the Court of King Henry VIII. Accused of treason in 1540, he was imprisoned, but set free after trial. He died in 1542.

Notes

BOOK SECOND

[This division, embracing generally the latter eighty years of the seventeenth century, contains the close of our early poetical style and the commencement of the modern. In Dryden we see the first master of the new; in Milton, whose genius dominates here as Shakespeare's in the former book, the crown and consummation of the early period. Their splendid odes are far in advance of any prior attempts, Spenser's excepted; they exhibit that wider and grander range which years and experience and the struggles of the time conferred on poetry. Our Muses now give expression to political feeling, to religious thought, to a high philosophic statesmanship in writers such as Marvell, Herbert, and Wotton; whilst in Marvell and Milton, again, we find noble attempts, hitherto rare in our literature, at pure description of nature, destined in our own age to be continued and equaled. Meanwhile the poetry of simple passion, although before 1660 often deformed by verbal fancies and conceits of thought, and afterwards by levity and an artificial tone, produced in Herrick and Waller some charming pieces of more finished art than the Elizabethan, until in the courtly compliments of Sedley it seems to exhaust itself and lie almost dormant for the hundred years between the days of Wither and Suckling and the days of Burns and Cowper. That the change from our early style to the modern brought with it at first a loss of nature and simplicity is undeniable; yet the bolder and wider scope which poetry took between 1620 and 1700, and the successful efforts then made to gain greater clearness in expression, in their results have been no slight compensation.]

85. This great ode was begun on Christmas Day, 1629. Milton was 21 years old, and was still at Cambridge, although he had taken his degree earlier in the year. The first four stanzas are written in the form known as "Rime Royal," with the last line an Alexandrine, or six feet, in place of the usual pentameter. The rest of the poem is composed in an eight-line stanza of singular dignity and force. The introduc-

Notes

tory portion shows the sonorous quality seen in perfection in *Paradise Lost*, and we note throughout the fullness and richness of allusion and the suggestive use of proper names. The splendid musical quality of the ode is evident when we read it aloud and this, like the other points mentioned, is characteristic of the poet.

5. **holy sages**: the writers of the Old Testament who foretold the coming of Christ. See, for example, *Isaiah*, ix, 1-7; liii. 6. **deadly forfeit**: the penalty of death — "for as in Adam all die, even so in Christ shall all be made alive." *I Corinthians*, xv, 22. **release**: remit, take away. 8. **unsufferable**: unbearable, insufferable. 11. **Trinal**: Threefold. 19-21. Before sunrise. Note the beauty of these lines; and note, too, the admixture of Greek mythology with Christian symbolism. This is true throughout the poem. Classical as well as Christian allusion came naturally to the deeply-stored mind of Milton. 23. **star-led wizards**: the "three Wise Men from the East." See *St. Matthew*, ii, 1. 24. **prevent**: come before — the original meaning of the word. 27. **quire**: old spelling for "choir." 28. **touch'd with hallow'd fire**: *i.e.*, touched with the fire of divine inspiration, that he may be able to sing of sacred things. See *Isaiah*, vi, 6-7: "Then flew one of the seraphims unto me, having a live coal in his hand, which he had taken with the tongs from off the altar; and he laid it upon my mouth."

41. polluted with sin and evil-doing. The earth is covered with snow, the symbol of purity, having taken off her "gaudy trim" of the summer. 45. **cease**: transitive; cause to cease, put a stop to. 48. **the turning sphere**: "According to the Ptolemaic system of astronomy, the Earth was a fixed body at the centre of eight globes or spheres which revolved round it and formed the paths of the Sun, the Moon, and the planets." (Wheeler.) As they revolved, they made what was called the "music of the spheres," to which reference is constant in poetry. Compare lines 134-141. 49. **harbinger**: forerunner, messenger. 50. **turtle wing**: the turtle-dove has always been the emblem of peace. 51. **myrtle wand**: the

myrtle, sacred to Venus, was the symbol of love. 53. **No war,** etc.: An allusion to the beautiful old legend that at the time of the birth of Christ there was no war throughout the world. 56. **hookéd chariot**: with hooks or scythes fixed to the axle. 59. **awful**: filled with awe or fear. 64. **whist**: hushed, silent. 68. **birds of calm**: according to the old legend, the halcyon or kingfisher bred during the winter in a nest floating on the sea, and at such time the water was always calm.

71. **one way**: towards Bethlehem. **influence**: a reference to astrology — the stars were supposed to exert a direct influence upon the lives of men. 74. **Lucifer**: the morning star, which warned of the approach of day. The word literally means "light-bringer." 78. **her room**: the space which she needed. 81. **As**: as though. 85. **lawn**: open field. 86. **point**: moment. 88. **than**: then — old alternative spelling. 89. **Pan**: the "Lord of all." In mythology, Pan was the god of shepherds. 92. **silly**: simple, innocent. 95. **strook**: old form for "struck." 97. **stringéd noise**: music of harps. 100. **close**: cadence. 103. **Cynthia's seat**: Cynthia was the moon; the "hollow round" would be the open sky. 116. **unexpressive**: not to be expressed in words, inexpressible. 119. **the Sons of Morning**: the angels — see *Job*, xxxviii, 6, 7: "Who laid the corner-stone thereof; when the morning stars sang together, and all the sons of God shouted for joy?" 124. **weltering**: surging, rolling. 125. **ye crystal spheres**: another reference (see line 48) to the music of the spheres. The planets, including the earth, were supposed to be set in nine concentric spheres, each with its own musical note, which could not be heard by human ears. Compare the famous passage in *The Merchant of Venice*, Act V, Scene 1:

"There's not the smallest orb which thou behold'st
  But in his motion like an angel sings,
  Still choiring to the young-ey'd cherubins;
  But while this muddy vesture of decay
  Doth grossly close it in, we cannot hear it."

Notes   513

131. ninefold: the full music of the nine spheres.   **132. [consort**: Milton's spelling of this word, here and elsewhere, has been followed, as it is uncertain if he used it in the sense of *accompanying*, or simply for *concert*.]   **135. the age of gold**: the age of universal happiness. In Greek mythology, the period when Saturn reigned upon earth.   **138. earthly mould**: the form of man.   **140. dolorous mansions**: gloomy dwellings.

145. sheen: brightness.   **155. ychain'd**: old past participle. The prefix y- was common in old English; see 144, line 12.   **156. Wakeful**: awakening, summoning.   **158. on Mount Sinai**: see *Exodus*, xix, 16.   **165-167.** Our bliss, which after the Day of Judgment will be perfect, is even now beginning.   **168. The old Dragon**: See *Revelation*, xx, 2.   **172. Swinges**: lashes, swings.   **173. The Oracles are dumb**: The famous Oracles of Greece were supposed to give help and guidance to those who consulted them. Tradition says that they ceased with the birth of Christ.   **175. archéd roof**: Oracles were sometimes established in caves. Note the skilful use of proper names in the following stanzas.   **178. Delphos**: the Oracle at Delphi, sacred to Apollo and the most famous of all.   **179. nightly**: in the night, by night.   **breathed**: inspired.   **183.** "Some sailors, who were on a voyage from Greece to Italy, were becalmed near the Island of Paxos, and heard a voice crying out to them over the waters bidding their pilot call out on reaching the mainland that great Pan was dead. On doing this, there was heard a great wailing of many voices, so that all wondered."   **191. Lars and Lemures**: household gods, and ghosts.   **194. Flamens**: Roman priests. **quaint**: familiar, well-known.   **195.** Statues were said to sweat before some happening of national import. The portent is mentioned frequently by Latin authors.   **196. peculiar**: special.

197. The next four stanzas mention Eastern deities. Peor and Baalim were Phoenician gods.   **199. twice-batter'd god**: Dagon, see *I Samuel*, v, 2-4.   **200. Ashtaroth**: the moon-goddess Astarte, worshipped in Phoenicia.   **203. Lybic Hammon**: an Ethiopian deity, represented as a man with a ram's head. **shrinks**: draws in, as if in fear. 204. **Thammuz**: see note on Osiris, line 213. 205. **Moloch**: god of the Ammonites, to whom human sacrifices were offered. 209. **grisly**: grim, horrible. 210. **furnace blue**: burning with blue flames. 211. **brutish gods**: most of the gods of Egypt were represented in the form of animals. Isis had the head of a cow; Horus, the head of a hawk; Anubis, the head of a jackal. 213. [The Egyptian god of agriculture was torn to pieces by Typho and embalmed after death in a sacred chest. This myth, reproduced in Syria and Greece in the legend of Thammuz and Adonis, may have originally signified the annual death of the Sun or the Year under the influence of the winter darkness.] 214. **Memphian**: Osiris was worshipped at Memphis. 215. **unshower'd grass**: because no rain falls in Egypt. The land is fertilized by the Nile flood. 219. **anthems dark**: mysterious anthems. 220. **sable-stoléd**: wearing black robes. **ark**: holy shrine containing the image of the god. 223. **eyn**: old plural for "eyes." 226. **Typhon**: brother of Osiris, represented sometimes as a serpent.

231. **orient**: eastern. It was an old tradition that all ghosts, free to roam by night, at sunrise must go to their own place. 234. **several**: separate. 236. **maze**: dancing-place. 240. [**youngest-teeméd**: last born.] This is the star referred to in line 23. 243. **courtly**: like a royal court for the new-born King. 244. **Bright-harness'd**: clad in gleaming armor. **serviceable**: ready for service.

86. St. Cecilia according to the old legend was the inventor of the organ, upon which she played so beautifully that an angel once appeared to listen. She became the patron saint of music. In 1683 a musical society was founded in London, the object of which was to celebrate St. Cecilia's Day — November 22 — with a cantata written especially for the occasion. The present Ode and *Alexander's Feast* (151), were written by Dryden for this purpose. Note the skilful use of onomatopeia in stanzas 3, 4, and 5. For the characteristics of the ode, see pages 461–462.

Notes 515

1–15. It was a very old theory, taught by the Greek philosopher Pythagoras, that music could build up a whole from scattered parts, and that in this way the universe was created from chaos. 2. **universal frame**: the Universe. 8. **cold and hot**, etc.: the four elements, according to ancient science. 15. **diapason**: the full range of notes — man completed the full harmony. 16. See 151, where Dryden works out this thought in detail. 17. **Jubal**: mentioned in *Genesis*, iv, 21, as " the father of all such as handle the harp and organ." **the corded shell**: the lyre. In the old myth it was invented by the god Hermes, who found an empty tortoise shell on the shore and stretched sinews across it. Compare with the following stanzas, Collins's *The Passions* (178). 33. **complaining**: sad, plaintive. 37. **sharp**: referring to the high-pitched notes of the violin. 47. **mend**: aid, assist. 48. **Orpheus**: a mythical Greek musician, who played so wonderfully that rocks and trees followed him. 50. **sequacious of**: following. 55–63. A very fine poetic conception of the power of music.

87. This sonnet was written in protest against the persecution of the Vaudois, or Waldenses, who lived in Piedmontese valleys of northern Italy. They had always been independent of the Church of Rome, and the Duke of Savoy moved against them in 1655. Milton, as Latin Secretary to the Commonwealth, was directed by Cromwell to write a letter of remonstrance to the Duke. This caused the persecution to cease for a time. The sonnet follows the original Italianate form (see page 461). Palgrave says that no more mighty sonnet than this " collect in verse " can be found in any language. It is worthy of note that eleven of the fourteen lines end with the long " o " sound, which gives a dignified and sonorous effect.

4. **stocks and stones**: idols. 12. **the triple Tyrant**: the Pope, who wore a triple crown emblematic of his power in heaven, on earth, and in purgatory. The Puritans regarded him as a " tyrant." 14. **the Babylonian woe**: the Puritans referred to Rome as Babylon — see *Revelations*, xvii, xviii.

Notes

88. For "Horatian" ode, see page 461. Cromwell was appointed lord-lieutenant of Ireland in 1649, in order to subdue the country, which was still largely loyal to King Charles I. He was successful after a campaign of nine months. [Cromwell returned from Ireland in 1650, and Marvell probably wrote his lines soon after, while living in the Fairfax household. It is hence not surprising that (St. 21–24) he should have been deceived by Cromwell's professed submissiveness to Parliament, which, when it declined to register his decrees, he expelled by armed violence: — one despotism, by natural law, replacing another. The poet's insight has, however, truly prophesied that result in his last two lines.]

1. **forward**: spirited, eager. **appear**: come out in the world. 8. **corslet**: body armor. 9. **cease**: remain quiet. 12. **Urgéd his active star**: made his own destiny. In astrology, man is controlled by the stars; but Cromwell forced his star to do what he wished. 15. **thorough**: alternative form for "through." **Side**: party. 17–20. [Rivalry or hostility are the same to a lofty spirit, and limitation more hateful than opposition.] 23. **Caesar's head**, etc.: a highly involved metaphor. Caesar stands for King Charles I, who was beheaded through the influence of Cromwell. Julius Caesar was accustomed to wear a laurel wreath, the sign of distinction in war; and, finally, the laurel was supposed to be a protection against lightning. 29. Cromwell was a quiet country gentleman until he was called to active life at the age of forty-one. 31. **plot**: scheme, plan, object. 32. **bergamot**: a species of pear-tree. 33–36. Cromwell overthrew the Kingdom and established the Commonwealth. 39–40. Right, if it is to survive, must be supported by Might. 41. [The allusion is to the old physical doctrines of the non-existence of a vacuum and the impenetrability of matter.]

45. **the civil war**: the struggle between King and Parliament, 1642–1649. 47. [**Hampton**: He contrived that Charles should remove himself, as a result of his own fears, from Hampton Court to Carisbrooke Castle.] 52. **case**: prison. 53–56. Charles was beheaded on January 30, 1649. 57–

Notes

64. Two beautiful stanzas. Marvell approved of Charles's execution, but he fully realized the noble qualities shown by the king at the time of his death. 66. secured the power that had been seized by force. 69. **a Bleeding Head**: an allusion to a legend of the founding of the temple of Jupiter at Rome. 87. **what he may**: as far as he can. 95. **lure**: technical term in falconry. 101-102. Caesar conquered Gaul; Hannibal overran Italy. 104. **climacteric**: bring to a climax, or crisis. Certain periods of life were supposed to be especially critical. The age of 63 was known as the "grand climacteric." 105. **The Pict**: Here used for the Scotch, whom Cromwell had beaten in the battle of Dunbar. 106. **parti-colour'd**: changeful, variable; with an incidental reference to the colors of the Scottish tartans. 107. **sad**: stern, severe. 109. **tufted brake**: bushes growing in thickets. 110. **him mistake**: fail to find him. 116. **erect**: ready for use. 117-120. The drawn sword can not only control the dark spirits of rebellion, but must also uphold what it has won.

89. [The person here lamented is Milton's college friend, Edward King, drowned in 1637 while crossing from Wales to Ireland. . . . Strict Pastoral Poetry was first written or perfected by the Dorian Greeks settled in Sicily: but the conventional use of it, exhibited more magnificently in *Lycidas* than in any other pastoral, is apparently of Roman origin. Milton, employing the noble freedom of a great artist, has here united ancient mythology with what may be called the modern mythology of Camus and Saint Peter, — to direct Christian images. Yet the poem, if it gains in historical interest, suffers in poetry by the harsh intrusion of the writer's narrow and violent theological politics.] *Lycidas* was written for a volume of elegies in memory of King, published in 1638. The poem is the most famous of English "threnodies," or laments for a dead friend. The general subject of the Pastoral elegy — the type to which *Lycidas* belongs — is discussed on page 462.

1. **Yet once more**: It has been pointed out that this was the second death within Milton's circle during the year; his

mother had died in April, and King was drowned in August. The laurels, myrtle, and ivy were all emblematic of poetry. 2. **sere**: dry. The general meaning of the whole passage seems to be that Milton is compelled by his grief to write before his powers are fully ripened by "the mellowing year." 6. **constraint**: compulsion. **dear**: used here in the sense of "grievous." Shelley has the phrase, "at my dearest need." 9. **peer**: equal. 10. **knew**: knew how. 13. **welter**: roll in the waves. 14. **melodious tear**: poem that shall bring tears to the eyes. 15. [**Sisters of the sacred well**: the Muses, said to frequent the Pierian spring at foot of Mount Olympus.] 19. **Muse**: poet. 22. **shroud**: grave. 23. **For we were nursed**, etc.: Milton and King were fellow-students at Christ's College, Cambridge. The metaphor of the shepherds is a familiar one in poetry; compare Arnold's *Thyrsis*, written in memory of his Oxford friend, Arthur Hugh Clough. 25. **lawns**: open fields. 28. **winds her sultry horn**: hums at the hot noontide hour. 29. **Battening**: feeding. 30. **the star**: Venus, the evening star. 33. **Temper'd**: sung in tune, modulated. **oaten flute**: made of reeds. The joint feeding of the flocks is companionship in study; the "rural ditties" are poems written in college. The Satyrs and Fauns represent Cambridge students, and "old Damoetas" is one of the Cambridge dons. The whole passage is drawn from classical imagery.

39–41. Note the emphasis upon the word "mourn," because of its position. 40. **gadding**: straggling. 45. **canker**: caterpillar. 46. **weanling**: the young of the herd. 49. Because they will no longer hear his music. 52. **steep**: the cliffs on the northwestern coast of Wales. 54. [**Mona**: Anglesey called by the Welsh poets the Dark Island, from its dense forests.] 55. [**Deva**: the Dee; a river which may have derived its magical character from Celtic traditions. These places are introduced as being near the scene of the shipwreck.] 56. **fondly**: foolishly. 58. **the Muse herself**: Calliope, mother of Orpheus. In the ancient myth, Orpheus was wandering in Thrace distracted with grief for the loss of his wife

Notes 519

Eurydice. He refused to join in the worship of Dionysus, and was torn to pieces by the Maenads, the female devotees of the god. His head was cast into the Hebrus and was finally washed ashore on the island of Lesbos in the Aegean Sea. See note on 144, line 145. 61. **rout**: disorderly crowd.

65–66. What advantage is it to devote oneself to poetry? 67. **use**: are accustomed to do. 68–69. Amaryllis and Neaera are names in classical love poetry. The "others" are Milton's contemporaries — Ben Jonson, Herrick, Lovelace, etc., examples of whose love lyrics may be found in this book. 70. **clear**: noble, illustrious. 71. **That last infirmity**, etc.: The "noble mind," which will not be tempted by wealth or power, may yet yield to the allurement of fame. 73. **guerdon**: reward. 75. **blind Fury**: Atropos, one of the three Fates or goddesses of destiny. Clotho spun the thread of life, Lachesis measured it, and Atropos cut it when the allotted end had come. Milton calls her here a Fury. The Furies were the three goddesses who punished men for crime. Milton calls Atropos "the blind Fury" because Fate so often seems to cut men off unjustly in the prime of life. 76. '**But not the praise**,' etc.: Phoebus, the god of poetry, says that fame is immortal, even though the poet may die. Jove will finally judge all aright. The general meaning may be paraphrased as "God seeth not as man seeth." 77. **touched my trembling ears**: *i.e.*, that he might hear the divine voice. 79: **glistering foil**: the mere show.

85–86. [**Arethuse . . . Mincius**: Sicilian and Italian waters are here referred to, as representing the pastoral poetry of Theocritus and Virgil.] 87. **That strain**, etc.: the passage in lines 76–84; the poet now returns to his former manner. 90. **in Neptune's plea**: to prove that the god of the sea was not guilty of the shipwreck. 91. **felon**: evil, cruel. 96. **Hippotades**: Eolus, the god of the winds. 99. **Panope**: a Nereid. Here personifying the open sea. 100. The ship struck a rock in calm weather, and was wrecked through no fault of the wind or sea. 101. **Built in the eclipse**: Built under unlucky omens.

103. **Camus**: God of the river Cam, on which Cambridge is situated. 104. Referring to the weeds of the river margin. 105. **figures dim**: because of the age of the University. 106. **that sanguine flower**: the hyacinth. Apollo loved a beautiful youth named Hyacinthus, whom he accidently killed as they were pitching quoits. From his blood the god caused a flower to spring, and marked on the petals the Greek exclamation of mourning — AI AI. 107. **reft**: snatched away. 109–129. Read Ruskin's highly suggestive comment upon these lines in *Sesame and Lilies.* 109. **The pilot of the Galilean lake**: St. Peter, who was a fisherman on the Sea of Galilee. Palgrave's note says that he is probably introduced as head of the Church on earth, to foretell "the ruin of our corrupted clergy," as Milton regarded them, "then in their heighth" under Laud's primacy. St. Peter bore the keys of Heaven and Hell. 111. **amain**: with force. 112. **mitered**: crowned with a bishop's mitre. 113. **How well**, etc.: King had intended to enter the Church. 115. **the fold**: the ministry of the Church. 117. **scramble at the shearer's feast**: get what they can in the way of rich ecclesiastical appointments. 119. **Blind mouths**: ignorant gluttons — they want only wealth and ease. 122. **What recks it them**: what do they care. **They are sped**: they have got what they wanted. 123. **lean and flashy songs**: dreary sermons. 124. **scrannel**: thin, meagre. The harsh line imitates the discordant notes of the false shepherds. 126. **draw**: breathe in. The people were poisoned by false spiritual pride ("wind") and false doctrines ("rank mist"). 128. [**wolf**: the Puritans of the time were excited to alarm and persecution by a few conversions to Roman Catholicism which had recently occurred.] 130. **that two-handed engine**: probably the executioner's axe.

132. **Return, Alpheus**: the poet renews his pastoral strain, after the stern interlude. Alpheus was a river-god who loved Arethusa. 133. **Sicilian Muse**: the Muse of pastoral poetry. **the dread voice**: that of St. Peter in lines 112–131. 136. **use**: dwell. 138. **the swart star**: Sirius, the Dog Star, which is in the ascendant during the hot weather of July and

Notes   521

August, when people become " swart," or sunburnt. **sparely**: seldom. 139. **quaint**: fine, exquisite. 141. **purple**: adorn, enrich, give color to. 142. **rathe**: early; it survives in *rather*, sooner. 143. **crow-toe**: species of butter-cup. 144. **freak'd**: streaked. 146. **woodbine**: honeysuckle.

151. **laureat**: crowned with laurel, the emblem of poetry. **hearse**: the bier. 152. Let us, to ease our sorrow, pretend that his body really has been found. 158. **the monstrous world**: the sea, teeming with monsters. 159. **moist vows**: tearful prayers. 160. [**Bellerus**: a giant, apparently created by Milton to personify Belerium, the ancient name of Land's End.] **fable**: for "fabled stronghold." 161. **the guarded mount**: Mount St. Michael, in Mount's Bay on the south coast of Cornwall. The legend was that the Archangel Michael had appeared there; he is pictured as still standing on the mount, looking southward. 162. **Namancos and Bayona's hold**: in an atlas of Milton's time these places were marked as close to Cape Finisterre, on the northwest of Spain. The poet beseeches St. Michael to turn his eyes homeward to the troubled waters off Land's End, and to pity Lycidas. 164. **dolphins**: in the Greek myth, Arion was carried by the dolphins safe to shore.

165-185. In these lines the poet finds consolation in the resurrection of Lycidas. 168. **the day-star**: the sun. 170. **tricks**: displays, sets off. **new-spangled ore**: gold shining with fresh brightness. 173. **Him that walked the waves**: See *St. Matthew*, xiv, 25. 175. **oozy**: defiled with mud and sand from the bottom of the sea. 176. **unexpressive**: inexpressible. **nuptial song**: see *Revelation*, xix, 9: "Blessed are they which are called to the marriage supper of the Lamb." 181. **wipe the tears**: see *Revelation*, vii, 17. 183. **Genius**: guardian deity. 184. **thy large recompense**: thy full reward.

186. Here Milton speaks of the poet as some one outside himself, singing about Lycidas all day among the hills. **uncouth**: unknown. 188. **quills**: the "oaten pipes" on which he played. 189. **Doric lay**: in reference to the origir

of pastoral elegiac poetry in ancient Greece.   190. the sun had cast long evening shadows from the hills.   192. **twitch'd**: hitched up.   193. The shepherd's grief for his dead companion causes him to leave the old places.

90. This poem and the two which follow deal with the same thought.

5. **had realms**: who had realms.   13. **birth**: noble birth. 18. **once dead**: when it is once dead.

91. Taken from a masque called *Cupid and Death*, published in 1653.

11. **servile emissaries**: slaves to do his bidding. 14. **quaint**: ingenious.

92. From *The Contention of Ajax and Ulysses*, a play published in 1659.

1. **blood and state**: birth and rank.   12. *i.e.*, they conquer one another, but they cannot conquer death.   19. **purple**: probably "royal."

93. [*The assault* was an attack on London expected in 1642, when the troops of Charles I reached Brentford. "Written on his door" was the original title of this sonnet.]

1. **Colonel**: originally a word of three syllables.   2. **Whose chance**: whose lot it may be.   5. **charms**: magic arts, *i.e.*, poetry.   10. **Emathian conqueror**: Alexander the Great. When he destroyed Thebes in 335 B.C., he ordered the house of Pindar, the great lyric poet, to be spared.   13. **sad Electra's poet**: When the Spartans took Athens in 404 B.C., they were about to destroy the city. An Athenian musician, however, sang a chorus from the *Electra* of Euripides, which so deeply affected the Spartan commanders that the city was spared.

94. Milton became totally blind in 1652, when he was forty-four years old.

3. **that one talent**: the power of writing. There is a reference to the parable in *St. Matthew*, xxiv, 14–30.   8. **fondly**: foolishly.   14. **post**: move swiftly.

Notes

95. [A fine example of a peculiar class of poetry, — that written by thoughtful men who practised this art but little.]
6. **still**: always. 9. **chance**: luck, fortune. 8. **private breath**: the opinion of ordinary individuals. 12. **state**: way of living. 13. Who never listens to, or repeats, mere gossip. 15–16. His condition on the one hand can give no occasion for flatterers, nor on the other will his fall make oppressors great. 21. **bands**: bonds.

96. This is the seventh stanza of a Pindaric ode entitled: *To the immortal memory and friendship of that noble pair, Sir Lucius Cary and Sir H. Morison*, in Jonson's *Underwoods* (1640).

97. Herbert called this beautiful little poem *The Pulley*, an awkward title indicating the means by which God raises man to himself.

98. This poem may well be compared with Wordsworth's *Ode on Intimations of Immortality* (338). The idea in each is that the world corrupts the purity of the child, who enters life from some happy stage of pre-existence.
4. **my second race**: *i.e.*, I had lived before, in another world. 18. **several**: separate. 24. **my glorious train**: the company of angels. 26. **City of palm trees**: the Heavenly City.

99. This graceful sonnet is addressed to the son of an important member of Cromwell's government. It was written when Milton was blind; with the following, it shows the more genial side of his character.
4. **help waste**: help each other to spend. 6. **Favonius**: the spring wind. 8. **that neither sow'd**, etc.: See *St. Matthew*, vi, 28. 10. **Attic taste**: refined taste. Athens was situated in Attica, and the Athenians were distinguished by their good taste and urbanity. 11. **artful**: skilful. 12. **Tuscan**: Italian — this music at the time was considered the best in Europe. 14. **spare**: refrain from indulging too freely.

524 Notes

100. Cyriack Skinner was the grandson of Sir Edward Coke, one of the most famous of English legal authorities.

2. Themis: the Greek goddess of law. **4. wrench**: distort to their own purposes. **7–8.** Lay aside your study of mathematics and foreign politics. Euclid was an Athenian geometer; Archimedes, a Syracusan mathematician and physicist. At this time (1655) Sweden was at war with Poland, and France with the Spanish Netherlands. **11. other things**: it is permissible to enjoy other pleasures besides the continual pursuit of "solid good." **12.** One should not make a show of unnecessary hard work. **14. refrains**: refuses to enjoy it. The sonnet is interesting as showing the "human" side of Milton's character, and his kindly interest in youth.

101. Somewhat in the spirit of Campion's lyrics in Book I; inserted here probably as reflecting the general tone of the numerous other songs in this book.

16. Syrens: beautiful women who lived on an island in the Mediterranean, and lured mariners to destruction by their sweet singing. Look up the story in the *Odyssey*. **20. empery**: empire.

102. From the masque called *Cynthia's Revels* (1601). Diana was worshipped as Cynthia, or the moon, in heaven; as Diana, goddess of hunting, on the earth; and as Hecate, in the world of the dead.

5. In the masque, Hesperus sings this song.

103. Palgrave has condensed this poem to about one half, and has altered the original order of the stanzas. As Crashaw wrote them, they stand as follows: 1–7, 9, 10, 30, 32, 31, 26, 27, 29, 35, 36, 38, 39, 41, 42. The justice of such a proceeding is open to question.

6. shady leaves of destiny: the Book of Fate. **19–21.** I wish her something more than the mere beauty of fine clothing. **28. Sidneian showers**: alluding either to the brilliant conversations in Sidney's *Arcadia*, or to the personal charm of the man himself. See note on Sir Philip Sidney, page 508. **29–37.** Days that owe nothing of their happiness to contrast

Notes

with sorrows gone before. **46-48.** I wish her so many blessings that she will have nothing more to desire. **51. Weave them**: weave for themselves. **59. fix**: settle. **60. determine**: give them the form. **63. her story**: the truth about her.

104. Printed in Percy's *Reliques*, a famous anthology of 1765, where it is called "ancient." It has been traced back as early as 1635.

12. for receipt of a fly: room for it to alight. **14. Lest she herself fast she lay**: get herself caught. **34. To stoop to your fist**: to come at your call, like a trained hawk. **35. inveigle**: entrap. The phoenix was a fabulous bird living in the Arabian desert.

105. [Delicate humor delightfully united to thought, at once simple and subtle. It is full of conceit and paradox, but these are imaginative, not intellectual only.] Read it carefully in order to appreciate this comment.

36. Flora: goddess of flowers. **38. Make th' example yours**: treat you in the same manner.

106. Note how neatly the thought of the preceding poem is continued in this. It is from Sedley's comedy *The Mulberry Garden* (1668), and illustrates the typically brilliant phrasing of the Cavalier poets.

19. his mother: Venus, goddess of beauty.

107. A critic said of this poem that it had "more wit than poetry." Can you see the reason for such a comment?

108. Herrick has been called "the author of the daintiest lyrics of the eighteenth century." The opinion is justified by the poems in this book.

2. still: always. **15.** Having once lost your period of perfection.

109. "A perfect piece of sincere gallantry." Poets of the time were fond of making up fanciful names for their lady-loves; Lucasta is coined from the Latin *Lux Casta*, "Pure Light."

4. **To war and arms**: This is no mere figure of speech: Lovelace fought for the King and spent all his fortune in his service. A young English army officer wrote in 1916 a poem called *To Lucasta on going to the War — for the Fourth Time*. The two form a most interesting contrast.

110. Elizabeth of Bohemia: daughter of James I, and Queen of Bohemia. She lost the kingdom and died in England in great poverty. These lines were written by a courtier, and are a fine example of gallant and courtly verse infused with real feeling.

6. **curious**: skilful.   10. **Philomel**: the nightingale.

111. [Lady M. Ley was daughter to Sir J. Ley, afterwards Earl of Marlborough, who died March, 1629, coincidently with the dissolution of the third Parliament of Charles' reign. Hence Milton poetically compares his death to that of the orator Isocrates of Athens, after Philip's victory.]

3. **unstain'd with gold or fee**: uninfluenced by corruption or bribery.   5. **the sad breaking**: The Parliament had passed the famous Petition of Right and after one year was arbitrarily dissolved by King Charles.   7. **Chaeroneia**: the battle where Philip of Macedon put an end to the freedom of Greece (338 B.C.). It was "dishonest" because of the wholesale bribery employed by Philip to subvert the friends of liberty.
8. **killed with report**: the news of it killed him.

112. Palgrave has been criticised because he included only one poem written by Carew, who is considered "the master of courtly compliment in verse."

113.   6. **wantons**: sports.   7. **Whenas**: since, whereas.

114. Closely resembling the work of Herrick, though we have no authority for assigning it to him.

10. **borrow**: take away.

115. This is the best of Waller's poems.

2. **wastes**: used in a double sense, with "time," and "me."
4. **resemble**: compare.   12. **retired**: withdrawn.

Notes

116. From a collection of Jonson's poems called *The Forest* (1616).

3. but: only. It goes with leave — "only leave a kiss."
9. rosy wreath: wreath of roses.

117. From Campion's *Third and Fourth Book of Airs* (1617).

6. Cherry-Ripe: the cry of the country-folk who sold cherries about the streets. No one may buy this fair maid's cherries, says the poet, until they offer themselves.
13. watch: guard, watch over.

118. [A masterpiece of grace and gentle feeling.] It was the custom for young people to get up a little after midnight on the first of May and go to the woods for flowers and hawthorn boughs, with which they would decorate the doors and windows.

2. the god unshorn: the new-risen sun. **10. matins**: morning prayers. **13. Whenas**: since. **22. Against you come**: in preparation for your coming. **orient**: brilliant. **24. dew-locks**: dewey locks. **Titan**: the sun. **48. left to**: ceased to. **57-70.** One of Herrick's most beautiful passages. Compare with his *To Daffodils* (140). **58. take**: enjoy.

119. 2. kindles in clothes a wantonness: produces a charming negligence. **4. fine distraction**: dainty disorder. **5. erring**: wandering. **7. thereby**: by its side. **12. a wild civility**: disordered neatness. This use of opposite terms is called "oxymoron." Milton employs it in *L'Allegro* (144), line 141: "Wanton heed and giddy cunning."

120. 1. Whenas: when. **5.** The beautiful play of light over the silk. **6. taketh me**: enchants me.

121. 1. wit: good taste, cleverness. **5. miss**: lack.

122. 5. My Heaven's extremest sphere: the utmost bound of my Heaven. **6. pale**: enclosure.

123. 8. became entire: were made one whole. **17. counter to**: an imitation as compared with.

Notes

124. 2. **Protestant**: champion. Literally, one who makes a solemn declaration.
18. **cypress**: because it was the emblem of mourning.

125. From a book of airs published in 1609.
7. **a true woman's eye**: a true woman's way of looking at things.

126. 1. The reason of my constancy is not that, etc. 5. **very thee**: thee, and thee only. 11. **afford**: produce, supply.

127. Lovelace was twice imprisoned for his active support of Charles I.
10. **With no allaying Thames**: not mixed with water. 17. A fine loyal spirit is shown in this stanza. **committed**: to prison. 23. **enlargèd**: free. **curl the flood**: make waves in the sea. 25–28. Four very familiar lines. 29. If I am free to love you.

128. Compare this poem with 109, in order to understand the appeal of greater simplicity.
10. **blue-god**: Neptune, god of the sea. 13. **betwixt**: that is, lie betwixt. The thought here is that the lovers can rise above all considerations of time and space, because of their faith and truth.

129. One of the few humorous poems included in *The Golden Treasury*. It occurs in the drama *Aglaura* (1637). Compare 131.

130. Taken from Cowley's epic, *Davideis*, which he called "a sacred poem of the troubles of David."
10. **awful**: full of fear. 11. **numerous**: musical, rhythmical; "numbers" was frequently used to mean poetry. 14. Conquer her through her ears as she has conquered me with her eyes. 15. **virtue**: power.

131. 9. **pined**: hurt, distressed. 14. The turtle-dove was an emblem of gentleness and love; the pelican was said to feed its young with blood from its own breast. 28. **outward**

Notes 529

helps: advantages of wealth or position. 33. A summary, in reverse order, of the qualities mentioned in the preceding stanzas.

132. From *The Nice Valour*, one of Fletcher's numerous plays, acted about 1624. It evidently exerted some influence upon Milton's *Il Penseroso* (145).
9. **mortifies**: chastens. 14. **fowls**: birds. 16. **parting**: dying. 18. **still**: ever, always.

133. One of the early "folk-songs" found in Percy's *Reliques*.
1. **waly waly**: an exclamation of sorrow (pronounce "wawly"). 2. **brae**: hillside. 3. **burn**: brook. 5. **aik**: oak. 7. **syne**: then, soon. 8. **did lichtly me**: treated me with scorn, made light of me. 13. **busk**: dress, attire. 17. **Arthur-seat**: a hill near Edinburgh. 19. [**Saint Anton's well**: below Arthur's Seat by Edinburgh.] 21. **Martimas**: St. Martin's Day was celebrated on November 11. 25. **fell**: cruelly, bitterly. 27. **sic**: such. 32. **cramasie**: crimson cloth. 33. **wist**: known, realized. 35. **gowd**: gold.

134. Part of a hymn entitled *Our Blessed Lady's Lullaby*, probably by Richard Verstegan. [This beautiful example of early simplicity is found in a song-book of 1620.] Compare the simplicity with that of 133 and 135. Which of the poems appeals to you most strongly?
4. **gives my sense her rest**: soothes my feelings. 21. **for**: in return for.

135. One of the old ballads found in Scott's *Minstrelsy of the Scottish Border*. It possesses a grim strength which is very effective.
7. **burd**: maiden. 11. **wi' meikle care**: with the greatest care. 14–15. The repetition marks the intentness with which the lover followed the murderer. The same effect is produced even more terribly in the next stanza. Note the desolate grief expressed by the close.

Notes

136. From Scott's *Minstrelsy*. Like 135, it has what may be called a fierce simplicity.

2. **corbies**: carrion crows. 2. **making a mane**: complaining together. 5. **auld fail dyke**: old turf wall. 6. **wot**: know. 13. **hause-bane**: collar-bone. 14. **een**: eyes. 16. **theek**: thatch. 17. **makes mane**: grieves.

137. [The poetic and the prosaic, after Cowley's fashion, blend curiously in this deeply-felt elegy.] Like *Lycidas*, it was written in memory of a college friend. Does it seem to you to express a more sincere grief?

26. **inform**: give life to, dwell in. 41. **spirits**: essence, distillation. Which are the "prosaic" stanzas?

138. A poem which will repay careful reading, because of certain curious survivals of the Shakespearean manner — "jewel of the just," for example.

5. **cloudy**: gloomy, sorrowful.

139. This and the poem which follows are difficult to characterize because of their singularly elusive charm. Few poems touch so lightly and so beautifully upon the deeper things of life. Note the dainty metrical form.

1. **pledges**: promises. 3. **date**: term of life. 15. **brave**: lovely, beautiful. 16. **pride**: beauty.

140. In the opinion of the present editor, the most charming of all Herrick's lyrics.

141. [Perhaps no poem is more adequately fancied, more exquisitely finished. By placing his description of a fawn in a young girl's mouth, Marvell has, as it were, legitimated that abundance of "imaginative hyperbole" to which he is always partial: he makes us feel it natural that a maiden's favorite should be whiter than milk, sweeter than sugar — "lilies without, roses within." The poet's imagination is justified in its seeming extravagance by the intensity and unity with which it invests his picture.] After reading this opinion of Palgrave, what do you yourself think about the poem?

Notes   531

142. Both this and the preceding should be compared with Marvell's *Horatian Ode* (88). [Marvell here throws himself into the very soul of the Garden with the imaginative intensity of Shelley in his *West Wind*.]

1. **amaze**: perplex, bewilder. 2. **the palm, the oak, the bay**: the rewards of the soldier, the citizen, and the poet. 5. **narrow-verged**: making a narrow shade. The general meaning is that honors in war, statesmanship, and letters are crowned with the narrow garland of a single plant, while Repose is crowned with garlands made from every tree and flower that grows. 7. **close**: combine. 15. **all but rude**: almost barbarous. 27–32. Allusions to the old Greek myths. 37. **curious**: rare. 41. **from pleasure less**: from the lesser pleasure of external life. 43. The mind can picture anything for itself; can even create new worlds of imagination. 47–48. **Annihilating all that's made**, etc.: the poet's imagination here is completely possessed by its garden surroundings. 51. **vest**: vesture, *i.e.*, the body itself. 56. **waves in its plumes**, etc.; causes the light to flicker through its wings. Have you ever watched a bird preening itself in a tree? The two stanzas closing with this line are imaginative to the highest degree. 57–60. The lines carry an allusion to the story of the Garden of Eden in *Genesis*, ii. 61. **beyond a mortal's share**: too much happiness for a mortal. 66. **this dial new**: a clock made of flowers that open at different times of the day. 68. **fragant zodiac**: *i.e.*, the sun runs its course through flowers. The zodiac literally is the division of the constellations along the path of the sun.

143. The title means "more than happy." The poem is much in the manner of Book I. 7. **Lash out**: spend freely. 9. **nappy**: strong. 12. **crabs**: crab-apples. 19. **tutties**: nosegays. 26. **strange**: unnatural. 32. **silly**: simple, innocent.

144. [It is a striking proof of Milton's astonishing power, that these, the earliest great Lyrics of the Landscape in our language, should still remain supreme in their style for range, variety, and melodious beauty. The Bright and the Thoughtful aspects of Nature and of Life are their subjects: but each is preceded by a mythological introduction in a mixed Classical and Italian manner.] *L'Allegro* means the Cheerful Man; *Il Penseroso*, the Thoughtful Man. The two poems were written about 1632, after Milton had left Cambridge and was living at Horton with his father. They reflect the lovely country scenery of that district. They should be studied together; they are composed upon the same constructive plan, but present a most interesting series of contrasted pictures.

2. **Cerberus**: the three-headed dog which guarded the entrance to the Lower World. 3. **Stygian**: adjective formed from Styx, the "River of Hate." 5. **uncouth**: unknown and repulsive. 6. **jealous wings**: grudging entrance to the light. 9. **ragged**: rough, unkempt. 10. **Cimmerian desert**: a land of perpetual darkness on the farthest West of the ancient world. 12. **yclept**: named — old form of the past participle. **Euphrosyne**: one of the three Graces; her sisters were Aglaia and Thalia. 17. **sager**: wiser. 24. **buxom, blithe, and debonair**: lively, joyous, and graceful. 27. Witty sayings, humorous turns of speech, and playful tricks. 28. **becks**: bows. 29. **Hebe**: goddess of youth, cup-bearer to the Gods. 36. The spirit of freedom is usually associated in poetry with mountainous countries. Compare Wordsworth's *England and Switzerland* (254). 40. **unreprovéd**: innocent. 43. **watch-tower**: the height where the lark hovers as he sings. 44. **dappled dawn**: a beautiful expression for the cloud-flecked sky of early morning. 45. **Then to come**: depending upon "admit me," in line 38, and coördinate with "To live" and "To hear." 45. **in spite of sorrow**: in defiance of sorrow. 55. **hoar**: gray with morning mists. 58. **hedge-row elms**: elms growing in the hedges — a familiar sight of the English country-side. 59. **right against**: straight towards — he walks towards the sunrise. 60. **his state**: his royal progress across the sky. 62. **dight**: richly dressed. 67. **tells his tale**: counts his sheep.

Notes

69. **Straight**: straightway, immediately. 71. **russet**: brownish. A lawn is any open grassy space. **fallows gray**: unsown land. 75. **pied**: variegated, modifying "meadows." 79. **lies**: dwells. 80. **Cynosure**: Literally, the North Star, the guide of sailors; hence, metaphorically, the centre of attraction. 83. **Corydon and Thyrsis**: conventional classic names for shepherds and shepherdesses, like Phyllis and Thestylis below. Milton uses them, of course, for country lads and lasses. 85. **messes**: dishes. 89. **if the earlier season lead**: if it is earlier in the season, she will go to the hayfield rather than to bind the sheaves of wheat.

91. **secure**: free from care. 92. **upland hamlets**: remote villages. 94. **jocund rebecks**: merry fiddles. 102. **Faery Mab**: the fairy who gave dreams to men. See *Romeo and Juliet*, Act I, Scene 4, lines 53–95. **junkets**: used generally, for "country delicacies." 104. **Friar's lantern**: the will-o'-the-wisp, a phosphorescent light over marshy ground. 105. **Tells**: supply a subject, "another." **drudging Goblin**: Robin Goodfellow, who performed household services and was rewarded by a bowl of cream set out for him. 108. **shadowy**: dim. **corn**: wheat. 110. **lubber**: probably, hard-working. 111. The old fashioned fireplace was often six or eight feet from side to side. 113. **crop-full**: full fed. 114. **his matin rings**: sounds his morning call. 117. When the country-folk are in bed, the poet loves to sit and read about the pleasures of great cities. Or perhaps L'Allegro actually goes to the city for music and the theatre. What do you think? 120. **weeds**: garments. 121. **store**: abundance. 122. **Rain influence**: like the stars, influence the destinies of men. 124. **her**: the most highly commended of the ladies, the "Queen of Beauty." 125. **Hymen**: god of marriage, represented as wearing a yellow robe and carrying a torch. If the torch burned clear, it was the omen of a happy marriage. 127. **pomp**: solemn procession. 131. **well-trod**: trodden by good actors. 132. **Jonson's learned sock**: Ben Jonson's comedies are strongly marked by his classical learning. The sock ("soccus") was the light shoe worn by the Roman comic

actor; the buskin, or cothurnus, was the high boot of the tragedian. 133–134. Milton wishes to contrast the rather heavy style of Jonson with the lighter side of Shakespeare's genius. He is thinking of the "woodland" plays, such as *As You Like It*, or *Midsummer Night's Dream*.

135. **eating cares**: cares that eat the heart. 136. **Lap**: enfold. [**Lydian airs**: used here to express a light and festive style of ancient music.] The Greeks employed three "modes": the Lydian, which was soft and pleasing; the Dorian, simple and solemn; and the Phrygian, warlike. 138. **meeting soul**: the soul which is drawn out to meet it. 139. **bout**: musical turn. 141. Another example of "oxymoron," the combination of opposite terms (see 119, line 12). The music is played with careful carelessness, and bewildering though skilful rapidity. 143–144. The music sets free the harmony in a man's soul. 145–150. Orpheus followed his wife to the Lower World after her death. By his glorious playing he won her back from Pluto, the King of Hades, on condition that he should not look back until he had led her to the upper world of life. But in his eagerness he turned as he reached the threshold, and Eurydice vanished from his eyes forever. 146. **golden**: delicious. 147. **Elysian**: heavenly. Elysium was the heaven of the ancients.

145. This poem is carefully balanced with *L'Allegro*, so as to emphasize the pleasures which appeal to the thoughtful man.

3. **bestead**: help, avail. 4. **toys**: trifles, a common meaning at the time. 6. Occupy foolish fancies with showy thoughts. 10. **pensioners**: followers. **Morpheus**: the god of sleep. 16. **staid**: solemn, sober. 17. **esteem**: estimation. 18. **Memnon's sister**: Prince Memnon was an Ethiopian ruler of great beauty and strength. Himera, his sister, was even more beautiful. **beseem**: suit, become. 19. **that starr'd Ethiop queen**: Cassopeia, Queen of Ethiopia, boasted that her beauty (according to some legends that of her daughter Andromeda) was greater than that of the sea nymphs, or Nereids. Poseidon, god of the sea, sent a sea monster to ravage the land, until Andromeda was chained to

Notes 535

a rock as a sacrifice. She was rescued by Perseus. Cassiopeia was placed among the stars after her death.   23. **Vesta**: Roman goddess of the hearth.   24. **Saturn**: King of the gods before Jove, who drove him out of Heaven.   29. **Ida**: a famous mountain in Crete.

31. **pensive**: thoughtful.   32. **Sober**: quiet. **demure**: grave.   33. **grain**: hue, color.   35. **sable stole**: black veil. For *Cipres lawn* see note on 62, line 2.   36. **decent**: comely. 37. **wonted state**: usual dignity.   39. **commercing**: holding intercourse.   40. **rapt**: absorbed.   41. kept motionless by a religious reverie.   42. **Forget thyself to marble**: stand as still as a statue.   46. **oft with gods doth diet**: enjoys spiritual food.   52. **Him that yon soars**, etc.: an allusion to *Ezekiel*, x.   55. **hist**: summon noiselessly.   57. **plight**: mood.   59. [**Cynthia**: the moon. Milton seems to have transferred to her chariot the dragons anciently assigned to Demeter and to Medea.]   60. "The oak over which I am accustomed to see her."   67. **the wandering Moon**: a beautiful and suggestive epithet, carried further in lines 69–72. 68. **her highest noon**: her highest point in the heavens.

73. **plat**: space, plot.   74. **Curfeu**: The bell rung about nine o'clock at night to warn householders to put out their lights and fires. From the French *Couvre feu*.   76. **Swinging slow with sullen roar**: *i.e.*, the sound of the bell mingles with the roar of the surf.   77. **air**: weather.   78. **still removéd place**: quiet, secluded place.   80. Light that only makes "darkness visible." See the fine passage in *Paradise Lost*, Book I, lines 62–64.   83. **the bellman's drowsy charm**: the night-watchman who patrolled the streets and called out the hours.   87. **out-watch the Bear**: as the constellation of the Great Bear never sets, to "out-watch" it would be to sit up till sunrise.   88. **thrice-great Hermes**: a Greek philosophical writer, known as *Trismegistus*, or "thrice-great."   88–96. The passage means that Il Penseroso will study the works of Plato as well as Hermes, in order to learn the secrets of the universe. **unsphere**: call from the unseen world.   92. **mansion**: dwelling-place.   93. **demons**:

spirits. 95. **consent**: agreement. 98. **In scepter'd pall**: in royal robes, because the great Greek tragedies dealt with the misfortunes of kings and royal houses. 99. **Thebes**: chief city of Bœotia and scene of the tragedy of *Oedipus Rex*. **Pelop's line**: an allusion to the trilogy of Æschylus on the subject of the murder of Agamemnon, a descendant of Pelops. 100. **Troy divine**: "divine" because founded by Poseidon, god of the sea. Sophocles and Euripides both touched upon the tale of Troy in their tragedies. 101–102. Probably referring to the tragedies of Shakespeare. **buskin'd stage**: because the ancient tragic actors wore a high boot, or "buskin." 104. **Musaeus**: a mythological Greek poet. 105. See note to 144, line 145. 107. **iron tears**: because of the stern character of Pluto. 109. **him that left half-told**, etc.: Chaucer, whose unfinished *Squire's Tale* is here referred to. 112. **And who had**, etc.: "and of him who had" — the tale does not go far enough to tell us. 113. **virtuous**: having magic powers. 117. **tunes**: verses, poetry. The "great bards" are probably Ariosto, Tasso, and Spenser, authors of romances and allegorical poetry. 118. **trophies hung**: arms of defeated knights hung up by the victor. 120. **Where more is meant**, etc.: as in Spenser's *Faerie Queene*.

122. **civil-suited**: quietly dressed. A "gray day," as contrasted with the bright sunrise of *L'Allegro*. 123. **trick'd and frounced**: gaily bedecked. 124. **the Attic Boy**: Cephalus, in the old myth beloved by Eos, the Dawn. 127. **still**: soft, gentle. 130. **minute drops**: falling slowly at regular intervals. 134. **Sylvan**: Latin god of the woods. 135. **monumental**: aged — a monument of other days. 140. **profaner**: unsympathetic. 145. **consort**: harmony. The murmur of the water mingles soothingly with the other woodland sounds. 148. **wave at his wings**: hover about the wings of Sleep. The passage is obscure; a good paraphrase is thus suggested: "Let some dream full of mystery hover over Sleep's wings, and display itself in an airy succession of lifelike pictures laid softly on my eyelids." 153. some spirit well-disposed to mortals. 154. **Genius**: guardian spirit.

Notes

156. **pale**: enclosure. 158. **massy-proof**: well able to bear the weight of the mass they support. 159. **storied windows richly dight**: rich stained-glass windows picturing a Bible story. 170. **spell**: interpret the meaning. 173. **old experience**: the ripe experience of old age. 174. **prophetic strain**: inspired teaching, inspiration.

146. The Bermudas were first colonized by England in 1612, and thirty years later received a number of refugees from the Civil War between King and Parliament. Among these was a friend of Marvell's, from whom he seems to have got his information.

7. **wracks**: destroys, wrecks. 12. **prelate's rage**: a reference to Laud, archbishop of Canterbury, who persecuted the Puritans. There does not seem to be historical foundation for the story that some of them took refuge here. 20. **Jewels**: the brilliant scarlet seeds of the pomegranate. **Ormus**: an ancient city at the mouth of the Persian Gulf, once famous for its wealth. 23. **apples**, etc.: [A fine example of Marvell's imaginative hyperbole.] 28. **ambergris**: a valuable waxlike substance found in tropical seas. It is the basis of many perfumes. 36. **the Mexique Bay**: the Gulf of Mexico.

147. One of the early poems, probably about 1630.

1. **Sirens**: Here, the Sirens of Plato who sang the music of the spheres. 4. Able to breathe feeling into inanimate things. 5. **high-raised fantasy**: lofty imagination. 6. **concent**: harmony. 10–11. These lines have the sonorous quality which is so characteristic of *Paradise Lost*. 14. **just spirits**: "The spirits of just men made perfect," *Hebrews*, xii. **palms**: the emblem of victory. 18. **noise**: the word is used by the early poets without any unpleasant meaning. 19. **disproportion'd**: out of harmony. 23. **diapason**: See note on 86, 15. 27. **consort**: harmony, as in 145, line 145.

148. The title means: "Night unto night showeth knowledge." It is from Psalm xix, beginning: "The heavens declare the glory of God, and the firmament showeth his handiwork." The whole psalm should be read in connection with this poem.

24. " Which he braves great danger to obtain."

149. [A lyric of a strange, fanciful, yet solemn beauty.]

1–8. See *Genesis*, i, 2–3 : " And the earth was without form, and void; and darkness was upon the face of the deep. . . . And God said, Let there be light: and there was light." 9. **monument**: the world. 11. **the folding circles**, etc.: the nine spheres in which, according to ancient belief, the planets were fixed: the next line refers to the Music of the Spheres. 14. **Before the council**, etc.: *i.e.*, before the creation of man. 24. A thought beautifully elaborated in Shelley's *To the Night* (232).

150. The opening verse of a long poem called *The World*, the rest of which does not attain the imaginative intensity shown here.

151. Dryden's sub-title is: " A Song in honour of St. Cecilia's Day: 1697." See note to 86. This is the greatest of the odes written by him. The poet represents the power of music to stir various emotions: pride, revelry, grief and pity, love and revenge. The structure is very skilfully arranged to express these feelings by the movement of the verse. Composed ten years after his first Ode for St. Cecilia's Day (86), it naturally shows a marked advance, combining with its lyric power a vivid dramatic and descriptive quality. Kipling's *Last Rime of True Thomas* is a modern treatment of a similar idea.

1. **for Persia won**: to celebrate the conquest of Persia. Alexander won a great victory over Darius, King of Persia, at Arbela (331 B.C.). The following year he entered Persepolis, the capital, which he gave up to plunder — not because he was instigated by Thais, as the Ode suggests, but in order to avenge himself on the Persians. 7. **roses and myrtles**: for victory and love. 10. Attired, decked out, like a beautiful Eastern bride. 12–15. The repetition is for emphasis and lends itself to musical treatment. 16. **Timotheus**: a famous

Notes

musician of Thebes. 21. **began with Jove**: took Jove for the opening theme. 24. **belied**: disguised. 26. **Olympia**: Olympias, mother of Alexander. 30. **lofty sound**: noble song. 31. **A present deity**: a god is with us. 32. **rebound**: re-echo. 35–37. Claiming to be the son of Jove, Alexander plays the part and imitates the solemn earth-shaking nod by which Jove signified approval at the Council of the Gods on Mount Olympus. 43. **honest**: kindly, jovial. 44. **hautboys**: oboes — soft-toned wooden wind-instruments. 57–58. A slight confusion of the pronouns: "he" and the second "his" refer to Alexander, the first "his" to Timotheus. 59. **mournful Muse**: sad music. 63–64. The repetition emphasizes the bitterness of the fall. 69. **With not a friend**: Darius was left dying on the field of battle, the pursuing Greeks coming up just as he expired.

76. **in the next degree**: the next stage, but one step from pity. 79. **Lydian**: See note on 144, line 136. 89. **The many**: the crowd of banqueters. 96. **at once opprest**: overcome at the same time. 97–126. Note how the meter reflects the thought; the whole passage moves with a rush, an effect produced by the skilful use of anapests. See especially 107–110 and 121–126. 107. **the Furies**: the goddesses who meted out just punishment for crime. They embodied the tortures of remorse, and were represented as winged figures with snakes for hair and flaming eyes. 108. **rear**: lift up. 114. **unburied**: the worst thing that could happen to a Greek. The soul could not pass to its rest until the funeral rites were properly performed. 120. **their hostile gods**: the gods of the Persians, hostile to the Greeks. 125. **Helen**: Helen of Troy, who caused the Trojan War which ended with the destruction of that city. 132. **Cecilia**: See note on 86. 133. **vocal frame**: the organ, with its pipes set in a frame. 136. referring to the sustained note of the organ. 137. **Nature's mother-wit**: natural ability, born genius.

Questions and Topics for Discussion

1. Estimate the difference in form, tone, and thought between any two sonnets by Shakespeare and Milton.

2. Make a study of the "Pastoral Elegy" — subject, form, style, etc. — as illustrated by *Lycidas*, Shelley's *Adonais*, and Arnold's *Thyrsis*.

3. Comment upon the "machinery" of *Lycidas*. How far does the use of the "shepherd" metaphor blend with the element of sadness?

4. What qualities are characteristic of the ode? How are these qualities evidenced by the odes in this Book?

5. Write a theme upon the relative appeal of *L'Allegro* and *Il Penseroso*. Show by means of a comparative table Milton's deliberate contrast of thought.

6. Select passages throughout the Book which show a love of nature.

7. Discuss the literary quality of the two ballads 135 and 136. Compare them with 133. Why does Palgrave include these ballads, when others are left out?

8. Write a critical appreciation of Dryden's use of metrical effects in *Alexander's Feast* (151).

9. Find instances of words and phrases used to produce definite effects of onomatopeia.

10. Compare the elements contributed by puritan and cavalier thought, respectively, to the poetry of this Book.

11. Discuss the lighter element in the Book — poems such as 106, 108, 112, etc. Point out the poetic value of this type of poetry.

BIOGRAPHICAL SKETCHES

FRANCIS BEAUMONT wrote in collaboration with John Fletcher, and they left the largest collection of printed plays attributed to any English authors. Fletcher seems to have been the creative spirit, while Beaumont criticised and revised. Of Beaumont's life we have little information. He was born in 1584, the son of a chief-justice; was educated at Oxford, passed most of his life in London, and died in 1616.

THOMAS CAMPION. See page 505. It would seem that the three poems given by Palgrave in Book II belong more fittingly with the other songs of the author in Book I.

THOMAS CAREW (1598–1638) was educated at Westminster School and Oxford. He has been called "one of the most perfect masters of lyrical form in English poetry." He was a friend of Ben Jonson, and among the most artistic of the Cavalier Poets at the Court of James I.

ABRAHAM COWLEY, born in 1618 and educated at Cambridge, was loyal to Charles I at the time of the Civil War, and assisted the Queen when she lived on the Continent after the death of the King. He returned to England during the Commonwealth, and after the Restoration in 1660 was highly honored as a poet. He died in 1667.

RICHARD CRASHAW, the son of a Puritan minister, was born in London in 1613. He was a Cambridge man, and made his mark as a religious poet. He lived in Paris during the Civil War; eventually joined the Roman Catholic Church, and at the time of his death in 1649 was a canon at Loretto.

JOHN DRYDEN, "Glorious John," was the leading man of letters during the last part of the seventeenth century. He was born in August, 1631, and died in London on May 1, 1700. A very notable poet, and a great critic, he exercised a sort of dictatorship in literary matters. His most memorable works, besides the Odes, are perhaps the remarkable satirical poem *Absalom and Achitophel* (1681), and *The Hind and the Panther* (1687), a defence of the Roman Catholic religion. He wrote a number of comedies and heroic plays, and a valuable *Essay on Dramatic Poesy*.

JOHN FLETCHER was the author, with Francis Beaumont, of a great number of plays. He was born in 1579 and died in 1625. His best work is found in his comedies and lyrics.

WILLIAM HABINGTON (1605–1654) was educated in France, and wrote poetry in the French manner. Much of his verse has a philosophic tendency.

Notes

GEORGE HERBERT, well-known among English religious poets, came of a noble Welsh family. His brother, Lord Herbert of Cherbury, was a statesman and historian, and the author of a famous autobiography. The poet was born in 1593, and educated at Cambridge, where he rose to a high University position. Towards the close of his career he became a clergyman, and lived a life of beautiful piety, which is reflected in his single volume of poetry, *The Temple*. He expresses the common needs and aspirations of the Christian in verse which is pleasantly quaint and attractive. He died in 1633.

ROBERT HERRICK, a lyric poet of singularly fine quality, was born in London in 1591. Educated at Cambridge, he led for several years a somewhat adventurous life. Finally he entered the Church, and in 1629 was vicar of a village in Devonshire. During the Civil War he was driven out by the Parliamentary forces, and went to London. Here he published his one volume of poems — *Hesperides*. At the Restoration, he returned to his vicarage, where he lived until his death in 1674. Herrick wrote many beautiful lyrics celebrating rustic festivals (like *Corinna's Maying*), superstitions, and country folk-lore. In his own way he was "an exquisite and complete poet."

BEN JONSON was a close personal friend of Shakespeare, and his greatest contemporary in the drama. He was born in 1573 and educated at Westminster School. He worked as a bricklayer in London, and afterwards was a soldier in the Netherlands. It is not known whether or not he had a University education. He became interested in dramatic writing, and produced *Every Man in His Humour* about 1598. Many other plays came from his pen, as well as some masques of high merit. After Shakespeare's death he was the acknowledged dictator in the literary world. He died on August 6, 1637.

RICHARD LOVELACE was one of the famous little band of "Cavalier Poets," to whom the words of Macaulay's poem would very well apply:

"To my true King I offered without stain
 Courage and faith; vain faith and courage vain."

Born in 1618, he passed through Oxford, became a favorite at Court, and when the Civil War came spent his fortune in the royal cause. He died, poor and deserted, in 1658. Like Suckling, Carew, and Herrick, Lovelace possessed a lyrical gift that was singularly pure and true.

ANDREW MARVELL was well qualified by training and experience for the posts under Government which he enjoyed in his lifetime. He was born in 1621, took his degree from Cambridge, and travelled on the Continent. He became private tutor in the family of Lord Fairfax and at the close of the Civil War held important positions under the Commonwealth. He was assistant to Milton and after the Restoration used his influence to protect the blind poet. Marvell was a political satirist as well as a lyric poet. He died in 1678.

JOHN MILTON, the greatest non-dramatic English poet, was born in London on December 9, 1608. He had a home life which was fortunate and happy. After attending St. Paul's School and Christ's College, Cambridge, he spent some years in travel and in pleasant retirement at Horton. To this time belong his early poems — *L'Allegro, Il Penseroso*, etc. When the Civil War broke out he turned to prose. Under Cromwell he was made Latin Secretary to the Commonwealth. The continuous devotion to his duties caused the loss of his eyesight. At the Restoration he was in some danger from the Royalists, though the menace was soon removed. In 1667 he published *Paradise Lost*, the greatest epic poem in our language. *Paradise Regained* and *Samson Agonistes*, a tragedy upon the Greek model, both appeared in 1671. Milton died on November 8, 1674.

JOHN NORRIS (1657–1711) was an Oxford man, entered the ministry, and became rector of Bemerton, George Herbert's parish, in 1692. His writings are chiefly couched in a vein of religious mysticism.

FRANCIS QUARLES was a kind of journalist "to whom the vehicle of verse came more easily than the vehicle of prose." His *Emblems* contains much poetry of a religious character which is sometimes eccentric. Quarles was born in 1592, educated at

Cambridge, spent some years on the Continent and in Ireland, and died in 1644.

Sir Charles Sedley studied for a time at Oxford, and entered Parliament after the Restoration. He became famous as a dramatist, a writer of songs, and a court wit. Like others of the court circle he led a dissipated life. He lived from 1639 to 1701.

James Shirley is sometimes called "the last of the Elizabethans," because he wrote plays which showed the characteristics of that great literary epoch. Born in 1596, he received his education at the Merchant Tailors' School in London, and at Oxford. He took orders in the Church of England, but later became a Roman Catholic. He died in 1666 from exposure during the Great Fire of London.

Sir John Suckling was born in 1609, and early became distinguished for his wit. Upon leaving Cambridge University he made a tour of the Continent. His verses and plays, as well as his gaming, made him a prominent figure at the court of Charles I. He was forced to leave England for political reasons, and died abroad about 1642. His career is not unlike that of Lovelace: both advocated a losing cause, both wrote some lyrics of exquisite beauty, and both met a melancholy end.

Henry Vaughan called himself the "Silurist" — a name derived from the ancient British tribe of the Silures — in order to distinguish himself from various other Vaughans. After an Oxford education, he led a quiet life as a physician with literary tastes. He was influenced by the work of George Herbert, and though not so generally successful, shows at times more depth and originality. He was born in 1622 and died in 1695.

Edmund Waller was in his own time an important literary figure. He was born in 1606, and educated at Eton and Cambridge. He entered Parliament very young and had a long, though not wholly creditable, political career. His fame rests chiefly upon his ability as an orator and the restrained charm of some of his poetry. He is considered to be the forerunner of the formal style in verse which characterized the poetry of the eighteenth century. He died in 1687.

Notes

JOHN WILMOT, second Earl of Rochester, has been termed "the chief of those dissolute, gifted youths who adorned and disgraced the Court of Charles II." He studied at Oxford, travelled in France and Italy, spent much of his time at Court, wrote some brilliant plays and poems, and died in 1680 at the age of thirty-three.

GEORGE WITHER was born in 1588, was educated at Oxford, tried farming, and eventually became a lawyer. At first an ardent Royalist, he changed his political views and became a supporter of Cromwell in the Civil War, and naturally got into trouble at the Restoration. His verse is very unequal; at its best it has a high degree of excellence. Wither died in 1667.

SIR HENRY WOTTON, writer of poetry of a quiet and dignified beauty, was born in 1568 and educated at Winchester School and Oxford. He had a distinguished public career, being ambassador to Venice and to the Holy Roman Empire under James I. He afterwards became Provost of Eton College, one of the most important positions in the educational world. He died at Eton in 1639.

BOOK THIRD

[It is more difficult to characterize the English poetry of the eighteenth century than that of any other, for it was an age not only of spontaneous transition, but of bold experiment: it includes not only such absolute contrasts as distinguish the "Rape of the Lock" from the "Parish Register" [of Crabbe], but such vast contemporaneous differences as lie between Pope and Collins, Burns and Cowper. Yet we may clearly trace three leading moods or tendencies: the aspects of courtly or educated life represented by Pope and carried to exhaustion by his followers; the poetry of nature and of man, viewed through a cultivated and at the same time an impassioned frame of mind by Collins and Gray; lastly, the study of vivid and simple narrative, including natural description, begun by Gay and Thomson, pursued by Burns and others in the north, and established in England by Goldsmith, Percy,

Crabbe, and Cowper. Great varieties in style accompanied these diversities in aim; poets could not always distinguish the manner suitable for subjects so far apart; and the union of conventional and of common language, exhibited most conspicuously by Burns, has given a tone to the poetry of that century which is better explained by reference to its historical origin than by naming it artificial. There is, again, a nobleness of thought, a courageous aim at high and, in a strict sense manly, excellence in many of the writers; nor can that period be justly termed tame and wanting in originality, which produced poems such as Pope's Satires, Gray's Odes and Elegy, the ballads of Gay and Carey, the songs of Burns and Cowper. In truth, poetry at this as at all times was a more or less unconscious mirror of the genius of the age; and the many complex causes which made the eighteenth century the turning time in modern European civilization are also more or less reflected in its verse. An intelligent reader will find the influence of Newton as markedly in the poems of Pope, as of Elizabeth in the plays of Shakespeare. On this great subject, however, these indications must here be sufficient.]

152. Gray wrote very little poetry; but what he did write was of the highest order of merit. This poem is incomplete; it was found in a pocket-book after his death, and probably was written about 1754. Note the finished metrical form of each stanza, and the easy grace of the whole.

3. **vermeil**: vermillion — an Elizabethan poet would have said "rosy." 11. **their wintry trance**: it was supposed at the time that birds slept through the winter. 23–24. Compare the thought of Burns in *To a Mouse* (184), lines 43–48. 25–26. An example of the tendency, common in this period, to personify the emotions; it means that quiet thought can make us smile at past sorrow. 30. **deepest shades**: object of "gilds." 39. **blended**: when blended together.

153. Palgrave points out that there is no poet more marked by "rapture and ecstacy" than Collins. Yet only once or twice do his lyrics reach the true Greek purity of utterance at

Notes

which he aimed, and of which this poem is an example. [His style, as his friend Dr. Johnson truly remarks, was obscure; he struggled nobly against the narrow, artificial manner of his age, but his too scanty years did not allow him to reach perfect mastery.] Such mastery, however, is undoubtedly found in his beautiful *Ode Written in 1746* (160).

9. **gauds**: ornaments. **pageant weeds**: rich garments. **pall**: robe. 10. **decent**: comely. 11. **Attic**: Greek. 14. **Hybla**: a mountain in Sicily, noted for its honey. 16. **her**: the nightingale. 18. The allusion is to a chorus in the *Oedipus at Colonus*, of Sophocles. Milton referred to Euripides in the same words; see note to 93, line 13. 19. **Cephisus**: a river near Athens. 22. **enamell'd**: bright with flowers. 34. [**stay'd to sing**: stayed her song when Imperial tyranny was established at Rome.] 37-42. In allusion to the love-poetry of the Italian Renaissance. Simplicity no longer inspires the poetry which once she influenced. 45. **thou**: *i.e.*, simplicity, or " poetic sincerity and singleness of aim and treatment." 48. [**meeting soul**: which moves sympathetically towards Simplicity as she comes to inspire the poet.] See a like usage in 145, line 136. 49. **Of these**: taste and genius.

154. Written when Pope was twelve years old. It is a short " Horatian Ode," and reflects exactly the spirit of Horace. For poems of a similar nature, compare 79 and 95.

155. Cibber's poetry is marked by a pleasant simplicity, but shows little power.

13-14. **With heavy sighs** modifies " mourn."

156. A clever bit of fooling, written about 1747. Gray's friend, Horace Walpole, was the owner of Selima.

3. **blow**: bloom. 4. **of the tabby kind**: of cats in general. 16. **Tyrian hue**: a beautiful dye produced at Tyre from a shell fish. 31. **eight times**: in allusion to the well known proverb that a cat has nine lives. 34. **Dolphin**: See note on 89, line 164. **Nereid**: water-nymph.

157. Addressed to the little daughter of Daniel Pulteney, a politician of some note.

1. **Timely**: coming just when you were wished for. 2. **fondling**: darling, pet. 13. **Yet**: as yet. 18. **Moduling**: tuning, modulating. 20. **Wanton**: capricious.

158. A good vigorous patriotic lyric, from the masque *Alfred*, produced in 1740. The fourth and fifth lines were changed by Dr. Arne, who wrote the music — " rule " to " rules," and " will " to " shall." The sense was thus materially altered from what Thomson intended.

17. **thy generous flame**: thy spirit of noble indignation. 19. **rural reign**: agriculture, as balanced with " commerce " in the next line.

159. Gray says that this ode was founded on a tradition that Edward I, when he conquered Wales in 1282, ordered all the bards (native poets) that fell into his hands to be put to death. This tradition has no foundation in history. [After lamenting his comrades (st. 2, 3) the Bard prophesies the fate of Edward II, and the conquests of Edward III (4); his death and that of the Black Prince (5); of Richard II, with the wars of York and Lancaster, the murder of Henry VI (*the meek usurper*), and of Edward V and his brother (6). He turns to the glory and prosperity following the accession of the Tudors (7), through Elizabeth's reign (8); and concludes with a vision of the poetry of Shakespeare and Milton.] This poem and the same author's *Progress of Poesy* are the two best examples of the English Pindaric Ode. See page 461.

1. **ruthless**: merciless, cruel. 5. **hauberk's**: the hauberk was a coat of mail. 8. **Cambria's**: Wales'. 13–14. **Glo'ster . . . Mortimer**: both " Lords Marchers " of Wales, holding lands on the marches, or borders, of the country. 16. The **Conway** was a river in the north of Wales; at its mouth Edward built a fine castle. 27. **Vocal no more**, etc.: *i.e.*, since the defeat of conquest, the woods and caves no longer echo back the songs of the old Welsh bards, Hoel and Llewllyn. 28. **soft**: gentle.

Notes 549

29–33. The names are those of ancient bards, here adopted by Gray as the names of the slain friends of the singer. 34. **Plinlimmon**: a mountain in Cardiganshire. 35. **Arvon's**: shore opposite Anglesea. 44. **griesly**: horrible, grim. 48. **weave . . . the tissue**: as they sang, the slain bards wove the web of fate. The joint prophecy is shown by the italics. 49. **the warp . . . the woof**: the warp ran crosswise, the woof lengthwise, of the loom. 51. **verge**: the edge where the pattern would be woven. 55. **Berkley's roof**: Edward II, son of Edward I, was murdered at Berkley Castle on the Severn in 1327. His wife Isabella, "she-wolf of France," instigated the deed. 59. **thy country**: France. Edward III, son of Edward II and Isabella, won the battles of Crécy and Poictiers. 63. **Mighty victor**, etc.: Edward III died deserted and alone. 67. **the sable warrior**: Edward the Black Prince, who died before his father. 70. **the rising morn**: the allusion here is to Richard II, who succeeded Edward III in 1377, and was soon afterwards starved to death in prison (lines 80–82). 71–76. Gray says these lines indicate the opening splendor of Richard's reign, followed by disaster and death. 83–86. The ruinous civil Wars of the Roses. 87. **Towers of Julius**: the Tower of London, said to have been founded by Julius Caesar. It is called "London's lasting shame" because of political murders committed there. 90. The "meek usurper" was Henry VI, slain in the Tower. His "consort" was Margaret of Anjou; his "father," Henry V. 91–94. The Houses of York and Lancaster, represented by the white and red roses respectively, were united in the person of Henry VII. At the battle of Bosworth (1487), he overcame Richard III; the "bristled boar" was the badge of this king, who was said to have caused the murder of his nephews, the two little princes, in the Tower. 99. **Half of thy heart**: Eleanor of Castile, queen of Edward I. She died suddenly in 1290.

100. The ghostly bards now vanish away, and a vision appears of the times succeeding Henry VII. 109. **Arthur**: Eldest son of Henry VII, who was himself the son of Owen

Tudor, a Welshman, and founded the House of Tudor. The Bard sees in him the restoration of the ancient British kings. 115. **a form divine**: Queen Elizabeth. 117. **lion-port**: proud, or lion-like, bearing. 119. **strings symphonious**; referring to the poets and dramatists of the Elizabethan age. 121. **Taliessin**: a famous ancient Welsh poet. 125–127. Spenser is here referred to. 128–130. The plays of Shakespeare. 131–134. The *Paradise Lost* of Milton, and the poetry that followed after his time. 135. **impious man**: King Edward II.

160. A fine example of the "ode in little." It commemorates the English soldiers who fell in Scotland in 1745–46. In the former year the "Young Pretender," Charles Edward Stuart, tried to gain back the throne of England for the Stuarts, who had been deposed by the Revolution of 1688. He won the battles of Falkirk and Prestonpans, but was defeated at Culloden in April 1746. Note the restrained pathos and simplicity of this poem.

6. **Than Fancy's feet**, etc.: than have ever been trodden in imagination.

161. 4. **saut**: salt. **blin's**: blinds. 5. **Drumossie moor**: the Highland name for Culloden. 13. **thou cruel lord**: the Duke of Cumberland, commander of the English forces.

162. Originally called *The Flowers of the Forest*, and written in 1756. It is sung to a very beautiful air of the same name. Flodden was a battle fought in the north of England, where James IV of Scotland was defeated and slain (1513). Scott's *Marmion* culminates with a fine description of the fight. The metre of the *Lament* is dactyllic tetrameter, treated in an unusual way.

1. **lilting**: singing. 2. **a'**: all. 3. **ilka**: every. **loaning**: piece of pasture land. 4. **The Flowers of the Forest**: the young men from Ettrick Forest. **wede away**: rooted out. 5. **bughts**: sheepfold. **scorning**: joking. 6. **dowie and wae**: dull and sad. 7. **Nae daffin', nae gabbin'**: no jesting and chattering. 8. **leglin**: milk pail. 9. **shearing**: reap-

ing. 10. **lyart and runkled**: grizzled and wrinkled. 11. **fleeching**: coaxing. 14. **bogle**: goblin, bogy. 17. **Dool**: grief, sorrow. 22. **heartless**: broken-hearted.

163. Based upon a tragedy which seems to have found favor with the poets. Compare this and following poem with the two written by Wordsworth, 305 and 306.
1. **braes**: banks, or hillsides near the river. 23. **water-wraith**: a river spirit, supposed to give warning of death. 42. **marrow**: mate.

164. [The Editor has found no authoritative text of this poem, to his mind superior to any of its class in melody and pathos. Part is probably not later than the Seventeenth Century: in other stanzas a more modern hand, much resembling Scott's, is traceable. Logan's poem (163) exhibits a knowledge rather of the old legend than of the old verses.]
7. **hecht**: promised. 8. **Gin**: if. 14. **marvis**: thrush. 16. **hinging**: hanging. 17. **lav'rock**: lark. 19. **eneuch**: enough. 20. **haughs**: valley-meadows. 21. **braid**: broad. 32. **twined o'**: separated from. 34. **pou'd**: pulled. 38. **braid and narrow**: far and wide. 39. **Syne**: then. **cleaving of a craig**: rift in a rock.

165. The *Royal George* was a man-o'-war of 108 guns, which sank at Portsmouth in August, 1782, while being partially careened for repairs. Of her total crew of 848 officers and men, only 330 were saved. The poem was written in September, 1782. [The reader who feels the vigour of description and force of pathos underlying Cowper's bare and truly Greek simplicity of phrase, may consider himself *se valde profecisse* in poetry.]
4. **Fast**: close. 25. **Weigh the vessel up**: *i.e.*, raise her. This was attempted but found impossible. She was finally blown up.

166. A delightful example of highly artificial ballad writing, for which a well-known air was composed. It is what would be called in the eighteenth century an " elegant production,"

Notes

and attempts to give a picture of lowly life. Compare it with the following poem, which is as simple as this is affected.

1. **Downs**: the anchorage off the east coast of Kent.

167. [A little masterpiece in a very difficult style. In grace, tenderness, simplicity, and humour, it is worthy of the Ancients; and even more so, from the completeness and unity of the picture presented.] It was written in 1725. You should by all means make yourself acquainted with the air that goes with it.

9. **cabbage-nets**: nets to boil cabbages in: 21. **bang his bellyful**: beat as much as he likes. 43. **box it**: make a "Christmas-box" of it. 53. **seven long years**: the term of his apprenticeship.

168. The sincere feeling of this poem may well be compared with the artificial note of *Black-eyed Susan*. It was sent by Burns in a letter to a friend in 1788.

2. **tassie**: cup. 5. **Leith**: the port of Edinburgh, at the mouth of the Firth of Forth. 6. **the Ferry**: Queensferry, nine miles up the Firth. 7. **Berwick-law**: Berwick hill, a conspicuous landmark southeast of Leith.

169. A vigorous and straightforward piece of writing, in the true vein of the Scotch lyric.

1. **doughty**: gallant. 3. **fast**: solid, steadfast. 4. **meed**: prize of victory. 8. **rue it to his smart**: suffer for it. 12. **trow**: believe. 14. **dight**: dress finely. 23. **skaith**: scathe, harm. 25. **ride the ring**: ride at the ring in a tournament. 26. **wear the blue**: as blue was the usual color for the uniforms of retainers, the phrase means: "I am your servant."

170. The four poems which now follow speak the language of courtly compliment. They form a marked contrast to the clear breezy note in those immediately preceding them.

171. Written in 1810, but preserving the eighteenth century style.

172. [Perhaps no writer who has given such strong proofs of the poetic nature has left less satisfactory poetry than Thomson. Yet this song, with *Rule Britannia* and a few others, must make us regret that he did not more seriously apply himself to lyrical writing.]

3. **mutual**: reciprocal, sharing the same feelings — frequently so used at the time.   10. To bring about marriages where there is no love or happiness.   11. **from pleasure to delude**: to entice from true happiness.   11. *i.e.*, to unite persons of unsuited dispositions.

173. Prior was a writer of clever trifles, of which this is a good sample.

1-2. Under a false name, as sometimes in wartime goods are sent under the label of a neutral.   3. **measure**: poetry, verse.   6. **toilet**: toilet-table.   7. **noted**: stated, expressed.

174. Here we have the mystic and suggestive element characteristic of Blake. It is the type of poem, as one critic has remarked, which may be hard to understand, but which is certainly hard to forget. The thought is of love and death. Note the simple beauty of the melody.

10. **a traveller**: death.

175. From *The Vicar of Wakefield*, Chapter xxiv.

176. This is the earlier and finer version of the famous little lyric. Burns wished it set to music, and to adapt it to a beautiful familiar air, lengthened the second and fourth lines of each stanza. From a literary point of view, the result was most unfortunate; the additions were chiefly padding, as may readily be seen:

" Ye banks and braes o' bonnie Doon
    How can ye blume sae fresh and fair;
How can ye chant, ye little birds,
    And I sae weary, fu' o' care!"

1. **Doon**: a river in Ayrshire, the county of Burns, running into the Firth of Clyde.   19. **staw**: stole.

554 Notes

177. An excellent type of the English Pindaric Ode; written in 1754, and published in 1757, with *The Bard*. Gray sets forth the benefits conferred by poetry on the human race: its impetuous power and soothing charm, its helpfulness in times of sorrow, its influence over barbarous minds, its aid in the growth of liberty. Then (stanzas 7 and 8) he traces the progress of poetry from the time of Greek supremacy to his own day.

1. [**Aeolian lyre**: the Greeks ascribed the origin of their lyrical poetry to the colonies of Æolis in Asia Minor.] 3. **Helicon's harmonious springs**: Hippocrene and Aganippe, springs sacred to the Muses. Gray compares the stream of poetry that rises on Mount Helicon to a river, now smooth and slow, now wild and tumultuous. 9. **Ceres' golden reign**: fields of ripe wheat. Ceres was the goddess of agriculture. 15. **Enchanting shell**: the lyre — here used for poetry in general. See note to 86, line 17. 17. **Thracia's hills**, etc.: Mars, the God of War, was especially worshipped in Thrace. 21. the **feather'd king**: the eagle, sacred to Jove. The passage is imitated from Pindar. 26. **Temper'd**: attuned. 27. [**Idalia**: in Crete, where **Cytherea** (Venus) was especially worshipped.] 42-48. "To compensate the real and imaginary ills of life, the Muse was given to mankind by the same Providence that sends the day by its cheerful presence to dispel the gloom and terror of the night." (Gray's note.) 43. **Penury**: poverty. 49-50. Gray follows the Roman idea of night as an unhealthy and even dangerous time. 53. **Hyperion's march**: sunrise. 54. **beyond the solar road**: within the Arctic circle where the sun is invisible for six months of the year. 61. **loose numbers**: rude poetry.

66-82. The progress of poetry is traced from Greece to Rome, and thence to England. 63-65. The structure is confused: "Where'er the goddess roves, Glory and generous Shame, etc., pursue her track . . ." 66. Delphi was a town at the foot of Mount Parnassus; it was sacred to Apollo, god of poetry. 67. Sappho, Alcaeus, and other Greek poets, came from the islands of the Aegean Sea. 68. **Ilissus**: a river near Athens, associated here with Greek tragic poetry. 69. **Maeander**: a winding river outside Troy — here used to suggest the epic poetry of Homer. The following passage laments the conquest of Greece by Rome, and the degeneration of the "lofty spirit" of Rome itself. 77. **the sad Nine**: the nine Muses, who inspired Art and Literature. 78. **the Latian plains**: Italy. 82. **Albion**: poetic name for England.

83. **Far from the sun**, etc.: *i.e.*, far from the southern countries, Greece and Italy. 84. **Nature's Darling**: Shakespeare who owed more to Nature than to the schools. 90. **vernal year**: spring season. 95. **Nor second He**, etc.: Milton, whom Gray ranks as equal to Shakespeare. 96. **Extasy**: inspired imagination — the reference is to *Paradise Lost*. 99. **The living Throne**, etc.: See *Ezekiel*, i, 26 also, 147, line 7. 101–102. A splendidly imaginative allusion to Milton's blindness. 105. **Two coursers**: a reference to Dryden's masterly use of the heroic couplet, in his *Absalom and Achitophel* and other poems and plays. 107. **the lyre**: alluding the Dryden's lyric poetry. Gray said in a note on this passage: "We have had in our language no other odes of the sublime kind, than that of Dryden on St. Cecilia's Day." 111. **'Tis heard no more**: Dryden died in 1700. 112. **what daring spirit**: Gray himself. 115. **the Theban Eagle**: Pindar, the greatest writer of odes. 120. **unborrow'd of the sun**: colored by the imagination. 121. Posterity has agreed with Gray's estimate of his posthumous fame. 122. **vulgar**: common, ordinary.

178. A critic said of this poem: "It is difficult to escape the impression that we are witnessing a 'performance,' in which the Passions go through their appointed parts. Hope smiles and waves her golden hair. Melancholy plays upon the horn with pensive prettiness. Revenge beats the drum and strains his eyeballs. We look on unmoved." What is your opinion after reading the poem? The "Passions" are the various emotions of the human mind, and the form of the stanzas corresponds to the feelings presented.

3. **shell**: See note on 86, line 17. 12. **instruments of sound**: the musical instruments referred to were: the lyre, the trumpet, the drum, the horn, the pipe, and the viol. 21–22. His rage was betrayed by the fire of his eyes. 43. **war-denouncing**: threatening war. 47. **doubling**: echoing. 53. **thy numbers**, etc.: thy song did not keep to one subject. 63. **bubbling runnels**: brooks — note the onomatopeia. 72. **buskins**: high boots. 74–76. **Faun . . . Dryad . . . Satyrs**: various woodland deities. **Chaste-eyed Queen**: Diana, goddess of the hunt. 78. **Brown**: tanned by the sun. 86. **Tempe's vale**: See note on 2, line 27. 95. **sphere-descended**: heaven-born. 106. **energic**: full of energy. 108. **thy recording Sister**: Clio, Muse of history. 114. **Cecilia**: See note on 86. 118. **Confirm the tales**, etc.: prove by your power the truth of the old Greek legends of Orpheus, Amphion, and other wonder-working musicians.

179. [From that wild rhapsody of mingled grandeur, tenderness, and obscurity, that "medley between inspiration and possession," which poor Smart is supposed to have written whilst in confinement for madness.] This poem, in which we can see both power and imagination, was omitted from the eighteenth century editions of his works.

5. **period**: time. 9. **champaign**: open country.

180. This possesses the peculiar mystical beauty which was characteristic of Blake. With the poem following it was taken from *Songs of Innocence*, published in 1789.

181. Note the change of tone in the last two lines. 16. [**the dreadful light**: of life and experience.]

182. An interesting comparison can be made between this poem and the *Elegy* (187).

1. **Hours**: the goddesses of the weather and the seasons. 4. **purple year**: the spring, the beautiful season. 5. **Attic warbler**: the nightingale. 27. **liquid**: clear. 29. **trim**: attire, dress. 42. **the sportive kind**: the dancing insects.

Notes

44. solitary: Gray was unmarried. **49. Thy sun is set**: thy day is over. This poem, however, was written about 1742, and Gray's best work was yet to come.

183. Here we have an example of the anapestic metre, the danger of which is that it tends to become "sing-song." Of this poem Tennyson wrote: "People nowadays hold this style and metre light; I wish there were any who could put words together with such exquisite flow and evenness." Other examples of the metre are 261 and 299.

4. **Ouse**: a river near Cowper's home.

184. From Burns's first book of poems, *Poems chiefly in the Scottish Dialect*, published at Kilmarnock in 1786. It illustrates the new sense of the unity of all created things which appeared about this time, and which was one of the essential features of the "Romantic Revival" of the late eighteenth century. Burns and Cowper were forerunners of this great movement, which was carried to its height by Wordsworth and Coleridge, by Byron, Shelley, and Keats.

1. **sleekit**: sleek. 4. **bickering brattle**: flickering flight. 5. **laith**: loath. 6. **pattle**: plough staff. 13. **whiles**: at times. 15. **daimen-icker in a thrave**: an occasional ear of corn in a sheaf. 17. **the lave**: what is left. 20. **silly wa's**: flimsy walls. 21. **big**: build. 22. **foggage**: after-grass. 24. **snell**: swift. 29. **coulter**: knife in front of the ploughshare. 34. **but . . . hald**: without dwelling-place. 35. **thole**: endure. 36. **cranreuch**: hoar-frost. 37. **thy lane**: alone. 40. **Gang aft a-gley**: often go awry. 43–48. Compare 152, lines 21–24.

185. Such a "wish" for solitude and cottage life was not uncommon in the artificial poetry of the eighteenth century. Compare 154 and 206. 11. **wheel**: spinning-wheel.

186. In the note of subdued and well-maintained repose, this poem resembles Gray's *Elegy* and is by some critics regarded as the finer piece of work. Note that it is an unrhymed lyric. For another example, see *The Old Familiar Faces*

(264). Some beautiful illustrations of the type will be found in Tennyson's *Princess*.

1. **oaten stop**: shepherd's pipe — a conventional phrase of the time.   7. **brede**: embroidery.   21. **folding-star**: the evening star, which warns the shepherd to bring his flocks to fold.   34–40. A picture of singular beauty.   50. **Science**: learning.

187. One of the most familiar poems in the whole collection. Its high literary value consists not only in the beauty of form, but also in "the perfection with which it phrases eternal truths in a form suggestive of emotion." It was begun at Stoke Poges in 1742, but was not published until 1751. The revisions made in the course of its composition form an interesting study.

1. **parting**: departing.   2. **lea**: pasture-land.   26. **glebe**: sods.   35. **hour** is the subject of "awaits."   39. **fretted vault**: carved roof.   41. Urn inscribed with the life story. **animated**: life-like.   47–48. Those who might have been mighty rulers or inspired poets.   51. **rage**: enthusiasm, fervor.   52. **genial**: kindly.   57. **Hampden**: John Hampden was a country squire who protested against the Ship Money tax levied by Charles I.   60. **Cromwell**, etc.: this point of view is the opposite of that taken by Marvell in his *Horatian Ode* (88).   64. See the results of their good government throughout the country.   71. To misuse their God-given talents by praising the rich and powerful. You might read, in this connection, Johnson's *Letter to Lord Chesterfield*.   73. **Far from**, etc.: Since they lived far from the maddening turmoil of the world.   76. **tenour**: course.   85–86. *I.e.*, resigned his life as a prey to dumb forgetfulness — was content that he should not be remembered.   91–92. Those who have passed away still exercise an influence upon the living.   93. **For thee**: as for thee (the poet) . . . if anyone shall ask thy fate, etc.   119. **Science**: knowledge, learning. **frown'd not on**: did not disdain, looked kindly upon.

188. This little group of Burns's love songs (188–191) are simple and sincere. The mythological references, so common

Notes

heretofore, have disappeared with the coming of a more natural view of life. They all belong to the year 1792–93.

2. **trysted**: appointed. 5. **bide the stoure**: endure the storm. 13. **braw**: gaily dressed. 20. **faut**: fault.

189. 13. **scaith**: harm. 17. **aboon**: above. **tent**: guard, protect. 18. **steer**: trouble, molest.

190. 8. **gang dry**: go dry, dry up.

191. "Highland Mary" was Mary Campbell, with whom Burns was deeply in love. The poem was written on the sixth anniversary of her death.

2. **castle of Montgomery**: where Burns met Mary. 4. **drumlie**: muddy. 5. *I.e.*, there may summer first unfold, etc. 9. **birk**: birch.

192. [There can hardly exist a poem more truly tragic in the highest sense than this; nor, perhaps, Sappho excepted, has any poetess equalled it.] It was composed to an old air in 1772; Lady Lindsay acknowledged the authorship in 1823. In direct tragic force it resembles the *Lament for Flodden* (162). The metre is excellently adapted to the tune to which it was written; in reading, four strong accents should be observed in each line.

1. **kye**: old plural for cow. 10. **stown**: stolen. 21. **urgit sair**: urged strongly. 27. **wraith**: ghost. 29. **greet**: cry. **muckle**: much. 34. **daurna**: dare not.

193. Written to a very attractive tune. The refrain in the first verse is repeated in the others.

3. **Yule**: Christmas. **fou**: merry with drink. 5. **coost**: tossed. 6. **asklent**: askance. **unco skeigh**: very proud. 7. **Gart**: made. **abeigh**: at a distance. 9. **fleech'd**: begged, coaxed. 10. **Ailsa Craig**: a rocky island in the Firth of Clyde. 12. [**Gart his een bleer't**: cried till his eyes were bleared.] 13. **lowpin o'er a linn**: jumping into a waterfall. 15. **sair to bide**: hard to put up with. 17. **hizzie**: hussy. 18. **for me**: for all I care. 24. **grace**: good feeling. 27. **smoor'd**: smothered. 28. **crouse and canty**: happy and merry.

Notes

194. Like the author of *The Burial of Sir John Moore* (262), Mickle's poetical fame rests upon one lyric. Burns called this poem "one of the most beautiful songs in the Scots or any other language."

13. **bigonet**: cap, head-dress. 14. **bishop's satin**: satin of specially fine quality. 15. **baillie's**: bailiff's, town officer's. 17. **Turkey**: red. 22. **muckle**: big. 25. **shoon**: old plural for "shoe." **slaes**: sloes. 31. **thraw**: twist. 34. Make everything look handsome. 38. **caller**: fresh. 44. **greet**: cry. 47. **gin**: if. 48. **aboon the lave**: above the rest.

195. [Burns himself, despite two attempts, failed to improve this little absolute masterpiece of music, tenderness, and simplicity: this "Romance of a life in eight lines."]

4. **eerie**: sad and lonely.

196. Written in 1788, shortly after Burns's marriage to Jean Armour. The last two stanzas were composed by John Hamilton, a music dealer of Edinburgh.

1. **airts**: quarters. 5. **row**: roll. 14. **shaw**: small wood, grove. 25. **knowes**: little hills.

197. 1. **jo**: sweetheart. 4. **brent**: smooth, unwrinkled. 7. **pow**: head. 10. **thegither**: together. 11. **canty**: happy, merry.

198. Lady Nairne was the author of several widely known songs: among them, *Caller Herrin'*, *Charley is my Darling*, and *Will ye no come back again?*

4. **leal**: loyal. 23. **fain**: happy.

199. Eton College, one of the most famous of English schools, was founded in 1440 by King Henry VI. The ode was written in 1742, after the death of one of Gray's old school friends.

3. **Science**: learning. 5. **ye**: the towers of Windsor Castle, just across the river from Eton. 9. **hoary Thames**: because "old in story." 14. The theory that childhood is a "stranger to pain," the happiest time of life, and so forth, is a favorite one with poets. Is it actually true in experience?

23. Playing on thy banks.   33. **'Gainst**: in preparation for.
60. Warn them beforehand of the troubles to come.
61. From here to the end the poet descends to the depths of pessimism.   82. **griesly**: horrible.   99–100. The quotation is familiar; do you think the idea is helpful?

200. [Written in 1773, towards the beginning of Cowper's second attack of melancholy madness — a time when he altogether gave up prayer, saying, " For him to implore mercy would only anger God the more."]

201. Written in the same year as 199.   Compare Wordsworth's *Ode to Duty* (252).
7. **purple tyrants**: kings in royal robes.   11. **birth**: child.
35. **Gorgon**: the three Gorgons were three terrible sisters, the worst being Medusa, whose face turned to stone those who looked at her.   36. **the vengeful band**: the avenging Furies. See note on 151, line 107.   43. **Thy philosophic train**: the lessons which we learn from adversity.

202. Selkirk was a sailor who was punished for insubordination by his captain, who put him ashore on the island of Juan Fernandez. Here he remained four years (1704–1709). His adventures suggested to Defoe the story of *Robinson Crusoe* (1719). Here and in *The Castaway* (205), Cowper sees his own loneliness of soul reflected in the physical loneliness of others.   27. **Some cordial endearing report**: some affectionate message.

203. Palgrave places this poem in the first rank of the sonnet, and adds: " There is much mannerism, much that is unimportant or of now exhausted interest in his poems; but where he is great, it is with that elementary greatness which rests on the most universal human feelings. Cowper is our highest master in simple pathos." Mrs. Unwin cared for him like a mother, and brought what brightness was possible into his unhappy life.
9. **There is a Book**: See *Revelation*, xx, 12.

204. Written in 1793, a few months after the preceding. It brings out the poignant pathos of simple things.

1. **The twentieth year**: in 1773 Cowper was prostrated by one of the severe attacks of melancholy, bordering upon insanity, to which he was liable.

205. [Cowper's last original poem, founded upon a story told in Anson's *Voyages*. It was written March, 1799; he died in next year's April.]

3. **destined**: ill-fated. 8. **he**: Sir George Anson, a celebrated English admiral who cruised round the world, 1740–44. 56. **Descanting**: speaking at length. 65–66. A pathetic reference to Cowper's mental misery.

206. Compare the metre of 183. A cheerful little poem. Palgrave calls it "truly noble"; another critic terms it "deplorable doggerel." What is your own opinion?

5. **pad-pony**: easy-pacing pony. 15. **Nabob**: rich man — originally used in this sense of one who had returned from India with a fortune. 28. **thread**: of life. 32. **Everlasting**: with a side reference to the cloth so-named at the time.

207. From a poem called *Life*. Palgrave has omitted eighteen lines after line 4.

Questions and Topics for Discussion

1. Discuss the "leading moods or tendencies" mentioned by Palgrave as characteristic of this Book. Cite passages to illustrate what you say.

2. Contrast the simplicity of Collins (160 and 186) with that of Cowper (183), Blake (180, 181), and Carey (167).

3. Write a comparative estimate of the two types of ode seen in this Book. Use *The Bard* (159) and the *Ode to Evening* (186) to illustrate what you say.

4. For what qualities of thought and expression do you find the following poems distinguished: *The Loss of the Royal George* (165) and *Black-eyed Susan* (166)?

5. Discuss the element of pathos in the *Ode Written in 1746* (160), *Lament for Flodden* (163), and *The Castaway* (205).

6. In which poems in the Book do you find the personality of the authors most strongly reflected? Are the poems so distinguished of less literary merit than those of an impersonal nature? Discuss fully.

7. Write a note upon the language of Burns's poems.

8. Analyze the stanza forms of the following poems: 183, 184, 187, 192. Comment upon their appropriateness for the subjects of the poems.

9. Find instances of personification throughout the Book. Comment upon their value as a means of poetic effect.

10. The attitude of the poets towards nature.

BIOGRAPHICAL SKETCHES

ANNA LETITIA BARBAULD (AIKIN) is remembered to-day as a writer "of more industry than genius." She lived from 1743 to 1825, and for many years was head of a school with her husband. She wrote for her pupils *Hymns in Prose for Children*, which attracted a good deal of attention. The lines selected (207) were much admired by Wordsworth.

WILLIAM BLAKE was a poet and an engraver, with astonishing genius in both capacities. He was born in 1757 and died in 1827. His poems have wonderful imaginative fervor, and the original illustrations which accompany them manifest a strange and beautiful art. His best work is found in his *Songs of Innocence* and *Songs of Experience*, and in his noble illustrations to the *Book of Job*. Blake was "a man of extraordinary powers, dominated by his imagination." He showed an eccentricity of genius which at times approached insanity.

ROBERT BURNS, best known and best loved of Scotch poets, was born at Alloway, Scotland, on January 25, 1759. He began life as a farmer, won fame by a volume of poetry (1786), and for a time was the centre of fashionable literary circles in Edinburgh.

Then he returned to his farm, later took a position as an exciseman, and died in 1796. He was a keen satirist, but a wonderfully sympathetic portrayer of Scotch rustic life. His best work is contained in his songs and lyrics; here the imagery is so brilliant and the melody so haunting that his verses are sung the world over. His *Auld Lang Syne* is one of the most familiar songs in the English language.

HENRY CAREY is a vague figure. The date of his birth is unknown; he died in 1743. He seems to have been at one time a teacher of music, and he was favorably known as a writer of songs and burlesques.

COLLEY CIBBER was a dramatist and for over forty years an actor at Drury Lane Theatre, of which he finally became manager. He was made Poet Laureate, got the better of Pope in a literary controversy, and by the latter was satirized as hero of the *Dunciad*, or "Epic of Dunces." He lived from 1671 to 1757.

JOHN COLLINS, the son of a tailor, became a moderately successful actor. He secured both fame and money by a novel form of entertainment which combined lecture, song, and story. The best of his poems is the one here included (206). He died in 1808 in his fifty-sixth year.

WILLIAM COLLINS was born in 1721, and educated at Winchester and Oxford. He began writing poetry while still at school, and adopted literature as a profession in the absence of any special tastes in other directions. His life ended sadly, under a cloud of insanity, in 1759. Collins, as a critic has said, has the touch of a sculptor; his poems are as pure, and as cold, as marble.

WILLIAM COWPER, like Burns, wrote of country life as he saw and knew it, and left some charming pictures of the English countryside. He was born in 1731, and educated at Westminster School. He studied for the Law, but a constitutional nervousness prevented him from taking the examination which would have ensured a permanent position under Government. He was actually insane for a time and upon his recovery went to Huntington, where he formed his well-known friendship with Mr. and

Notes

Mrs. Unwin. In 1767 he removed to Olney. Here the famous "Olney Hymns" were written. The melancholy which was his besetting weakness slowly increased, but he was able to write a good deal of poetry: the familiar humorous ballad *John Gilpin* appeared in 1783; *The Task*, which introduced a new note into English poetry, in 1785. These established him as the greatest living English poet. His last poem, *The Castaway*, reflects the mental unhappiness which in the end completely overshadowed his life. He died in 1800. The personal letters of Cowper possess a singular delicacy and charm.

JEAN ELLIOTT was born in Scotland in 1727, of a somewhat literary family. The fine poem given in this book (162) was the result of a wager with her brother, who said that she could not write a poem on the subject of Flodden Field. It appeared anonymously in 1756, and was thought by many to be a genuine old ballad. Burns, and later Scott, detected the modern note; the latter published it as a modern ballad in his *Minstrelsy of the Scottish Border*. The author passed her last years in Edinburgh, and died in 1805.

JOHN GAY is best remembered by his highly successful play, *The Beggar's Opera* (1728), which has proved capable of holding the stage at the present day. He was born in 1685, and became one of the leading men of letters of his time, and a personal friend of Pope and Swift. His *Trivia* is a brilliant poetical account of the London of the early eighteenth century. He died in 1732.

OLIVER GOLDSMITH, in spite of certain weaknesses, won the affectionate esteem of such men as Dr. Johnson and Sir Joshua Reynolds, the great portrait painter. He was born in Ireland in 1728, educated at Trinity College, Dublin, and led a restless, uncertain kind of life as a writer in England. His three chief works were extremely popular in their time, and are ranked to-day among the treasures of English literature. They are: his poem *The Deserted Village*, his novel *The Vicar of Wakefield*, and his delightful play *She Stoops to Conquer*. He died in London in 1774.

ROBERT GRAHAM (1735?–1797) was educated at Glasgow University, of which he was many years later elected Rector. He had a wide experience of life, having been a planter in the West Indies, and a member of parliament from 1794-1796. His songs in their day enjoyed a good deal of popularity.

THOMAS GRAY was characterized by the critic Arnold as the least prolific of classical writers, but a classic none the less. He wrote little, but what he did write was perfect in its kind. The *Elegy* and *The Bard* show his poetic genius at its best. He was born on December 26, 1716, educated at Eton and Cambridge, and travelled for a time on the Continent with Horace Walpole, the famous wit and critic. He was a profound scholar and his personal correspondence makes delightful reading. It is interesting to note that he was one of the first among English writers to travel solely for the sake of beautiful scenery. Most of his life was passed at Cambridge University, where he died in 1771.

LADY ANNE LINDSAY (1750-1825) was the eldest daughter of a Scottish Earl, and connected with the literary world through her friendship with Dr. Johnson, Sheridan, and Burke.

JOHN LOGAN was born 1748, in Midlothian, Scotland. Educated at the University of Edinburgh, he was ordained a minister of the Scottish Church, but became unpopular with his co-religionists because he composed a tragedy for the stage. His *Poems* appeared in 1783; he died in London in 1788.

WILLIAM JULIUS MICKLE (1735-1788) was educated in the Edinburgh schools. His literary tastes caused him to fail in business. He was for a time connected with the Clarendon Press of Oxford University, attempted dramatic composition, and eventually settled down in a government sinecure. He was author of the beautiful ballad *Cumnor Hall*, to which Scott refers in his novel *Kenilworth*.

LADY NAIRNE (Carolina Oliphant) was a Scotchwoman born in 1766. Her admiration of Burns's poems led her to write some imitations of the old Scottish ballads. *The Land o' the Leal* was composed in 1798 to comfort a friend who had lost her child. Lady Nairne died in 1845.

Notes

AMBROSE PHILIPS was successful enough as a poet to arouse the jealousy of Pope. He was a friend of Swift, Addison, and Steele. Born about 1675, he was educated at Shrewsbury and Cambridge, and rose to a high legal position. He died in 1749.

ALEXANDER POPE was born in London on May 21, 1688. He was brought up as a Roman Catholic, suffered much from ill-health, turned eagerly to poetry and eventually became a master of satiric and didactic verse. He first won his place by his *Pastorals* (1709) and *The Rape of the Lock* (1714). He established certain poetic principles which were followed until the "Romantic Revival" which began with Burns and Cowper. Pope died at Twickenham in 1744.

MATTHEW PRIOR (1664–1721), one of the leading English poets in light verse, was educated at Cambridge. Besides winning distinction in literature, he had a notable diplomatic career.

SAMUEL ROGERS was born in 1763, and began life as a banker, but soon turned to literature. While not attaining the highest rank, he wrote much pleasing verse, and his cultivated tastes and knowledge of the world won him many friends among the poets, artists, and statesmen of his time. He died in 1855.

CHRISTOPHER SMART was born in 1722, and was educated at Cambridge University. During much of his life he suffered from attacks of insanity. In a lucid interval he wrote the extraordinary *Song of David*, from which the lines in this book are taken. His other work was of little value. He died in London in 1771.

JAMES THOMSON was born in 1700, and educated at the University of Edinburgh. His great works were *The Seasons* (1726–1730), and *The Castle of Indolence*, written in the Spenserian stanza, and well known in its day. He died in 1748.

BOOK FOURTH

[It proves sufficiently the lavish wealth of our own age in poetry, that the pieces which, without conscious departure from the standard of excellence, render this book by far the longest, were with very few exceptions composed during the first thirty years of the nineteenth century. Exhaustive reasons can hardly be given for the strangely sudden appearance of individual genius; that, however, which assigns the splendid national achievements of our recent poetry to an impulse from the France of the first Republic and Empire is inadequate. The first French Revolution was rather one result — the most conspicuous, indeed, yet itself in great measure essentially retrogressive — of that wider and more potent spirit which through inquiry and attempt, through strength and weakness, sweeps mankind round the circles (not, as some too confidently argue, of advance, but) of gradual transformation; and it is to this that we must trace the literature of modern Europe. But without attempting discussion on the motive causes of Scott, Wordsworth, Shelley, and others, we may observe that these poets carried to further perfection the later tendencies of the century preceding, in simplicity of narrative, reverence for human passion and character in every sphere, and love of nature for herself; that, while maintaining on the whole the advances in art made since the Restoration, they renewed the half-forgotten melody and depth of tone which marked the best Elizabethan writers; that, lastly, to what was thus inherited they added a richness in language and a variety in metre, a force and fire in narrative, a tenderness and bloom in feeling, an insight into the finer passages of the soul and the inner meanings of the landscape, a larger sense of humanity, hitherto scarcely attained, and perhaps unattainable even by predecessors of not inferior individual genius. In a word, the nation which, after the Greeks in their glory, may fairly claim that during six centuries it has proved itself the most richly gifted of all nations for poetry, expressed in these men the highest strength and prodigality of its nature. They interpreted the age to itself; hence the many phases of thought and style they present. To sympathize with each fervently and impartially, without fear and without fancifulness, is no doubtful step in the higher education of the soul. For purity in taste is absolutely proportionate to strength, and when once the mind has raised itself to grasp and to delight in excellence, those who love most will be found to love most wisely.

But the gallery which this book offers to the reader will aid him more than any preface. It is a royal palace of poetry which he is invited to enter:

Adparet domus intus, et atria longa patescunt [1] —

though it is, indeed, to the sympathetic eye only that its treasures will be visible.]

208. [This beautiful lyric, printed in 1783, seems to anticipate in its imaginative music that return to our great early age of song, which in Blake's own lifetime was to prove that the English Muses had resumed their "ancient melody": — Keats, Shelley, Byron, — he overlived them all.] Can you give any reasons why Blake should feel discouraged, as the poem implies, about the future of English poetry?

1. **Ida** was the mountain near Troy.

209. The souls of poets have a double life — one in heaven, where they enjoy the highest pleasures; and one on earth, where they teach mortals insight and wisdom. 8. **parle**: speech — surviving in *parley, parliament*. 11. **Elysian**: heavenly. 12. **Dian's fawns**: Diana was the goddess of hunting, and of animals of the chase. 13. **tented**: coördinate with "seated." 18. See what Keats says of the nightingale in his *Ode* (290). 28. **cloying**: satiated. 30. **little week**: short life.

210. [To find in Chapman's Homer the "pure serene" of the original, the reader must bring with him the imagination of the youthful poet; — he must be a "Greek himself," as Shelley finely said of Keats.] George Chapman, an Elizabethan poet, finished his translation of Homer in 1616.

1. **the realms of gold**: the kingdom of literature. 3-4. A reference to the poetry of England. 6. **demesne**: domain.

---

[1] "The interior of the house appears, and the long halls open out" (Virgil, *Æneid*, II, 483).

11. **Cortez**: a slip for Balboa, the actual discoverer of the Pacific in 1513.

211. It is interesting that we have here all the "machinery" of Romance — love, moonlight, ruins, knights, and so on. The form is very simple and approximates the ballad type. But the imaginative appeal is not comparable to that found in Coleridge's best poetry, such as *Kubla Khan* (316).

212. Palgrave called this "the most tender and true of Byron's smaller poems." Do you agree with this estimate, after reading Byron's lyrics in this book?

3. **myrtle and ivy**: typical of love and feasting. The **laurel** was the badge of success. 11. **discover**: show.

213. Scott had a wonderful gift for ballad-writing; no other author has been able to reproduce the past so vividly. These lines are from his *Rokeby*, iii, 16 (1813). Note the skilful use of proper names.

1. **Brignall**: a village in Yorkshire. Greta and Dalton are close by. 17. **read**: interpret — the original meaning of the word. 37. **brand and musketoon**: sword and musket. 40. **tuck**: beat. 43. **when the beetle**, etc.: at night. 51. **The fiend**: the "will-o'-the-wisp."

214. Called by Byron "Stanzas for Music"; published in the *Poems* of 1816.

10. **Her bright chain**: her reflection.

215. Named by the author "Song written for an Indian Air." It appeared in 1822, the year of Shelley's death.

11. **champak**: a beautiful and fragrant Indian tree.

216. Compare this poem with that which follows; each is considered to be characteristic of the author. Which do you prefer? Why? It has been said that Byron's lyric concerns itself with beauty, Wordsworth's with character. Comment upon this statement.

217. Written in 1804, two years after Wordsworth's marriage — his wife is the "She" referred to. 22. **machine**: Does the metaphor appeal to you?

Notes

218. Hartley Coleridge was the son of the greater poet, Samuel Taylor Coleridge. He did a good deal of writing, but this is the only poem which has lived.

219. For an exercise in critical appreciation, compare this lyric with the lines *To Helen*, by Edgar Allan Poe.

220. This group of Wordsworth's poems (220–223) gives an excellent illustration of his theory that poetry could reach the heart through unadorned simplicity. Here, this simplicity is seen in its best sense. But Wordsworth's poetry was very unequal, and the reader would do well to compare *Simon Lee* (263) with the masterly selections given here.

10. It does not matter who "Lucy" was — though there has been much discussion on the subject. The thing to note in this, as in the others of the group, is the elemental truth and beauty of Wordsworth at his best.

221. 1. Written in 1799, when the poet was on a visit to Germany. 6. Wordsworth did not live up to this thought; he was in Calais in 1802, and made other journeys through Europe. 11. **wheel**: spinning-wheel.

222. This was written in the Hartz Forest, in Germany, in 1799. It was Wordsworth's theory that nature — or rather God through nature — has a message of the deepest meaning for the human mind. This theory is very beautifully expressed in a poem not included here — *Tintern Abbey*. Other references are found in his *Ode on Immortality* (338).

223. A poem of elemental power.

224. Written by the author of the well-known hymn, *Abide with Me*, which is a finer piece of work than the poem.

225. Campbell was a successful ballad-writer, although his fame during his lifetime was considerably higher than it is today. This ballad was written in Scotland about 1796; the scene of the tragedy was on the west coast, near the island of Mull.

3. **a silver pound**: a pound of silver. 5. **Lochgyle**: arm of the sea, about two miles wide. 7. **Ulva's Isle** lay westward

of Mull. 26. **water-wraith**: a water-spirit that gave warning of death. See 163, line 23. 25–32. A fine bit of descriptive writing.

226. [Simple as *Lucy Gray* seems, a mere narrative of " what has been, and may be again," yet every touch in the child's picture is marked by the deepest and purest ideal character.] Note the severe simplicity of the diction. Many readers think it is one of the most moving of English poems. Can you see why?

227. Written in 1816. This, like so many of the short poems of Scott and Burns, seems almost to " sing itself "; like others of the kind, it goes to a charming tune. All the place-names refer to Border localities.

7. **loot**: let. 19. **mettled**: thoroughbred. **managed**: trained. 20. **palfrey**: horse for a lady. 29. **bower and ha'**: bower and hall, *i.e.*, throughout the whole castle.

228. Published in 1819. Note the lightness and grace with which the subject is treated.

229. Moore was an accomplished writer of songs, and this is one of the daintiest of his poems. Compare Tennyson's song in *The Princess*, beginning: " The splendor falls on castle walls."

230. From *Quentin Durward* (1823), Chapter iv.
1. **County**: count.

231. Part of a longer poem, written in 1796. There is an odd survival of the eighteenth century love for personification — see stanza 3. The " evening star " is Venus.
5. **pensile**: hanging in mid air.

232. This poem shows the magic imagery of Shelley, as well as his mastery over the pure music of language.

233. Suggested to Wordsworth by " a forsaken bird's-nest filled with snow," which he saw during a winter walk. He wrote the sonnet, as he tells us, to prove to himself that he could write in a strain that poets had been fond of.

7-8. My least generous thought only asked for what you could easily spare me — a letter, or a message.

234. The metre is similar to *The Bridge of Sighs*, but the thought is widely different. Which of the two poems seems to you the better to express the emotions involved?

235. [In this, as in other instances, the addition (or the change) of a Title has been risked in hope that the aim of the piece following may be grasped more clearly and immediately.]
5. **undo them:** ruin them. 8. **prime:** spring-time. 15. **petting:** worrying. 21–24. *I.e.*, the bitterness of this feeling has never been expressed in poetry. Shelley says, however, that " our sweetest songs are those which tell of saddest thought." Which of the two great poets is right?

236. From *Marmion*, Canto iii. " Eleu loro " is a cry of grief.

237. Reminiscent of the old ballads, but far more highly imaginative. It appeared in 1819. The title is from an ancient French ballad, and means, " the beautiful lady without mercy." Note the grim effect produced by the shortened fourth line in each stanza.
32. **With kisses four:** Keats wrote to his brother George: " Why four kisses, you will say, why four? Because I wish to restrain the headlong impetuosity of my Muse — she would fain have said 'score' without hurting the rhyme — but we must temper the imagination, as the critics say, with judgment."

238. From *Rokeby*, iii, 28.
4. **rue:** a bitter herb, typical of repentance. 7. **Lincoln:** a town long famous for the green cloth produced there. 12. **fain:** gladly, beautifully.

239. 19. **singled:** " singled out." 20. **To endure:** to endure the loss of. 23. **the frailest:** *i.e.*, the human heart.

240. Written in 1806, and founded upon a tradition of Neidpath Castle, to the effect that the Earl of March in order

Notes

to save his daughter's life recalled a young knight whom he had banished, and for love of whom the girl was dying. Tennyson said that this poem was "almost more pathetic than a man has a right to be."

21. **kenn'd**: recognized.

241. Upon the same subject as the preceding. In what respects is it inferior?

242. [This beautiful Sonnet was the last word of a youth, in whom, if the fulfilment may ever safely be prophesied from the promise, England lost one of the most rarely gifted in the long roll of her poets. Shakespeare and Milton, had their lives been closed at twenty-five, would (so far as we know) have left poems of less excellence and hope.]

4. **Eremite**: hermit.

243. A poem of the deepest pathos, when we remember Keats's high promise and early death.

3. **charact'ry**: writing. 8. **magic hand of chance**: imaginative inspiration. 11. **faery**: magic.

244. "This was in fact suggested by my daughter Catherine, long after her death." — Wordsworth's note. The title (supplied by Palgrave) means, "things longed for."

11. **when I stood forlorn**: *i.e.*, immediately after his daughter's death.

245. [It is impossible not to regret that Moore has written so little in this sweet and genuinely national style.]

1. **When stars were weeping**: poetic expression for "when the dew is falling." 8. **orison**: memorial prayer.

246. [A masterly example of Byron's command of strong thought and close reasoning in verse; — as the next is equally characteristic of Shelley's wayward intensity.] Compare these poems with 220 and 223, noting how they express the personality of the authors.

18. **'Tis Nothing**, etc.: that what I loved so well has passed into nothingness. 62. Supply "which" after "love." 68–72. Thy immortal soul returns to me and makes thy memory dearer than anything else, except thy love when alive.

247. Published in 1824.

8. **Than that**: *i.e.*, love, the " word," the " hope," and the " feeling," mentioned above.

248. Written in 1816, to the air of an old song of the Clan MacDonald. Note the vigor and sweep of the stanzas.

1. **pibroch**: war-song to the bag-pipe. **Donuil Dhu** means " Donald the Black." 12. **Inverlocky**: in the central part of the Highlands. 24. **targes**: shields.

249. One of the best of sea-songs for its freshness and sincerity. Compare it with Masefield's *Sea-Fever*, or Kipling's *Anchor-Song*, or Tennyson's *The Sailor-boy*. Each of these four poems is excellent, yet each is different from the others.

1. **sheet**: the rope by which the sail is controlled.

250. Published in 1801, and signed " Amator Patriae " (lover of his country). At the moment, there was danger of a war with Russia. The poem shows intense feeling and has a stirring rhythm.

15. **Blake and mighty Nelson**: Robert Blake (1599–1657) and Horatio Nelson (1758–1805) were two of England's greatest naval heroes; the former fought under the Commonwealth, and the latter won the battle of Trafalgar. 31. **meteor**: streaming like a meteor; Campbell had in mind also the superstitious fears with which meteors were regarded.

251. Written in the winter of 1804–5. The battle was won by Nelson off Copenhagen on April 2, 1801, and the union of the northern nations with Napoleon against England was thus prevented. See Southey's *Life of Nelson*. As in the preceding, the rhythm is very effective.

6. **lighted brand**: the old-fashioned muzzle-loading cannon was fired by means of a slow-match applied to the touch-hole. 20. **To anticipate the scene**: in anticipation of. 26. **hurricane eclipse**: The smoke of battle hid the sun like the clouds of some great storm. 34. **strike**: lower. 53. **fires of funeral light**: the burning ships. 63. **Elsinore**: a small port near by; the scene of *Hamlet*. 67. **Riou**: an English captain.

252. Published in 1807, though written earlier. This poem might have been written by Milton; it expresses very finely one side of Wordsworth's character. Note the consistently lofty quality of thought and expression.

11–16. rely Upon the genial sense of youth, etc.: *i.e.*, there are some fortunate characters who act from their own inner kindliness and not from a sense of duty; if this trust in themselves brings failure, then they may be saved by the sterner power. **20. security**: safeguard. **37. uncharter'd freedom**: liberty not limited by set bounds. **41–56.** The thought in these stanzas lies at the heart of Wordsworth's theory of life.

253. This sonnet was prefixed to the first edition of *The Prisoner of Chillon* (1816). [Bonnivard, a Genevese, was imprisoned (1530–6) by the Duke of Savoy in Chillon on the Lake of Geneva for his courageous defence of his country against the tyranny with which Piedmont threatened it during the first half of the Seventeenth Century. — This noble sonnet is worthy to stand near Milton's on the Vaudois massacre.]

254. The strong political feelings of the time are reflected in this sonnet and the next. The Swiss Confederation had broken up through internal troubles, and in 1802 Napoleon set up a new government.

5. There came a tyrant: Napoleon.

255. Venice had been an independent state since 997, and had held for centuries a position of great strength. Napoleon occupied the city and dissolved the Venetian Republic in 1797. This sonnet was written in 1802.

1. in fee: in subjection — at one time Venice owned Cyprus and parts of Greece. **2. safeguard of the West**: through her fleet and her strategic position. **4. eldest child of Liberty**: Venice was founded in 697, when refugees from some of the northern Italian towns fled from the invading Huns under Attila, and settled on an inaccessible chain of islands in the Adriatic. **8. espouse the everlasting Sea**: the wedding of Venice and the Adriatic was celebrated each year with

Notes

great magnificence. It symbolized the city's guardianship of the Adriatic.

256. The three sonnets now following form a poetic indictment of the evils of the day. They were published together in 1807. Note the noble use of the Italianate sonnet form.

10. **This is idolatry**: these are our idols. 13. **fearful**: fearing to do wrong.

257. 3-4. Note the effective metaphor. **hall and bower**: the resorts, respectively, of the knight and the lady. 8. **manners**: used broadly of moral character.

258. Here Wordsworth feels that he had allowed too free rein to his indignation. Other great nations have been ruined by excess, and he had " unfilial fears " for England. But he has allowed his view of the whole to be unduly influenced by the actions of a part; his very love has moved his depth of feeling.

10. **a bulwark for the cause of men**: at the time, England stood alone against the power of Napoleon, who had said: " Give me command of the English Channel for twenty-four hours, and I am master of the world."

259. Another of Campbell's stirring " battle-pieces," written in 1801. [This battle was fought December 3, 1800, between the Austrians under Archduke John and the French under Moreau, in a forest near Munich. *Hohen Linden* means *High Limetrees*.] Note the strong effect of the unrhymed last line.

4. **Iser**: river near Munich. 21. **level**: *i.e.*, low on the horizon.

260. This poem was written in 1798, and is decidedly ironical in general meaning. Blenheim was a great battle which was fought in 1704.

23. **many thousand men**: the allies, who won, are said to have lost 11,000 men; the French and Bavarians, 40,000. 63. **what good came of it**: as a matter of fact, the battle was by no means fought in vain. Louis XIV of France was aim-

ing at a French domination of Europe, very much as Napoleon did a century later. At Blenheim his ambitions were definitely checked.

261. These lines, published in 1807, were written to commemorate the death of Robert Emmet, who organized an unsuccessful rising against the Irish government in 1803. *Pro Patria Mori* means "to die for one's country" — Palgrave's title. The metre is well adapted to music.

1. **thee**: Ireland.

262. Byron first called attention to the excellence of this poem — the only one by which its author is remembered today. It was published in 1817. Sir John Moore was in command of the English troops at the battle of Vimiera (1808) in the Peninsular War. Out-numbered and almost cut off by Napoleon, he retreated 250 miles to Corunna, on the north coast of Spain. Here he fought an action to cover the embarcation of his troops. The French were beaten off, and the troops safely embarked; but Sir John Moore was killed by a cannon ball and buried at midnight on the ramparts of the town.

263. Published in the *Lyrical Ballads* (1798). The weakness of Wordsworth's theory of extreme simplicity in poetry is illustrated in this poem, and even more in his *Ruth* (320). They should be compared with the *Lucy* poems (220-223), or with *To the Cuckoo* (289), where simplicity of diction is combined with the loftiest poetic feeling.

1. **Cardigan**: in Wales. 23. **chiming hounds**: referring to the musical cry of the foxhounds. 68. Such was Wordsworth's theory, and it led him sometimes into very trivial matters. 95-96. An extreme display of gratitude, such as that of old Simon, shows that the man has received very little kindness in the course of his life.

264. Lamb is one of the most delightful of essayists; he is little known as a poet. These lines, however, possess true lyrical feeling and deep pathos. They were first published in

Notes

1798. The peculiar metrical form is not assignable to any of the common metres; it resembles the Greek "Sapphic." Tennyson has a poem in similar metre, beginning: "Faded every violet, all the roses."

7. **fairest among women**: Ann Simmonds, to whom Lamb refers as "Alice W—n" in his *Dream Children*. 10. **I have a friend**: Charles Lloyd, a poet and friend of Lamb and Coleridge. 16. **Friend of my bosom**: Coleridge. Lamb had been a school friend of his at Christ's Hospital, and the friendship lasted throughout their lives.

265. Typical of Moore in the sentiment and the easy flowing metre. It was written to the tune of *The Girl I Left behind Me*.

266. Written in 1815, and characteristic of Byron. The gloomy outlook on life and the note of self-pity were constantly recurring in his poetry.

267. It would be well to read this poem in connection with the two other poems by Wordsworth about flowers, *The Daffodils* (301) and *To a Daisy* (302). Which seems to you the best poetry? Why?

20. **spleen**: gloom. 21-22. Youth overloads us with good things, and Age allows us too little.

268. Hood was best-known in his own day as a humorist; but he had the gift of sincere pathos, as may be seen here and in *The Bridge of Sighs* (274).

269. In a key similar to the preceding. The unusual stanza form is gracefully handled, and the pathos rises above mere sentiment.

270. A sea-picture of singular beauty. Note that nature can bring peace, but not consolation, to the poet's sadness of heart. Wordsworth found something more; as may be seen, to cite one example, in the last stanza of his *Intimations of Immortality*.

Notes

7. **of one delight**: expressing the same happiness. 35-36. We remember that Shelley was drowned at sea. Read the last stanza of his *Adonais*.

271. This has been called "a pleasing little poem"; it is doubtful if any of Southey's rather voluminous poetical writings deserves much more emphatic praise.

23. **a name**: although his name has not actually "perished," yet only one or two of Southey's poems are now remembered.

272. [The Mermaid was the club-house of Shakespeare, Ben Jonson, and other choice spirits of that age.] You should read some of the poems in *Tales of the Mermaid Tavern*, by Alfred Noyes.
6. **Canary wine**: a sweet yellow wine, a favorite drink of the Elizabethans, imported from the Canary Islands. 10. **Robin Hood**: the famous outlaw whose exploits are celebrated in a series of old ballads. 12. **bowse**: drink heavily, "booze." 22. **Zodiac**: The path of the sun in the heavens. It was divided into twelve parts, each containing a constellation. These were called the "Signs of the Zodiac."

273. From *The Heart of Midlothian*, chapter xl. [Scott has given us nothing more complete and lovely than this little song, which unites simplicity and dramatic power to a wildwood quality of the rarest quality. No moral is drawn, far less any conscious analysis of feeling attempted: — the pathetic feeling is left to be suggested by the mere presentment of the situation.] There is a very grim touch here which is seldom found in Scott's poetry.

8. **Kirkward**: to the church — for your funeral service. The "six braw gentlemen" are the pall-bearers.

274. Published in 1843. The "bridge" was Waterloo Bridge, over the Thames. It was less used at the time than other bridges, and hence was chosen by such "unfortunates" as the one in the poem. The difficult metre (dactyllic dimeter) is handled with rare skill and restraint.

Notes 581

10. **cerements**: grave-clothes. 22. **mutiny**: against life. 96. **contumely**: insult, scorn.

275. Compare this lyric with the four which follow. Each possesses features, both in form and thought, that are typical of the author. Byron's *Elegy* was written in 1815. Note the pathetic quality of the two closing lines.

13. **unteach**: teach us not to.

276. A touching memorial of a beautiful young Quaker girl whom Lamb frequently met on his way to his office in the South Sea House. It is a little character sketch, with the note of tenderness that is so often found in the *Essays of Elia*.

21. **prying**: searching, inquiring. 32. **forewarning**: a foretaste of the pleasure of her friendship.

277. [Wolfe resembled Keats, not only in his early death by consumption and the fluent freshness of his poetical style, but in beauty of character.] We must be careful, however, not to press too far Palgrave's highly complimentary estimate. How do you think this poem compares with the same author's *Burial of Sir John Moore* (262)?

278. From *The Lady of the Lake* (1810), iii, 16. "Coronach" is Gaelic for a funeral dirge.

15. **in flushing**: in full bloom. 17. **correi**: hollow on a mountain-side. 18. **cumber**: trouble, difficulty. 19. **foray**: raiding expedition.

279. In memory of his sister. Some critics feel that the third stanza is a little too "ingenious" for the subdued pathos of the poem. What is your opinion?

280. [This book has not a few poems of greater power and more perfect execution than *Agnes* and the extract which we have ventured to make from the deep-hearted author's *Sad Thoughts* (224). But none are more definitely marked by the note of exquisiteness.] Do you agree with this enthusiastic appreciation?

Notes

281. From *The Lay of the Last Minstrel* (1805), vi, 23.

7. **Ravensheuch**: a castle, now in ruins, on the north shore of the Firth of Forth. 10. **inch**: islet. 13-14. An instance of "second-sight," or power to foresee death, widely believed in at the time, and even today not altogether discredited in some parts of the Highlands. 18. **Roslin**: a famous castle, with a beautiful chapel, not far from Edinburgh on the south shore of the Firth. 31. An estate near Roslin, famous for its oaks. 32. **Hawthornden**: another place near Roslin; the home of William Drummond, some of whose poems appear in Book I. 36. **panoply**: armor. 38. **sacristry**: room where sacred vessels of the chapel were kept. **altar's pale**: the enclosure of the altar. 39. The pillars of Roslin Chapel are very beautifully carved. 41. **pinnet**: pinnacle. 50. *I.e.*, with all the rites of the funeral service.

282. The "infant" was the first child of Hood, to whom Lamb sent the poem.

21. **the Promethean fire**: the fire of life. Prometheus was the mortal who stole fire from heaven to give to men. 38. **economy**: management. **dark**: mysterious. 39. **clerks**: scholars. 41. **ephemeral**: living only for a day.

283. [From *Poetry for Children* (1809), by Charles and Mary Lamb. This tender and original little piece seems clearly to reveal the work of that noble-minded and afflicted sister, who was at once the happiness, the misery, and the life-long blessing of her equally noble-minded brother.]

284. Written in 1801 of an old village woman in whom Wordsworth was interested. The simplicity of utterance here rises to a fine dignity; mother-love has never been more nobly expressed. See especially the last two stanzas.

285. Written in 1808, and published in a romance called *Queen-Hoo Hall*, which was left incomplete by its author and finished by Scott. Note the change of tone in the last stanza.
6. **knelling**: ringing out. 29. **baulk**: check, restrain.

Notes 583

286. This poem should be carefully compared with that of Shelley on the same subject. To Wordsworth, the skylark is a real, actual bird, with a nest to which it can return at will. To Shelley, it is a spirit — "bird thou never wert" — springing from the earth "like a cloud of fire," until it is lost in "the golden lightning of the sunken sun." Try to understand fully, and to appreciate thoroughly, the peculiar beauties of each of these wonderful lyrics.

14. **A privacy of glorious light**: *i.e.*, the lark, when soaring at its height, is as much alone as the nightingale in "her shady wood." 16. **more divine**: than the nightingale.

287. This is probably the best known of Shelley's poems, and it shows all the qualities which make him the most lyrical of lyric poets. He tries to make us feel his delight in the song of the skylark by a series of exquisite similes; see especially the figures of light and sound in stanzas 3, 5, 6, 7, 10, and 12. We notice, too, the touch of sadness which always creeps into Shelley's verse.

22. **that silver sphere**: the moon, fading out at sunrise. 36–37. **hidden In the light of thought**: as a poet whose songs stir the world, though he himself is unknown. 53. **deflower'd**: robbed. 56. **vernal**: spring-time. 66. **Chorus hymeneal**: marriage song.

288. Written in 1803; a pure picture, without any interpretative element.

18. **paramours**: lovers — see 74, line 16. 34. **brother**: *i.e.*, green, like the leaves.

289. [This poem has an exultation and a glory, joined with an exquisiteness of expression, which place it in the highest rank among the many masterpieces of its illustrious author.] Do you feel that the praise is too high in this instance? Compare this poem, in thought and expression, with Shelley's *Skylark* and Keats's *Nightingale*. What do you consider to be the special excellences of Wordsworth's lyric?

8. **far off and near**: it is very difficult to locate the bird by its call; see also line 19.

290. Keats wrote this in 1819, soon after the death of his brother. It is the poem of a mood — the thoughts aroused by the nightingale, rather than the bird itself. The imagery is that of the physical senses, not the spirit; in this respect it is far removed from Shelley's *Skylark*. The tone of luxuriant melancholy is, however, almost equally beautiful.

2. **hemlock**: a numbing poison. Socrates was put to death, under the Athenian law, by drinking hemlock. 4. **Lethe-wards**: towards Lethe, the River of Forgetfulness in the world of the dead. 7. **That**: in the thought that, because. **Dryad**: wood-nymph. 13. **Flora**: the goddess of flowers. 14. **Provençal song**: the poetry of the troubadours, who came from Provence in southern France. 16. **Hippocrene**: the fountain of the Muses, on Mount Helicon. 20–21. Note the effect of the repetition; it is used even more beautifully in lines 70–71. 32. **Bacchus and his pards**: the leopard, or panther, was sacred to Dionysus (Bacchus) the Greek god of wine. 33. **viewless**: invisible. 51. **Darkling**: in the darkness. 60. **requiem**: song for the dead; literally, a service for the repose of the dead. 64. **clown**: peasant, rustic. 66. **Ruth**: see the Bible story *Ruth*, ii. 68–70. Of these lines, and of lines 14–16 in *Kubla Khan* (316), Kipling wrote: "These are the pure Magic. These are the clear Vision. The rest is only Poetry." See if you can understand what he meant. 73. **fancy**: imagination.

291. Composed "on the roof of a coach" leaving London in the early morning. Wordsworth was on his way to France.

7. **Open unto the fields**: plainly visible from the outskirts of the city.

292. Note the subtle connection with the thought of the preceding sonnet.

7. **debonair**: graceful, pleasantly told. 10. **Philomel**: the nightingale.

293. Published in 1818. In its irony and stern restraint, the poem is unlike anything else that Shelley wrote. Ozymandias was a warlike king who lived about 1200 B.C.

Notes 585

7-8. survive . . . The hand, etc.: *i.e.*, the expression carved on the ruined face has outlived the hand of the sculptor and the heart of the king.

294. The lover of trees will sympathize with the sentiments expressed in this poem and that which follows. Which appeals to you more strongly? Neidpath Castle is mentioned in Scott's *Maid of Neidpath* (240). Scott himself greatly admired the sonnet, of which Wordsworth sent him a copy. "Few lines," says his biographer, Lockhart, "were more often in his mouth."

1. **Douglas**: William Douglas, Duke of Queensberry, who was said to have sold the timber on his estates to raise money for the race-course and the prize-ring. 11-14. Nature does not heed the havoc wrought by man. 12. **bays**: deep recesses in the woods.

295. Do you find an artificial note here? Campbell often followed the methods of eighteenth century poetry; see such expressions as "murmuring tribes," "ambrosial amber," and lines 25-27.

296. The three poems which are placed here were derived from incidents in Wordsworth's travels in the Highlands of Scotland. They were all written between 1803 and 1807.

297. Inversneyde is on Loch Lomond. 20. I know neither thee nor thy companions. 42. **a bondage sweetly brook'd**: *i.e.*, she bore gracefully her lack of English speech. 51. **homely ways and dress**: the customs and garb of your country. 72. **pleased at heart**: *i.e.*, pleased to have seen her.

298. A recent critic says that this poem is full of "magical" lines. One example of what he means is found in lines 17-20. Can you find some others?

299. Wood Street, Lothbury, and Cheapside are all in the heart of London. The subject is a common one — the lonely country girl in the city. How has Wordsworth lifted it above the commonplace?

Notes

300. This poem, with 307 and 308, was addressed to Mrs. Jane Williams, a close friend of Shelley and his wife while they lived in Italy. Ariel stands for Shelley; Ferdinand and Miranda for Mr. and Mrs. Williams. See Shakespeare's *The Tempest* for the names. The thought is developed with high imaginative grace.

7–12. In the last scene of *The Tempest*, Prospero commands Ariel to guide Ferdinand and Miranda safely home to Naples. 24. **her interlunar swoon**: the period of her invisibility. 39. Compare *Ode to the West Wind* (322), lines 55–56. 43. **idol**: the guitar. 57. **beneath heaven's fairest star**: in a most fortunate hour. 75. **mysterious sound**, etc.: the music made by the earth as it rolls through space. A reference to the "music of the spheres"; see note to 85, line 125.

301. One of the most familiar, as it is one of the most completely satisfying, of Wordsworth's shorter lyrics. He tells us that the flowers were growing on the banks of Ullswater, in the Lake District, near his home.

302. Burns wrote a poem *On a Mountain Daisy*, which might well be compared with this in order to study the difference in treatment. Wordsworth is cheered; Burns is saddened by the thoughts suggested.

9. **dappled**: spotted, or variegated, with daisies. 25. **Cyclops**: a mythical giant, with a single eye in the middle of his forehead.

303. A beautiful picture, full of rich imagery and the suggestion of peace. Note how the slow-moving stanzas, and the careful selection of musical words, add to the general effect. The poem was published in 1820.

2. **maturing**: ripening, bringing to maturity. 17. **Drows'd**: made drowsy. 18. **swath**: a row of wheat waiting to be reaped. 20. **laden head**: carrying a sheaf of wheat. 25. **barréd clouds**: lines of level clouds. **bloom**: tint with glowing colors. 30. **hilly bourn**: boundary of hills. 32. **garden-croft**: piece of land enclosed for a garden.

304. Published in 1801. The poem shows in a striking way the eighteenth century influences on Campbell's work. Note, in particular, the personification used throughout. It presents an interesting contrast in tone to the poems which precede and follow it.

11. **Calpe**: ancient name for Gibraltar — here used to indicate the Mediterranean lands in general. 14. **The Queen of vintage**: autumn, when the grape harvest is gathered. 19. **deer-borne car**: sledge drawn by reindeer. 21. **Lofoden**: a famous whirlpool (the maelstrom) off the northwest coast of Norway. 23. **Runic Odin**: the chief god of northern mythology; **Runic** stands for Scandinavian. 25. *I.e.*, when Winter moves south. 29. **light's returning Lord**: the summer sun. 34. **The Lapland drum**: the Lapps formerly had a wide reputation for divination and witchcraft, in which the drum played a prominent part. 54. **yonder tented shores**: this refers to the war between the French and Austrians, in which the battle of Hohenlinden was fought (see 259). 61–64. Pure eighteenth century moralizing.

305. [This lovely poem refers here and there to a ballad by Hamilton on the subject better treated in 163 and 164.] Yarrow is frequently mentioned in ballads of the Scottish Border.

5. **Clovenford**: where the road to Selkirk and Yarrow turns off. 6. **winsome Marrow**: the poet's sister Dorothy. 17. **Gala Water**: a tributary of the Tweed. **Leader Haughs**: see note to 164, line 20. 19. **Dryburgh**: east of Melrose, on the Tweed. 20. **lintwhites**: linnets. 21. **Tiviot-dale**: or Teviotdale, a district north of the Tweed. 33. **holms**: meadows by a river. 35. Taken directly from Hamilton's ballad. 37. **strath**: valley. 43. **St. Mary's Lake**: the Yarrow flows through this lake.

306. Written on a tour of the Highlands eleven years later. 25–32. See 163; but Wordsworth was thinking also of the other ballad by Hamilton, where the youth "lay bleeding." 40. **rueful**: melancholy. 55–56. **Newark's towers**: on the

Yarrow, five miles west of Selkirk. It is the scene of Scott's *Lay of the Last Minstrel*. 80. **Accordant**: in tune.

307. Originally published in 1824 as part of the poem which follows; the division was made in a later edition. The poems are addressed, as noted above, to Shelley's friend, Mrs. Williams. A very interesting study can be made here of the poet's treatment of light, and of his reaction to natural beauty.

9. **halcyon**: calm and beautiful; see note on 85, line 68. 28. Here Palgrave omits eighteen lines. Such omissions are always questionable, but in this case the passage is inferior to the rest of the poem. 40. **sets**: *i.e.*, closes. 41. **windflowers**: anemones. 45. **dun**: dark.

308. A fine example of memory colored by the light of imagination. Note the touch of melancholy at the close of the poem.

25. **azure breath**: the wind from the blue sky. Compare 307, line 11, and 322, line 9. 35–37. A remarkable touch of imaginative observation. 53–76. The intensity of feeling for beauty is characteristic of Shelley. 80. Compare 322, lines 33–36. 85–88. How do these lines blend themselves with the thought of the whole poem?

309. Wordsworth wrote this at Calais in August, 1802.

9. The poet's sister, Dorothy. 12. See *St. Luke*, xvi, 22. These closing lines refer very beautifully to purity of thought and life.

310. The first two lines, and the whole of the second stanza, show a sincerity of feeling which Campbell did not often command.

9. **herds are heard**: this must be noted as an example of faulty "assonance."

311. From a tragedy called *The Doom of Devorgoil*, which was published in 1830, but which was never acted. This song appears in the first act. The title (supplied by Palgrave) means "The hour is given to rest." 17. **row**: swim, paddle.

Notes 589

312. One is reminded of Sir Philip Sidney's sonnet beginning "With how sad steps, O Moon" (58). Shelley's lines form a fragment of an intended longer poem, which was not finished.

313. A good example, like *The Daffodils* (301), of Wordsworth's power to perceive the poetry of the commonplace. Most of us have tried to soothe ourselves to sleep; but the poet transmutes this familiar experience into something "rich and strange."

314. The thought and the metre are both conventional; does Campbell succeed in raising his poem above the commonplace?
6. **wolf-scaring faggot**: fires were lighted to keep the wolves away from the dead on the battle-field. The poem was written in 1807, when Europe was very familiar with war.

315. Published in 1822 and entitled *The Question*. Do you prefer Palgrave's title? What is the significance of the poem?
9. **pied wind-flowers**: vari-colored anemones. [10. **Arcturi**: seemingly used for *northern stars*.] Arcturus is the brightest star in the northern constellation Boötes. 11. **constellated**: star-like. **that never sets**: see 307, line 40. 13. **that tall flower**: probably the lily. 15. **Its mother's face**: the earth. 17. **eglantine**: sweet briar. 18. **cowbind**: bryony. **moonlight-colour'd May**: white hawthorn. 26. **prank'd**: decked out. 37. **imprison'd**: by the hand which held them. **Hours**: see note on 182, line 1.

316. [Coleridge describes this poem as the fragment of a dream-vision which composed itself in his mind when he had fallen asleep after reading a few lines about "the Khan Kubla" in Purchas's *Pilgrimage*.] His dream was interrupted by "a person on business from Porlock," and the marvellous fantasy was never finished. It must be read aloud (as indeed all poetry should be) to get the full effect.
14-16. See note on 290, lines 68-70.

317. Written in 1833. The title was given by Palgrave. Note that the sestet, in the manner of the Italianate sonnet, develops fully the thought of the octave. It is furthermore a statement of Wordsworth's theory that nothing was too humble for imaginative treatment in poetry.

10. **commerce:** intercourse, communion.

318. Published in 1820. Compare this poem with Milton's *L'Allegro* (144) and *Il Penseroso* (145). Fine as Keats's poem is, the reader will observe that Milton is more direct, less luxuriant, and touches a higher plane both of imagination and expression. It may be mentioned, incidentally, that Milton was 24 and Keats 25 when their respective poems were written.

2. The mind must range freely, to gain true pleasure. 16. **ingle:** chimney-corner, fire-place. Compare with this whole passage *Il Penseroso*, lines 77–120. 21. **shoon:** old form of "shoes." 22. *I.e.*, on dark winter afternoons. 38. **fit:** suitable. 51. **Shaded:** growing in the shade. 56. Thin from its winter sleep. 68. "Familiarity breeds contempt." 81. **Ceres' daughter:** Persephone, or Proserpina, who, in Greek mythology, was carried off by Pluto to the Underworld. He is called the God of Torment because he was in charge of sinners who were punished in Hades. 85. Hebe was the goddess of youth, and cup-bearer to the gods. 89. **languid:** Compare *Alexander's Feast* (151), line 96.

319. This is a bit of poetical moralizing. From what you have read in the poetry of Shelley and Keats, can you suggest the kind of inspiration which they would have received under like circumstances?

320. "This regrettable poem was the outcome of Wordsworth's theory that there is no essential difference between the language of poetry and that of prose." What should you say of this criticism after reading the poem?

20. **casque:** helmet. 22. **Cherokees:** an Indian tribe living, at the time, in Georgia. 28. The War of Independence ended in 1781. 55–72. Wordsworth had never been

in the tropics; note how his imagination transmutes book-knowledge into reality and beauty. 67. **savannahs**: wide plains. 203. **cheerful knell**: Compare 285, line 6. 214. **Tone**: a river in Somersetshire. 217. **The engines of her pain**: the elements of nature that had caused her sorrow. 246. **Quantock**: the Quantock Hills are in West Somersetshire. 254. **hallow'd mould**: the churchyard. Wordsworth has pictured here the influence of nature in forming an evil character; compare 222, which shows her influence for goodness and purity.

321. [The leading idea of this beautiful description of a day's landscape in Italy appears to be — On the voyage of life are many moments of pleasure, given by the sight of Nature, who has power to heal even the worldliness and uncharity of man.] The main idea is accompanied with many ethereal images, beautiful in themselves, and typical of the poet. Palgrave has omitted 182 lines. The Euganean Hills are in Italy, between Padua and Verona.

3–26. Compare the characteristic passage in Arnold's *A Summer Night*, lines 51–73. 32. **paean**: hymn to Apollo, the Sun-god. 41. **grain**: texture. 56. **Venice**: plainly visible, twenty miles away. 58. [**Amphitrite**: daughter to Ocean.] Venice stands on land reclaimed from the sea. 74. **the dome of gold**: the oracle of Apollo at Delphi. 76–102. Shelley here speaks of the political troubles of Venice. The city was annexed by the Austrians in 1814, and the poet suggests that she will be ruined by tyranny and abandoned to the sea. 83. **conquest-branded brow**: referring to the occupation by Napoleon in 1797; he is called "slave of slaves" in the next line. 101. **masque**: dance. 110. the highest point in the heavens. 124. **olive-sandall'd**: clothed with olive-trees at the foot. 133–137. Whether it (the "glory of the sky") be the spirit of nature, or come from my own mind which peoples a dead universe. 141. **her**: evening. 147. **that silent isle**: see lines 1, 2 and 27–30. 170–191. Such a "healing paradise" of beauty as the poet imagines would cure all the evil of the world. 180–187. The intervals in the music of nature would be filled with the music of the soul, and universal Love would bring the sense of brotherhood to all. 188. **They, not it**: the "polluting multitude," not the "healing paradise."

322. This poem was published in 1820. Shelley wrote it "on a day when that tempestuous wind, whose temperature is at once mild and animating, was collecting the vapours which pour down the autumnal rains." For general comment, see page 467. Note, throughout, the vigor and sustained imagery. A study of the words and phrases offers a valuable training for the reader.

9. **Thine azure sister of the Spring**: the east wind, bringing the blue skies of spring. 21. [**Maenad**: a frenzied Nymph, attendant on Dionysus.] 24. **closing**: coming, closing in. 32. **pumice**: a kind of lava — the whole district near Naples is volcanic. **Baiae's bay**: a beautiful inlet on the Bay of Naples, formerly a resort of the wealthy Romans. 41. [Plants under water sympathize with the seasons of the land, and hence with the winds which affect them.] 49. race with the wind and the clouds. 57. **Make me thy lyre**: use me to sound high thoughts throughout the world. 64. **quicken**: bring to life. Shelley longs for freedom, truth, and happiness for all mankind, and — like all great poets — he wants to play his part in bringing the new age.

323. [Written soon after the death, by shipwreck, of Wordsworth's brother John. The poem may be profitably compared with Shelley's following it. Each is the most complete expression of the innermost spirit of his art given by these great Poets: — of that Idea which, as in the case of the true Painter (to quote the words of Reynolds,) "subsists only in the mind: the sight never beheld it, nor has the hand expressed it: it is an idea residing in the breast of the artist, which he is always laboring to impart, and which he dies at last without imparting."] Peele Castle (or Piel) is a ruined keep on Piel Island off the coast of Lancashire. Sir George Beaumont was an

Notes

artist and a friend of Wordsworth's. The poem was written in 1805.

13–15. These famous lines express the magic nature of poetic inspiration. 36. *I.e.*, the death of his brother. 54. **the Kind**: the human race. 56–60. Judging from these lines, what should you say of Wordsworth's views as to the attitude of the human mind towards trouble and sorrow? How does his thought gain by being expressed in poetical form?

324. From the first act of *Prometheus Unbound*, published in 1820. In the play this song is sung by a Spirit. The thought in the last three lines is similar to lines 14–16 in the preceding poem; both may be compared to the famous passage in Shakespeare's *Midsummer Night's Dream*, Act V, Scene 1, lines 12–17.

325. Note the restraint and singleness of thought. Ossian was an ancient Gaelic poet. Some critics question the authenticity of his work.

326. A protest against the artificiality of life which deadens the soul to all the finer influences of nature. The sonnet might very well have been written at the present day, instead of more than a century ago.

3. **that is ours**: that makes any appeal to us. 10. **outworn**: obsolete, out of date. 13. **Proteus**: the old man of the sea, who looked after Neptune's seals. 14. **Triton**: son of Neptune; he calmed the sea by blowing a large conch-shell.

327. Said to have been written during a visit to his brother Christopher, Master of Trinity College, Cambridge, in 1820.

1. **Tax**: accuse. **the Royal Saint**: King Henry VI, who caused the chapel to be built. See notes to 160, line 89, and 199, line 4. 2. **ill-match'd aims**: in planning so magnificent a chapel for such a small number of scholars. 6–7. This might well serve as a motto for the builders of the great cathedrals and chapels of mediaeval times. 8. **for the sense**: *i.e.*, to delight the eye.

328. [Every one knows the general story of the Italian Renaissance, of the Revival of Letters. — From Petrarch's day to our own that ancient world has renewed its youth; poets and artists, students and thinkers, have yielded themselves wholly to its even fascination, and deeply penetrated its spirit. Yet perhaps no one more truly has vivified, whilst idealizing, the picture of Greek country life in the fancied Golden Age, than Keats in these lovely stanzas: — his quick imagination, by a kind of " natural magic," more than supplying the scholarship which his youth had no opportunity of gaining.] The central thought is that life and its pleasures must pass away, but beauty is eternal.

3. **Sylvan historian**: because its rustic decorations tell us of days long past. 7. **Tempe**: a vale in Thessaly. **Arcady**: in the Peloponnesus and always associated with pastoral life and pastoral poetry. 13. **sensual ear**: bodily ear. 35–40. This passage is infused with the purest imaginative beauty. 41. **Attic**: Attica was the centre of the highest Greek art. **brede**: decoration, adornment. 45. **Cold Pastoral**: because the scene is not living, but wrought on the urn. 49. '**Beauty is truth, truth beauty**': this idea lies at the basis of Keats's poetry.

329. Completed in 1832.

9. **This body that does me grievous wrong**: Coleridge had only himself to blame; he had ruined his health by the habit of taking opium. 12. **those trim skiffs**, etc.: steamboats. Steam navigation was tried in France as early as 1783, and on the Thames in 1801; a regular steamer service was established on the Clyde, in Scotland, in 1812. 27. **fond conceit**: foolish fancy. 34. **this alter'd size**: in his later years Coleridge became fat and unwieldy. 36. Tears are brightened with the sunshine from thine eyes. 49. **without the smile**: without winning a smile.

330. Like *Lucy Gray* (226), these two poems are marked by absolute simplicity. They were both written in 1799.

10. **steaming rills**: with the early morning mist. Compare 285, line 11.   56. **And did not wish her mine**: the memory of his dead daughter was more to him than any living child could be.   60. **wilding**: wild apple blossom.

331. This poem has some of the weaknesses that are seen in *Simon Lee* (263) and *Ruth* (320).

11. **catch**: round, or part-song.   41–44. Do you suppose that a student of bird-life would agree with this pleasant statement?   67. **glide**: "The use of this word here," says a critic, "is simply deplorable." Why?

332. A skilful treatment of a somewhat conventional idea. Note, however, the lack of true poetic feeling when compared with *The Human Seasons* (333) or *Threnos* (335).

333. Published in 1819. It has the tone of some of Shakespeare's sonnets; their joy in life and shrinking from death. Note especially the grim closing couplet.

4. **span**: grasp.   13. **misfeature**: when everything goes wrong, disaster, misfortune.

334. While he was not a pessimist, Shelley felt too deeply the sorrow of the world and of humanity to write always in a hopeful vein of life as he saw it.

3. **cloud**: thunder-cloud.   6. **stain**: probably the word ought to be "strain."

335. Written in 1821, a year before his death, with a sad premonition of what was coming. "Threnos" means a lament.

2–3. As when, in climbing a lofty cliff, one looks back in fear to the height traversed, but has to keep on climbing. 8. Possibly the word "autumn" should be inserted after "summer"; but Shelley did not write it, and no one else has the right to put it in.

336. The best description of the Trosachs is found in the famous passage in Scott's *Lady of the Lake*, Canto I. This is purely "objective," or concerned with the beauty of natural scenery; Wordsworth's sonnet is "subjective," dealing with the effect of this scenery upon the mind. 11. The robin redbreast. This line is a little labored.

337. Written in 1802. The poet hopes that the love of nature may be a consolation to him through life.

9. **natural piety**: the feeling of God's presence in nature.

338. This poem was written between 1802 and 1806. By many it is regarded as the greatest ode in our language. It will repay the most careful study both because of the sheer beauty of the language, and because it so admirably evinces that "high truth and seriousness" which characterizes the noblest poetry.

The actual meaning may be briefly paraphrased. The poet no longer finds in the world the keen delight which it gave in his childhood, yet the children he sees appear still to enjoy this. He feels, therefore, that the sense of glory — "the vision splendid" — which we bring with us from some previous existence is gradually lost as we acquire worldly growth and worldly customs. Yet it is not altogether lost; there come "obstinate questionings," and "high instincts," which help us to realize the deeper meaning of life.

We find here also the thought that underlies all Wordsworth's poetry. God is in the world and speaks to us through nature; customs and conventions, "getting and spending," should not be allowed to blind us to the deep truths of life — "truths that wake, to perish never." There is a divine meaning, says the poet, in all the beauty we see about us; to this meaning our own inner consciousness will respond; hence

"Thanks to the human heart by which we live . . .
   To me the meanest flower that blows can give
   Thoughts that do often lie too deep for tears."

21. **the tabor's sound**: the tabor was a small drum. 28. The figure here conveys the idea of peace and refreshment. 38. **jubilee**: rejoicing. 40. **coronal**: wreath. 58–65. Compare Vaughan's *The Retreat* (98). The doctrine of

Notes

the existence of the soul in a previous state is taught by the Buddhists and Brahmins; it enters also into Greek and Roman philosophy. Plato may be considered as a chief exponent of the theory. It is doubtful if Wordsworth held the belief literally. "It is far too shadowy a notion," he said, "to be recommended to faith as more than an element in our instincts of immortality. . . . I took hold of the notion of pre-existence as having sufficient foundation in humanity for authorizing me to make for my purpose the best use of it I could as a poet." 67. **Shades of the prison-house**: the cares and sorrows that life brings as we grow up. 71. **daily farther from the east**, etc.: *i.e.*, farther from the joys and ideals of childhood. 72. **Nature's priest**: still consecrated to the service of nature.

85. **the Child**: Hartley Coleridge, son of the poet, is referred to here. For the whole passage, compare Pope's *Essay on Man*, II, lines 275–282. 102. **cons**: studies. 103. '**humorous stage**': compare *As You Like It*, Act II, Scene 7, lines 139–166. "Humorous" means showing various moods, or humors. 104. **Persons**: characters in the play. 108. **Thou**: *i.e.*, the child. Coleridge, in his *Biographia Literaria*, made a sharp criticism of this stanza. "Now here, not to stop at the daring spirit of metaphor which connects the epithets 'deaf and silent' with the apostrophised *eye:* or (if we are to refer it to the preceding word 'Philosopher') the faulty and equivocal syntax of the passage; and without examining the propriety of making a 'Master *brood* o'er a slave,' or 'the Day' brood at all; we will merely ask, what does all this mean? In what sense is a child of that age a *Philosopher?*" The closing lines (123–128), however, need no defence. 123. **provoke**: call on, challenge. 141–142. Those doubts as to whether outward things are actually more real than the things of the imagination. To a child, especially, the world of the imagination is sometimes the more real of the two. 143. **Fallings from us**, etc.: the falling away, for a time, of the material world — as in moments of intense spiritual emotion. 148. **But for**: I raise the song of

thanks for. 160–167. A fine example of Wordsworth's high imaginative power. Note how the exaltation of thought is sustained throughout the two following stanzas. They are couched in a strain of lofty imagery, and infused with a noble wisdom.

339. Written in 1821. A simple and melodious little poem, beautifully contrasted with the deep thought and rich harmony of Wordsworth's lines.

3. **sicken**: lose their scent.   7. **thy thoughts**: the thoughts of thee — " Love shall find rest in thinking of thee, when thou art gone."

Questions and Topics for Discussion

1. Discuss the points of view suggested in the first two poems in this Book.

2. Make a list of the " bird " and the " flower " poems found in the Book. In each case, what is the dominant motive?

3. In what respects does the " personal lyric " in Book IV differ from the same type in Book I?

4. Comment upon the attitude of Wordsworth towards nature.

5. Compare, as regards diction and thought, the following sonnets: *On His Blindness* (94), *Bright Star!* (242), *Ozymandias of Egypt* (293).

6. Select a characteristic poem of Scott's. What are its intrinsic qualities? How do these qualities differentiate it from the work of Shelley?

7. Compare Wordsworth's poems on Yarrow (305, 306) with those in Book III on the same subject (163, 164).

8. Comment upon the ideas of war presented in *Hohenlinden* (259), *After Blenheim* (260), and *The Soldier's Dream* (314).

9. Select three short poems as characteristic of Byron, Shelley, and Keats, respectively. In each case, what do you

consider the most poetical quality? By what qualities, poetical and other, is each distinguished?

10. Write a comparative note on Wordsworth's *To the Skylark* (286) and Shelley's *To a Skylark* (287). Wherein is each poem characteristic of its author?

BIOGRAPHICAL SKETCHES

WILLIAM BLAKE (see page 563), because of the romantic element in his verse, might well have been placed in this book. Palgrave has chosen to represent him by one poem here, thus suggesting his connection with the later age.

GEORGE GORDON BYRON, Lord Byron, the English poet who, with the exception of Shakespeare, is most widely known on the Continent, was born in London on January 22, 1788. He was educated at Harrow School and Cambridge. He began to write poetry early; his first book, *Hours of Idleness*, appearing in 1807. When this volume was harshly treated by the critics, he turned upon them in his powerful satire, *English Bards and Scotch Reviewers*. In 1812, on his return from a tour of Europe and the Mediterranean, he published the first two Cantos of *Childe Harold's Pilgrimage*. This poem won for him instant fame — "I awoke one morning," he said, "to find myself famous." He left England in 1816, and passed the rest of his life on the Continent. Among his other works, besides a number of beautiful lyrics, may be mentioned *The Giaour*, *The Bride of Abydos*, Cantos III and IV of *Childe Harold*, and his unfinished masterpiece, *Don Juan*. He went to Greece to help in the War of Independence; contracted fever at Missolonghi, and died there on April 19, 1824.

THOMAS CAMPBELL is best known as a writer of battle lyrics. He was born at Glasgow in 1777, and first attracted attention by *The Pleasures of Hope* in 1799. He wrote several other long poems (*Gertrude of Wyoming*, *Theodoric*), but none of them have the poetic value of the shorter pieces included in this book. He died in 1844.

Notes

HARTLEY COLERIDGE, son of the great poet, was born in 1796. He went to Oxford, and then devoted himself to miscellaneous literary work. He was befriended by Wordsworth, and died at Grasmere in 1849.

SAMUEL TAYLOR COLERIDGE was born at Ottery St. Mary, in Devonshire, on October 21, 1772. He went to Christ's Hospital — the "Bluecoat School" — where he formed a lifelong friendship with Charles Lamb. His university training was received at Cambridge. Soon after leaving, he met Wordsworth, who exercised a profound influence upon him. Together they brought out the famous collection of poetry called *Lyrical Ballads* (1798), to which Coleridge's contribution was *The Ancient Mariner*. His poetry was very small in actual bulk, but its best showed a quality of imaginative beauty which has never been surpassed. All his best poetry was written before 1800. His splendid genius never attained its full development, chiefly owing to his fatal indulgence in opium. At the same time, he showed remarkable powers as critic, lecturer, and conversationalist. All in all, he was one of the most variously gifted among modern literary men. He died at Highgate, near London, on July 25, 1834.

ALLAN CUNNINGHAM was a Scotchman and was brought up as a stone-mason, but early showed a taste for writing poetry. His first poems were published in the guise of Scotch ballads in 1810. He issued a collection of English and Scotch folk-tales, and a large edition of *Songs of Scotland*. The latter included his famous sea-song (249). Cunningham was born in 1784, and died in 1842.

THOMAS HOOD, "the witty and the tender," as a friend called him, was a Londoner, born in 1799. His literary career concerned itself almost entirely with magazine writing and editing. From 1830 to the end of his life, he edited the *London Magazine*, the *Comic Annual*, the *New Monthly Magazine*, and *Hood's Magazine*. He was a master of the art of clever punning; but his serious poems, such as *The Bridge of Sighs* (274), show a far higher quality. He suffered much from ill-health, and died in 1845.

Notes

JOHN KEATS stands with Shelley and Byron in a group remembered for the glory of their poetic achievement and the untimely fate which cut them down. He was born in London on October 31, 1795, and began life as apprentice to a surgeon. But his tastes were not for medical studies. In 1812 a reading of Spenser's *Faery Queene* stirred him to a knowledge of his true bent. The first of his great sonnets — that on Chapman's Homer — appeared in 1815. His first volume of poems came out two years later; *Endymion* in 1818. His last volume was published in 1820; it contained, among other excellent poems, the two odes, *The Eve of Saint Agnes*, and the masterly fragment, *Hyperion*. He left England in 1820, and went to Italy in the vain hope of recovery from consumption. He died at Rome on February 23, 1821. Although his work was bitterly assailed by the reviewers during his life, his fame steadily grew. Today, he is ranked among the greatest English poets; it is a question, indeed, whether any other writer has achieved, at Keats's age, such sure mastery of his art.

CHARLES LAMB, loved by all who knew him not only for himself but also for the whimsical personal charm of his essays, was born in London on February 10, 1775. He was educated at Christ's Hospital — the "Bluecoat School," which he commemorated in one of the most interesting of the *Essays of Elia*. Here, as noted above, a warm friendship sprang up between him and Coleridge. Lamb entered the South Sea House, and in 1792 became a clerk in the East India Company, where he remained until superannuated in 1825. His best-known work is the *Essays of Elia*, published originally in the *London Magazine*. He was a keen critic of Shakespeare and the Elizabethan dramatists. With his sister, Mary, he wrote the famous *Tales from Shakespeare*. To the care of this sister Lamb's whole life was devoted; few things in literature are more touching than the essays (such as *Old China* and *Mackery End*) which reveal the affection that subsisted between them. He died at Edmonton, a London suburb, on December 27, 1834.

MARY LAMB was born in 1764. The tragedy of her life was a

tendency to insanity, which manifested itself in 1796 in a very dreadful way. Her brother Charles, as mentioned above, undertook the responsibility of her care; his devotion and her love form a pathetic and beautiful story. Mary collaborated with her brother in the *Tales from Shakespeare* and also in a collection of *Poetry for Children* (1809). She died in 1847.

HENRY FRANCIS LYTE is remembered chiefly for his beautiful hymn, *Abide with Me*. He was born in 1793, was educated at Trinity College, Dublin, and spent much of his time travelling on the Continent in search of health. He died at Nice in 1847.

THOMAS MOORE, very popular in his day as a writer of melodious lyrics, was born in Dublin on May 28, 1779. He was a close friend of Byron, of whom he published a voluminous biography. His chief poetical works were the *Irish Melodies* (1807-1834), and *Lalla Rookh*, a tale with an Eastern setting. He died on February 25, 1852.

SIR WALTER SCOTT was not only a poet and the creator of the historical novel, but a deep scholar and the author of excellent critical editions of Dryden and Swift. Tennyson called him the greatest man of letters of the nineteenth century. He was born at Edinburgh on August 15, 1771. He graduated from Edinburgh University, and became a lawyer, but was always strongly drawn to literature. In 1802 he published *The Minstrelsy of the Scottish Border*. This was followed by a series of great romantic poems — including *The Lay of the Last Minstrel* (1805), and *The Lady of the Lake* (1810). In 1814 he published his first novel, *Waverley*, the success of which determined his future career. In all, he wrote 32 novels. The short lyrics scattered through his works are invariably sincere and musical, and not seldom strike a high note of poetic feeling. He died at Abbotsford on September 21, 1832. His death is generally taken to mark the close of the "Romantic Revival."

PERCY BYSSHE SHELLEY, the most ethereal of English lyric poets, was born in Sussex on August 4, 1792. He was educated at Eton and Oxford, but was expelled from the University for publishing a tract on *The Necessity of Atheism*. His radical ideas led to a separation from his father, and later to his departure from England. On the Continent he became a close friend of Byron. The last years of his life were spent in Italy. He was drowned while sailing in the Adriatic off Spezzia on July 8, 1822. One of his greatest poems was the pastoral elegy *Adonais* (1821), written in memory of Keats. Other poems were: *Queen Mab, The Revolt of Islam, Prometheus Unbound,* and *The Cenci*, a tragedy.

ROBERT SOUTHEY was a voluminous writer of both prose and verse, including a few memorable ballads, such as *The Inchcape Rock*, and an excellent *Life of Nelson*. He was born on August 12, 1774, and educated at Westminster School and Oxford. After leaving the University he became deeply interested in the French Revolution, and like Coleridge and Wordsworth was for a time a strong radical. He married the sister of Coleridge's wife; when the latter proved incapable of supporting his family, Southey cared for them himself. Most of his life was passed at Keswick, in the Lake District. He wrote a number of epic poems which had a certain vogue in their day, and was made Poet Laureate in 1813. He lived a life, in a word, of honest literary labor, and died at Keswick on March 21, 1843.

CHARLES WOLFE was the author of one famous poem — 262 in this Book. He was born in Ireland in 1791, educated at Trinity College, Dublin, and went into the Church. He died at Queenstown in 1823.

WILLIAM WORDSWORTH, one of the greatest English poets, was born at Cockermouth, Cumberland, on April 7, 1770. He was educated at Cambridge, and having been strongly moved by the French Revolution, went to Paris with some idea of joining the Revolutionary army. He was extricated by his friends, however, and turned his energies to poetry. In 1798 he published with Coleridge the *Lyrical Ballads*. This has come to be recognized as the beginning of a new era in English poetry. For the Second Series, 1800, he wrote the well-known Preface that formulated his theory of perfect naturalness in poetic diction and thought.

Most of his life was passed in the Lake District, chiefly at Grasmere, where he exemplified the "plain living and high thinking" of one of his sonnets. On the death of Southey he was made Poet Laureate. He died at his home, Rydal Mount, on April 23, 1850. Although his poetry was not popular during his life, it has come to be acknowledged as attaining at its best the loftiest heights of English literature.

GENERAL QUESTIONS ON THE FOUR BOOKS

1. Compare some typical sonnets from Books I, II, and IV, treating them from the point of view of subject, tone, and diction.

2. Speaking of sonnets, Wordsworth said:

> "With this same key
> Shakespeare unlocked his heart."

To which Browning answered:

"*Did* Shakespeare? If so, the less Shakespeare he!"

What is your opinion, after reading the sonnets?

3. Make a list of the types of lyric poetry contained in the four Books — ode, sonnet, elegy, etc. What are the essential features of each?

4. Write an essay on the use of nature subjects in English poetry, illustrating from material drawn from the four Books.

5. Palgrave's inclusion of humorous poetry.

6. Compare the treatment of nature and natural objects in any selected group from the four Books. One such group might be, for example: *Summons to Love* (4), *L'Allegro* (144), *The Poplar Field* (183), and *Ode to a Nightingale* (290).

7. Make a list of the various stanza forms included in *The Golden Treasury*.

8. Compare poems dealing with similar subjects from different Books. For example: Marvell's *Thoughts in a Garden* (142) and Wordsworth's *Written in Early Spring* (319).

9. Make a detailed study of a single poet, as he is represented in *The Golden Treasury*. William Blake, for instance, forms a fruitful subject for investigation.

10. Study the poem as reflecting the mood of the poet. For example, in lighter mood: 26, 129, 173, 229; in a more serious vein: 46, 94, 162, 244.

11. Make a collection of your favorite poems from *The Golden Treasury*. Base your choice solely upon your personal taste and liking.

12. Compile groups of poems according to subject. For example, lyrics dealing with: Sleep, Death, War, Ingratitude, Ideals of Womanhood, The Poor, Music, and so forth.

EXAMINATION QUESTIONS

(The following questions are taken from examinations copyrighted by the College Entrance Examination Board, and are used by permission.)

1. Briefly show how, in choice of subject and in other respects, the lyric differs from other kinds of poetry. (You may illustrate your answer by referring by title to poems, by quoting single lines or short passages, or by using a longer continuous passage.)

2. What are the qualities of lyric poetry? Mention examples from Palgrave's *Golden Treasury* of (i) an ode, (ii) a sonnet, (iii) a song.

3. Name the author of each of *five* of the following quotations from *The Golden Treasury*, and the titles of *three* of the poems in which they occur. Give the thought of *one* poem in full, or quote at least twelve consecutive lines of *one* poem. [Eight quotations are given.]

4. [Keats's sonnet, *The Terror of Death*, is quoted in full.] How does the form of the foregoing sonnet differ from the sonnet form used by Wordsworth? Explain why Keats should be writing of death, and show how his desires as here expressed are partially, at least, realized in the *Ode to Autumn* and *Ode on a Grecian Urn*, or any other of his poems to which you may wish to refer.

5. [Wordsworth's *To a Skylark* is quoted in full.] (*a*) Why is *To a Skylark* correctly classed as a lyric? How does it differ in form from a sonnet? (*b*) If the poem contains a prominent idea, express it as definitely as you can in a sentence or two. (*c*) In what respects is the poem characteristic of Wordsworth rather than of Shelley?

6. (*a*) What resemblances do you find between *The Reaper* and *To the Highland Girl of Inversneyde?* Who wrote these two poems? (*b*) Name four odes you have studied in Book IV of *The Golden Treasury*. Give the author of each.

7. (*a*) What representative ideas of Wordsworth are found in the following poems: *The Daffodils, The Reverie of Poor Susan, Simon Lee, The Reaper, The World is Too Much with Us.* (*b*) In what other poems of the period are there similar ideas? Illustrate.

8. Show wherein the poet has advantages over the writer of prose. Support your argument by definite examples or references.

9. Characterize the man Milton from *L'Allegro, Il Penseroso,* and *Lycidas.*

10. In what poems of Scott, Coleridge, Wordsworth, and Shelley that you have read is there significant use of lake, river, or sea?

11. Choose from your reading five different poems. Make such a selection that in the five poems named the following characteristics shall be represented: (*a*) praise of a national hero, (*b*) a view of life, (*c*) melodious sound, (*d*) a description of humble and poor people, (*e*) allusions to Greek and Roman mythology. Summarize, or describe, in a sentence or two at least four of these poems.

12. There is poetry of thought, poetry of feeling, poetry of incident. Name one poem of each kind and state its main theme.

13. What pleasure and interest do you find in reading poetry that you do not find in reading prose? Illustrate your answer by reference to specific poems.

14. Choose from the poems that you have read six which

you would recommend to a friend of your own age. Give in each case the reasons for your choice.

15. "Most of the great poets have done their best work in lyric form." — Tennyson. Comment upon this statement in the light of your reading in *The Golden Treasury*.

In general, the questions asked in class or set for school examinations may be based upon the following scheme:

1. Questions on the characteristics of the Book.
2. Questions on the poem-group of each writer.
3. Questions on certain individual poems.
4. Questions involving a comparison or a contrast.
5. Questions correlating the poem with literary history.

Certain men and certain poetical types may call for more detailed study. For example: in Book I, the sonnet and the songs from Shakespeare; in Book II the Milton poems and the Italianate sonnet form; in Book III, the ode, and the Scotch lyrics; in Book IV, the freedom of poetic form, the development in choice of topic, the poetical theories of Wordsworth, Byron, Shelley, and Keats.

The books listed below may be profitably used in connection with the study of Palgrave.

English Lyrical Poetry, Edward Bliss Reed. Yale University Press.

A History of English Literature, W. A. Neilson and A. H. Thorndike. The Macmillan Company.

Essentials of Poetry, W. A. Neilson. Houghton Mifflin Company.

Classic Myths in English Literature, C. M. Gayley. Ginn and Company.

Excellent literary biographies are found in *The Dictionary of National Biography*, Oxford University Press; *English Men of Letters*, The Macmillan Company; and *Great Writers*, Charles Scribner's Sons. Separate works dealing with individual poets are too numerous to mention; literary criticism of great value, however, is contained in *Elizabethan Literature* and *Nineteenth Century Literature*, by George Saintsbury, and in *Eighteenth Century Literature*, by Edmund Gosse.

INDEX

INCLUDING AUTHORS, TITLES, AND FIRST LINES

[References are to pages.]

A Chieftain to the Highlands bound, 271
A child's a plaything for an hour, 346
A flock of sheep that leisurely pass by, 394
A slumber did my spirit seal, 270
A sweet disorder in the dress, 120
A weary lot is thine, fair maid, 289
A wet sheet and a flowing sea, 301
Absence, 11
Absence, 234
Absence, hear thou this protestation, 10
Admonition to a Traveller, 366
Advice to a Girl, 20
Advice to a Lover, 40
Affliction of Margaret, The, 347
After Blenheim, 313
Agnes, 341
Ah, Chloris! could I now but sit, 109
Ah! County Guy, the hour is nigh, 279
Alexander's Feast, or, the Power of Music, 163
ALEXANDER, WILLIAM (1567?–1640), 505
All for Love, 260
All in the Downs the fleet was moor'd, 191
All thoughts, all passions, all delights, 256
And are ye sure the news is true? 231
And is this — Yarrow? — This the Stream, 383
And thou art dead, as young and fair, 296
And wilt thou leave me thus? 32
Ariel to Miranda: — Take, 371
Art thou pale for weariness, 394

609

Index

Art thou poor, yet hast thou golden slumbers? 61
As it fell upon a day, 33
As I was walking all alane, 135
As slow our ship her foamy track, 322
At a Solemn Music, 158
At the corner of Wood Street, when daylight appears, 370
At the mid hour of night, when stars are weeping, I fly, 295
Auld Robin Gray, 229
Avenge, O Lord! Thy slaughter'd saints, whose bones, 80
Awake, Aeolian lyre, awake, 201
Awake, awake, my Lyre! 127

Ballad, 452
BARBAULD, ANNA LETITIA (1743–1825), 563
Bard, The, 179
Bards of Passion and of Mirth, 254
BARNARD (*See* Lindsay)
BARNEFIELD, RICHARD (1574–1627), 505
Basia, 19
Battle of the Baltic, 303
BEAUMONT, FRANCIS (1584–1616), 540
Beauty sat bathing by a spring, 16
Beech Tree's Petition, The, 365
Behold her, single in the field, 369
Being your slave, what should I do but tend, 11
Beneath these fruit-tree boughs that shed, 356
Best and brightest, come away, 386
Bid me to live, and I will live, 122
Black-Eyed Susan, 191
BLAKE, WILLIAM (1757–1827), 563
Blest pair of Sirens, pledges of Heaven's joy, 158
Blind Boy, The, 174
Blind Love, 37
Blow, blow, thou winter wind, 41
Bonnie Lesley, 226
Braes of Yarrow, The, 186
Bridge of Sighs, The, 332

Index

Bright Star! would I were steadfast as thou art, 293
Burial of Sir John Moore at Corunna, The, 316
BURNS, ROBERT (1759–1796), 563
By the Sea, 391
BYRON, GEORGE NOEL GORDON (1788–1824), 599

Call for the robin-redbreast and the wren, 49
Calm was the day, and through the trembling air, 55
CAMPBELL, THOMAS (1777–1844), 599
CAMPION, THOMAS (c. 1567–1619), 505
Captain, or Colonel, or Knight in Arms, 95
Care-charmer Sleep, son of the sable Night, 34
CAREW, THOMAS (1598?–1638), 541
CAREY, HENRY (— –1743), 564
Carpe Diem, 26
Castaway, The, 248
Character of a Happy Life, 96
Cherry-Ripe, 116
Child and Maiden, 109
CIBBER, COLLEY (1671–1757), 564
COLERIDGE, HARTLEY (1796–1849), 600
COLERIDGE, SAMUEL TAYLOR (1772–1834), 600
Colin, 16
COLLINS, JOHN (1752–1808), 564
COLLINS, WILLIAM (1721–1759), 564
Come away, come away, Death, 47
Come, cheerful day, part of my life to me, 62
Come little babe, come silly soul, 42
Come live with me and be my Love, 6
Come Sleep: O Sleep! the certain knot of peace, 29
Come unto these yellow sands, 2
Composed at Neidpath Castle, the Property of Lord Queensberry, 1803, 364
Consolation, A, 12
Constancy, 110
Corinna's Maying, 117
Coronach, 339

Index

Counsel to Girls, 110
COWLEY, ABRAHAM (1618-1667), 541
COWPER, WILLIAM (1731-1800), 564
Crabbed Age and Youth, 8
Cradle Song, A, 211
CRASHAW, RICHARD (1613?-1649), 541
CUNNINGHAM, ALLAN (1784-1842), 600
Cupid and Campaspe, 53
Cupid and my Campaspé play'd, 53
Cyriack, whose grandsire, on the royal bench, 101

Daffodils, The, 374
DANIEL, SAMUEL (1562-1619), 505
Datur Hora Quieti, 393
Daughter of Jove, relentless power, 242
Daughter to that good Earl, once President, 113
Death Bed, The, 340
Death the Leveller, 94
Degenerate Douglas! oh, the unworthy lord! 364
DEKKER, THOMAS (1570?-1641?), 505
Desideria, 294
DEVEREUX, ROBERT, Earl of Essex (1566-1601), 505
Dilemma, A, 51
Dirge, A, 439
Dirge of Love, 47
Ditty, A, 24
DONNE, JOHN (1573?-1631), 506
Doth then the world go thus, doth all thus move? 65
Down in yon garden sweet and gay, 188
Dramatic Poetry, 452
DRAYTON, MICHAEL (1563-1631), 506
Dream of the Unknown, A, 396
Drink to me only with thine eyes, 116
DRUMMOND, WILLIAM (1585-1649), 506
DRYDEN, JOHN (1631-1700), 541
Duncan Gray, 230
Duncan Gray cam here to woo, 230

Index

Earl March look'd on his dying child, 292
Earth has not anything to show more fair, 362
Echoes, 278
Education of Nature, The, 268
E'en like two little bank-dividing brooks, 122
Elegy, 462, 463
Elegy, 336
Elegy on Thyrza, 296
Elegy Written in a Country Churchyard, 220
Elizabeth of Bohemia, 112
ELLIOT, JEAN (1727–1805), 565
Encouragements to a Lover, 127
England and Switzerland, 1802, 308
Epic, 451
Eternal Spirit of the chainless Mind! 308
Ethereal minstrel! pilgrim of the sky! 351
Ever let the Fancy roam, 400

Fain would I change that note, 7
Fair Daffodils, we weep to see, 140
Fair pledges of a fruitful tree, 139
Fair Helen, 133
Fairy Life, The, (i), 2; (ii), 2
Farewell, A, 195
Farewell! thou art too dear for my possessing, 30
Fear no more the heat o' the sun, 48
Fidele, 48
Figures of Speech, 463–465
Fine knacks for ladies, cheap, choice, brave, and new, 26
FLETCHER, JOHN (1579–1625), 541
Flight of Love, The, 290
Follow thy fair sun, unhappy shadow! 36
For ever, Fortune, wilt thou prove, 198
Forget not yet the tried intent, 21
Forsaken, 131
Fortunati Nimium, 145
Fountain, The, 434

Index

Four Seasons fill the measure of the year, 438
Friends in Paradise, 138
From Harmony, from heavenly Harmony, 78
From Stirling Castle we had seen, 381
Frustra, 35
Full fathom five thy father lies, 49

Gather ye rose-buds while ye may, 110
Gathering Song of Donald the Black, 299
GAY, JOHN (1685–1732), 565
Gem of the crimson-colour'd Even, 280
Get up, get up, for shame! The blooming morn, 117
Gifts of God, The, 98
Girl Describes Her Fawn, The, 141
Glen-Almain, the Narrow Glen, 426
Go fetch to me a pint o' wine, 195
Go, lovely Rose, 115
GOLDSMITH, OLIVER (1728–1774), 565
GRAHAM, ROBERT (1735–1797), 565
GRAY, THOMAS (1716–1771), 566
Great Adventurer, The, 105
Green Linnet, The, 356
GREENE, ROBERT (1558?–1592), 506

HABINGTON, WILLIAM (1605–1654), 541
Hail thou most sacred venerable thing! 161
Hail to thee, blithe Spirit! 352
Happy Heart, The, 61
Happy Insensibility, 285
Happy the man, whose wish and care, 173
Happy those early days, when I, 99
Happy were he could finish forth his fate, 66
He is gone on the mountain, 339
He sang of God, the mighty source, 210
He that loves a rosy cheek, 113
Hence, all you vain delights, 130
Hence, loathéd Melancholy, 146

Index

Hence, vain deluding Joys, 151
HERBERT, GEORGE (1593–1633), 542
HERRICK, ROBERT (1591–1674), 542
Hester, 337
HEYWOOD, THOMAS (1575?–1648?), 506
Highland Mary, 227
High-way, since you my chief Parnassus be, 10
Hohenlinden, 312
Honest Autolycus, An, 26
HOOD, THOMAS (1799–1845), 600
Horatian Ode upon Cromwell's Return from Ireland, 81
How happy is he born and taught, 96
How like a winter hath my absence been, 12
How sleep the brave, who sink to rest, 184
How sweet the answer Echo makes, 278
How vainly men themselves amaze, 142
Human Seasons, The, 438
Hunting Song, 350
Hymn in Praise of Neptune, A, 101
Hymn to Adversity, 242
Hymn to Darkness, 161
Hymn to Diana, 102

I am monarch of all I survey, 243
I arise from dreams of Thee, 263
I cannot change, as others do, 110
I dream'd that as I wander'd by the way, 396
I fear thy kisses, gentle maiden, 267
I have had playmates, I have had companions, 321
'I have no name,' 210
I heard a thousand blended notes, 403
I meet thy pensive, moonlight face, 270
I met a traveller from an antique land, 363
I remember, I remember, 326
I saw Eternity the other night, 162
I saw her in childhood, 341
I saw my Lady weep, 23

I saw where in the shroud did lurk, 344
I travell'd among unknown men, 268
I wander'd lonely as a cloud, 374
I was thy neighbour once, thou rugged Pile! 423
I wish I were where Helen lies, 133
Idyl, 452
If aught of oaten stop or pastoral song, 217
If doughty deeds my lady please, 195
If I had thought thou couldst have died, 338
If Thou survive my well-contented day, 50
If to be absent were to be, 126
Il Penseroso, 151
I'm wearing awa', Jean, 236
In a drear-nighted December, 285
In Imagine Pertransit Homo, 36
In Lacrimas, 23
In Memoriam, 346
In the downhill of life, when I find I'm declining, 251
In the sweet shire of Cardigan, 317
In this still place, remote from men, 426
In Xanadu did Kubla Khan, 397
Indian Serenade, The, 263
Infant Joy, 210
Inner Vision, The, 399
Invitation, The, 386
It is a beauteous evening, calm and free, 391
It is not growing like a tree, 97
It was a dismal and a fearful night, 136
It was a lover and his lass, 9
It was a summer evening, 313
I've heard them lilting at our ewe-milking, 185

Jack and Joan, they think no ill, 145
Jean, 234
Jock of Hazeldean, 276
John Anderson, 235
John Anderson my jo, John, 235

Index

JONSON, BEN (1573–1637), 542
Journey Onwards, The, 322

KEATS, JOHN (1795–1821), 601
Kubla Khan, 397

La Belle Dame sans Merci, 287
Lady, when I behold the roses sprouting, 51
L'Allegro, 146
LAMB, CHARLES (1775–1834), 601
LAMB, MARY (1764–1847), 601
Lament, A, 46
Lament for Culloden, 184
Lament for Flodden, 185
Land Dirge, A, 49
Land o' the Leal, The, 236
Last Conqueror, The, 93
Lawrence, of virtuous father virtuous son, 100
Lesson, A, 325
Lessons of Nature, The, 64
Let me not to the marriage of true minds, 24
Life! I know not what thou art, 252
Life without Passion, The, 31
Light of Other Days, The, 327
Like as the waves make towards the pebbled shore, 30
Like to the clear in highest sphere, 14
LINDSAY, LADY ANNE (1750–1825), 566
Lo! where the rosy-bosom'd Hours, 212
LODGE, THOMAS (1558?–1625), 507
LOGAN, JOHN (1748–1788), 566
London, 1802, 310
Lord Ullin's Daughter, 271
Loss of the Royal George, 189
Lost Love, A, 270
Love, 256
Love in my bosom like a bee, 52
Love in thy youth, fair Maid, be wise, 114

Index

Love not me for comely grace, 123
LOVELACE, RICHARD (1618–1658), 542
Lover's Appeal, The, 32
Love's Farewell, 36
Love's Insight, 25
Love's Omnipresence, 25
Love's Perjuries, 21
Love's Philosophy, 278
Love's Secret, 199
Lucy Gray, 274
Lycidas, 86
LYLY, JOHN (1553–1606), 507
LYTE, HENRY FRANCIS (1793–1847), 602

Madrigal, A, 8
Maid of Neidpath, The, 291
The man of life upright, 63
Manly Heart, The, 128
Many a green isle needs must be, 414
MARLOWE, CHRISTOPHER (1564–1593), 507
MARVELL, ANDREW (1621–1678), 543
Mary! I want a lyre with other strings, 245
Mary Morison, 225
Melancholy, 130
Memory, 28
Mermaid Tavern, The, 330
Metre, 455–459
MICKLE, WILLIAM JULIUS (1735–1788), 566
MILTON, JOHN (1608–1674), 543
Milton! thou shouldst be living at this hour, 310
Mine be a cot beside the hill, 217
Moon, The, 44
MOORE, THOMAS (1779–1852), 602
Mortality, behold and fear, 92
Most sweet it is with unuplifted eyes, 399
Much have I travell'd in the realms of gold, 255
MUNDAY, ANTHONY (1553–1633) (*See* The Shepherd Tonie)

Index 619

Music, when soft voices die, 448
Musical Settings, 477–484
My days among the Dead are past, 329
My heart aches, and a drowsy numbness pains, 359
My heart leaps up when I behold, 440
My love in her attire doth shew her wit, 121
My lute, be as thou wert when thou didst grow, 47
My thoughts hold mortal strife, 46
My true-love hath my heart, and I have his, 24
Mystical Ecstasy, A, 122

NAIRNE, CAROLINA OLIPHANT, Baroness (1766–1845), 566
Narrative Poetry, 451, 452
NASH, THOMAS (1567–1600?), 507
Nature and the Poet, 423
Never love unless you can, 20
Never seek to tell thy love, 199
Nightingale, The, 33
No longer mourn for me when I am dead, 50
Noble Nature, The, 97
NORRIS, JOHN (1657–1711), 543
Not a drum was heard, not a funeral note, 316
Not, Celia, that I juster am, 124
Now the golden Morn aloft, 169
Now the last day of many days, 388
Nox Nocti Indicat Scientiam, 159

O blithe new-comer! I have heard, 358
O Brignall banks are wild and fair, 261
O Crudelis Amor, 44
O Friend! I know not which way I must look, 310
O happy shades! to me unblest! 241
O if thou knew'st how thou thyself dost harm, 22
O leave this barren spot to me! 365
O listen, listen, ladies gay! 342
O lovers' eyes are sharp to see, 291
O Mary, at thy window be, 225

O me! what eyes hath Love put in my head, 37
O Mistress mine, where are you roaming? 26
O my Luve's like a red, red rose, 227
O never say that I was false of heart, 13
O saw ye bonnie Lesley, 226
O say what is this thing call'd Light, 174
O talk not to me of a name great in story, 260
O Thou, by Nature taught, 171
O waly waly up the bank, 131
'O what can ail thee, knight-at-arms,' 287
O wild West Wind, thou breath of Autumn's being, 420
O World! O Life! O Time! 439
Obscurest night involved the sky, 248
Ode, 461–462
Ode on a Distant Prospect of Eton College, 237
Ode on a Grecian Urn, 428
Ode on Intimations of Immortality from Recollections of Early Childhood, 441
Ode on the Morning of Christ's Nativity, 69
Ode on the Pleasure Arising from Vicissitude, 169
Ode on the Poets, 254
Ode on the Spring, 212
Ode to a Nightingale, 359
Ode to Autumn, 377
Ode to Duty, 306
Ode to Evening, 217
Ode to Simplicity, 171
Ode to the West Wind, 420
Ode to Winter, 378
Ode Written in 1746, 184
Of all the girls that are so smart, 193
Of a' the airts the wind can blaw, 234
Of Nelson and the North, 303
Of Neptune's empire let us sing, 101
Of this fair volume which we World do name, 64
Oft I had heard of Lucy Gray, 274
Oft in the stilly night, 327

Index

Oh snatch'd away in beauty's bloom! 336
Old Familiar Faces, The, 321
Omnia Vincit, 7
On a day, alack the day! 21
On a Favourite Cat, Drowned in a Tub of Gold Fishes, 175
On a Girdle, 121
On a Poet's lips I slept, 425
On an Infant Dying as Soon as Born, 344
On First Looking into Chapman's Homer, 255
On His Blindness, 95
On Linden, when the sun was low, 312
On the Castle of Chillon, 308
On the Death of Mr. William Hervey, 136
On the Extinction of the Venetian Republic, 309
On the Late Massacre in Piedmont, 80
On the Tombs in Westminster Abbey, 92
Once did She hold the gorgeous East in fee, 309
One more Unfortunate, 332
One word is too often profaned, 298
Oral Work, 474–477
Our bugles sang truce, for the night-cloud had lower'd, 395
Outlaw, The, 261
Over the mountains, 105
Ozymandias of Egypt, 363

Pack, clouds, away, and welcome day, 54
PALGRAVE, FRANCIS TURNER (1824–1897), 504
Passionate Shepherd to His Love, The, 6
Passions, The, 205
Past and Present, 326
PHILIPS, AMBROSE (1675–1749), 567
Phoebus, arise, 3
Pibroch of Donuil Dhu, 299
Picture, A, 17
Picture of Little T. C. in a Prospect of Flowers, The, 107
Poet's Dream, The, 425
Poetry of Dress, The (i, ii), 120; (iii), 121

Index

Poor Soul, the centre of my sinful earth, 63
POPE, ALEXANDER (1688–1744), 567
Poplar Field, The, 214
Post Mortem, 50
Present in Absence, 10
Pride of Youth, The, 331
PRIOR, MATTHEW (1664–1721), 567
Pro Patria Mori, 315
Progress of Poesy, The, 201
Prothalamion, 55
Proud Maisie is in the wood, 331

QUARLES, FRANCIS (1592–1644), 543
Queen and Huntress, chaste and fair, 102

Realm of Fancy, The, 400
Reaper, The, 369
Recollection, The, 388
Renunciation, A, 40
Retreat, The, 99
Reverie of Poor Susan, The, 370
Revolutions, 30
Rhythm, 455
River of Life, The, 437
ROGERS, SAMUEL (1763–1855), 567
Romance, 452
Rosabelle, 342
Rosaline, 14
Rosalynd's Madrigal, 52
Rough wind, that moanest loud, 439
Rover, The, 289
'Ruin seize thee, ruthless King!' 179
Rule Britannia, 177
Ruth: or the Influences of Nature, 404

Sailor's Wife, The, 231
Saint John Baptist, 67

Index

Sally in Our Alley, 193
Same, The (See *London, 1802*), 310
Scholar, The, 329
SCOTT, SIR WALTER (1771–1832), 602
Sea Dirge, A, 49
Season of mists and mellow fruitfulness, 377
SEDLEY, SIR CHARLES (1639–1701), 544
See with what simplicity, 107
Sephestia's Song to Her Child, 45
Serenade, A, 279
SHAKESPEARE, WILLIAM (1564–1616), 507
Shall I compare thee to a summer's day? 18
Shall I, wasting in despair, 128
She dwelt among the untrodden ways, 267
She is not fair to outward view, 266
She walks in beauty, like the night, 264
She was a Phantom of delight, 265
SHELLEY, PERCY BYSSHE (1792–1822), 602
SHEPHERD TONIE, THE, 507
SHIRLEY, JAMES (1596–1666), 544
Shrubbery, The, 241
Sic Transit, 62
SIDNEY, SIR PHILIP (1554–1586), 508
Simon Lee the Old Huntsman, 317
Since brass, nor stone, nor earth, nor boundless sea, 5
Since there's no help, come let us kiss and part, 36
Sleep, 29
Sleep, angry beauty, sleep and fear not me! 38
Sleep on, and dream of Heaven awhile, 197
Sleep, sleep, beauty bright, 211
Sleeping Beauty, The, 197
SMART, CHRISTOPHER (1722–1771), 567
Soldier's Dream, The, 395
Solitude, 173
Solitude of Alexander Selkirk, The, 243
Song for Music, A, 17
Song for St. Cecilia's Day, 1687, 78

Song of David, The, 210
Song of the Emigrants in Bermuda, 157
Song to the Evening Star, 392
Sonnet, 460, 461
Soul and Body, 63
Souls of Poets dead and gone, 330
SOUTHEY, ROBERT (1774–1843), 603
SPENSER, EDMUND (1552–1599), 508
Spring, 1
Spring, the sweet Spring, is the year's pleasant king, 1
Stanza, 459, 460
Stanzas Written in Dejection near Naples, 328
Star that bringest home the bee, 392
Stern Daughter of the Voice of God! 306
SUCKLING, SIR JOHN (1609–1642), 544
Suggestions for Study, 465–473
Summons to Love, 3
Supplication, A, 21
Supplication, A, 127
Surprized by joy — impatient as the wind, 294
Sweet, be not proud of those two eyes, 114
Sweet Highland Girl, a very shower, 366
Sweet Love, if thou wilt gain a monarch's glory, 17
Sweet Lullaby, A, 42
Sweet stream, that winds through yonder glade, 197
Swiftly walk over the western wave, 281
SYLVESTER, JOSHUA (1563–1618), 509

Take, O take those lips away, 35
Tax not the royal Saint with vain expense, 428
Tell me not, Sweet, I am unkind, 111
Tell me where is Fancy bred, 51
Terror of Death, The, 294
That time of year thou may'st in me behold, 28
That which her slender waist confined, 121
The curfew tolls the knell of parting day, 220
The forward youth that would appear, 81

Index

The fountains mingle with the river, 278
The glories of our blood and state, 94
The last and greatest Herald of Heaven's King, 67
The lovely lass o' Inverness, 184
The man of life upright, 63
The merchant, to secure his treasure, 198
The more we live, more brief appear, 437
The nightingale, as soon as April bringeth, 34
The poplars are fell'd; farewell to the shade, 214
The sea hath many thousand sands, 40
The sun is warm, the sky is clear, 328
The sun upon the lake is low, 393
The twentieth year is well-nigh past, 246
The World is too much with us; late and soon, 427
There be none of Beauty's daughters, 263
There is a Flower, the lesser Celandine, 325
There is a garden in her face, 116
There's not a joy the world can give like that it takes away, 323
There's not a nook within this solemn Pass, 440
There was a time when meadow, grove, and stream, 441
They are all gone into the world of light! 138
They that have power to hurt, and will do none, 31
This is the month, and this the happy morn, 69
This Life, which seems so fair, 62
THOMSON, JAMES (1700-1748), 567
Thou art not fair, for all thy red and white, 40
Thou still unravish'd bride of quietness, 428
Though others may Her brow adore, 25
Thoughts in a Garden, 142
Three years she grew in sun and shower, 268
Threnos, 439
Thy braes were bonny, Yarrow stream, 186
Time and Love, (i), 4; (ii), 5
Timely blossom, Infant fair, 176
Tired with all these, for restful death I cry, 66
To a Distant Friend, 283
To a Lady, with a Guitar, 371

Index

To a Mouse, 215
To a Skylark, 352
To a Young Lady, 197
To Althea from Prison, 124
To Anthea Who May Command Him Any Thing, 122
To Aurora, 22
To Blossoms, 139
To Celia, 116
To Charlotte Pulteney, 176
To Cyriack Skinner, 101
To Daffodils, 140
To Dianeme, 114
To His Love, 18
To His Love, 18
To His Lute, 47
To Life, 252
To Lucasta, on Going beyond the Seas, 126
To Lucasta, on Going to the Wars, 111
To Mary, 338
To Mary Unwin, 245
To me, fair Friend, you never can be old, 14
To Mr. Lawrence, 100
To one who has been long in city pent, 363
To Sleep, 394
To the Cuckoo, 358
To the Daisy, 375
To the Evening Star, 280
To the Highland Girl of Inversneyde, 366
To the Lady Margaret Ley, 113
To the Moon, 394
To the Muses, 253
To the Night, 281
To the Same (See *To Mary Unwin*), 246
To the Skylark, 351
Toll for the Brave! 189
Tomorrow, 251
Triumph of Death, The, 50

Index

Trosachs, The, 440
True Beauty, The, 113
True Love, 24
Turn back, you wanton flyer, 19
Twa Corbies, The, 135
'Twas at the royal feast for Persia won, 163
'Twas on a lofty vase's side, 175
Two April Mornings, The, 432
Two Voices are there; one is of the Sea, 308

Unchangeable, The, 13
Under the greenwood tree, 8
Unfaithful Shepherdess, The, 38
Upon my lap my sovereign sits, 132
Upon Westminster Bridge, Sept. 3, 1802, 362

VAUGHAN, HENRY (1622–1695), 544
Verse, a breeze 'mid blossoms straying, 430
Via Amoris, 10
Victorious men of earth, no more, 93
Vision, A, 162

Waken, lords and ladies gay, 350
WALLER, EDMUND (1606–1687), 544
We talk'd with open heart, and tongue, 434
We walk'd along, while bright and red, 432
We watch'd her breathing thro' the night, 340
WEBSTER, JOHN (1580?–1625), 509
Wee, sleekit, cow'rin', tim'rous beastie, 215
Weep not, my wanton, smile upon my knee, 45
Weep you no more, sad fountains, 17
Were I as base as is the lowly plain, 25
Whenas in silks my Julia goes, 120
When Britain first at Heaven's command, 177
When first the fiery-mantled Sun, 378
When God at first made Man, 98
When he who adores thee has left but the name, 315

When icicles hang by the wall, 27
When I consider how my light is spent, 95
When I have borne in memory what has tamed, 311
When I have fears that I may cease to be, 294
When I have seen by Time's fell hand defaced, 4
When I survey the bright, 159
When I think on the happy days, 234
When in disgrace with fortune and men's eyes, 12
When in the chronicle of wasted time, 18
When lovely woman stoops to folly, 200
When Love with unconfinèd wings, 124
When maidens such as Hester die, 337
When Music, heavenly maid, was young, 205
When Ruth was left half desolate, 404
When the Assault Was Intended to the City, 95
When the lamp is shatter'd, 290
When the sheep are in the fauld, and the kye at hame, 229
When thou must home to shades of underground, 44
When to the sessions of sweet silent thought, 28
When we two parted, 283
Where art thou, my beloved Son, 347
Where shall the lover rest, 286
Where the bee sucks, there suck I, 2
Where the remote Bermudas ride, 157
Whether on Ida's shady brow, 253
While that the sun with his beams hot, 38
Whoe'er she be, 103
Why art thou silent? Is thy love a plant, 283
Why so pale and wan, fond lover? 127
'Why weep ye by the tide, ladie?' 276
Willy Drowned in Yarrow, 188
WILMOT, JOHN, Earl of Rochester (1647–1680), 545
Winter, 27
Wish, A, 66
Wish, A, 217
Wishes for the Supposed Mistress, 103
With how sad steps, O Moon, thou climb'st the skies! 44

Index

With little here to do or see, 375
With sweetest milk and sugar first, 141
WITHER, GEORGE (1588–1667), 545
Within King's College Chapel, Cambridge, 428
WOLFE, CHARLES (1791–1823), 603
WORDSWORTH, WILLIAM (1770–1850), 603
World's Way, The, 66
WOTTON, HENRY (1568–1639), 545
Written among the Euganean Hills, 414
Written in Early Spring, 403
WYATT, SIR THOMAS (1503–1542), 509

Yarrow Unvisited, 1803, 381
Yarrow Visited, 1814, 383
Ye banks and braes and streams around, 227
Ye banks and braes o' bonnie Doon, 200
Ye distant spires, ye antique towers, 237
Ye Mariners of England, 302
Yes, there is holy pleasure in thine eye! 366
Yet once more, O ye laurels, and once more, 86
You meaner beauties of the night, 112
Young Love, 51
Youth and Age, 323
Youth and Age, 430

GROUP-INDEX OF POEMS

In the following Index the poems are grouped under the respective authors. The pupil will thus be enabled to see at a glance how many poems were chosen from each author, and what these poems were. He will also be able to judge for himself, in a convenient way, the wisdom and good taste shown by Palgrave and Tennyson in their selections for *The Golden Treasury*.

ALEXANDER, WILLIAM (1567?–1640)   PAGE
   To Aurora 22

ANONYMOUS
   Omnia Vincit 7
   A Picture 17
   A Song for Music 17
   In Lacrimas 23
   Love's Insight 25
   An Honest Autolycus 26
   The Unfaithful Shepherdess 38
   Advice to a Lover 40
   A sweet Lullaby 42
   A Dilemma 51
   The Great Adventurer 105
   Love in thy youth, fair Maid 114
   My love in her attire 121
   Love not me for comely grace 123
   Forsaken 131
   Upon my lap my sovereign sits 132
   Fair Helen 133
   The Twa Corbies 135
   Willy Drowned in Yarrow 188
   Absence 234

BARBAULD, ANNA LETITIA (1743–1825)
   To Life 252

Group-Index of Poems

	PAGE
BARNFIELD, RICHARD (1574–1627)	
The Nightingale	33
BEAUMONT, FRANCIS (1584–1616)	
On the Tombs in Westminster Abbey	92
BLAKE, WILLIAM (1757–1827)	
Love's Secret	199
Infant Joy	210
A Cradle Song	211
To the Muses	253
BURNS, ROBERT (1759–1796)	
Lament for Culloden	184
A Farewell	195
Ye banks and braes o' bonnie Doon	200
To a Mouse	215
Mary Morison	225
Bonnie Lesley	226
O my Luve's like a red, red rose	227
Highland Mary	227
Duncan Gray	230
Jean	234
John Anderson	235
BYRON, GEORGE NOEL GORDON (1788–1824)	
All for Love *lyric*	260
There be none of Beauty's daughters *lyric*	263
She walks in beauty, like the night *lyric*	264
When we two parted *lyric*	283
Elegy on Thyrza *elegy*	296
On the Castle of Chillon *Ital sonnet*	308
Youth and Age *lyric*	323
Elegy *elegy*	336
CAMPBELL, THOMAS (1777–1844)	
Lord Ullin's Daughter	271
To the Evening Star	280
Earl March look'd on his dying child	292
Ye Mariners of England	302

Long poems — "Don Juan," "Child Harows," "Giaour"

Group-Index of Poems

	PAGE
Battle of the Baltic	303
Hohenlinden	312
The Beech Tree's Petition	365
Ode to Winter	378
Song to the Evening Star	392
The Soldier's Dream	395
The River of Life	437

CAMPION, THOMAS (c. 1597–1619)

Basia	19
Advice to a Girl	20
In Imagine Pertransit Homo	36
Sleep, angry beauty, sleep	38
A Renunciation	40
O Crudelis Amor	44
Sic Transit	62
The man of life upright	63
A Hymn in Praise of Neptune	101
Cherry-Ripe	116
Fortunati Nimium	145

CAREW, THOMAS (1598–1638)

The True Beauty	113

CAREY, HENRY (–1743)

Sally in our Alley	193

CIBBER, COLLEY (1671–1757)

The Blind Boy	174

COLERIDGE, HARTLEY (1796–1849)

She is not fair to outward view	266

COLERIDGE, SAMUEL TAYLOR (1772–1834)

Love	256
Kubla Khan	397
Youth and Age	430

COLLINS, JOHN (1752–1808)

Tomorrow	251

COLLINS, WILLIAM (1721–1759)

Ode to Simplicity	171

Group-Index of Poems

	PAGE
Ode Written in 1746	184
The Passions	205
Ode to Evening	217

COWLEY, ABRAHAM (1618–1667)
| A Supplication | 127 |
| On the Death of Mr. William Hervey | 136 |

COWPER, WILLIAM (1731–1800)
Loss of the Royal George	189
To a Young Lady	197
The Poplar Field	214
The Shrubbery	241
The Solitude of Alexander Selkirk	243
To Mary Unwin (i, ii)	245
The Castaway	248

CRASHAW, RICHARD (1613?–1649)
| Wishes for the Supposed Mistress | 103 |

CUNNINGHAM, ALLAN (1784–1842)
| A wet sheet and a flowing sea | 301 |

DANIEL, SAMUEL (1562–1619)
| Care-charmer Sleep | 34 |

DEKKER, THOMAS (1570–1641?)
| The Happy Heart | 61 |

DEVEREUX, ROBERT, EARL OF SUSSEX (1566–1601)
| A Wish | 66 |

DONNE, JOHN (1573?–1631)
| Present in Absence | 10 |

DRAYTON, MICHAEL (1563–1631)
| Love's Farewell | 36 |

DRUMMOND, WILLIAM (1585–1649)
Summons to Love	3
A Lament	46
To His Lute	47
This Life, which seems so fair	62

Group-Index of Poems

	PAGE
The Lessons of Nature	64
Doth then the world go thus?	65
Saint John Baptist	67

DRYDEN, JOHN (1631–1700)
Song for St. Cecilia's Day	78
Alexander's Feast	163

ELLIOT, JEAN (1727–1805)
Lament for Flodden (Flowers of the Forest)	185

FLETCHER, JOHN (1579–1625)
Melancholy	130

GAY, JOHN (1685–1732)
Black-eyed Susan	191

GOLDSMITH, OLIVER (1728–1774)
When lovely woman stoops to folly	200

GRAHAM, ROBERT (1735–1797)
If doughty deeds my lady please	195

GRAY, THOMAS (1716–1771)
Ode on the Pleasure arising from Vicissitude	169
On a Favorite Cat	175
The Bard	179
The Progress of Poesy	201
Ode on the Spring	212
Elegy Written in a Country Churchyard	220
Ode on a Distant Prospect of Eton College	237
Hymn to Adversity	242

GREENE, ROBERT (1558?–1592)
Sephestia's Song to her Child	45

HABINGTON, WILLIAM (1605–1654)
Nox Nocti Indicat Scientiam	159

HERBERT, GEORGE (1593–1633)
The Gifts of God	98

HERRICK, ROBERT (1591–1674)
Counsel to Girls	110
To Dianeme	114

Group-Index of Poems

	PAGE
Corinna's Maying	117
The Poetry of Dress (i, ii)	120
To Anthea	122
To Blossoms	139
To Daffodils	140

HEYWOOD, THOMAS (1575?–1648?)
Pack, clouds, away, and welcome day 54

HOOD, THOMAS (1799–1845)
Past and Present 326
The Bridge of Sighs 332
The Death Bed 340

JONSON, BEN (1573–1637)
The Noble Nature 97
Hymn to Diana 102
To Celia 116

KEATS, JOHN (1795–1821)
Ode on the Poets 254
On First Looking into Chapman's Homer . . . 255
Happy Insensibility 285
La Belle Dame sans Merci 287
Bright Star! 293
The Terror of Death 294
The Mermaid Tavern 330
Ode to a Nightingale 359
To one who has been long in city pent . . . 363
Ode to Autumn 377
The Realm of Fancy 400
Ode on a Grecian Urn 428
The Human Seasons 438

LAMB, CHARLES (1775–1835)
The Old Familiar Faces 321
Hester 337
On an Infant Dying as soon as Born . . . 344

LAMB, MARY (1764–1847)
In Memoriam 346

Group-Index of Poems

	PAGE
LINDSAY, LADY ANNE (1750–1825)	
Auld Robin Gray	229
LODGE, THOMAS (1558?–1625)	
Rosaline	14
Rosalynd's Madrigal	52
LOGAN, JOHN (1748–1788)	
The Braes of Yarrow	186
LOVELACE, RICHARD (1618–1658)	
To Lucasta, on Going to the Wars	111
To Althea from Prison	124
To Lucasta, on Going beyond the Seas	126
LYLY, JOHN (1553–1606)	
Cupid and Campaspe	53
LYTE, HENRY FRANCIS (1793–1847)	
A Lost Love	270
Agnes	341
MARLOWE, CHRISTOPHER (1564–1593)	
The Passionate Shepherd to his Love	6
MARVELL, ANDREW (1621–1678)	
Horatian Ode upon Cromwell's Return from Ireland	81
The Picture of Little T. C. in a Prospect of Flowers	107
The Girl Describes her Fawn	141
Thoughts in a Garden	142
Song of the Emigrants in Bermuda	157
MICKLE, WILLIAM JULIUS (1735–1788)	
The Sailor's Wife	231
MILTON, JOHN (1608–1674)	
Ode on the Morning of Christ's Nativity	69
On the Late Massacre in Piedmont	80
Lycidas	86
When the Assault was intended to the City	95
On his Blindness	95
To Mr. Lawrence	100

Group-Index of Poems

	PAGE
To Cyriack Skinner	101
To the Lady Margaret Ley	113
L'Allegro	146
Il Penseroso	151
At a Solemn Music	158

MOORE, THOMAS (1779–1852)
Echoes	278
At the mid hour of night	295
Pro Patria Mori	315
The Journey Onwards	322
The Light of Other Days	327

MUNDAY, ANTHONY (The Shepherd Tonie), (1553–1633)
Colin	16

NAIRNE, CAROLINA OLIPHANT, BARONESS (1766–1845)
The Land o' the Leal	236

NASH, THOMAS (1567–1600?)
Spring	1

NORRIS, JOHN (1657–1711)
Hymn to Darkness	161

PHILIPS, AMBROSE (1675–1749)
To Charlotte Pulteney	176

POPE, ALEXANDER (1688–1744)
Solitude	173

PRIOR, MATTHEW (1664–1721)
The merchant, to secure his treasure	198

QUARLES, FRANCIS (1592–1644)
A Mystical Ecstasy	122

ROGERS, SAMUEL (1762–1855)
The Sleeping Beauty	197
A Wish	217

SCOTT, SIR WALTER (1771–1832)
The Outlaw	261
Jock o' Hazeldean	276
A Serenade	279

Group-Index of Poems

	PAGE
Where shall the lover rest	286
The Rover	289
The Maid of Neidpath	291
Gathering Song of Donald the Black	299
The Pride of Youth	331
Coronach	339
Rosabelle	342
Hunting Song	350
Datur Hora Quieti	393

SEDLEY, SIR CHARLES (1639–1701)

Child and Maiden	109
Not, Celia, that I juster am	124

SHAKESPEARE, WILLIAM (1564–1616)

The Fairy Life (i, ii)	2
Sonnet — Time and Love (i)	4
Sonnet — Time and Love (ii)	5
A Madrigal	8
Under the greenwood tree	8
It was a lover and his lass	9
Sonnet — Absence (i)	11
Sonnet — Absence (ii)	12
Sonnet — A Consolation	12
Sonnet — The Unchangeable (i)	13
Sonnet — The Unchangeable (ii)	14
Sonnet — To His Love (i)	18
Sonnet — To His Love (ii)	18
Love's Perjuries	21
Sonnet — True Love	24
Carpe Diem	26
Winter	27
Sonnet — That time of year	28
Sonnet — Memory	28
Sonnet — Revolutions	30
Sonnet — Farewell	30
Sonnet — The Life without Passion	31

Group-Index of Poems

	PAGE
Frustra — Take, O take those lips away	35
Sonnet — Blind Love	37
Blow, blow, thou winter wind	41
Dirge of Love	47
Fidele — Fear no more the heat o' the sun	48
A Sea Dirge	49
Sonnet — Post Mortem	50
Sonnet — The Triumph of Death	50
Young Love	51
Sonnet — Soul and Body	63
Sonnet — The World's Way	66

SHELLEY, PERCY BYSSHE (1792–1822)

	PAGE	
The Indian Serenade	263	song
I fear thy kisses, gentle maiden	267	lyric
Love's Philosophy	278	"
To the Night	281	"
The Flight of Love	290	"
One word is too often profaned	298	"
Stanzas Written in Dejection near Naples	328	"
To a Skylark	352	Horat. ode
Ozymandias of Egypt	363	Ital. son.
To a Lady, with a Guitar	371	lyric
The Invitation	386	"
The Recollection	388	"
To the Moon	394	"
A Dream of the Unknown	396	"
Written among the Euganean Hills	414	"
Ode to the West Wind	420	pin. ode
The Poet's Dream	425	lyric
A Dirge	439	song
Threnos	439	song
Music, when soft voices die	448	lyric

SHIRLEY, JAMES (1596–1666)

	PAGE
The Last Conqueror	93
Death the Leveller	94

Long poems = "Adonais" on Keats "Cenci" - crime in Ital

Group-Index of Poems

	PAGE
SIDNEY, SIR PHILIP (1554–1586)	
Via Amoris	10
A Ditty	24
Sleep	29
The Nightingale	34
The Moon	44
SMART, CHRISTOPHER (1722–1771)	
The Song of David	210
SOUTHEY, ROBERT (1774–1843)	
After Blenheim	313
The Scholar	329
SPENSER, EDMUND (1552–1599)	
Prothalamion	55
SUCKLING, SIR JOHN (1609–1642)	
Encouragements to a Lover	127
SYLVESTER, JOSHUA (1563–1618)	
Love's Omnipresence	25
THOMSON, JAMES (1700–1748)	
Rule Britannia	177
For ever, Fortune, wilt thou prove	198
VAUGHAN, HENRY (1622–1695)	
The Retreat	99
Friends in Paradise	138
A Vision	162
WALLER, EDMUND (1606–1687)	
Go, lovely Rose	115
On a Girdle	121
WEBSTER, JOHN (1580?–1625)	
A Land Dirge	49
WILMOT, JOHN, EARL OF ROCHESTER (1647–1680)	
Constancy	110
WITHER, GEORGE (1588–1667)	
The Manly Heart	128

Group-Index of Poems 641

PAGE

WOLFE, CHARLES (1791–1823)
The Burial of Sir John Moore 316
To Mary 338

WORDSWORTH, WILLIAM (1770–1850)
She was a Phantom of delight *lyric* 265
She dwelt among the untrodden ways *lyric* . . 267
I travell'd among unknown men 268
The Education of Nature *l* 268
A slumber did my spirit seal *l* 270
Lucy Gray *ballad* 274
To a Distant Friend *ital sonnet* 283
Desideria *italyn sonnet* 294
Ode to Duty *pindaric ode* 306
England and Switzerland, 1802 *sonnet* . . . 308
On the Extinction of the Venetian Republic " . 309
London, 1802 310
Milton! thou shouldst be living at this hour " . 310
When I have borne in memory what has tamed *lyric* 311
Simon Lee, the Old Huntsman *ballad* . . . 317
A Lesson 325
The Affliction of Margaret *lyric* 347
To the Skylark . " 351
The Green Linnet . " 356
To the Cuckoo . " 358
Upon Westminster Bridge *sonnet* 362
Composed at Neidpath Castle . " 364
Admonition to a Traveller . " 366
To the Highland Girl of Inversneyde *lyric* . . 366
The Reaper *lyric* 369
The Reverie of Poor Susan *lyric* 370
The Daffodils *lyric* 374
To the Daisy *ode* 375
Yarrow Unvisited, 1803 *lyric* 381
Yarrow Visited, 1814 383
By the Sea *sonnet* 391
To Sleep . . " 394

Long poems — "The Prelude", "The Excursion"

Group-Index of Poems

	PAGE
The Inner Vision	399
Written in Early Spring	403
Ruth, or the Influences of Nature	404
Nature and the Poet	423
Glen-Almain, the Narrow Glen	426
The World is too much with us	427
Within King's College Chapel, Cambridge	428
The Two April Mornings	432
The Fountain	434
The Trosachs	440
My heart leaps up	440
Ode on Intimations of Immortality	441

WOTTON, HENRY (1568–1639)

Character of a Happy Life	96
Elizabeth of Bohemia	112

WYATT, SIR THOMAS (1503–1542)

A Supplication	21
The Lover's Appeal	32

WORD–LISTS

The true poet is a master of words; he chooses what one critic has called the "inevitable phrase" to express the exact shade of meaning which he wishes to convey. Sometimes the words add beauty to the poem by their own quality, as in the famous lines from the *Ode to a Nightingale*:

> " magic casements, opening on the foam
> Of perilous seas, in faery lands forlorn."

Sometimes the effect is produced by sheer simplicity:

> " A violet by a mossy stone
> Half-hidden from the eye!
> Fair as a star, when only one
> Is shining in the sky."

The study of words is not least among the pleasures of reading poetry. Such a study will help us to appreciate more fully both the skill shown in the selection of the words, and the charm or significance which the words themselves add to the general effect of the poem. The following lists will facilitate the study. Short definitions can be found in the Notes; for more exhaustive investigation consult a large dictionary.

BOOK FIRST

whist	swains	wasted
featly	hie	wights
burthen	prime	blazon
decore	mettle	forsworn
orient	bootless	assays
madrigals	flame	swain
kirtle	woe-begone	sweeting

644 Word-Lists

knacks	up-till	featerously
guiles	ill-adventur'd	vermeil
saw	warp	eftsoons
crabs	dole	assoil
keel	cypress	shend
knot	harbinger	whilom
baiting-place	turtle	ensuing
prease	equipage	baldric
nativity	prothalamion	aggravate
flourish	paramours	disabled
misprision	entrailéd	simplicity
grame	flasket	uncouth

BOOK SECOND

forfeit	climacteric	taffeta
unsufferable	peer	civility
prevent	welter	'suage
doff'd	battening	mortifies
gaudy	oaten flute	nappy
silly	weanling	yclept
close	guerdon	buxom
unexpressive	foil	debonair
consort	eclipse	dight
mold	reft	tale
sheen	mitered	fallows
tissued	recks	pied
ychain'd	flashy	upland hamlets
divine	scrannel	lubber
eyn	swart	matin
fays	enamel'd	haunted
youngest-teemed	rathe	pensioners
courtly	amaranthus	grain
bright-harnessed	freak'd	commercing
diapason	laureat	hist
numbers	monstrous	bless
bergamot	tricks	scepter'd pall

Word-Lists

buskin'd	pale	assumes
monumental	spell	mother-wit
garish	enamels	

BOOK THIRD

moduling	oaten stop	ingenuous
ruthless	folding-star	madding
lilting	incense-breathing	sequester'd
doughty	glebe	unletter'd
boding	fretted	trysted
energic	chill penury	fearful
ecstatic	rage	pad-pony
champaign	senates	

BOOK FOURTH

chambers	in fee	darkling
parle	homely	requiem
cloying	bowse	plaintive
fealty	contumely	swath
demesne	unteach	wailful
wend	inch	bourn
down (n.)	panoply	croft
musketoon	sacristy	dulcimer
diurnal	pale	savannahs
pensive	chapelle	voluptuous
water-wraith	incommunicable	masque
bower	participation	congregated
pensile	unbodied	crystalline
winnow'd	vernal	love-adept
fretting	hymeneal	brede
rue	visionary	wilding
charact'ry	charioted	tabor
orison	pards	habitual
native oak	viewless	fret
uncharter'd	enbalmed	

A LIST OF PROPER NAMES

Many names are found throughout *The Golden Treasury* which have an interesting significance, mythological or other. The list that follows will show how rich the collection is in such references. The student should be familiar with the "background" of the poetry as suggested by these names. They may be looked up in the Notes; if fuller information is needed a good encyclopedia should be consulted.

BOOK FIRST

Phoebus	King Pandion	Tempe
Memnon	Tereus	Thessaly
Tithon (Tithonus)	Philomena	Echo
Peneus	Cassandra	Cynthia
Flora	Iope	Templar knights
Zephyr	Helen	Hercules
Parnassus	Cupid	Elisa
Aurora	Venus	Hesper

BOOK SECOND

Pan	Lybic Hammon	Orpheus
Mount Sinai	Thammuz	Cecilia
Delphos	Moloch	Piemontese
Genius	Isis	Cromwell
Lars	Orus	Caesar
Lemures	Osiris	Hampton
Peor	Memphian grove	Carisbrook
Baalim	Typhon	Capitol
Ashtaroth	Jubal	Hannibal

A List of Proper Names 647

Satyrs	Themis	Hebe
Fauns	Euclid	Lydian airs
Druids	Archimedes	Eurydice
Mona	Neptune	Vesta
Deva	Tritons	Saturn
Arethusa	Sirens	Hermes
Mincius	Chaeronea	Plato
Galilean lake	Cambridge	Thebes
Alpheus	Apollo	Pelops' line
Sicilian Muse	Daphne	Troy
Emathian conqueror	Syrinx	Musaeus
Pindarus	Cimmerian	Alexander
Electra's poet	Graces	Philip
Favonius	Bacchus	Darius
Attic	Cynosure	Timotheus
Tuscan	Faery Mab	

BOOK THIRD

Hybla	towers of Julius	Cytherea
Cephisus	Taliessin	Hyperion
Tyrian hue	Culloden	Chili
Nereid	Inverness	Aegean
Cambria	Drumossie Moor	Ilissus
Snowdon	Flodden	Maeander
Conway	Yarrow	Albion
Cadwallo	Leith	Avon
Plinlimmon	Aeolian lyre	Hampden
Arvon	Helicon	Windsor
Severn	Ceres	Gorgon terrors
Berkley	Thracia	Anson

BOOK FOURTH

Ida	Darien	Eremite
Chapman	Dove	Nelson
Cortez	Neidpath	Chillon

A List of Proper Names

Bonnivard	Promethean fire	Danube
Venetian Republic	Lethe	Stirling
Hohenlinden	Dryad	Clyde
Blenheim	Provençal	Tweed
Corunna	Hippocrene	Mount Abora
Cardigan	Ruth	Cherokees
Naples	Cheapside	Quantock
Mermaid Tavern	Miranda	Euganean Hills
Robin Hood	Ferdinand	Lombardy
Maid Marian	Ariel	Amphitrite
Elysium	Cyclops	Apennine
Zodiac	Calpe	Arcady
Roslin	Rhine	Trosachs

POETS' CORNER, WESTMINSTER ABBEY